SOCIAL POLICY

Third Edition

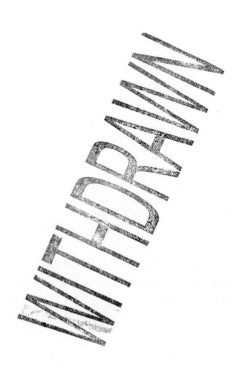

SOCIAL POLICY

AN INTRODUCTION

Third Edition

Ken Blakemore and Edwin Griggs

 McGraw Hill

Open University Press

Open University Press
McGraw-Hill Education
McGraw-Hill House
Shoppenhangers Road
Maidenhead
Berkshire
England
SL6 2QL

email: enquiries@openup.co.uk
world wide web: www.openup.co.uk

and Two Penn Plaza, New York, NY 10121–2289, USA

First published 2007

A catalogue record of this book is available from the British Library

ISBN 10: 0335 218 741
ISBN 13: 978 0335 218 745

Library of Congress Cataloguing-in-Publication Data
CIP data applied for

Typeset by YHT Ltd, London
Printed in Great Britain by Cromwell Press, Trowbridge, Wiltshire

The *McGraw·Hill* Companies

To the Coventry Lanchester Polytechnic – one of the best of its kind

Contents

The Authors

Ken Blakemore is a senior research fellow in social policy in the School of Human Sciences at Swansea University. He has previously taught in Africa, in the USA (UCLA) and at universities in Coventry, Warwick and Birmingham, as well as Swansea. He has researched and written widely in several fields of social policy, including comparative education, diversity and equal opportunities, and policies on care of older people.

Edwin Griggs has taught social policy and politics at a number of higher education institutions over the years, including Coventry, Teesside, Leeds and City of London Polytechnics, Keele University and Coventry University, and continues to teach at universities in the West Midlands.

Preface

This third edition of *Social Policy: An Introduction* has been revised throughout to take account of policy changes and developments since the second edition, published in 2003. The framework of the book is substantially that of the earlier edition, but some new material has been incorporated, mainly in the form of a chapter on criminal justice policy (Chapter 4). This has the purpose of providing a brief introduction to comparative analysis, supplementing the section on different models of social policy in Chapter 3. It also serves to introduce students to an area of public policy which is the subject of lively interest at the present time, as well as overlapping to some extent with social policy.

Four more years of New Labour government since the previous edition provide an opportunity to explore the extent to which that government has made a difference to social policy and general well-being, and to provide a clearer picture of its achievements and failures. To that extent the book attempts, as did its predecessors, to provide a commentary on current developments, as well as providing a foundational account of welfare institutions and policies for the beginner.

The aims of this book, like those of its predecessors, are simple: to offer a text that can be consulted briefly for single items or insights, but also to offer a piece of writing about social policy that you, the reader, might enjoy reading chapter by chapter. Let's hope that you agree.

Ken Blakemore
Edwin Griggs

Acknowledgements

Space does not permit us to mention everyone who has contributed in various ways both to the creative process in developing the third edition of this book and to its revision from the second. However, Ken Blakemore would particularly like to acknowledge the help of friends and former colleagues at the University in Swansea, and most notably among these Bob Drake and Anthea Symonds. Ken Blakemore would also like to acknowledge the friendly advice and inspiration provided by others working in social policy research or connected fields – particularly Bill Bytheway and Julia Johnson, Steve Smith and Tim Stainton.

Edwin Griggs would like to be able to acknowledge, as many academics do, the academic and other support provided by his former university, but is unable to do so. However, he can acknowledge the support of individual former colleagues, especially Dr Alf Barrett. Finally, he would also like to thank Pam, Alex, Will and Lizzie for making such a difference to his life in recent years.

Any writer who claims to have surveyed the field owes an enormous debt, both to fellow scholars and to students. However, the responsibility for this book of course lies solely with both of us.

We must acknowledge the support of Catriona Watson and Rachel Gear at McGraw-Hill, and Laura Dent, formerly of McGraw-Hill, and especially their encouragement and unwavering patience when confronted with one missed deadline after another.

Finally, we should like to acknowledge the following for their kind permission to reproduce copyright material in this book:

The Controller of HMSO and the Queen's Printer for Scotland, for use of Crown Copyright material in Figures 4.1, 4.2 and 5.1; and *The Times Educational Supplement* for a summary of 'Education in the UK – How Countries Compare' in Box 12.1.

1 THE SUBJECT OF SOCIAL POLICY

Social policy: an identity problem?

Social policy can be defined in two ways. First, it is an academic subject to research and to study. The aim of this first chapter is to introduce you to it. Second, policies have an impact on the 'real' world. Government, business and voluntary organizations all have policies which are experienced by families and individuals.

What are 'policies'? In one way they can be seen as aims or goals, or statements of what ought to happen. *Social* policies aim to improve human welfare (though they often fail to do so) and to meet human needs for education, health, housing and social security.

As goals, intentions and ideas, policies can be found in the form of official government policy (legislation, or the guidelines that govern how laws should be put into operation). The ideas and proposals put forward in manifestos and glossy leaflets by the Conservative, Labour, Liberal Democrat and other political parties are examples of policies as broad ideas and stirring goals. Outside government, a company's or an organization's statement of policy on something – for instance, an equal opportunity policy – is also an example of policy expressing ideas about what ought to happen.

However, policies are living things, not just static lists of goals, rules or laws. Policy blueprints have to be implemented, often with unexpected and sometimes with disastrous results. Therefore, social policies are what happens 'on the ground' when they are implemented, as well as what happens at the preliminary decision-making or legislative stage. There is often a gulf between the concepts and goals that inspire policy and 'real' policy, the ugly result of compromise.

Studying social policy will involve you in thinking about:

- *What* social policies are: that is, what the content of specific government policies is, such as an Education Act or a policy on abortion in a National Health Service (NHS) hospital.
- *How* policies are developed, administered and implemented: for instance, how a new policy on tackling youth unemployment was conceived, what its stated and hidden aims are, how it is funded and how far it meets its objectives.
- *Why* policies exist (or do not exist). Why, for example, was a market approach to providing health and social services introduced in the 1980s and early 1990s? Or why, in Britain, has there never been – until recently – a concerted policy on nursery provision and preschool care for children?

Social policy and other subjects

Although preliminary definitions of social policy might be helpful, no definition tells the whole story. The challenge facing us, therefore, is more than that of moving from simple to slightly more complicated definitions of social policy, and descriptions of various policies in areas such as education and health.

Definitions and descriptions are not enough. Anyone new to a subject needs something else: an image of the subject to identify with, or a glimpse of the whole thing which gives a feel for the subject, and some way of anticipating what is coming next.

To demonstrate the importance of these things, you might briefly think about a range of subjects that you are already familiar with: English literature, perhaps, or media studies, sociology, geography, history or economics. Now think of the images that each one calls up in your mind.

English and media studies bring images from drama, film and novels – some of which, incidentally, are very useful for a broader understanding of social policy and changing social conditions (see suggestions for further reading at the end of Chapter 3). Geography helps us to visualize the globe, space and particular environments such as a tropical rain forest or mountain ranges. History and sociology might prompt images of particular periods that you have been interested in – how ordinary people fared in Hitler's Germany in the 1930s, for instance. Depending on the health of your bank balance, economics might give an image of either a looming overdraft or fountains of golden coins.

Now try the same exercise with the words 'social policy' in mind. Do any images appear? If they do, you might be sufficiently well informed to consider shelving this book. If you have no clear image or impression of the subject, on the other hand, this is perfectly understandable – and you need to read on.

Social policy's identity problem – or, more precisely, its problem of *lack* of identity – has a number of causes. As with sociology, perhaps social policy's lack of a clear image is due to it being a relatively new subject compared with traditional disciplines such as history and geography. Also, social policy has only just been introduced as an advanced level subject. To date, very few schools and colleges have included it in their A-level programmes. Consequently, not many people considering a course in social policy have a clear idea of what is entailed because they are unfamiliar with it as a taught subject.

There is another reason for social policy's identity problem. It is a 'magpie' subject – a discipline that has taken bright and sparkling treasures from other disciplines such as economics, philosophy, politics and sociology. For this reason social policy is sometimes seen as an interdisciplinary subject rather than an academic discipline in its own right. As argued later, however, there is a strong case for viewing social policy as a discipline. Like the magpie's nest, social policy's base contains others' pearls of wisdom, but social policy has also developed insights, theories and empirical research of its own.

Like any other discipline, social policy employs a distinctive body of theory that individual scholars and researchers have used to test hypotheses about the impact of social policies on people's lives (see Box 1.1). Through the study of social policy as a discipline, therefore, you will gain a view of the world that is distinctly different from, but related to, the perspectives of sociology, politics and the other social sciences.

BOX 1.1   Social policy research – an example

Example of a theory	*Some possible hypotheses to test the theory*
Public provision (for example of social housing) maintains some fairness in allocation of goods and services; market provision is bound to exclude disadvantaged groups.	1 Where social housing is sold off, poorer families tend to get left behind in substandard housing; they are excluded from better quality flats or houses.
	or
	2 Where social housing is sold off, the purchasers are more likely to stay; there is a better mix than if people have to leave their estates to purchase a home.

An example of research that examines these hypotheses – in relation to council house sales and the African-Caribbean community – can be found in a study by Peach and Byron (1994). See Chapter 9 for further discussion of Peach and Byron's study.

Before we leave initial impressions and images, it is important to realize that experienced scholars in social policy have their personal images of the subject, just as much as do people who have only recently begun to study it. For example, Nicholas Deakin (1994: 1) gives us this personal impression:

> *Towards the end of the War (which is how people of my generation still habitually refer to the Second World War) my mother took to bringing home from our visits to the children's clinic . . . small brown bottles labelled 'welfare orange juice'. My brother and I gulped down the contents willingly enough: the flavour, bland, but with a slightly bitter chemical back taste, was in every way preferable to the only other alternative on offer: cod liver oil. Now, forty years later, the ghost of the tang that the juice once left still appears unbidden on my palate whenever I first see the word 'welfare'; and it illustrates in a trivial but (to me) highly immediate way how the terms employed in the debate about the future of welfare have developed associations and personal references which are lodged deep in the collective unconscious of the nation.*

For the millions of people of Nicholas Deakin's generation and of preceding generations, this particular impression has a lot of resonance. It expresses a deep attachment to the welfare state and might be termed a welfarist image of social policy.

More recent impressions among younger generations might be less pro-welfare or welfarist. For instance, the term welfare might be more readily associated with the frustrations of dealing with a benefits office, or with the suspicion that sometimes poverty is made worse by the welfare system rather than relieved by it (see Chapters 5 and 6).

Images of welfare and social policy (assuming these two terms are used synonymously) can therefore be negative as well as positive. The study of social policy must include a critical element. Social policies are 'nasty' as well as 'nice'. The aims and impact of social policies and the welfare system (either deliberately or unintentionally) can as often be to control people and to keep them in their place (see Chapter 6) as to liberate them or to give them a better life than they would otherwise have.

Thus, a major aim of the subject of social policy is to *evaluate critically* the impact of social policies on people's lives. As already mentioned, this involves developing theories about the role of welfare and using hypotheses to test out what is happening. As an example, we might consider the impact of standard assessment tests (SATs) in (English and Welsh) primary and secondary schools (see Chapter 7), and whether these have really helped to improve children's education.

To engage in an honest and objective appraisal, the social policy researcher must, like any other social scientist, try to lay aside personal views and political opinions. A teacher overwhelmed by the work of administering SATs, and whose school is not performing very well in the 'league tables' of SATs results, would probably not be the best choice of person to research the value of standard testing of schoolchildren. But then neither would a government spokesperson committed to this policy.

Despite the importance of objectivity, though, the identity of social policy as a subject *is* simultaneously bound up with values: that is, expressing what you believe in, and what you think social policies *should be* trying to achieve to make society better for everyone.

How can there be a commitment to objectivity on the one hand, and to personal and political values on the other? The tension between these two opposites will be explored by looking at the life and work of Richard Titmuss, who is perhaps the most important founder of the subject of social policy. He argued strongly that it is possible to be committed to one's values and political standpoint *and* to be objective about social conditions and the need for social reform.

We shall also explore the way in which social policy developed as a subject both before and after Titmuss made his important contribution. Before this, however, it might help to review these opening remarks about social policy by comparing the ways in which different academic subjects relate to social policy (see Box 1.2).

Box 1.2 Examples of links between social policy and other disciplines

Discipline	Examples of social policy relevance
Anthropology	Study of family, kinship and differences in household composition and living arrangements. Social security entitlements depend on official policy of 'what counts' as a recognized household unit.

Economics	Looking at the economic costs and 'payoffs' of particular policies and social benefits, for example child benefit.
Geography	Insights into the spatial patterns of the distribution and take-up of services, for example maps of the boundaries of general practitioners' practices, numbers of patients and visits to the doctor.
History	Study of the development of social policies through time: comparing present-day services and attitudes to them with examples from the past, for example hostels for the homeless today could be compared with 'Poor Law' institutions in the past.
Philosophy	Examining the reasons or justifications for choosing one kind of policy rather than another; discussing ethical questions, such as the right of health authorities not to provide certain kinds of treatment, drugs or therapy.
Politics	Investigating the social policy aims of the Labour, Conservative, Liberal Democrat, Green and nationalist parties; or, conversely, looking at the political impact of social policies, for example what have been the effects of council house sales on voting patterns?
Psychology	Studying personal perceptions of, and attitudes towards, welfare services. Psychological perspectives are important in investigating individual need and design of services, for example the way prostate cancer screening is advertised and provided, and men's perceptions of this service.
Sociology	Researching the norms, values and other social pressures that affect the relationship between the welfare system and different groups, for example reasons for racial inequalities in access to social services.

The story of social policy

In order to understand the distinctive character of social policy as a subject, we need briefly to examine its roots and the way it developed in the UK.

Early roots: social work, sociology and social administration

Concern about questions of social policy grew throughout the nineteenth century. For instance, there was mounting concern about poverty and the squalid conditions that many people had to live in at that time, concern about child labour in mills, factories and mines, and concern about lack of literacy and the threatening power of the uneducated masses (see Chapter 3).

As the end of the nineteenth century neared, it became increasingly clear to a growing number of reformers that government would have to play a much larger role than before in dealing with the social problems of the day. Although some of this concern was motivated by genuine and progressive aims to improve social conditions for ordinary people, it was mixed with other more controlling and reactionary motivations.

The work of those who led the Charity Organisation Society (COS) is a good example of this mix of motivations and aims. The COS, set up to coordinate charitable efforts and to eliminate problems of charities duplicating one another's work, became a highly influential advisory body in late Victorian and early twentieth-century Britain. For instance, several of its members, including Octavia Hill (see Chapter 10), served on a government commission on the reform of the Poor Law between 1905 and 1909.

In general, the COS and those who shared similar opinions were looking for a more efficient way of managing the existing system of poverty relief, rather than a radical overhaul of social policy and the introduction of universal state benefits. The COS had pioneered the development of a new kind of occupation – the social caseworker – who was often a volunteer and often a (middle- or upper-class) woman. 'Social workers', as they gradually came to be known, were responsible for investigating the needs of poor families and for finding out whether they were 'deserving' cases. There was great concern among those who ran charities at the time that no one who was 'undeserving' should receive any help, because undeserved help would compound the character faults that were then thought to cause poverty and unemployment: laziness, ignorance, immoral behaviour and dependence.

Social work in its early days was arguably more concerned with social control and with trying to make the poor 'respectable' than with helping them on their own terms. But the very fact that social casework was thought necessary did succeed in bringing the problems of poverty and social inequality to the attention of middle-class volunteers and opinion-formers on a scale that had never been seen before.

At the same time, journalists, radical politicians and other commentators were writing about the appalling conditions in which many British people lived. They gave first-hand accounts and vivid descriptions of slum life that were as shocking to 'respectable' society as reports of other cultures and ways of life among the 'savages' in newly-conquered parts of the Empire.

As a result of both social casework investigation and journalistic reports, philanthropists began to provide funds for research on poverty and social problems as well as for schemes to help the poor directly. One famous example of this was Seebohm Rowntree's survey of poverty in York in 1901, *Poverty: A Study of Town Life* (discussed by Fraser 1984: 136–7). It showed that an alarmingly high proportion of York's population (28 per cent) was then living below subsistence level. Rowntree's survey, which was followed by other Rowntree investigations after the First World War, is a prime example of the way in which the social conscience of leading manufacturing firms (in this case, the well-known chocolate and cocoa-processing firm) was translated into social research.

Rowntree's study was more progressive and less moralistic about the poor than an earlier study by Charles Booth, *The Life and Labour of the People in London*. This was an extremely lengthy and exhaustive study of poverty carried out between 1889 and 1903. All the studies of social conditions during this period were marked by an overriding concern to discover the 'facts' of poverty. Providing statistics of poverty and simply drawing the public's attention to social problems would make a conclusive case for urgent social reform, it was thought, and would galvanize government into action.

Therefore, the key to understanding these early, problem-focused pieces of research is to realize that they were strongly motivated by a desire to be *scientific*. Rather than an appeal for social reform and action based solely upon grounds of conscience or morality, the case put forward by Booth, Rowntree and others was to be based on irrefutable evidence and an objective approach to social problems.

It is about this time – the beginning of the twentieth century – that the term 'sociology' began to gain currency as a way of summing up this scientific, statistical approach to understanding social problems. Early sociology, reflecting as it did the passion for collecting facts and statistics, came to be known as 'blue book sociology', because it was based so heavily on official reports and population censuses (published in blue covers).

All this rapidly accumulating knowledge about social conditions and social problems fostered the development of new kinds of training courses and university degrees in social work. In the relatively new municipal 'redbrick' universities of the time, such as Birmingham, and in the newly-established London School of Economics and Political Science (LSE), three important strands of learning and training were fused together. These were social work, sociology and social administration, the last being the study of local and central government institutions, and of the framework in which services to the poor and needy were to be delivered.

The early roots of the subject of social policy (or its forerunner, social administration) were therefore entwined inextricably with practical action (social work) and research (sociology). Later, as sociology developed a more independent identity, sociologists began to deplore the idea of their subject being a problem-focused or policy-oriented discipline. Sociology became more theoretical in its concerns, though some sociologists retain an interest in 'real world' and policy issues.

The main aim of sociology, however, is to discover knowledge about society for its own sake. The main aim in social policy is to research the impact of social policies on people and society. Thus a key question for social policy is, 'what difference does a policy make?' At the same time, the subject of social policy raises other questions, focusing upon how policies develop, why certain policies are chosen over others and what the economic, political and social implications of policies are.

Box 1.3 Richard Titmuss, 1907–73

When Richard Titmuss became Professor of Social Administration at the LSE at the age of 43, he was one of the few non-graduates to have ever become a professor. Titmuss had had to leave school at the age of 14. His father, who had been thrown out of work on a small farm and became heavily indebted, died before Richard was 20. As a result, Titmuss had experienced first-hand the shock of financial insecurity.

After leaving school, Titmuss worked as a clerk, then as a more senior inspector, for an insurance company. This work deepened his knowledge of both social welfare and inequality. As Kincaid explains, 'During the 1930s Titmuss lived a double life. In working hours, the insurance office – but in the evenings and at the weekends, the actuarial skills learned in the insurance office were brought to bear on data about birth-rates, poverty and ill-health' (Kincaid 1984: 115).

By this time Richard Titmuss had married, and his wife, Kay Titmuss, further encouraged his social conscience and his drive to write on policy and welfare matters. During the Second World War, Titmuss was appointed as an official war historian, and subsequently wrote a masterpiece on the civilian experience of wartime, called *Problems of Social Policy* (1950). Of many later works, among the more important are *Essays on the Welfare State* (1958), *Commitment to Welfare* (1968) and *The Gift Relationship* (1970), the last being a study of blood donation and the significance of this as a model of altruism for the provision of welfare generally.

Richard Titmuss died of cancer in an NHS hospital and, at the time, his daughter Ann Oakley (well known for her feminist analyses of family life and housework) wrote a moving tribute to his life and work.

Coming of age: the welfare state and social administration

In 1950, Richard Titmuss was appointed as the first professor of social administration at the London School of Economics (see Box 1.3). The subject had 'come of age' and was fast becoming recognized as a university discipline in many other British universities.

Titmuss's department at the LSE became a central influence on the subject in the 1950s and 1960s. The LSE itself had been set up in the early years of the twentieth century, largely as a result of the efforts of energetic and pioneering socialist thinkers such as Sidney and Beatrice Webb. It was envisaged as a powerhouse of progressive political ideas and adult education. Its chief aims were, first, to provide a route into higher education for able students from working-class backgrounds and, second, to build a solid base of research studies on economic and social problems. Both of these functions were thought to be vital for developing the planned society led by enlightened experts that the Webbs and other socialists believed in at the time.

Under the directorship of William Beveridge (see Chapter 3, Box 3.4) in the 1920s and 1930s, the LSE became an internationally renowned centre of learning. Among the scholars who joined the LSE during Beveridge's time was Friedrich von Hayek, an exponent of right-wing ideas on economics and politics who was to have a profound effect on future leaders such as Margaret Thatcher.

Thus the early development of social administration and social policy as university subjects took place in an environment in which a variety of views and a commitment to scholarly research were highly valued.

Richard Titmuss's teaching and research activities ably met these standards. He was not only highly prolific as a writer and researcher (see suggestions for further reading at the end of this chapter). Like those who had worked in the early poverty research tradition of Booth, Rowntree and other important reformers, his aim was not simply to do factual research for its own sake. It was also to engage in research which, while still based on *empirical studies* (that is, observation of factual evidence and real-life experience), would be directed by the aims of exposing unmet need, social inequality and the ways in which policies seemed to be failing to bring social justice.

Why was Titmuss so committed to such values as equality and social justice, and what were the implications of this commitment for the development of social policy as a subject? See, first, the brief summary of his life and work in Box 1.3. As the thumbnail sketch of Titmuss's life indicates, the twin strands in his approach to writing about social welfare go back to his own experience.

There was the dispassionate critic of social inequalities and of 'who gets what' in a society dominated by class privilege and an unfair labour market (see Chapter 5). Titmuss succeeded in elevating the subject of social administration from the tedious study of how the welfare system is administered to a more questioning analysis of why inequalities persist, even in a welfare state such as the one developed in Britain after 1945.

It was Titmuss who first pointed out that there are two welfare states: the obvious welfare system that provides education, health services and social security, and a less obvious system that particularly benefits the middle classes. The latter, 'hidden welfare state' includes subsidies to better-off groups in the form of tax advantages, public support for higher education (a near monopoly of students from middle-class families when Titmuss was writing) and mortgage interest tax relief (also benefiting better-off households at that time).

Second, though, there was the Titmuss who celebrated the welfare state that had been built in Britain after 1945 (see Chapter 3). He defended not only the actual services provided 'free' at the point of use, but also the values that underpinned the welfare state: the values of altruism, of community and of the collective will to improve people's lives. By contrast, the values that underpinned the market – individualism and competition – seemed to Titmuss to be destructive of human welfare.

Not surprisingly, therefore, many have seen marked inconsistencies in Titmuss's ideas. How could there be a unified subject of social policy based on Titmuss's approach if it included on the one hand a strong defence of the existing welfare system, and on the other a devastating critique of the inequalities and injustices that it masked?

In retrospect, it is not too difficult to see how both of these views can be reconciled even though there is some tension between them. It is quite possible to point out the weaknesses and injustices of the present welfare system while at the same time drawing attention to the possibility of greater inequalities and problems if the system were to be scrapped. For instance, the NHS, despite being a largely 'free at the point of use' service, has not succeeded in eradicating inequalities in health and use of health services (see Chapter 9). But Titmuss argued that the replacement of the NHS with a completely privatized health system, as in the USA, would lead to health inequalities even greater than already existed.

Crisis and change: the development of social policy as a subject

In the 1970s, the Titmussian approach to the study of the welfare state was challenged from a number of directions. This was partly because, despite Titmuss's lively criticisms of the flaws in the welfare state, much of the subject of social administration seemed to have developed into a rather complacent and technical description of existing social services and how they were to be delivered.

What criticisms there were of existing social problems, unmet need and inequality seemed to be dominated by the Titmussian assumption that all would be well if a left of centre, planned and rather paternalistic approach to providing state welfare was followed. But what if there was something more fundamentally wrong with the whole approach to providing welfare through state institutions?

It was this latter question that provoked much interest in the 1970s, when 'social policy' began to replace 'social administration' as the heading or title of university courses in the subject. Students of social policy were increasingly exposed to a range of critiques of the welfare state and of the traditional welfare values that had been contained in the old subject of social administration.

These critiques (critical discussions) may be divided into *culturalist* criticisms and *materialist* criticisms of state welfare. Culturalist critiques are those that challenge the *way* that welfare services are designed and provided, and the cultural assumptions (for example about men's and women's roles in society) that underpin the manner in which services are delivered. For instance, in the 1970s a growing feminist and women's studies literature raised questions about the sexist assumptions behind many health, education and social services, and the ways in which those services could reinforce gender inequality (see Chapter 6). Similarly, growing awareness of racism and studies of racial discrimination pinpointed the inappropriateness of many social services to the needs of minority ethnic groups, as well as the paternalistic, 'culture blind' attitudes of those who ran them.

Materialist critiques, on the other hand, focused on material factors and the economic crisis apparently facing the welfare state. On the political left, Marxists and other kinds of socialists concentrated on the material inequalities that seemed to be inherent in the welfare state: for instance, in the provision of housing, schools and hospitals of unequal quality or standards. This kind of critique (as an example, see Gough 1979) paid less attention to the way in which welfare services are run, and was more concerned that *not enough* welfare was being provided to poorer and working-class groups in society. At the same time, though, Marxists pointed to what they saw as an uncontainable and rising demand from the working classes for more welfare services and higher social security benefits – a demand that would spiral out of control and lead to a fundamental crisis in the capitalist system.

For entirely different reasons, commentators on the political right shared with Marxists a view of the welfare state as an unmanageable economic burden upon the capitalist economy. Therefore, they too were putting forward materialist criticisms of the welfare state. However, unlike the Marxists, right-wing commentators based their criticisms on the belief that *too much* state welfare was being provided.

Conclusions: the subject today

From today's vantage point many of the debates about social policy that used to take place in the 1970s and 1980s now seem out of date. In those days, debates were rather polarized. On the one hand, Marxist and left-wing critics of the welfare state were combining dreams of a socialist future with dire predictions of the end of capitalism. On the other, the so-called 'New Right' called for the privatization of much of the welfare system.

Neither school of thought proved to be much good at forecasting the actual development of social policy. As will be shown elsewhere in this book, Conservative government in the 1980s and 1990s did not lead to the full-scale implementation of all 'New

Right' ideas, nor to the scrapping of the welfare state (though there were many significant changes). The massive rise in unemployment during the 1980s and large increases in social security spending did not result, as many Marxists had suggested, in the breakdown of the capitalist system.

The writings of Titmuss about the social policy dilemmas of the 1950s and 1960s seem in some ways to be more pertinent than the theories of the 1970s and 1980s to an understanding of today's social policy questions and the approach of government to dealing with these questions. When Titmuss was writing about the welfare state in the 1950s it was a relatively new and untried institution. Though public welfare and institutions such as the NHS enjoyed popular approval, there were strong pressures in a newly 'affluent society' to develop separate, market-based provision for the better-off and to leave the stretched public services for everyone else. There was a certain fragility about the welfare state then, and the prospect of returning to a more divided, private-insurance based system, which has strong echoes today. For instance in 1959, in a Fabian Society lecture, Titmuss warned of growing inequality in an 'irresponsible society' – a society in which a two-tier welfare system could develop if its middle- and upper-class members opted out of the system. This seems highly relevant to today's context. Those who can afford it are being encouraged to take out private health insurance, and there are government incentives to make personal arrangements for our pensions (instead of relying on standard state pensions), and for funding any long-term care that we might need in the future. Therefore a rereading of Titmuss's concerns about the future of the welfare state has a resonance with today's dilemmas over what direction social policy should take.

By contrast, the radical left-wing ideas of the 1970s and 1980s, preoccupied as they were with over-abstract theories about class conflict and the end of capitalism, now seem rather archaic. They did not anticipate a future in which there could be significant reversals of social welfare policy without great political upheavals and crisis. In the event, there have been fundamental changes in social policy since 1979 without the scale of social crisis envisaged by Marxists.

Equally, the ideas of the New Right, which placed the market above the value of any state-provided health, education or social service, now have a rather tired and discredited appearance. Almost 20 years of Conservative government (1979–97) saw the implementation of *some* of these ideas but there is now a widespread realization that privatization, market competition and other New Right ideas have marked limitations as well as the supposed advantages that were advocated by the government at the time.

However, this is not to say that the debate between right and left did not have its uses in the development of social policy as a subject. As pointed out above, Titmuss's strong influence over the subject in the 1950s and 1960s led to the dominance of a rather cosy view of the world. The British approach to welfare was thought to be the best and a planned, state-run welfare system was seen as inevitably superior to anything the private or voluntary sector could do.

In Britain, this was largely a result of the way the subject developed as an independent discipline. In universities in other countries, it is rare to find 'social policy' as a separate undergraduate course. Social policy is often subsumed under politics, sociology or public administration in other European countries, while in the USA 'social welfare' and social policy studies are often linked with social work education. British social policy and administration grew rather more separately as a university discipline in the 1950s and 1960s.

Thus the traditional approach to the subject in Britain did establish a strong foundation of social policy studies, but it had its limitations. The explosion of debate about social policy and the welfare state in the 1970s blew fresh air into the subject and established the fundamental point that there are many ways of providing welfare. There is a range of competing models or types of welfare system to discuss, a point that is further explored at the end of Chapter 3, where Britain's welfare system or the 'British model' is compared with other models.

Plan of the book

In this chapter we have begun to explore how social policy has developed in recent times, both as a subject and as a programme of action 'out there' in the 'real' world. In Chapter 13 we shall return to these themes. The impact of the 'New' Labour government which came to power in 1997 will be assessed, together with broader questions about the interrelationship between social policy, economic change and social trends – for instance, the value of the concept of a 'postmodern' or 'late modern' world and its contribution to understanding current trends in social policy.

As for the filling in the sandwich – that is, all the intervening chapters – the choices that had to be made were difficult ones. For instance, there is a fundamental choice to be made between writing a book which is all 'isms and ologies' – that is, concerned primarily with theories of welfare and society – or another kind of book which provides a 'Cook's tour' of the welfare system. The drawback with the first kind is that it can easily become a semi-sociological or philosophical discussion, relatively abstract and timeless, and without much relevance to the world outside the university gates. That kind of book would not tell you much about the content of actual policies or how they were decided upon. The drawback with the second kind of book is that, after a few months, it begins to look like last summer's travel brochure. Time moves on, policies change and new Acts of Parliament are passed.

The plan of this book represents an attempt to bridge the gap between the two basic choices outlined above. The next four chapters deal with the big picture and with some important general themes in social policy, as follows:

- Chapter 2: the key ideas and principles upon which social policies are based.
- Chapter 3: the historical development of social policy.
- Chapter 4: criminal justice policy, which also explores the boundaries of social policy and considers the usefulness of comparative approaches to the study of policy.
- Chapter 5: 'who gets what?' Questions of social and economic inequality raised by social policy, and current issues of poverty and income maintenance.
- Chapter 6: the connections between social policy, social control and liberation.

Although these chapters focus on general themes, they also refer to specific policy areas and examples. Chapters 5 and 6, for instance, discuss social security benefits policy as an illustration of both the 'who gets what?' question and the question of 'how much control do social policies exercise over us?'

The remaining chapters (before the concluding Chapter 13) also try to marry thematic approaches with specific policy areas, though the emphasis is more upon the latter than the former.

- Chapter 7 discusses education policy, using the example of the Education Reform Act 1988 and its impact on education today to reflect upon how policies are made in Britain.
- Chapter 8 traces the links between welfare and work, looking at government employment policy and its impact on the well-being of different groups, including youth, low-income workers and older workers.
- Chapter 9 defines and explores health policy, examining recent changes in the structure of the NHS and the ways in which professional groups shape the design of health services.
- Chapter 10 takes the example of housing to examine how rival ideologies, values and utopian dreams influence policy.
- Chapter 11 gives an account of recent community care policy, exploring at the same time 'who cares?' in today's welfare system.
- Chapter 12 discusses important changes in the way that policy is being created and implemented in the UK as a result of devolution of power from Westminster to the National Assembly for Wales, the Scottish Parliament and to other regional and devolved bodies. It focuses on the significance of these changes for growing differences in social policy within the UK, and it also includes a discussion of the impact of European Union (EU) social policy.

A final point, assuming that you have decided to launch into the rest of the book, is that the term 'welfare *system*' is preferred throughout the book to that of 'welfare *state*'. Interestingly, William Beveridge – a key founder of Britain's welfare system (see Chapter 3) – strongly disliked the 'welfare state' tag. As a supporter of insurance and the principle of saving for a rainy day, he disapproved of any term that seemed to encourage the idea of welfare being a bottomless pit of resources, or an institution which would unquestioningly look after people however 'undeserving' of help they were.

However, avoiding the 'welfare state' term in this book has little to do with Beveridge's preferences. Rather, it is to signal some sort of recognition that we have moved out of the twentieth-century, postwar era of 'big government' in which the state was expected to play the leading role as provider of every major welfare service.

At the same time, there is still a 'system' of welfare. Though inadequate and badly coordinated in parts (see Chapter 11 on community care for examples), there is a connected set of agencies making decisions about, paying for, or providing services. The structure of the welfare system is composed of: central and local government; quangos or quasi-autonomous non-governmental organizations (see Chapter 7 for examples in education); the voluntary (non-profit-making) sector; the private (for-profit) sector; and the informal sector of the family and community. This book is about the system, why it is run according to certain principles and not others and – in the next chapter – what these principles mean.

Key terms and concepts

critique
disciplines
empirical research
hypothesis
implementation
models (of welfare or social policy)
objectivity
public administration
quangos
social administration
theory
values
welfare
welfare system
welfarism

Suggestions for further reading

A book written by Nicholas Deakin, *Politics of Welfare* (1994) represents a good start in reading about social policy. The introduction and Chapters 1 and 2 of his book provide a helpful historical framework that discusses the development of social policy in Britain. Another authentic taste of social policy can be obtained by dipping into one or more of the books written by Richard Titmuss; *Problems of Social Policy* (1950), for instance, is a huge work and contains a lot of detail, but there are some genuinely moving and ex-tremely well-written passages on Britain's response to wartime problems. Any of Tit-muss's later books, such as *Essays on the Welfare State* (1958), *Commitment to Welfare* (1968) and *The Gift Relationship* (1970) give an impression of social policy's roots. A convenient collection of Titmuss's writing about welfare is *The Philosophy of Welfare: Selected Writings of Richard M. Titmuss* (1987), edited by Brian Abel-Smith and Kay Tit-muss. Another period piece, Ian Gough's *The Political Economy of the Welfare State* (1979) provides a readable example of late 1970s radicalism. A collection of papers, *The Goals of Social Policy* (1989), edited by M. Bulmer and colleagues, contains some useful reflective and historical essays from a largely mainstream perspective on the state of social policy as it appeared in the late 1980s.

Finally, recent 'postmodernist' or 'poststructuralist' styles of thinking about social policy are exemplified in *Embodying the Social: Constructions of Difference* (1998), edited by Esther Saraga.

2   IDEAS AND CONCEPTS IN SOCIAL POLICY

Introduction

The principles of social policy are the guiding ideas that underlie policies for social welfare, education, health services and the like. For instance, one policy might make the principle of *equality* a priority, while another might stress choice or freedom. This chapter is about such principles – equality, equity, need, freedom and rights – and how these words can be interpreted in different ways.

While the term 'principle' is both useful and widely used, it has a very general meaning and is potentially rather confusing. In fact it has several different but *interconnected* meanings.

First, a principle might be said to have a *moral* or ethical meaning. If someone takes a 'principled stand', they will be standing up for certain beliefs in what is right and wrong and upholding certain moral standards. A moral standard in social policy could be represented, for instance, by the principle that no individual in need, no matter how poor or for whatever reasons, should be left without access to health care. Another more contentious example might be the principle, advocated by some, that housing and social benefits should either be reduced for lone parents or be withheld unless they fulfil certain conditions, such as finding work or employment training.

As can be seen from these examples, the moralistic side of a welfare principle contains a vision of how things ought or ought not to be. Social policy reflects the *norms* and *values* of society. Many social policies have a normative element, and are drafted with the intent of influencing society or the behaviour of individuals in line with deeply-held convictions and values. Thus there are left-wing normative principles which would include, among other things, the idea of equalizing outcomes for people. Conservative normative views tend to stress the idea that social policies should uphold 'traditional family values', or wherever possible make greater use of the voluntary sector in providing welfare services rather than expanding the role of government.

A second way of defining principles is to see them as *rules*. To take an example from the physical world, the human body – or any part of it, such as the heart – operates according to certain principles: for instance, the physical laws governing blood pressure and muscle tension.

However, the principles of social policy are not the same as the principles of human biology or the laws of nature. When New Labour formed a government in 1997, much was made of the idea of making policy 'evidence-based': the intention was to use social scientific evidence and hard evidence from public enquiry to decide 'what works', rather than basing policy on ideology or values. However, while efforts to use objective evidence undoubtedly increased, there remain many examples of recent policy change that seem to be based more on the government's determination to push through certain reforms irrespective of the evidence for or against them. Government proposals to greatly increase the number of city academies are just one example of this, in education policy (see Chapter 7). But even if policies are based on evidence, we could not expect to scientifically predict what the effects of social policies will be in the way that a scientist or doctor can predict what will happen if a certain medical operation or treatment is carried out (though even here we must be careful not to expect too much certainty).

On the other hand, there is an important sense in which principles do convey an idea of the rules of social policy. Each welfare system creates a welfare bureaucracy: government departments with thousands of staff and a framework of laws and rules to regulate the work. Users of services will be affected by the rules: for example, in relation to eligibility for a service or a grant.

Third, 'principles of social policy' refer to the *ideas* and theories that underpin social policy. This definition very much overlaps with the first: principles as morals, norms or value judgements.

However, there is a valid and useful distinction between a principle as a moral statement and a principle as an idea or a theory. It is possible, as we saw in Chapter 1, to have theories about social policy that are not based *primarily* on morals or value judgements, even though such ideas might be coloured *partly* by political opinions or other biases.

For example, we may seek to define, in as objective a way as possible, what such ideas as 'freedom', 'liberty', 'justice' and 'equality' mean in social policy terms. Another example of a leading idea in social policy, which was developed in the early nineteenth century, is utilitarianism: a set of principles outlined by Jeremy Bentham (1748–1832) to offer what he saw as a rational alternative to governing on the basis of values or religious morals (see Box 2.1).

Box 2.1   An early principle still relevant? The example of Bentham and utilitarianism

Jeremy Bentham was born in 1748 into a prosperous middle-class family. At the age of 7 he was sent to Westminster school and, at the tender age of 12, he entered Queen's College Oxford, which 'he hated even more' than school (Warnock 1966: 7). By the age of 20 he had received five years of training in London as a lawyer, but his brilliant mind and wide-ranging interests led him into the world of publishing and discourse on philosophy.

Between early adulthood and middle age, Bentham established himself as a radical thinker on social, political and moral issues. Together with a circle of friends, writers and publishers, he became an influential figure, challenging government inefficiency and abuse and recommending radical and rational solutions to social problems. His influences on policy were especially noticeable in the field of poverty and 'poor relief' (see Chapter 3), though he also put forward an ambitious scheme to reform and redesign prisons, as well as many other constitutional and administrative proposals.

In 1788, he published his *An Introduction to the Principles of Morals and Legislation* (see Bentham 1982), which contains all the main elements of what became known as 'utilitarianism' or 'Benthamism'. Though not a socialist (socialism was in its infancy), Jeremy Bentham did advocate changes that were revolutionary in their time: the vote for all adult men and women, annual parliaments, open and accountable government based on rational or scientific principles. Above all, he firmly believed that the value of any policy should be decided on its objective merits, not whether it fitted with custom and practice or with any particular religious viewpoint.

In this way, Bentham's philosophy could be summarized as 'radical and ruthless'. There is no room for sentiment, or tradition, or for policies that support unearned privilege. The basic question, according to Bentham, is whether any government policy or institution serves any valuable purpose or has any *utility* (use) – hence 'utilitarianism'.

But how do we decide whether a policy has a useful function or not? Bentham's answer – and the principle he is perhaps most famous for – was to suggest that we find out what would bring 'the greatest happiness of the greatest number'. The best policy is one that minimizes the harm or discomfort to the greatest possible number of individuals, or that brings 'happiness' to the majority, even if there is a cost to the minority.

Bentham's method or 'calculus' for working this out was based on the degree of pleasure or pain involved in any course of action. Not surprisingly, he was denounced by leading religious authorities of the day because he appeared to be advancing a godless doctrine that appealed to primitive or basic human instincts. In defence, Bentham's calculus of pleasures included the 'higher' things – for example, education and artistic achievement – and he suggested that policies that promote these have the greatest utility.

How does utilitarianism apply to modern dilemmas of rationing services or calculating who should benefit from welfare? The utilitarian approach to these dilemmas is to apply 'the greatest happiness of the greatest number' principle. It therefore questions whether all human life is of equal value, and whether it is immoral to weigh some people's happiness or continued life against that of others. These questions are still very much with us, as illustrated by moral dilemmas in the provision of scarce health care resources (see Chapter 9). When health service professionals make judgements about patients on other than medical criteria, they may stray into making utilitarian judgements: for example, whether a patient is young or old, is married or has dependants. Consciously or not, they may be asking themselves, 'What use does saving or prolonging this life have, and how far would medical help in this case add to the sum of human happiness?'

On the one hand, utilitarianism can be seen as realistic: in this world, hard choices have to be made and it is better to be clearheaded about the relative costs and gains of a policy so that welfare can be maximized. On the other, utilitarianism can be seen as one element in an overarching Victorian philosophy of self-interest and a penny-pinching approach to public services. It would be unfair to portray Bentham as someone who advocated pure self-interest. After all, he believed in the idea of expanding public education and other services to benefit the majority. However, it was the case that a cruder kind of utilitarian thinking gained ground in the nineteenth century and helped to justify the harsh treatment of the poor.

Equality, equity and justice

Equality and politics

The principle of equality occupies a central place in debates about social policy. For those on the left of the political spectrum, social policies are ideally the tools or mechanisms with which to create a fairer society by equalizing benefits from health, education and other services.

But from the perspectives of the political right and centre, social policies that attempt to equalize outcomes for people do so at considerable cost. Not only do they impose a burden of high taxation on people with average and higher incomes, with the suggested effect of dampening incentives and *economic growth*, but also they require a highly interventionist state and an army of bureaucrats and professionals.

Robert Nozick, a philosopher who published an influential book, *Anarchy, State and Utopia*, in 1974, powerfully attacked the goal of using social policies and other forms of government intervention (such as taxation) to increase equality. He based his argument on a distinction between 'patterned' and 'non-patterned' forms of justice. To summarize Nozick's complex and interesting argument, his fundamental point is that patterned justice involves the idea of continual interference in people's lives in order to bring about a particular distribution (pattern) of property, goods and other things of value (for instance, employment opportunities). The pattern would be based upon a particular goal. For instance, in one society there might be a particularly strong attachment to the idea of rewarding merit and of distributing resources and rewards on that basis. Conversely, another society might stress the goal of equality between individuals irrespective of merit or performance.

However, according to Nozick, any attempt to enforce patterns of justice will tend to undermine the supremely important value of liberty – hence Nozick's philosophy is an example of 'libertarian' principles. It is wrong and unjust, according to these principles, for any government to take away the individual's property or income in order to redistribute it in the attempt to create patterned justice: for instance, by taxing individuals to fund social welfare. Nozick's approach therefore emphasizes the idea that there is justice in wealth and property being owned in 'non-patterned' ways (for instance, according to historical factors and chance). For him, the only moral form of government is one that is minimal in its interventions and actions; any 'more extensive state would (will) violate the rights of individuals' (Nozick 1974: 333).

Note how perspectives of the 'right', including libertarian principles such as Nozick's, often suggest that the principle of *freedom* is threatened if social policies are too concerned with equality, while 'left' perspectives often defend equality by reference to people's *needs*. Thus, arguments about the value of equality, and whether promoting it is a good idea, cannot be fully understood in isolation from either of these other concepts.

However, it is misleading to package all ideas about equality and policy neatly into either a left-wing or right-wing perspective. To begin with, and despite the popularity of the terms, there is little consensus on what being 'left wing' or 'right wing' actually means. The distinction between left and right in politics is thought to originate from the days of the French Revolution in the late eighteenth century, when the more liberal and radical representatives in the newly-formed National Assembly were seated to the left of the presiding officer, while the more conservative members of the legislature sat on the right. As democracy developed in Europe, a similar seating arrangement became common practice in a number of parliaments. Thus a tradition grew up, associating 'left' with principles that favoured equality, radical reform and 'bigger government', and 'right' with principles that favour individual freedom and liberty over equality of outcome, a more cautious approach to change and reform, and an emphasis on reducing the role of 'big government' in people's lives.

In the contemporary **postmodern** political context, however, these earlier distinctions between left and right have become blurred (see concluding chapter for further discussion). But also, there have always been considerable differences *among* fellow socialists, liberals and conservatives on the question of how much equality is desirable and how far social policies should attempt to 'correct' the inequalities and injustices of society.

For instance, a liberal thinker on equality, John Rawls (1972), argues that a basic goal of every policy should be one of equality. As far as possible, the 'good things' of life should be shared equally: education and career opportunities, welfare services, leisure and so on. Further, Rawls regards the right to liberty as fundamental in a just society. Everyone should be treated equally in this respect.

However, Rawls also argues that a certain amount of inequality – just enough to create rewards and incentives for the better-off people in society – will benefit not only the advantaged *but also the least advantaged*. With the right amount of incentive, the better-off groups in society will work at an optimum level of efficiency. This will mean that everyone will benefit from well-run public services and private businesses. But if rewards for the better-off exceed the optimum level, the poorer groups begin to lose out. The better-off contribute less than they should in the form of taxes (wealth and income that can be redistributed) and have fewer incentives to be efficient, because their incomes are high irrespective of their work efforts. Rawls termed the idea of achieving just about the right amount of inequality the 'difference principle' (see Rawls 1972).

It has always been the case that some thinkers on the left have believed that certain inequalities are unavoidable. Some kinds of inequality might even be encouraged if they are based on rewarding merit. Conversely, it is also true that some thinkers on the right have subscribed to the idea that there should be certain basic equalities between people.

In Britain, the old left–right battle lines between the Labour and Conservative parties have been redrawn in recent times. Partly, this is a reflection of international events – in particular, the downfall of communism in the former Soviet Union (Russia) and its satellite states in eastern and central Europe. Though almost all western European socialists had already distanced themselves from repressive, corrupt and highly unequal communist regimes, the end of communism nevertheless removed an important reference point.

In short, socialism may live on as an idea, but if we define it as a set of policies to redistribute resources and to make society substantially more equal than it was, it is dead. No major political party in Britain – including the Labour Party – now supports principles of equality in the traditional socialist sense.

There is another strong reason for this. In the first half of the twentieth century, policies to redistribute wealth and to make society more equal than before held some appeal for the majority of the population. Approximately a third of the British population enjoyed relatively high incomes and considerable wealth, while the remaining two thirds lived either on moderate and static incomes, or in poverty. Most people could agree with the idea of redistribution, knowing that it would be likely to benefit them.

In more recent decades, however, the pattern of income and wealth has shifted. Although inequalities have widened, living standards for a two-thirds majority have steadily improved at the same time. A political party that stands for equality and a substantial redistribution of resources therefore no longer has the appeal it may have had. The Labour Party in Britain painfully discovered this in election defeat after election defeat between 1979 and 1992. Its victory in 1997 was largely attributable to its ability to distance itself from the idea that it was a high tax party with policies to help the poorer third of the population at the expense of the majority (see Chapter 13).

Justifying policies for equality

Given these changes in the political context and the lack of support for full-blooded socialism, can equality still be defended as an important principle of social policy? As with every principle, the answer to this question depends on how equality is interpreted. Three basically different views can be identified: the goal of near-equality or egalitarianism; equity; and equality of opportunity. Attached to each of these definitions are somewhat different justifications for equality.

Egalitarianism
This is an ideal, an expression of equality in its 'purest' or most utopian form (Drabble 1988). It is about finding ways of ensuring that people enjoy the same results or *outcomes* in life: the same incomes, the same life span, similar levels of education and health and so on.

What would be the justification for policies to bring about a state of near-equality? Again, much would depend on the egalitarian's values or morality. The example of communism has already been mentioned. There has also been a thread of ethical or

Christian socialism in British egalitarianism, and this has been a recurrent influence on thinking about social policy (see, for example, Tawney 1964). In communism or Marxism, the ultimate objective was a society in which no one unfairly exploited the labour of anyone else. Ethical socialists, however, stressed the *moral* dimension: gross inequalities are morally wrong, whereas a society of near-equals is one in which community, brotherhood and sisterhood will flourish. Note the normative ideas underlying this principle of equality.

Tawney was a Christian socialist and a leading figure in debates about equality in a welfare society. For him, equality amounted to much more than 'distributive justice' or making sure that incomes and the benefits of the welfare system were distributed equally among individuals and classes. Julian Le Grand's study, *Strategy of Equality* (1982) is an example of how the concept of distributive justice can be applied to research on 'who gets what' from the welfare system. Tawney held to a wider socialistic vision of equality. His goal and his vision of social policy was to help create a society in which people felt that they belonged to a common community – a society in which they would feel free to participate in making political decisions about their own future, and in which everyone was valued equally.

In a similar vein, Marshall – another founder of the principles of an egalitarian welfare society – argued that: 'The extension of the social services is not primarily a means of equalising incomes ... What matters is that there is a general enrichment of the concrete substance of civilized life, a general reduction of risk and insecurity, an equalisation between the more and less fortunate at all levels ... Equality of status is more important than equality of income' (1963: 107).

However, *inequality* of income is important to egalitarians in one important respect. Large inequalities, it is argued, lead to social division and are, in themselves, morally wrong. For instance, public concern has been expressed about the enormous annual pay increases (of over 30 per cent and totalling thousands of pounds) awarded to the heads of government agencies. This has been at a time when the great majority of public sector employees, working in the same agencies, have been expected to accept much lower annual pay increases.

Thus, the egalitarian's argument against inequality is relatively easy to invoke, as did Charles Dickens in his scathing attacks on the greed and selfishness of Victorian business people and corrupt public servants. However, a critique of gross inequality is not the same as making a case for *near-equality*. Here the egalitarians' arguments are harder to sustain, for a number of reasons.

First, *individuals differ*. Whether as a result of nature or nurture, every individual has a unique combination of talents, abilities, temperament and motivation. Policies trying to bring about absolute or near-equality would work against these differences, rewarding the lazy, the incompetent and the dishonest as well as the innovative, intelligent or honest.

There is a lack of justice in policies that try to ensure equal outcomes for all. Would it be just, for example, to ensure that all 16-year-olds 'achieved' the same number of GCSE passes at the same grades, even though everyone knew that a proportion of the 'successful' candidates were being rewarded for either mediocre efforts or none at all? Such a policy would immediately devalue the GCSE qualification but, more importantly, would be unjust to those who had worked hard or had the ability to achieve the better results.

The second factor is coercion and *lack of freedom*. In order for a state of near-equality to be maintained, very strong regulatory authorities would be needed to survey constantly individuals' incomes, redistribute wealth and monitor who was being appointed to each and every job. Not only would this cost a great deal to implement, but it would also bring about a very invasive state. Everyone's private life would have to be scrutinized regularly and closely to make sure that no one was becoming better off than anyone else. So while inequality spells lack of freedom for some because better-off individuals and groups may gain at the expense of the poor, a state of *imposed equality* would severely reduce everyone's freedom.

However, these criticisms of equality are valid only where policies are taken to extremes. It is relatively easy to put up a 'straw man' of absolute equality and then knock it down, as gurus of the New Right such as Hayek (1944), Worsthorne (1971) and Scruton (1984) have done. In arguing that the goal of equality is unattainable, they have always told cautionary tales of the horrors of repressive state socialist regimes such as the former Soviet Union. But they have never carefully considered the achievements of countries that successfully applied social democratic principles in the past. Countries such as Sweden and Denmark have not sought to abolish inequality completely, but have acted to reduce the extremes that arise in other capitalist economies.

So while everyone agrees that near-equality is an impossible dream, perhaps even a nightmare, this does not mean that the equality principle need be rejected altogether. In policy terms, a more acceptable and practical principle might be that of *making society more equal than it was*, rather than trying to bring about absolute equality. This is in one way a utilitarian consideration, increasing social equality not so much for the sake of it but more to maintain social order and to ensure 'the greatest happiness of the greatest number'. But, more importantly, there is also the justification of fairness – making sure that less well-off or disadvantaged groups are treated with justice.

A policy to bring about near-equality might look more justifiable if we think about it in relation to *groups* rather than individuals. For example, while accepting that individual men and women differ – the more and the less intelligent, able, rich and poor individuals – there is a strong argument that men and women as groups should be near-equals. This would mean that approximately equal proportions of women and men would occupy each occupational or income level. Sweden, for instance, has set policy targets to do just this, and aims to achieve a balance of no more than 60 per cent or less than 40 per cent of either men or women in a comprehensive list of occupations (Blakemore and Drake 1995).

Similar arguments about equality and the representation of different groups at every level of society can be applied to minority groups as well as to men and women. Equal opportunity policies (see pp. 24–26), for instance, aim to increase opportunities for people who have experienced discrimination in the past because of their disability, age, sexual orientation or 'race'. As they are minority groups in the population, however, this means that equality in terms of numbers is achieved once the *proportions* of black, gay, disabled and older people in a given occupation or at a given income level match the proportions in the population as a whole. This notion of equality based on proportions – 'proportionality' – is a relatively limited definition of equality, however, because it does not include any reference to *power*. A business firm or a government department might employ representative proportions of women and disabled people, for instance, but this does not necessarily mean that women and disabled employees have an equal say in the shaping of policy or in sharing managerial control of the organization.

Equity

This is a useful idea that extends the concept of equality. The notion of equality tends to make us focus on sameness or similarity. Thus, if neighbours X and Y are equal, we tend to think of them having similar incomes, houses, type of car, number of children and so on. But if such an end-state were to be brought about by social and taxation policies, what would be required?

This is where the concept of equity is useful because, to reach a similar end-state or outcome, it is usually necessary to treat individuals, families and groups *equitably* rather than *equally*. An equitable approach means treating people fairly, but differently, to ensure that there is some equality between them at the end.

Dividing a cake gives a homely example to illustrate equity. Assuming that one guest feels full, two are not very hungry and a fourth is ravenous, equitable slicing would mean no cake for the first, two thin slices and one large wedge. After this, all guests should be in an equal state – full – but they have been treated unequally to achieve this. Treating them all equally, on the other hand, would have resulted in unequal or undesirable outcomes.

In social policy terms, and returning to our neighbouring families X and Y, equitable social policies would treat each household differently depending on its needs and circumstances. For example, if X's son is disabled or has special educational needs, there might be targeted grants, benefits or school facilities that would have the object of compensating the X family for additional expenditure and bringing them back to a state of near-equality with the Y family.

The problem with equitable social policies is that sometimes they do not *look* fair. Treating everyone in the same way is seen as fair, whereas treating them differently seems to smack of injustice or special favours. For example, equitable cake slicing might work with adults but try it with small children, who expect equal slices of a birthday cake. In this situation equity will almost certainly end in tears.

A more serious example is provided by public reaction to William Beveridge's wartime proposals for social security reform, which might be regarded as the cornerstone of Britain's welfare state (see Chapter 3). Above all, it was the fairness and perceived equality of the scheme that gripped the public imagination, made Beveridge into something of a hero and the 'Beveridge Report' into a best seller (Beveridge 1942). Beveridge's proposal that all contributors be treated equally, paying the same (flat-rate) National Insurance contributions and being able to draw the same flat-rate benefits when in need, seemed to tune in perfectly with the wartime collective spirit of equality.

Yet, in essence, Beveridge's plan owed more to liberal principles of equality than to socialist ones. Treating people 'equally' meant that the scheme did not substantially redistribute resources from the better-off social classes to the less well-off, although of course it did redistribute from the healthy to the temporarily sick and from the employed to the temporarily unemployed. A more equitable social security policy, it could be argued, would have asked the better-off to pay a little more into the scheme in return for the same benefits as everyone else – but would this have looked fair?

Applying the equity principle can also raise problems because fairness demands an accurate and accepted definition of people's *needs*. Suppose that you are again faced with a table of squabbling children at mealtime and that you have decided to distribute food in unequal, equitable portions. If you are both a parent and a student of social policy, perhaps the children will already have grudgingly learned to put up with the principle of equity. However, this does not solve the problem of deciding whose definitions of need to take into account – yours or theirs? There might be vociferous objections from the children to the *grounds* on which the size of each child's portion has been decided: 'That's not fair, he had a big slice yesterday', 'She said she's going to be sick if you give her any vegetables' and so on. You may yourself be unsure of each child's 'real' needs: is Matthew clamouring for more simply because he is showing off; is Alison hungrier than she is prepared to say, and should she be encouraged to eat more? Faced with all this, it is not surprising that parents, like welfare systems, resort to giving equal, but inequitable, benefits.

Equality of opportunity

This is another useful refinement of the meaning of equality. The equal opportunity concept might be applied first to *employment*, through policies to remove barriers of discrimination, improving access to jobs, education and training. In an age of temporary work contracts and part-time jobs, this is important. Work, despite its drawbacks, raises incomes, usually provides social contact and reduces social exclusion (see Chapter 8). Second, equal opportunity principles can be applied to improving access to, and use of, *health and social services*.

However, as with other equality principles, equal opportunity means different things to different people. Conservatives, as well as those on the left, subscribe to 'equality of opportunity'. Views from the political right stress *opportunity*, while those from the left stress the *equality* side of the equation. These differences of emphasis can result in substantial practical differences in the ways that equal opportunity policies are applied. Distinctions can be made between (a) relatively limited and modest definitions of equal opportunity, and (b) more ambitious and 'tougher' approaches. These distinctions are summarized in Box 2.2.

Under British law – for example, the anti-discrimination laws planned for 2007 that will combine legislation against discrimination on the basis of gender, race, disability, age and other categories for the first time – policy and practice are much closer to (a) than to (b). But it is better to think of equal opportunity policies on a spectrum from 'modest' to 'tough'. Particular examples do not necessarily fit neatly into either category. In the UK, for example, not all equal opportunity policies can be pigeonholed as weak. A certain amount of 'positive action' to correct gender and 'race' discrimination is allowed under British law, and in Northern Ireland a Fair Employment Act and other government action has endorsed the principle of 'proportionality' mentioned above. In the Northern Ireland case proportionality means a more equal sharing of job opportunities between the Protestant and Catholic communities than before. Although a strict policy of reserving jobs for the under-represented Catholic minority has not been introduced, it is in Northern Ireland that the UK has moved closest to the principle of a 'tougher' approach to equal opportunities.

The summarized distinctions between minimalist policies and maximalist policies (or 'weak' and 'tough') of equal opportunity (see Box 2.2) suggest sharp differences between two types of equality policy. However, it is worth re-emphasizing that in reality these distinctions are blurred. If policies favour positive action rather than positive discrimination, for instance, we can describe them as being midway between 'weak' and 'tough'.

Positive action refers to policies that stop short of positive discrimination. Under Britain's Race Relations Act 1976, for example, it was permissible to take positive steps to encourage members of under-represented groups to apply for work in an organization (for instance, in the way that job advertisements were worded). Other forms of positive action include additional training courses to meet the needs of under-represented groups, career breaks for women, and improvements in facilities in the workplace that enhance disabled people's opportunities.

All these measures were designed to develop a workforce that was more representative of the population, but that did not rely on a quota system of reserving jobs for each under-represented group. Similar principles apply to the distribution of benefits or access to social and health services. Positive action here would entail taking steps to encourage access and to enable under-represented or disadvantaged groups to make fuller use of the services available.

However, positive action does not mean that people will automatically qualify for a service or a benefit *because* they are members of a minority or a disadvantaged group. *Need* remains the basic criterion. The object of positive action is therefore to equalize access and to ensure that everyone with needs is heard: for instance, by providing translation services to hospital patients whose first language is other than English.

Box 2.2 Equal opportunity strategies

'Minimalist' principles	*'Maximalist' principles*
Equality policies aim to ensure that people are *treated* fairly or on an equal basis.	Equality policies aim to create *equal outcomes*. Policies and the law must go further than banning unfair or negative discrimination; they must also positively encourage or discriminate so that minorities and other disadvantaged groups benefit equally from employment opportunities or the welfare system.
Discrimination on grounds of gender, 'race', disability or other irrelevant criteria is unjust and illegal in most cases.	
'Fair competition' on a 'level playing field' is the hallmark of this approach. The end result or outcome (for example, being employed or receiving a benefit) must be decided on *merit* or according to *need*.	There is no 'level playing field'. Historic advantages enjoyed by those in control now mean that they decide how 'merit' and 'need' are defined. Though merit is important, it may have to be redefined to avoid in-built bias against women, disabled people and others.

Individuals must be treated 'in like fashion'. The end result is unequal, but fair. *Any* discrimination, positive or negative, is wrong.	Individuals may be treated differently according to the social group or category they belong to. 'Positive action' or 'positive discrimination' might be necessary to make sure that underrepresented groups obtain benefits or employment from which they have previously been excluded.
Quotas, or reserving a certain number of jobs, educational places or services for members of minority and disadvantaged groups, are unjust.	Quotas, or at least targets, to bring the *proportions* of people in various groups (women, disabled people and others) in line with the proportions receiving employment, education and welfare are necessary because without them little will change.
'Minimalist' principles fit best with liberal or conservative principles and values.	'Maximalist' principles fit best with social democratic or egalitarian principles, though 'tough' equal opportunities policies are found in the right-of-centre dominated USA.

Having said this, the distinction between (a) providing services strictly according to need and (b) positive discrimination in favour of a certain group, is not as clear-cut as it might first appear. Some social benefits combine (a) need criteria with (b): a kind of positive discrimination. For example, child benefit is distributed to mothers (or the father, if he is the main carer). The idea behind this benefit is to meet need by offsetting partly the expenses incurred in bringing up children. Parents receive this benefit because they are parents, not because every one of them is in need. Thus recipients of child benefit are in one sense the beneficiaries of a form of positive discrimination, in that they are singled out as a group or category rather than being treated as individuals, some of whom actually do not need the benefit and some of whom do.

This point is linked to arguments about whether benefits should be universal benefits – that is, available to everyone in a certain category, such as child benefit for parents – or whether they should be targeted or selective benefits. This is discussed further in Chapter 5.

Need

This brings us to the important concept of need. We have already seen that 'need' is a *problematic* concept (by 'problematic', we mean a term that is not easy to define and where there is a lack of consensus about what it means). This causes difficulties when, for example, we try to decide whether one person's or one group's needs are greater than another's.

Before you read any further, it might help at this point to spend five minutes writing a short list of what you think are the most important human needs. Try to list at least ten.

Now ask yourself these questions. Is there any pattern or logic in the list you have drawn up? For example, do some needs come before others and if so, why? Are some more basic or fundamental? (If you do not see a pattern, add some more needs and then try to prioritize the needs in some way.)

Are your definitions of need culture-free, or do they relate only to a particular country or social group? To test this, think about whether your list would be as applicable in India or Mali, say, as in Britain or another economically developed country. Try constructing a list as if *you* were living in a village in the African Sahel, or on the streets of an Indian city. How does your list compare with that of Doyal and Gough (1991), presented a little further on?

Writing your own list of human needs and the questions this poses in your mind should help to identify two fundamental points about need. These points have been at the centre of social policy ever since the state began to take on certain basic responsibilities for people's welfare. The first is a central question about objectivity. Is it possible to establish a commonly accepted or objective definition of need and to distinguish clearly between those who are in need and those who are not? The second point relates to questions of responsibility and duty. How far is the state responsible for meeting certain needs? Should every citizen have *rights* to have their needs met, and does the community have a *duty* to meet them?

These questions not only are of great interest today, but also vexed the conscience of nineteenth-century Britain. In Britain, the 'new' Poor Law of 1834 showed official acceptance of a very basic responsibility of the state towards the poorest citizens. Workhouses and 'parish relief' were organized into a system that was designed to provide for only the absolutely destitute (see Chapter 3). In return for their freedom and loss of *civil rights*, paupers could obtain just enough from the public purse to survive. In this early example of social policy we have a definition of basic needs: shelter, food and perhaps some very limited medical care.

Doyal and Gough (1991: 56–9) point out that survival is too limited a definition even of basic need. As they suggest, the victim of a serious accident who is in a coma is surviving but is not able to achieve anything or to satisfy any other needs. Similarly, the example of severely malnourished victims of famine shows that people might be surviving – just – but are hardly having their basic needs met. Another problem with 'survival' as a definition of basic need is that it is rather circular: it is rather like saying that human beings 'need to live'.

For these reasons, Doyal and Gough suggest that *physical health* is a better definition of basic need, because 'to complete a range of practical tasks in daily life requires manual, mental and emotional abilities with which poor physical health usually interferes' (1991: 56).

The advantage of using physical health as a criterion of basic need is that it suggests certain *goals*. Note that Doyal and Gough talk of 'good' physical health, which takes us away from mere survival to a goal that people can aim for. However, the concept of 'physical health' also opens up problems of definition: how healthy do people have to be before we can say that their needs can be met?

Thus, it might not be possible to find completely objective definitions, even of basic needs. This is more apparent when we include Doyal and Gough's second criterion of basic needs, *autonomy*. Without autonomy, or the freedom to be able to decide and choose, human beings are arguably deprived of a need as basic as physical health. It is no use being physically healthy without the ability to realize the aspirations or objectives that make us human – secondary needs such as the need to develop oneself in various ways, to communicate and to form relationships with other human beings. As with physical health, however, autonomy is a matter of degree. There is bound to be debate about how much autonomy human beings need or, more negatively, how much they can do without. Related to this is the question of mental health. It is hard to see why only physical health should be seen as a basic need when mental illness can seriously impair quality of life and can remove people's ability to live autonomous, independent lives.

Sadly, loss or lack of autonomy is not difficult to find in the field of welfare and social policy. Older people, for example, are particularly vulnerable in this respect, because they might have been judged to be incapable of exercising autonomy. The very old are often written off as too mentally confused or frail to exercise any autonomy. Studies of confused older people in residential care suggest that the staff or 'carers' might exaggerate these infirmities and might actually increase them (Kitwood 1997). Such residents are not even allowed to exercise choice or autonomy in matters that they can still comprehend. Similar issues of loss of autonomy and the controlling aspects of residential care are discussed further in Chapter 6.

Box 2.3 Universal human needs?

Doyal and Gough (1991) argue that it is relatively easy to make up a list of needs – social policy research abounds with them. However, it is more difficult to decide which needs are *universal* and which definitions would permit us to compare need satisfaction in different countries or cultures.

Their list (below) has been drawn up according to one main criterion. To be included, each item must contribute towards satisfying the two most *basic* needs (physical health and autonomy). For example, they suggest that sexual relationships need not be included 'because some people manage to live healthy and autonomous lives without sex with others' (1991: 158). Do you agree with this, and in general what do you think of their list of needs?

- nutritional food and clean water
- protective housing
- a non-hazardous work environment
- a non-hazardous physical environment
- appropriate health care
- security in childhood
- significant primary relationships
- physical security
- economic security

- appropriate education

- safe birth control and childbearing.

To sum up, physical health and autonomy can be seen as basic needs that, if denied, will result in people being unable to meet other, secondary needs. Putting it another way, *needs could be defined as basic if being deprived of them will lead to serious harm*.

Once basic needs have been discussed, however, there remains the question of how secondary or intermediate needs are to be identified. This is the point at which to compare your own list with that of Doyal and Gough (see Box 2.3).

Needs, wants and satisfaction

So far, our discussion of need has highlighted some of the problems encountered in trying objectively to define 'real' needs. But while difficult, this is not an impossible task as long as we remember that there has to be some argument. In fact, debate about needs is a healthy phenomenon. For instance, it might be prompted by attempts to improve standards of welfare or to expose the hidden needs of disadvantaged groups.

Bradshaw (1972), in a pioneering discussion, suggested that there are four main ways in which people define needs.

- *Felt need*, according to Bradshaw, occurs when individuals are conscious of their needs. This, however, leaves open the question of whether they decide to express their felt needs or whether they are able to do so. Not all felt needs are expressed, either because those in need choose not to express them or because inequalities of power and status prevent oppressed and less powerful groups from voicing their needs. For example, older Asian women's needs have been neglected in the provision of community services because of the subordinate position of many of these women (see Blakemore and Boneham 1994).
- *Expressed needs* are publicized and known about. They become *demands*, as opposed to the hidden needs of those who are unwilling or too powerless or otherwise unable to express what they need, as just mentioned.
- *Normative needs* are those defined according to professional norms or standards; they are needs defined by outside observers or experts. For example, a professional counsellor might identify a need in a client that the client might accept, or on the other hand reject or fail to comprehend. Or, to give another example, social workers responsible for finding foster homes will judge whether a particular home is adequate to meet the needs of a child, as defined by their professional view and the standards laid down by their employer.
- *Comparative need* introduces the concept of relative judgement – that is, the needs of a group are defined relative to what other groups have or do not have. There is an element of justice here. If there are two similar groups, but only one is receiving a benefit or a service, the group not receiving welfare could be unjustly deprived and in comparative need.

The first definition – felt need – introduces a subjective element into the discussion. On the one hand, there are some needs that can be defined objectively (albeit with some disagreement among observers) and, on the other, wants that are apparently more to do with subjective or personal states of mind or desires. For example, a person might need a certain medical treatment that is invasive or painful, but not want it. Or a hypochondriac will be obsessed with medical treatments even though objectively these are not needed.

Remember that one way of defining a *need* is that being deprived of it causes serious harm, whereas this is not the case with things that are purely *wants*. A child might desperately want the latest computer game but arguably being deprived of it will not cause harm and might even do some good.

This distinction between wants and needs is not a clear-cut one, however. The very idea of 'felt needs' suggests that a strongly subjective element *can* enter into definitions of need. For example, pensioners on a low income might decide that keeping in touch with their grandchildren is a basic requirement (and a need to sustain important family relationships). They might decide that it is vitally important to spend a lot of their money on cards and gifts, especially on the grandchildren's birthdays or at seasonal holidays such as Christmas. But in refusing to compromise on this, they might well have to economize on heating or food costs. In this case, what appear to be unnecessary wants (cards, gifts) take the place of things that safeguard a basic need, such as physical health. For instance, they might decide that their heating must be switched off to save money, possibly risking death from hypothermia for the sake of being able to afford Christmas cards and presents.

Therefore, although being deprived of needs can be said to cause serious harm, so in some ways could being deprived of wants. The teenager who is deprived of the latest fashion item might take this want so seriously that they become depressed, feel that they are a social outcast and that their whole life has been blighted. If this happens, then we might have to take the consequences seriously: for example, shoplifting or other forms of offending.

The value of bringing the subjective element into any discussion of needs and wants is that it helps to answer the question of why *satisfaction* levels are not rising markedly in industrialized countries when, according to many objective economic criteria, needs are being met more fully than ever before.

For instance, if economic indicators of well-being are anything to go by, great progress has been made in the past few decades. British incomes rose by 230 per cent in real terms between 1950 and 1990 (Vidal 1994: 4), life expectancy has increased and ordinary people now own many more consumer goods – television sets, computers, cars, freezers and refrigerators – than could have been dreamt of in the 1950s. But whether there has been progress in meeting the full range of human needs is a much more debatable point.

This is where the subjective element is important, for as Vidal (1994: 4–5) notes,

> *many people feel intuitively that growth has not necessarily made people better off. Evidence that quality of life is declining is all around. The British now work the longest average weekly hours in the European Union ... We appear to have invented new illnesses – from chronic fatigue syndrome to anorexia – and we have increased our vulnerability to older ones, such as asthma, ulcers and diabetes ... Job stress may cost*

> *the UK ten per cent of GNP [gross national product] annually. And so on, through jammed-up cities, loss of greenbelt, more noise, increasing need for the car ... the abuse of natural resources ... pollution, and inner city blight.*

We do not have to accept the whole of this negative message. For instance, there are objective grounds for saying that health is better now than it was in the early 1960s (see Chapter 9). However, an equally important factor is whether people *feel* that their needs are being met and whether their quality of life is failing to improve. As societies with welfare systems become more affluent than before, perhaps they can increasingly 'afford' to be disenchanted with the costs of progress (pollution, erosion of public amenities and loss of community life) in a way that poorer, less industrialized countries cannot.

Sen's theory: 'commodities', 'capabilities' and 'functionings'

The eminent Indian economist Amartya Sen has developed a view of poverty, and more generally of well-being and the standard of living, which has attracted a great deal of attention in the 20 years or so since he first put them forward. Sen's theory may be regarded as a critique and revision of economic views about well-being and at the same time his approach can be viewed as a variant of, or an application of, a 'needs' approach.

Sen criticizes what he calls the economist's and utilitarian's definitions of welfare or of value in terms of 'happiness' or utility. These, he argues, neglect a range of moral and economic issues that are important, such as exploitation (Sen 1980). He points to the urgency of basic wants and needs and the objectivity of such facts as whether a person is 'hungry, cold or oppressed' (1980: 154). Utility information (pleasure, desire–satisfaction) must be supplemented by such objective assessments. Sen therefore suggests that it is more appropriate to see demands for freedom from exploitation as a moral claim for just rewards ('equality of desert') than as 'lack of well-being' (1980: 155). Similarly, the demand for 'equal pay for equal work' is not a purely instrumental claim, which in welfarist/utilitarian terms it would be.

In developing his theory, Sen has identified, and distinguishes between, three concepts: 'commodities', 'capabilities' and 'functionings'. Commodities (which can be defined as resources, including income, health care and education) have tended to be the focus in most research on needs, poverty and social policy. The notion of a poverty line or subsistence, minimum income level is based on the idea of such commodities, or the lack of them. But Sen suggests that focusing only on commodities is an inadequate basis for poverty research and for defining needs. This is because people vary in their capacities to transform commodities into 'capabilities' and 'functionings' (Sen 1980: 161).

'Capabilities' can be defined objectively, according to Sen, and they describe the necessary conditions human beings need to enable them to function fully. Examples of basic capabilities would include the following: the ability to move about; the ability to meet our nutritional requirements; the wherewithal to be clothed and sheltered; and the ability to participate in the social life of the community.

The object of public policy, according to Sen, is therefore to try to ensure as fair a distribution as possible of both commodities and capabilities. Functionings, which can be at the social or the individual level, involve the idea of activity, or of 'being and doing'.

So, in sum, capabilities are necessary conditions to achieve functionings. They relate directly to the kinds of lives that people are able to lead – the kinds of activities they can pursue, or 'being and doing' (which, he argues, is what our concern with the standard of living and poverty is all about). Commodities by themselves are described as 'opaque' by Sen; it is what people are able to *do* with them that matters.

A useful feature of the capabilities concept is its connection with the idea of positive freedom – freedom as 'empowerment' or as opportunity (see the next section for further discussion of 'positive' and 'negative' definitions of freedom). Capabilities seem to involve choice and the range of choice that individuals have: 'Capabilities ... are notions of freedom, in the positive sense: what real opportunities you may have regarding the life you may lead' (Sen 1987: 36). So, in contrasting a capability and a functioning, the latter is an achievement and the former is 'the *ability* to achieve' (1987: 36) (italics added).

Sen's theory is valuable for a number of reasons. It provides a systematic attempt to explore and develop a more precise characterization of well-being for social science and policy purposes than that provided by some of the standard theories on offer. It provides a corrective to some established views. Sen has drawn attention to what commodities are *for*. His theory attempts to integrate economic and sociological ideas about inequality, poverty and need – that is, economic theory based on the idea of utility or subjective preference, and social science and policy ideas based on objective notions such as need. Finally, Sen's contribution has the great merit of internationalizing the debate about issues such as poverty and need, and the political questions and moral principles these issues provoke. His discussion is as applicable to economically developed countries such as the UK as it is to developing countries such as India.

Freedom and rights

If we are coerced or told what to do throughout our lives and are deprived of rights, we cannot realize our potential to become fully human beings. However, as with equality, 'freedom' and 'rights' can easily become slogans. Difficulties begin when policy-makers or those who deliver welfare services have to decide what 'freedom' and 'rights' mean in practical terms, and on what grounds some people's freedoms might have to be removed or curtailed.

For instance, there might be a need to suspend the driving licence of a driver whose seriously failing vision and hearing pose grave dangers to other road users and pedestrians. However, difficulties arise in defining safety limits for the majority of older drivers, most of whom are safe drivers and enjoy lower insurance premiums as a result. What if a driver's vision is poor but just about adequate to drive a car along familiar routes? Or what if the driver and their partner live in a rural area, where without the use of a car it would be very difficult to visit a chemist's shop or buy groceries? Should such drivers have the freedom to take moderate risks with their own and others' safety?

Disability throws up a range of even deeper questions about freedoms and rights. The right to vote, for example, signifies an individual's full membership of society as a citizen. But should people with significant learning difficulties have the right to vote and, if not, how can their voices be heard and rights as citizens be respected?

Those who champion the rights of disabled people (for instance, Oliver 1990) argue that most, if not all, of the problems they face have been created by the society around them rather than directly by their disabilities. This is a 'social' model of disability, as opposed to a 'charity' or 'victim' model. It suggests that rather than pitying disabled people as victims of their own physical or mental states, society is responsible for improving their freedoms and guaranteeing their rights. Considerable investment in redesigning housing, work environments and transport facilities is needed in order to remove the barriers to freedom experienced by disabled people.

How far and in what ways society should be expected to make such a full commitment to the rights of disabled people is an open question, and is likely to cause continuing arguments about how to balance the rights and freedoms of disabled and non-disabled people. However, any discussion of freedom and rights will be unproductive unless these principles are broken down into different elements.

One way of doing this is to follow Marshall's (1950) classic distinction between civil, political and social rights. It is possible for individuals and groups to enjoy one or more of these types of right and the freedoms that are associated with them.

- *Civil rights* include basic freedoms under the law: for instance, freedom from discrimination, arbitrary arrest and detention, freedom to meet in groups and to have open discussion, freedom of the press and of expression.
- *Political rights* extend these freedoms to include the right to vote, to join and participate in political parties and to hold government accountable to democratic opinion.
- *Social rights*, according to Marshall, are of a rather different order. They involve a greater commitment of resources and are represented by rights to education, social welfare and social security; in short, rights to the benefits of a welfare system.

Viewed historically, in Britain, the three categories of rights can be seen to have developed gradually, with civil rights being established first, then political rights (for men first, and for women substantially later) and finally social rights. However, Marshall stressed that there is not necessarily an inevitable process of evolution at work here, involving automatic or continued progress towards social rights.

Some countries, such as present-day Singapore, combine substantial social rights and a well-organized welfare system with rather limited political rights (see Chapter 6). Thus one kind of freedom and one set of rights does not necessarily lead to another. In fact, social welfare can bolster paternalistic governments by making them appear fair and reasonable, thus reducing basic political freedoms.

To return to particular groups in society, such as disabled people, older people or children, we may apply Marshall's distinctions to questions about the rights of each. For example, with regard to children, electoral democracies have nowhere extended them *political* rights – they cannot vote or send their own representatives to parliament. However, this does not mean that they cannot have their *civil* rights improved and, under the Children Act 1989 and many other pieces of legislation, children have legal rights to education and welfare services: *social* rights.

If we consider people with learning difficulties, it may well be that they enjoy social protection and certain social rights, but they may never be granted civil and political rights even though, in some cases, they are capable of exercising political preferences or participating in decisions made about their welfare.

Another way of looking at both rights and freedoms is to think of them either as *negative* principles ('freedom *from*' certain things that endanger liberty) or as *positive* principles ('freedom *to*' do certain things).

A negative definition of freedom would give every citizen the right to be protected from harm from others – for example, from physical assault, burglary or discrimination. Negative definitions of freedom are very much part of a classical liberal or laissez-faire philosophy. In this view, people should be allowed as many freedoms as possible. However, complete freedom, or free-for-all anarchy, would not bring genuine liberty. Laissez-faire must be coupled with strong laws to restrain those who would intentionally seek to harm or reduce the freedoms of others. Thus a liberal society such as the USA has always had relatively strong laws to limit the power of both the state and of private monopolies (which form to fix prices unfairly and exploit consumers).

A strong belief among those on the political right who subscribe to the negative view of freedom (for example, Joseph and Sumption 1979) is that *to be poor is not to be unfree*. In other words, the poor and the rich alike enjoy political rights – all can vote in parliamentary elections, for instance – and civil rights, such as freedom from arbitrary arrest. According to this view, it is not up to society or a government to bring about a state of affairs in which everyone has equal freedom of action.

To those on the political right, freedom can be fully guaranteed only in a society organized by the market, in which people are free to own as much property as they can amass and in which there is competition between individuals and businesses. Markets are seen as vital in ensuring not only freedom but also efficiency. But by their very nature, markets lead to differences and they expose inequalities. People are bound to have different amounts of talent and ability, luck and spending power. In a 'free' market, there cannot be equal freedom for everyone to be able to afford tea at the Ritz.

Why do defenders of this view, such as Hayek (1944), argue that the poor – the losers in a market-based society – are not deprived of freedom? First, civil and political freedoms are still protected. For example, a family on income support probably could not afford tea at the Ritz, but they would have as much (civil) right to enter as anyone else (in contrast to a society in which discrimination against certain groups was legal, as in the former South Africa, where a black person could legally be denied entry to a hotel). They would also have the political right to meet with others on the street outside to demonstrate about poverty, if they wished, or to write to their Members of Parliament (MPs) to complain about the inadequacy of benefit payments.

Second, this argument runs, loss of freedom involves coercion or the *intention* of someone to deprive others of freedom. In a true market, though, there is no planned intention to reduce anyone's freedom. The market operates impersonally, and its outcomes (for example, rising or falling house prices, booming demand in one industry, layoffs in another) are apparently unknowable in advance.

Does this argument ring true, especially to anyone who happens to be poor in a society dominated by the market? First, we may question the suggestion that the outcomes of living in a market-based society are unknowable. There *is* clear evidence that, if unchecked, inequalities tend to widen. The social gap increases between wealthy elites and a more or less permanent group of disadvantaged people, while those in the middle feel increasingly insecure about their position. Rather than an increase in freedom and the creation of a mobile society in which enterprise and individuality are rewarded, there is an argument that increasing numbers of people begin to feel unfree and the better-off tend to monopolize positions of power and influence.

Also there is an assumption that, because market forces are blind, nothing should be done to 'tinker' with them, apart from ensuring that the rules of fair competition are enforced. But it is on this point that many, including some conservatives as well as those in the political centre and on the left, agree that it is both unethical and unwise to allow the market full rein. A more positive view of freedom involves policies to make sure that it is possible for those disadvantaged by a market society to have or to do certain things: for instance, to be able to purchase adequate food or housing, to be educated or to use a public library.

In one sense, the whole of social policy and its history revolves around this question: *how far* should the state step in to mitigate the effects of a society based on the market and on competition? How far can it guarantee rights to both freedom and security for every citizen, which implies not only 'freedom from' discrimination or harm, but also 'freedom to' enjoy a certain standard of living and welfare?

As we have seen, there are flaws in the pro-market, 'negative' concept of freedom. On the other hand, there is also growing acceptance in social policy of the limits of 'positive' views of freedom. Partly because of the spiralling costs of welfare systems and also because of worries about the creation of welfare dependency, politicians and policy-makers in every major industrial country have introduced reforms to limit the automatic right to welfare. For example, recent policies to shift people on benefit 'from welfare to work' in Britain, the USA and elsewhere, emphasize the *responsibilities* of the young unemployed rather than their *rights*.

Citizenship

Having looked, in the previous sections, at ideas about equality, needs, rights and freedom, let us now turn to look at a concept which puts together all these ideas, and which is important for thinking about the meaning and purpose of the welfare state. This concept, citizenship, is one that has undergone something of a revival and reformulation in recent decades. But what is 'citizenship'?

First, citizenship implies membership – membership of a particular type of community, namely, the nation-state: 'Citizenship is a status bestowed on those who are full members of a community' (Marshall 1964: 92). How is such membership defined, and what are the markers or identifiers of citizenship? They include, for example, nationality and right of residence, the possession of a passport and the right to participate in elections. They also include the right to work and the right to a range of social benefits. Thus the general principle of citizenship poses some fundamental questions, such as 'who is a citizen?' and, perhaps more importantly, 'who are non-citizens'? What is citizenship's connection with social policy, and do the formal rights attached to being a citizen match up with substantial rights, or the experiences people have when they make use of the health service or a social service, or when they claim benefits or try to enter the job market to find work?

In social policy, the concept of citizenship was developed by T.H. Marshall in 1949, in a series of lectures exploring the nature of the recently developed welfare state. Marshall was offering an account of the remodelling of the social services by the post-war Labour government, interpreting these in the light of an expanded conception of citizenship as an expression of social rights (see previous section). Marshall was the first to suggest that the concept of citizenship had mutated and developed in the modern period, so that by the mid-twentieth century it had come to include welfare entitlements. Marshall debated the nature of modern capitalism and its relation to democracy, and of the competing conceptions of equality and inequality that arise from the conflict and conjunction of these two. His contribution to the understanding of a modern conception of citizenship is, therefore, a major one and continues to be vigorously explored (Bulmer and Rees 1996).

Social and policy changes since the late 1970s arguably helped to revive interest in the concept of citizenship. One social change was the dramatic increase in income inequality in the UK, USA and other Anglophone countries resulting from greater inequality in earnings from paid employment, the growth of unemployment and growing polarization between two-earner and no-earner households (see Chapter 5). There was a growth, in the 1980s, of social polarization, of a 'North–South divide', of a '30-30-40' society and of social exclusion.

Accompanying these developments and associated with them was the discovery, or rediscovery, of the contentious concept of an 'underclass', a class with, allegedly, only a tenuous connection with mainstream norms and values, to the labour market and paid work, and to conventional family life. Murray's (1994) writings on the underclass associated it with the rise in criminality in this period, and defined the underclass not simply as a group defined by its poverty or unemployment but one outside, and sometimes in opposition to, mainstream society. Although many of Murray's conclusions were subsequently challenged and shown to be unfounded, they nevertheless stimulated a debate about the degree to which some sections of the population had come to be seen – and maybe saw themselves – as 'non citizens'. Another important social development of the last three decades has been the advent of movements – so-called 'new social movements', associated with, among others, gender, race, disability and sexuality – for liberation and empowerment, which have explicitly questioned the extent to which citizenship rights had been equalized in postwar Britain (Lister 1998).

Marshall believed that citizenship was a dynamic and developing concept and he certainly did not believe that Britain had reached the end of the road with regard to bringing equal citizenship rights to all. For him, social class differences and inequalities still seemed to raise barriers to full and equal use of the welfare state. He also devoted some space to discussing the extent to which there could be genuine equality in the possession of civil rights, given unequal access to courts and litigation because of their costs.

The aforementioned 'new social movements', to do with gender, race, disability and sexuality, among others, have reignited the debate about the boundaries of citizenship in contemporary societies such as Britain, and have posed again the question of the extent to which citizenship's formal attributes are matched by substantial ones. In other words, is the equal status which is the promise of citizenship matched by real equality of rights? Formally, every adult British national resident in the UK is a citizen, equal in the possession of the basic package of citizenship rights described above (with some limited exceptions, including peers and criminals!), but real equality of status, it is claimed, does not exist.

Marshall neglected the dimensions of race, ethnicity and culture, understandably, perhaps, since the UK had a much smaller ethnic minority population at the time of his lectures. These are issues of great interest and importance at the present time because of their significance as sources of social division – for instance, in relation to heated public debates about the social rights of migrants, particularly those who have travelled to work in the UK from new member states of the EU in eastern Europe. Marshall's focus was on class divisions as the major determinant of social inequality and the main challenge to citizenship, and he could not have foreseen the difficulties that were to arise in deciding how far social rights should be extended to include not only EU migrants but also to people migrating to the UK from countries outside the EU, and to those seeking asylum.

Conclusions

From this chapter you should have gained an insight into some basic principles of social policy: equality, need, freedom and rights. But before leaving this discussion, a word of warning: any debate about concepts is bound to exaggerate their importance. It is easy to elevate them to a position of influence over social policy that in reality they do not always have. Therefore, to end the chapter, it might be worth thinking about the following points in order to keep the principles of social policy in perspective.

First, *in reality, social policies are based on conflicting principles.* There is rarely, if ever, a clear and unambiguous set of principles underlying any single policy or welfare system. Sometimes rival groups, each with its own set of principles, support the same policy. The Child Support Agency (CSA), for example, was in the beginning supported by both feminist opinion (because it seemed as though more absent fathers than before would have to recognize their responsibilities) and conservatives who subscribe to 'traditional family values' and responsibilities. Similarly, feminists and conservatives might combine to support a policy to restrict or ban pornography. When a new policy comes to be implemented, though, these temporary alliances of principles and groups easily shatter.

Second, *rarely, if ever, do the ideas and stated principles put forward by a government actually determine policy.* For instance, looking back to the 1980s, it would be misleading to use a checklist of 'Thatcherite' principles (such as introducing business principles into welfare provision) to show how British social policy changed course in the space of a few years *as a direct result* of changed ideas in government. Even reforming governments such as those of Mrs Thatcher could not rip up every existing principle and start afresh the next day. The British welfare system today continues to operate on a mix of conservative and social democratic principles (see the last section of Chapter 3). Arguably, the introduction of new principles and ideas by Tony Blair's 'New' Labour government – summarized as the 'Third Way' – have not had a significant effect on the direction of social policy either. Policy has broadly continued along the lines set by previous Conservative governments (see Chapter 13). In this sense the principles and ideas which are supposed to guide policy are actually more like fig leaves that vainly attempt to disguise what governments are doing.

Third, *so-called principles are often rationalizations for decisions that would have been taken anyway.* For instance, continuing the example of the impact of 'Thatcherite' principles, it is likely that the slow-down in Britain's economic growth in the 1970s and early 1980s would have led to a sharp brake on welfare expenditure, whichever political party had come to power in 1979. Thatcherism could be seen as one of several possible ways in which British politicians and policy-makers could have tried to justify to the electorate what was inevitable: tougher limits to welfare expenditure. The popularity of the Conservative message in some quarters may have derived from the way it attempted to make a virtue of the 'tough' approach to welfare (whereas previous governments had been defensive and apologetic about reducing expenditure).

Despite these three points, however, principles can still be seen as important – even if they do not always play a strong, decisive role in shaping policy. For one thing, they act as signposts towards new developments in social policy and they can be invoked as goals or targets by those who wish to move policies in a new direction. Mrs Thatcher's drive to inject market and business principles into the welfare system is a case in point.

This chapter has examined principles, such as equality and need, that were once the bedrock of social policy. As mentioned in Chapter 1, students of social policy were traditionally tutored in a framework of mainly social democratic principles (see the last section of Chapter 3 for an explanation of social democracy). The merits of the welfare state would have largely been taken for granted, just as there would have been trust in the idea of improving state-provided welfare services to meet needs.

However, as a result of profound economic and social change, including the splintering of former class divisions and allegiances, we can no longer take for granted all the old aims and principles of the welfare state. This does not mean that principles or concepts of equality and inequality are irrelevant, but it does mean that such principles have to be rethought and reconsidered to understand better the role of social policy in a more uncertain world.

Key terms and concepts

autonomy
basic needs
civil rights
comparative need
egalitarianism
equality
equality of opportunity
equity
expressed needs
felt need

freedom
justice
minimalist and maximalist policies (of equal opportunity)
need
normative needs
normative policies
political rights
positive action
principles
social rights
utilitarianism
wants

Suggestions for further reading

If you are interested in the ideas discussed in this chapter and would like to read more about them, there is no better way of starting than with Robert Drake's excellent overview, *The Principles of Social Policy* (2001). This book wrestles with complex ideas – and wins! – and in the process provides an admirably clear and stimulating range of examples of the ways in which principles and ideas shape social policy.

For a specialized discussion of Bentham and utilitarianism, see Steintrager's book, *Bentham* (1977). For more general purposes, though, concise and readable introductions to utilitarianism can be found in Eric Midwinter's *The Development of Social Welfare in Britain* (1994) and Derek Fraser's *The Evolution of the British Welfare State* (3rd edn, 2003).

To get a flavour of the stirring yet scholarly and well-reasoned debates about equality that used to permeate British social policy, try any book by R.H. Tawney, but especially *Equality*. The 1964 edition – if you come across it in a library – has an introduction by Richard Titmuss, which is interesting in itself as a commentary on ideas about equality in the postwar period. T.H. Marshall's *Sociology at the Crossroads* (1963) or *Citizenship and Social Class* (1950) provide essential historical background to the development of welfare principles.

At the other end of the political spectrum, Hayek's *The Road to Serfdom* (1944), written before the end of the Second World War and the beginning of the Cold War, offers a passionate defence of freedom and the principles of a property-owning, market society. And for an overview of both 'old' and 'new' right thinking on concepts of equality and inequality, freedom, justice and so on, see Roger Scruton's collection of short articles, *The Meaning of Conservatism* (1984).

For more contemporary reading, my book with Robert Drake, *Understanding Equal Opportunity Policies* (Blakemore and Drake 1995, especially Chapter 2) offers discussion of the principles of, and justifications for, equality policies. Finally, Doyal and Gough's *A Theory of Human Needs* (1991) provides a thorough exploration of concepts of need and the policy dilemmas that arise in trying to meet them.

3 THE DEVELOPMENT OF SOCIAL POLICY IN BRITAIN

Introduction

In Chapter 2 we looked at social policy in a general way, focusing on key principles that are not specific to any particular time or place. However, in this chapter we will focus on welfare development in Britain for two key reasons. First, to provide some historical background to particular social policy areas discussed elsewhere in the book: notably, education (Chapter 7) and health policy (Chapter 9). There will also be some discussion of the history of the Poor Law and nineteenth-century attempts to deal with the problem of poverty. This has relevance for social security and poverty today (Chapter 5) and for social control and social policy (Chapter 6).

The second aim is to put Britain's overall approach to social policy in its historical context. Any country's social policy can be seen as part of what Jones (1985) calls a **whole system**: that is, its economy and level of development, political system and social structure.

As Jones warns, it is easy to make shallow generalizations about a whole system. There is always the danger of jumping to conclusions about the way British social policy developed, and what this means today. To understand fully a particular area of policy, there is no substitute for careful study of the history books. Further reading suggestions on the history and development of the British welfare state are given at the end of the chapter.

Box 3.1   Themes in present-day and historical social policy

Key issues in present-day social policy	*Historical examples and comparisons*
Welfare dependency; 'workfare'; dealing with problems of social exclusion and the possible formation of an underclass. Renewed interest in public health and preventive policies; health promotion; sanitation.	The reform of the Poor Law; the 'workhouse test' and distinctions between the 'deserving' and 'undeserving' poor. Public health reforms: government regulation of housing and working conditions.
Centralized control of the curriculum and assessment in schools, coupled with more local management of schools; tighter inspection procedures; publishing school league tables.	Developing a system of state education; deciding the appropriate roles of central government, local authorities and churches; 'payment by results'.

However, as Jones also points out, looking at the big picture of social policy development helps to put the issues of today in perspective. Present-day policy changes can be attributed with earth-shattering importance when, in the broader context of the past 50 or 100 years, they are relatively minor adjustments. The second part of this chapter will therefore provide you with a sketch of Britain's social policy development, concentrating on how the welfare state was affected by the turning point of the Second World War and by William Beveridge's plan for a new welfare system. We shall then be in a better position to compare Britain's current state of welfare with that of other countries.

Before we consider recent and current policy, though, the next section will explore some of the key developments in social policy that occurred before the welfare state was born. Though these are influences from much further back in time, they have a relevance to modern social policy. This is partly because nineteenth-century policies towards poverty, for instance, left a deep and lasting impression on British culture and on attitudes to the state and welfare. Understanding the significance of history also helps us to see that there are certain long-lasting *themes* in social policy, as indicated by the examples in Box 3.1.

Example 1: from workhouse to workfare?

Laws governing the provision of help to the poor have long existed in Britain. Such 'poor laws' are among the earliest forms of social policy. The first comprehensive Poor Law in England and Wales was passed at the end of Elizabeth I's reign, in 1601. In 1834, however, there came a major turning point. Previous legislation about how the poor should be helped was superseded by a revised or 'New' Poor Law that departed from previous policy in a number of important ways. This change illustrates a common theme and a central debate in social policy, about *how much* welfare should be provided to the poor and *what kind* of welfare it should be.

From the earliest days, and including the original 1601 Act, poor laws had always emphasized this distinction between the **'deserving'** poor and the **'undeserving'**

poor. However, nineteenth-century critics of the old system for helping the poor pointed out that it did not have a sufficiently *deterrent* effect. Under the 'New' Poor Law, individuals were expected to submit to degrading and shameful procedures to receive any benefit. Thus only the truly deserving, the completely destitute, would be prepared to come forward for help. It is for this reason that we link the poor laws with **stigmatization**, for to be seen as a pauper or – in the old language – to 'go on the parish', was a permanent scar or blight upon one's reputation and that of one's family.

The last remnants of the Poor Law system were scrapped in 1948. The mental scars and the deterrent effects of the system have faded, except perhaps in the minds of people in their seventies or older. However, it is still possible to show how the tougher attitudes towards the poor evident in the 1834 Act had a long-lasting and deeply transforming effect on British social policy and public attitudes towards poverty. It increased the shame and stigma associated with being poor and being dependent on public welfare. It also cemented the connection between work and respectability on the one hand, and between unemployment and irresponsibility on the other. This deep-rooted idea, that it is only through being in paid work that one can fully demonstrate responsibility as a citizen, is still evident in the aims and values that underlie the policies of **workfare** developed in the USA and adopted, to an extent, in the UK.

The concept of *eligibility* is highly important to an understanding of the historical preoccupation with how to distinguish between 'deserving' and 'undeserving' poor people. To be eligible for assistance under the nineteenth-century Poor Law, a person in poverty not only had to be willing to forgo certain liberties and to experience degrading conditions, but also had to fit into one of several tightly-defined categories of 'deservingness'. There were not only the simply destitute, for example, but also those who had been abandoned or orphaned, women who had been widowed and had no family support, or disabled or chronically ill people.

Throwing greater responsibility for welfare upon individuals and their families is bound to increase the role and significance of *means tests*, or assessments of people's incomes, savings and ability to draw upon family help. Therefore the example of the Poor Law of 1834 also helps us to review the history of the means test and to appreciate its significance in the development of British social policy.

From the present-day standpoint, and from the point of view of the poor in the nineteenth century, the Poor Law of 1834 represented a step backwards. It removed traditional 'rights' to assistance, however limited, and challenged the idea that social policies should automatically evolve towards a more generous treatment of the disadvantaged.

The *workhouse* was a central element in the earliest Poor Laws, aiming to make those who received public assistance contribute to their own keep. However, there was always a moral aim too. The workhouse was to be an institution to correct laziness and to reform the character. It would also serve as an example to others, acting as a harsh reminder of what could happen to those who turned to the public authorities for help.

Thus treatment of the poor was demonstrably more punitive and less open-handed after the 1834 Poor Law than before. Historically, harsh treatment of the 'undeserving' had been accompanied by traditions of providing charitable support to the needy and deserving. And to supplement this there had developed a widespread informal practice of giving a **dole** of bread, the staple food, or an equivalent weekly payment in money, to low-paid labourers and their families who would otherwise starve.

The latter form of support, an early form of income support, was tagged with the name of the parish said to exemplify the practice: Speenhamland. But although the *Speenhamland system* was widespread, it was not based on law or formal rights. Nevertheless it represented an expectation that the working poor would be helped, and that they could receive such help while continuing to work from, and live in, their own homes.

The Poor Law of 1834 represented a new body of thought that sought to challenge all this. Not only did it seem to reformers that relief of poverty was leading to ever-rising and unmanageable public expenditure, but also the rising laissez-faire orthodoxy in economics suggested that it was wrong to interfere in the labour market by subsidizing poorer workers' wages. Such subsidies were encouraging employers to pay their workers a lower wage because they knew that the parish would make up each labourer's income to subsistence level. In a free market, it was held that supply and demand should determine the price of labour, as it does any other commodity.

In the Poor Law reforms of 1834, the distinction between *poverty* and *pauperism* or 'indigence' was redrawn and reaffirmed. The law accepted no responsibility for trying to reduce inequality and poverty in the broader sense. The poor laws were only to assist the completely destitute – the paupers.

Second, the *workhouse test* was to replace other kinds of means tests, or assessments, of able-bodied people as to whether they needed assistance. The workhouse test was a chillingly simple one. To qualify for assistance under the new law, the individual had to be prepared to lose his or her freedom and civil rights, and enter a Poor Law institution. Families would be split up, mothers separated from their children and husbands separated from their wives. According to the legislation, outdoor relief – that is, support to individuals and their families at home or outside the workhouse – would no longer be an option.

Reformed workhouses and other institutions were to be run according to centrally defined principles and rules, so that no paupers would be treated better in some workhouses than in others. The rationale for this was the principle of *less eligibility*, the idea that no one receiving public assistance should be in a more 'eligible' (satisfactory) position than any wage earner. To have paupers in a better financial position than wage earners would undermine the wage economy. Less eligibility and the uniformly harsh conditions of the workhouse were introduced to prevent the poor from seeking out the more generous or liberal institutions, and to deter the 'roving beggar'.

As an example of the regulated uniformity of the workhouse, there is the famous scene in Dickens's *Oliver Twist*, when Oliver asks for more gruel. This scene was a criticism not simply of individual cruelty but also of the tight bureaucratic regulations that governed workhouses. The diets of inmates, and the weights and quantities of every ingredient, were carefully controlled down to the tiniest quantity – or at least, had to appear to be under control (corruption and misuse of funds meant for inmates was quite common).

Gradually, the Poor Law institutions took on more specialized functions, some becoming infirmaries or hospitals where people without any means could obtain medical treatment, many becoming mental asylums, others institutions for older people and so on. Eventually, as local government was reformed and expanded, it took over Poor Law institutions: for example, there were municipal or local authority-run hospitals before the NHS was introduced in 1948. As it turned out, the great majority of 'paupers' receiving assistance continued to do so outside workhouses and other institutions. Fraser, for example, quotes evidence to show that approximately five out of six received 'outdoor' relief in the middle of the nineteenth century (1984: 51). The workhouse test was never applied comprehensively because many local areas refused to build the number of workhouses envisaged in the original policy because of the costs involved.

Thus the results of the 1834 legislation provide a classic example of the gap between a stated policy and outcomes. Not only did the policy raise questions about the cost and practicability of workhouses, but also it appeared to be designed for a rural and a parish-based world rather than the new industrial age. In the large and rapidly growing urban centres of industrial Britain it was not uncommon to find that many thousands of workers could be thrown out of work overnight as one or more factories or companies suddenly went out of business. To expect masses of labourers to submit to the workhouse test, with possibly permanent effects on workers' family stability, earning power and respectability, was simply unrealistic.

Example 2: public health reform

One of the leading policy issues today is about the balance of resources to be devoted, on the one hand, to **public health** and preventive strategies, and on the other to individual care and curative strategies in medicine.

Box 3.2   Nineteenth-century health reforms

- *A Central Board of Health* was set up in 1831 by government to deal with a major outbreak of cholera.

- *Report on the Sanitary Condition of the Labouring Population of Great Britain*, 1842: a pioneering and scathing report on the environmental causes of disease led by Edwin Chadwick.

- *Liverpool Sanitary Act 1846*: this was an example of how all the major cities required specific parliamentary legislation to permit them to bring about public health improvements. Liverpool's was a model for the times: a local medical officer and staff were appointed to oversee water supply and sewerage improvements.

- *The Public Health Act 1848* set up a national General Health Board. Local authorities were permitted, but not obliged, to set up local boards to improve sanitation, build waterworks and so on.

- *The Medical Act 1858* established a General Medical Council to control a register of qualified doctors and to regulate training.

- *The Sewage Utilization Act 1865* laid down national standards for safe sewage disposal.

- *The Sanitary Act 1866* for the first time *obliged* local authorities to comply with previous legislation, as under the 1848 Act.

- *The Public Health Acts 1872 and 1875* were two pieces of legislation that consolidated and clarified all earlier regulations. Together, they laid down the duties of local authorities with regard to environmental health (for example, duties to inspect housing and maintain sanitary standards) up to 1936.

Everyone agrees that it is much better to prevent illness in the first place than to have to deal with its consequences. However, a certain amount of illness cannot be prevented. This means that there will always be a demand for individual solutions and treatments for illnesses.

The history of public health in Britain illustrates both the connection between environment and health and the conflict of interests between public needs (public health, preventive strategies) and individual needs (for *curative medicine*).

The nineteenth century was *the* age of public health and environmental improvement. This is not to say that progress in health was smoothly achieved or always centrally planned. Public health reforms were brought about after protracted struggles between progressives and reactionaries, between central government and local authorities, and between the mean-spirited and those who championed public spending on unglamorous sewer-building, better water supplies and health inspectors. However, by the end of the century, Britain had developed a comprehensive system of laws governing health standards (see Box 3.2).

Why did the Victorians put so much effort into improving public health? First, there was an increasing threat of infectious disease in the squalid conditions of Britain's rapidly expanding towns and cities. As a result of rural–urban migration the populations of Birmingham and Manchester doubled between 1801 and 1831, while those of Glasgow tripled and of Leeds more than quadrupled in the same period (Fraser 1984: 57).

Historians are uncertain about how much the death rate went up in the first quarter of the nineteenth century, but it is certain that there was a marked increase. Overcrowding and inadequate housing, poor or non-existent sanitation and infected water supplies all contributed to a high death toll and worsening health.

Urbanization on such a vast scale and at such a pace was unprecedented. Further, in a profoundly unequal society, most members of the privileged classes had little or no idea of the changing circumstances of the mass of the working population, or of the impact of death and disease upon them. Fear filled the vacuum left by lack of knowledge – fear of cholera and other deadly diseases, and fear of the contaminating mob. By preventing infectious disease in the general population, the middle and upper classes were protecting themselves.

More than narrow self-interest was involved, however, because concern with public health was inextricably bound up with a mission to control and to 'civilize' the masses. The Victorians often mixed together images of the poor, of slums and of contamination. Moral improvement of the masses came to be seen as part and parcel of improving physical health, communicated in the motto 'cleanliness is next to Godliness'.

No one illustrates the public health mission more aptly than Edwin Chadwick, whose zeal and energy were stimulated by a desire to bring order where disorder, squalor and filth coexisted. He had been a leading architect of the 'New' Poor Law (see pp. 42–43), but his later studies of the costs of illness to the poor relief system (caused by the need to support the sick) led him in a new direction. Chadwick's crusade 'soon embraced wholeheartedly the environmental theory of disease prevention, brushing aside the claims of curative medicine' (Klein 1984: 13).

Basing his conclusions on varying rates of disease and death in different localities, Chadwick traced the connection between poor social conditions, inadequate sanitation and illness. But he was by no means the first or the only person to conduct research on the social causes of disease. From the late eighteenth century onwards, doctors carried out a number of studies of the connections between urban living conditions and disease. Though the scientific causes of infection were not fully understood, the medical profession had therefore played a leading part in establishing the evidence for *public* health reform.

As medicine developed in the nineteenth century, this early link between medical research and public health began to wane. Gradually, doctors for a variety of reasons began to focus less on public health and more on individualized and curative care.

Historical evidence shows that the commonest illnesses of the nineteenth century were acute infectious diseases such as typhoid, influenza, tuberculosis and pneumonia, which had little or no medical remedy at the time (McKeown 1979). From the late nineteenth century and through the first half of the twentieth, the terrible toll of the acute killing diseases, which were particularly prevalent among children, was gradually reduced. But in most cases this was *not* achieved by medical discoveries or by improvements in individual medical treatment such as immunization. Social policies on public health and sanitation, housing and the working environment, and the regulation of food storage and hygiene, all reduced the opportunities for infectious diseases to spread. As McKeown has demonstrated, much if not all the improvement in death rates in the twentieth century came *before* the introduction of effective medical treatments such as immunization against tuberculosis and diptheria or the introduction of antibiotics to counter respiratory infections.

Thus modern medicine has its limitations and has not single-handedly reduced the death rate. However, this does not devalue the contribution of medicine to the management of illness and pain (see Chapter 9). As long as individualized medical care retains the lion's share of the resources devoted to health, though, there is likely to be continuing conflict of interests between what individuals want and public health interests.

Example 3: education, the roles of central and local government and the concept of the 'contract state'

'Must welfare be provided by the state?' is a leading question in social policy. One way of answering it is to look at what happened in history when the state, or government, did *not* take on a welfare-providing role. In the times before the era of 'big government' and the twentieth-century expansion of the state, people asked whether it was right for central government to provide any services at all.

Education is a good example of this debate because, in Britain, arguments about the proper role of central government have continued uninterruptedly from the nineteenth to the twenty-first centuries. Compared with other educational systems, Britain's had been relatively decentralized (Rust and Blakemore 1990). For example, only since 1988 have we had a National Curriculum defined by central government. In this and in other ways, British educational policy has been rather different from the French, German and other European systems.

The development of a 'contract state' in education

Before 1870, the responsibility for providing, paying for and running schools lay largely in the hands of the voluntary sector (churches and charitable institutions) and the private sector ('public' schools, many of which were then of inferior quality but some of which were to become exclusive, elite institutions). As Best (1979: 173) explains, 'Readers ... will perhaps be astonished to learn that there were few primary schools ... for which the state had full responsibility in 1850, very many for which it had no responsibility at all, and that its responsibility for the rest lay with a variety of religious organisations'.

In a slow process of educational reform from about 1850, the state did come to accept growing responsibility. But the idea that government should actually provide education continued to be resisted strongly. Government's first duty, it was thought, was to regulate providers: to ensure that education of a sufficient standard was being provided, but by other providers than government itself.

However, the *contract state* is a term that implies more than regulation. It also includes the idea of government (central or local) paying for services and entering into contracts with non-governmental organizations (NGOs) to provide services. The authorities laid down standard definitions of quality (for example, mastering the 'three Rs' of reading, writing and arithmetic) and tried to enforce these standards in contracts with providers. For instance, in the nineteenth century, churches agreed to have their schools regulated and inspected in return for religious freedom, grants from government and the right to run the schools.

Why did central government not play a more active role in providing state education? A number of reasons have been advanced. The prevailing ideology of laissez-faire and individualism militated against spending public money on education. The *nature* and *timing* of industrialization in Britain also played a part. As the first country to industrialize on a large scale, Britain enjoyed 50 or more years of dominance in world markets with little apparent need for state education. There was disdain among the elite for scientific, technical and applied education. Classics and the arts became by far the more prestigious and valued part of the curriculum in elite public schools, while science was neglected.

However, there were progressive voices in the nineteenth century advocating much greater government commitment to the provision of schools. For instance, John Stuart Mill, a leading writer and liberal, championed the cause of public education. Lord Shaftesbury, an aristocrat who (in modern language) became a 'born again' evangelical Christian, was passionately committed to education as part of the campaign for factory reform, the abolition of child exploitation and the provision of factory schools. And

Charles Dickens, a tremendously popular writer, both celebrated the importance of education and highlighted the scandal of child abuse in existing boarding institutions (see, for instance, *Nicholas Nickleby*).

There was also concern about Britain's international competitors, and the fact that other industrializing nations were demonstrating greater public commitment to education. At the same time, demand for child labour began to decline. Regular schooling would keep troublesome young people off the streets and help to inculcate them with industrial disciplines such as time-keeping and 'knowing your place'.

Despite these pressures for change, government policy continued to be one of delay. In the words of Best, the period up to 1870 can be seen as 'thirty and more years of dithering' in education policy (1979: 177). A review of education policy in 1861 (the Newcastle Commission) advised that the voluntary, largely church-run system should remain, but should be improved in efficiency by a system of *payment by results*. This policy not only delayed direct state involvement in providing education but also perpetuated rivalries in the voluntary sector of churches.

However, the efficiency drive after 1861 had a dramatic effect on the classroom. Individual schools' grants, and thus teachers' salaries, were dependent upon how many children attended the school regularly, and whether performance in standard tests of numeracy, literacy and basic factual knowledge was satisfactory. Less efficient schools would get less support, while the schools that boosted attendance and successfully drilled children in the three Rs would be rewarded. As might be expected, rote-learning and strict discipline in the classroom overshadowed interest and educational stimulation, while anything like fun or enjoyment would have been very rare indeed. Also, payment by results did nothing to reduce the huge class sizes that were prevalent in urban schools at the time. Sometimes a single teacher would be responsible for over 100 pupils, aided by monitors or pupil-teachers.

At this stage, British education policy illustrates clearly the meaning of a contract state: that is, regulation by central government, a 'purchaser' role for the government department responsible for a particular service such as education, and competition between providers.

It is valuable to compare Lowe's payment by results scheme of the nineteenth century with the education reforms of the Conservative government in 1988 (see Chapter 7). The Education Reform Act 1988 introduced a competitive market into the school system, standard ways of assessing children's school performance and the publication of school results in attainment 'league tables' in England and Wales.

As another step towards the reintroduction of a 'contract state' approach, Blair's government has developed a policy of removing 'failing' schools and 'failing' local education authorities from the state sector altogether. A number of schools and local education authorities have been placed under the control of private companies, signalling the return of the state's regulator role, while private or non-governmental agencies manage provision of the service (see Chapter 7).

In the late nineteenth century, however, the contract state principle of funding and providing education was on the wane. It was supplemented, at first, by another way of organizing education – the direct provision of schools by public bodies known as School Boards. Then, from the early 1900s on, local education authorities increasingly took over and developed a state sector of education. In the twentieth century, the state (local education authorities and a central Department for Education) became the main provider.

The development of a welfare state

In the first four decades of the twentieth century, a different set of principles and a different model of social policy gradually replaced the classic, laissez-faire ideas of the nineteenth century (see Chapter 6 for further discussion of the development of social policy in the twentieth century).

In health, income maintenance, housing and other important policy areas, as well as in education, government began to act according to more interventionist principles. These have been summed up as *social liberalism* (to distinguish them from classical, nineteenth-century liberalism) and, in health care and income maintenance, were based on the idea of individuals protecting themselves with insurance from the risks of illness, unemployment and other causes of loss of income.

However, to see the early decades of the twentieth century as a complete change from nineteenth-century laissez-faire would be wrong. Despite a growing willingness by governments to improve social welfare and to build up a system of social insurance, economic policies were still largely constrained by the thinking of classical liberalism. In the face of economic slumps in the 1920s and 1930s, governments could think of little else to do but reduce public expenditure, balance the books and try to alleviate the worst effects of economic depression – unemployment and poverty – by providing meagre and strictly means-tested benefits.

Nevertheless, and despite these limitations, the landmarks of social policy in the 1920s and 1930s represent some achievement in the face of economic adversity, as the list in Box 3.3 indicates.

The interwar period of social policy demonstrated that there were severe limitations to the insurance principle as a way of providing security of income and health care for everyone. Though government schemes for pensions, health and unemployment insurance were extended and improved in the 1920s and 1930s, mass unemployment and the persistence of poverty meant that millions of people could not adequately insure themselves. The poor were forced to rely on the dole and, as in the nineteenth century, had to submit to degrading and humiliating means tests to obtain any assistance.

Beveridge: the man and the plan

It is against this historical background that the contribution of one man, William Beveridge (see Box 3.4), should be judged. Perhaps more than anyone else, Beveridge can be seen as the main architect of Britain's welfare system.

His plan for a complete overhaul of Britain's social policies was written in the middle of the Second World War, in 1942. Full-scale war had dramatic effects on social policy, just as it did upon the role of government in all areas of life. The war was a particularly distinctive experience for Britain because the country successfully resisted invasion but, in the early years of the war, was brought to the brink of defeat. It was also a war that involved the whole population. In these extreme times, and as a result of the Blitz, food rationing and other common adversities, British people discovered a new sense of equality and purpose.

The significance of the so-called 'wartime spirit' can be overemphasized. There is no doubt, however, that Beveridge's proposals on welfare were hugely popular because they chimed in with wartime hopes and goals: the idea that, if the war was to be won, it had to be won for the purpose of creating a better society than that of the 1930s.

Box 3.3   Landmarks of social policy in the 1920s and 1930s

- *The Housing Act 1919* launched an ambitious postwar house-building programme (see Chapter 10).

- *The Unemployment Insurance Act 1920* extended insurance cover under the state insurance scheme (introduced in 1911) to almost all workers, except those in agriculture, earning up to £250 per year.

- *The Contributory Pensions Act 1925* replaced the original 1908 (non-contributory) old age pension scheme and extended benefits to widows and orphans.

- *The Hadow Report 1926* on the future of education firmly established the notion of 'primary' and 'secondary' stages and paved the way for later reform in 1944.

- *The Unemployment Insurance Act 1927* provided help for long-term unemployed people who had insufficient contributions to benefit from the scheme, but also toughened benefit rules and the 'seeking work' test of eligibility.

- *The Local Government Act 1928* transferred many of the functions of the Poor Law guardians (officials) to local authority committees (public assistance committees), including responsibility for administering means tests. It also exhorted local authorities to reorganize services according to function (for instance, a health services committee to supervise services for all in the local area) rather than a public assistance committee to deal with the health needs of 'ex-paupers'.

- *The Unemployment Act 1934* restored cuts to dole payments which had been made in 1931; it also clearly separated poverty relief from unemployment insurance.

The Beveridge report was a revolutionary step forward in British social policy in the sense that it revised the social security system completely. Implementation of the social security reforms was carried out by the Labour government elected after the war, apart from legislation on family allowances that had already been passed by the preceding coalition government. Clement Attlee's Labour government introduced the following social security schemes in the National Insurance Act 1946 and the National Assistance Act 1948:

- sickness and unemployment benefits;
- retirement pensions (for men at 65 and women at 60);

- maternity benefits, widows' benefits and a death grant;
- a National Assistance Board to replace the Poor Law.

The Beveridge report had also established the need for policies of full employment and a national health service. Without these two supporting planks, Beveridge argued, his proposals for children's and family allowances, pensions and unemployment insurance would not work. His plan was also revolutionary in that it suggested *universal* coverage of the whole population (wage earners, the self-employed, people not employed, dependants) and provision of a wide range of benefits *without having to submit to a means test*.

Box 3.4   William Beveridge, 1879–1963

William Beveridge came from a well-off, upper-middle-class background. His father was a prominent judge who worked for the colonial service in India. After a public school education, followed by a classics degree at Oxford University and law in London, Beveridge decided not to follow his father into a career in law, but went to live in a university settlement house, Toynbee Hall.

In doing this, Beveridge demonstrated that he had both a social conscience and an interest in social questions. University settlements were charitable institutions for graduates with reforming ideas to engage in social work with the poor. Although Beveridge's work at Toynbee Hall, as a warden, was more like that of a university tutor than a community worker, and did not involve him very much in contact with local people, he began to establish himself as an influential commentator on social issues, and especially on problems of unemployment and poverty.

In 1906, Beveridge left Toynbee Hall to work as a journalist, reporting mainly on social policy issues for the *Morning Post*. Then, in 1908, he became a civil servant and an important government adviser (to Winston Churchill at the Board of Trade), helping to frame legislation on labour exchanges (job centres) and advocating the introduction of compulsory insurance of workers against loss of income from unemployment.

Thus William Beveridge's formative years were very much tied up with the social reforms of the Liberal government of 1906–14, and it was this commitment to both Liberal ideas and social insurance which shaped his later, and much greater, impact on social policy in the 1940s. Between the wars, however, Beveridge took an academic post as Director of the LSE, successfully building it up from a relatively small workers' education college to a leading university institution (see Chapter 1).

Though concentrating on academic affairs at this time, Beveridge maintained a strong interest in practical action and in devising more efficient and comprehensive approaches to social insurance than the piecemeal system that developed in the 1920s and 1930s. For instance, he was in close communication with Seebohm Rowntree, the social reformer and investigator of poverty, whose 1937 book, *The Human Needs of Labour*, was very influential in shaping Beveridge's ideas on minimum incomes and the levels of benefit necessary to maintain subsistence.

In the early years of the Second World War the government cold-shouldered Beveridge's earnest desire to help with the emergencies of wartime planning and, as has often been reported, he rather unwillingly (and with tears in his eyes) accepted what seemed to be the rather mundane task of tidying up workers' insurance schemes.

The government report that emerged from this effort in 1942, *Social Insurance and Allied Services*, was a triumph. It was a tribute not only to Beveridge's outstanding ability to bring order and simplicity to complex administrative matters, but also to his bold and imaginative use of language. His scheme promised to vanquish the five 'giants' of Want, Ignorance, Squalor, Disease and Idleness and, for the first time in British history, presented both a vision of a community in which everyone would be cared for and the practical means for attaining that vision.

The Beveridge report became a huge best-seller. People formed long queues to obtain copies and a quarter of a million were sold in the first year. It had caught the mood for welfare reform and became an important element in wartime propaganda.

As a result, Beveridge's plan became the most significant part of the blueprint for the welfare state created by the postwar Labour government of 1945–51. However, it is important to remember that although Beveridge's plan became part of a Labour programme, neither Beveridge himself nor the underlying principles of the social security system he devised were particularly socialistic. William Beveridge had always resisted the idea of joining left-wing groups such as the Fabian Society or the Labour Party and, in 1944, he became a Liberal MP (losing the seat in the 1945 election). Similarly, his blueprint for social security, though comprehensive and universal in its coverage, did not involve redistribution of money from richer to poorer sections of society. Rather, it was intended to provide a basic foundation of support for everyone, and Beveridge assumed that many would turn to the private sector of insurance to add to the coverage provided by state schemes.

On the other hand, Beveridge's plan in some ways looked back to the problems of the 1930s rather than forward to a postwar world. First, it was based on a principle of *flat-rate contributions and benefits*. That is, everyone paid in the same amounts of National Insurance and received the same benefits. This appealed to people's sense of equality and fairness (see the discussion of equality and equity in Chapter 2), but it meant that contributions had to be geared to what the lowest earners could afford. As a result, the National Insurance scheme could gather in only relatively modest sums and – if the system had continued to run according to the strict insurance principles advocated by Beveridge – only inadequate benefits could be paid out.

Second, Beveridge's idea of a *national minimum standard of living*, though in one respect a radical breakthrough, assumed a very meagre definition of basic necessities for survival. Beveridge's calculations of benefit levels were derived in part from surveys of poverty conducted by Seebohm Rowntree and others during the 1930s, and what these researchers had suggested the poor could survive upon. Thus the retirement pension introduced in 1946, for instance, amounted to less than £30 per week for a single person in today's (beginning of the twenty-first century) money.

Therefore, while Beveridge's welfare system did bring a comprehensive range of benefits to all and successfully established the notion of care 'from the cradle to the grave', it had three main flaws. First, poverty persisted because benefits for older people, disabled people and the long-term unemployed were set at low levels. Increasingly, people on low incomes had to turn to means-tested National Assistance benefits. Beveridge had intended means-tested benefits to be a little-used safety net, but for a growing number of people on low incomes they became an indispensable and long-term support. Thus Beveridge's vision of a welfare system with little or no use of means tests was never realized.

Second, as demands upon the benefit system grew in the postwar period, the government soon found that it was impossible to find the money for benefits from National Insurance contributions alone and the social security coffers had to be topped up from tax revenues. The idea that state benefits are paid from insurance funds – a pot of gold to which people have contributed over the years – is a fiction. Britain's benefits are paid for mainly by *current* contributions to the system through tax and National Insurance contributions, not by contributions made in the past. The entire system runs with only a few months' money in hand.

Third, Beveridge's plan, as adopted and revised by the Labour government in its Social Security Act 1946, contained the old-fashioned sexist assumption that married women would be treated mainly as dependants of their husbands, not as wage earners or breadwinners in their own right. The gendered nature of the welfare system is further discussed in Chapter 6.

Conclusions: Britain's welfare history in comparative context

The years 1945–51 can be seen as the period in which the main structure of Britain's welfare system was built. From 1951 to 1964, a period of Conservative administration, Beveridge's system was continued, but earnings-related contributions and benefits were introduced. As mentioned, there were difficulties in funding the system from flat-rate contributions.

In the 1960s and early 1970s, a wider range of benefits and support for families, the unemployed, the disabled and chronically ill people extended the Beveridgian welfare system. Against a background of economic growth and rising prosperity for the majority, coupled with the 'rediscovery' of poverty among a minority, expectations of the welfare system grew.

Although there were clear differences of emphasis in social policies between the two main political parties, Conservative and Labour, the period up to 1979 can be seen as one of basic consensus or agreement about welfare. In other words, as Conservative and Labour governments succeeded one another, they were unlikely to rip up the social policies of the previous government and were predisposed to expand the role of the state as a provider of welfare.

Margaret Thatcher's period of office as a Conservative Prime Minister from 1979 to 1990 is often presented as a radical break with the past and as the period in which Britain turned its back on the Beveridgian welfare state. In the following chapters on social security, education, employment, health and housing, you will be able to make your own judgements about how far this was actually the case. However, radical and across-the-board changes in social policy certainly did not occur in the first two governments led by Mrs Thatcher (1979–87), when economic policy and political items dominated the agenda (Deakin 1994). It was during Mrs Thatcher's third term that important social policy reforms began in earnest. There were major reforms in education, health and **community care**, and additional reforms in housing, where policies had already brought great change through the sale of council houses to council tenants (see Chapter 10).

However, as far as social security – the cornerstone of the Beveridgian welfare system – was concerned, the fundamental structure of the old Beveridge system was left untouched by the social security reforms of the 1980s. The Conservatives' Social Security Act 1985 introduced some important and contentious changes, such as the Social Fund, which replaced certain rights to benefits with a more discretionary relief system. Also, the names of the major benefits and welfare schemes were changed, but the underlying system of benefits designed and established in the 1940s could still be seen.

Change to the 'British model' or the basic Beveridgian welfare state is therefore proving to be more evolutionary than revolutionary. However, evolutionary change can be fundamental in the long run. There are already signs that within one or two decades some of the key elements in the original Beveridge scheme could disappear into the sands.

For instance, though the state retirement pension was maintained at a value of about 20 per cent of average male earnings between 1980 and 1989, since then it has dipped to less than 16 per cent. This was a result of the Conservative government's decision to uprate pensions in line with prices rather than wages. If price inflation is low, the annual increase to the pension will be correspondingly low. At the same time, wages have tended to increase faster than inflation, meaning that annual increases in the state pension have been noticeably falling behind the improving incomes of wage earners. The Labour government elected in 1997 decided to continue the Conservatives' policy of uprating state pensions in line with prices rather than average wage increases, with the effect that in one year, 2000, the increase announced in the basic state pension was a footling 75 pence. The political cost of this was experienced in late 2000, when pensioners' grievances added significantly to a marked drop in the government's popularity. If the present policy of tying pension increases to price increases continues, by the year 2010 the state retirement pension will shrink to only 10 per cent of average earnings and, in the years that follow, it will become an insignificant element in older people's incomes.

How then can the British experience of the development of a welfare system be summed up? What sort of welfare system has Britain developed, and how does it compare with others? For purposes of comparison it is worth considering three main types or clusters of welfare state or 'welfare regimes' in Europe, which have been identified by Esping-Andersen (1990).

Liberal welfare states are those in which government provides only a minimum level of welfare services. Examples are the USA and Australia, and southern European countries such as Portugal, Spain and Greece (though Esping-Andersen did not include Greece in his survey). Health and welfare services are typically rather basic. As state-provided services are **residual** – that is, mainly for the poor – it is expected in liberal welfare states that the family and religious or charitable institutions will play a major part in providing health and social welfare services. However, the state organizes and subsidizes social insurance schemes that protect the better-off and those in middle-class occupations.

Corporatist welfare states, exemplified by Belgium, France, Germany and Ireland, are less dependent on the market and a laissez-faire approach than liberal welfare states. They have well-developed welfare systems in which the government takes a leading role in organizing and providing health, welfare and education services. These services are often of high quality and are typically funded by a mixture of private and social (state) insurance schemes. However, other non-government institutions or corporate bodies, such as the churches, trade unions and employers' organizations, are also important in welfare provision. Hence corporatist welfare states are often rather conservative in their approach to welfare issues: for instance, with regard to the family, the role of women in the labour force and the rights of single women.

Social democratic welfare states place more emphasis on social equality than either liberal or corporatist types. The Scandinavian countries, especially Sweden, can be seen as representatives of this type. These countries lead the world in terms of the amount of public money spent on welfare services and social security. Consequently, services are comprehensive, available to all and of a very high standard. Social security benefits are also high (along with the taxes to fund them). However, social democratic welfare states such as Sweden place a lot of emphasis on the work ethic and the importance of keeping people in work. For example, one of the main reasons for Sweden's extensive system of parental benefits and nursery care is to facilitate women's return to work after they have had children. The aim, then, is to reduce welfare dependency by a joint policy of full employment and of benefits that are geared to being in work.

It is very important to note that the classification of different countries' welfare systems into 'liberal', 'corporatist' and 'social democratic' types is an oversimplification. Any attempt to sketch the big picture, which Esping-Andersen (1990) has done with these three models, is bound to mean that particular countries do not fit a particular model exactly, and that countries contain elements of more than one type of welfare system. Sweden, for instance, has been portrayed as a corporatist welfare state (Mishra 1990). Further, recent economic change and the integration of Sweden into the European monetary union means that the 'traditional' Swedish welfare state is under threat. On the other hand, economic growth and policy reforms in the southern European countries mean that they are adopting elements of the corporatist and social democratic models.

Interestingly, Britain does not easily fit any of these models. This could mean that Britain genuinely differs from all of Europe in its approach to social policy and is better compared with countries outside Europe, such as Canada or the USA, or that Britain is a 'one-off' and very distinctive example unlike any other welfare system. However, it could also mean that the models themselves are flawed and must be adapted in some way to incorporate the British case.

Britain's history of welfare development has shown that, along with Sweden (which interestingly did not, as a neutral country, share the direct impact of war on welfare), it led Europe in introducing a comprehensive and universal welfare system. In that sense, the early emphasis on equality and citizenship, rights to a wide range of benefits and 'free' health care all point to Britain being a prototype of the social democratic model. However, as the above summary of Beveridge's plan and its underlying philosophy has shown, Britain developed a welfare system that was founded upon liberal rather than social democratic principles and a rather basic or minimal idea of how much help people should receive in times of need.

Although the welfare state of the 1940s represented a tremendous leap forward, once the system was in place the British approach has been to expand it cautiously. Britain is not easily portrayed as a 'liberal' type of welfare system (as in southern Europe) but, as a medium spender on welfare, neither has it kept up with social democratic regimes to develop as comprehensive and advanced a welfare state as exists in Denmark, Norway and Sweden. Nor has the corporatist system of joint provision of welfare by the government, employers and unions – as in Germany – ever been developed in Britain.

In conclusion, Britain's welfare system today represents an interesting mix of principles and influences from the past. There is still a relatively strong foundation of welfare state principles and a commitment to provision of universal benefits. As will be shown in Chapter 5, the proportion of the nation's wealth spent on welfare services and social security has not changed much since the 1970s, despite Mrs Thatcher's pledge to cut back the welfare state.

However, a significant change in the direction of policy, especially since the late 1980s, has reintroduced into the 'British model' elements of the pre-1940s or even the nineteenth-century approach to social welfare. This trend is noticeable, for instance, in the tightening of rules governing eligibility for benefits and making some benefit conditional upon claimants' 'good behaviour' (such as seeking work or training). It also appears in the stress upon individual responsibility for welfare (as in official views of the causes of illness) and in the revival of the concept of a contract state through the privatization of services and the development of a market in public welfare services. For all these reasons, therefore, the British model combines elements of the liberal or residual type of welfare system with remnants of a social democratic approach.

Key terms and concepts

contract state
corporatist welfare states
deserving and undeserving poor
dole
flat-rate
less eligibility
liberal welfare states
means tests
pauperism
payment by results (in education)
public health
residual (approach to provision of state services)
social democratic welfare states
Speenhamland system
stigmatization
welfare dependency

'whole systems' comparisons
workfare
workhouse

Suggestions for further reading

There is now a wide range of texts that give concise and readable accounts of the history of British social welfare. For instance, at the more accessible and concise end of the spectrum there are Kathleen Jones's *The Making of Social Policy in Britain 1830–1900* (3rd edn, 2000) or Eric Midwinter's *The Development of Social Welfare in Britain* (1994). For fuller and more detailed historical accounts, try Derek Fraser's *The Evolution of the British Welfare State* (1984) which, though rather dull in places, is still one of the best. Pat Thane's *The Foundations of the Welfare State* (1996) concentrates on the period 1870–1945. It is an extremely thorough and readable history and, like Fraser's book, contains an interesting appendix with examples of historical documents.

There are also books that specialize in the interwar period: for instance, John Stevenson's *British Society 1914–45* (1984), which provides an interesting discussion of the social context as well as detailed coverage of various areas of social policy, such as housing, health services and education. Another discussion of the interwar period is Anne Crowther's *Social Policy in Britain 1914–39* (1988), a short and readable specialist book that makes occasional reference to policies in Scotland as well as to the situation in Britain as a whole.

Useful general texts that throw light on the postwar history of social policy include Howard Glennerster's *British Social Policy since 1945* (1995) and Rodney Lowe's *The Welfare State in Britain Since 1945* (1993), while Nicholas Timmins's *The Five Giants: A Biography of the Welfare State* (1995) offers an outstandingly enjoyable and informative read: it is written in a pacy and readable style that brings the subject fully alive.

For a history that is not specifically focused on social welfare yet which offers valuable background on political, social and economic change, Edward Royle's *Modern Britain: A Social History 1750–1985* (1987) is a good choice. Similarly, Paul Addison's *The Road to 1945* (1994) gives insights into the political context in which the welfare state emerged and includes a chapter (Chapter 8) on Beveridge and social policy.

Just as future generations watching television serials such as the BBC's *EastEnders* or ITV's *Coronation Street* would not necessarily gain an accurate picture of Britain at the beginning of the twenty-first century, so we must be cautious about reading too much into Charles Dickens's portrayals of life in the nineteenth century. His novels were the sentimental potboiler serials of their day. However, taken with a pinch of salt, novels such as *Oliver Twist* and *Nicholas Nickleby* do offer interesting insights into Victorian social conditions and attitudes, as well as being an enjoyable read.

For quite different reasons, José Harris's masterly biography of *William Beveridge* (1977) provides stimulating reading. It is a long and densely detailed book, but worth reading for the way in which it relates the great man's life to the development of social thought and social policy from the early 1900s to the early 1950s. A good companion to this biography would be Peter Hennessy's award-winning book *Never Again* (1992), which expertly captures the spirit and the achievements of the immediate postwar years, 1945–51; the chapter titled 'Building Jerusalem' focuses on the achievements of Beveridge and other architects of the welfare state.

Finally, for comparative insights in social policy and discussions of the global context, Patricia Kennett's *Comparative Social Policy* (2001) provides a stimulating collection of chapters by Kennett and other comparative specialists.

4 THE CONTESTED BOUNDARIES OF SOCIAL POLICY: THE CASE OF CRIMINAL JUSTICE

Introduction: what is criminal justice policy?

In this chapter we introduce the reader to the subject of criminal justice policy. Its purpose is to consider some aspects of the English criminal justice system and its workings (the Scottish system is different), but space permits only the briefest account of its structure. Further detail may be sought in the many available excellent texts on criminal justice, for example that of Maguire (Maguire *et al.* 2002). Another purpose of this chapter is to examine the connection between criminal justice policy and social policy, and to suggest that the links between the two are close, while the boundaries between the two policy areas are somewhat vague. In this sense we might say that the subject matter of social policy is wider in scope than it is conventional to suppose. A final purpose is to provide a brief introduction to the topic of **comparative analysis** in social policy and suggest that it can provide a valuable perspective on UK policies. Comparative study, in our context, means the examination of the policies, programmes and services of more than one country.

We should begin by noting that 'criminal justice', like most other concepts in social life and the social sciences, is fuzzy, inexact and contestable in character. (The term 'penal policy' is also sometimes used to refer to the subject, but perhaps implying a more specialized focus on punishment and the treatment of offenders.) 'Law and order' is also a rough and ready term with approximately the same meaning with which you may be more familiar. So under this heading we would expect to find descriptions and discussions of such topics as the roles of police forces, courts, sentencing, punishment, prisons, probation and of what is sometimes referred to as the criminal justice 'process' generally, as well as debates on the merits of particular approaches to the problem of crime. Much criminal justice research is concerned with evaluation of the effectiveness and fairness (or lack of it) of these institutions and their workings, and this is where comparisons with other countries' policies are often made.

There are, however, broader and narrower definitions. Thus the United Nations (UN) affiliated research agency concerned with crime and criminal justice, HEUNI, employs a broad concept, 'public safety', to refer to the subject matter of criminal justice (Kangas-punta *et al.* 1998: 2). A recent evaluation of the performance of the UK's New Labour government contains a chapter entitled 'Safer?', most of which is a straightforward dis-cussion of 'law and order' issues. Significantly, this chapter also includes discussions of such topics as migration, asylum-seeking, refugees, citizenship, the secret services and national security, and the emergency services (Toynbee and Walker 2005: 6). These are topics which we might not always spontaneously associate with 'law and order', but some at least of which certainly make sense in terms of a general concept of 'safety'.

There are various analytical perspectives on crime and criminal justice. On one level, a traditional focus of much criminological research has been on the workings of the criminal justice system – on how such agencies as the police, courts and prisons *actually* work, as opposed to how they are *supposed* to work (Maguire *et al.* 2002: Part 5). On another level, there are political science or 'public policy' perspectives which analyse the politics of criminal justice in terms of the outcome of interactions between institutions and groups, such as government, Parliament, the Home Office, political parties, pressure groups, voters and public opinion (Morris 1989; Downes and Morgan 2002). In some recent criminological writing we find, at yet another level, attempts to locate and analyse the criminal justice system within a larger societal framework. This research calls atten-tion to the impact of broad social and economic trends on crime, for example, changes in the family, an ageing population, globalization and capitalist 'restructuring' (Loader and Sparks 2002).

This issue of definitions and subject boundaries is significant when we come to consider the issue of the relationship of criminal justice to social policy, because it will be seen that there are areas of overlap – drug policy and mental health, for example, are matters of concern within both the health and criminal justice systems.

Criminal justice, social control and social policy: a 'penal–welfare state'?

An immediate context for thinking about the connection between criminal justice and social policy has been the way that New Labour, in opposition, and then in government, have deliberately made the link. Tony Blair remarked in 1993, when Labour Shadow Home Secretary, that a Labour government would be 'tough on crime and tough on the causes of crime'. This explicitly makes a connection between crime and social conditions which can be altered by forms of social intervention – that is, social policy. This approach will be fully explored in the later section on New Labour's policies.

One way of thinking about the connection between criminal justice and social policy is in terms of the concept of *social control*. In Chapter 6 we examine the relationship between social policy and **social control**. Social policy can be regarded as something positive or negative, as welfare-enhancing or welfare-negating. Social control can be more or less overt, more or less concealed. In looking at criminal justice policy, we are concerned with another aspect of the state's relationship with society. In this case, it is that of public safety or the maintenance of law and order.

Criminal justice is concerned with coercion, or at least the possibility of coercion, and the state's power to coerce individuals to do things they would not otherwise do. It is concerned with one of the most basic aspects of the state – its use, or potential use, of force. Historically this has been a fraught and contested issue in the justification and legitimation of political authority. The tradition of liberal political thought has, for example, been uneasy about the coercive powers of the state, and liberals have, historically, been those who sought to limit and circumscribe that authority and have been associated with such legal–constitutional principles as **'the rule of law'** and **'due process'** (Gray 1986). Other traditions, such as anarchism, have rejected the claim of the state to coerce and regulate its members.

This brings us to the concept of the **'penal–welfare state'** (Garland 2001: Ch. 2; Loader and Sparks 2002: 84), a concept which owes something to the work of social theorists such as Foucault (Foucault 1977; Hudson 2002: 238–40). Foucault proposed a connection between welfare and criminal justice. The welfare state is also a 'penal state' – a state based on regulation, control and punishment. 'Penality' – crime control and punishment – and welfare are two sides of the same coin, Foucault argued, and historically both developed together as aspects of the modern state, or the 'policeman state' (Gatrell 1990). This perspective highlights the ambiguity of the modern state and its functions.

There have been various approaches to justification and legitimation of the state's coercive authority from within the liberal–individualist tradition, from a position broadly sympathetic to the modern state. The criminal law – that area of public law with which the criminal justice system and policy are concerned – may be justified in terms of protecting human rights; in terms of the utilitarian moral principle of maximizing overall happiness, 'utility' or well-being (see Chapter 2); or in terms of so-called 'contractarian' approaches, such as that of the celebrated theory of justice of John Rawls (see Chapter 2) (Rawls 1972). In the first case, the criminal law may be understood as protecting people's human rights to personal freedom from harm and to the ownership of property – and as imposing duties on people to respect these rights. Such rights – often referred to as 'civil rights' – may be incorporated in charters of human rights, such as those in the *European Charter of Human Rights* and its English legal manifestation in the Human Rights Act 1998. From this point of view, criminal justice is concerned with preventing and punishing rights violations or compensating victims of such violations. From this perspective, also, the state's claim to legitimacy lies in its protection of citizens' rights. There is a connection here with social policy, because one way of viewing welfare state programmes is in terms of protecting or promoting people's rights, in this case, 'social' rather than 'civil' rights (see Chapter 2).

On the other hand, the criminal law may be seen as enhancing the security and well-being of citizens, in so far as property and person are safer than they would otherwise be.

People's well-being, 'utility' or happiness is enhanced. (There is a kind of cost–benefit calculation involved in this kind of reasoning. The benefits of criminal justice must be set against the costs of it, in terms of, for example, the costs of law enforcement and possible negative effects, such as punishment of the innocent, corruption, discrimination, unfair treatment, etc.)

Social policy and criminal justice exhibit a concern with similar topics and issues. The latest edition of a recent handbook includes chapters with titles like 'Governance, Risk and Globalization', 'Social exclusion', 'Mentally-disordered Offenders', 'Probation' and 'Drugs and Alcohol' (Maguire *et al.* 2002). This looks much like social policy; many of the issues highlighted and discussed therein are also dealt with in social policy texts. The agencies and functions of welfare overlap with those of the criminal justice system, and the objects of the two systems are to some extent the same. The criminal justice system is in practice mostly concerned with a substratum of society – the poor, the marginalized and the excluded, who make up a disproportionate share of the system's 'clients' – which is also to some extent the focus of at least some parts of the welfare system. If one's view of welfare is to see it as especially concerned with 'social problems', one would certainly be inclined to make a clear link. The probation service, for example, in terms of its methods and in terms of its client base, overlaps considerably with voluntary and statutory social work. Penal policy is much concerned with appropriate models of treatment of convicted offenders. **Rehabilitation** is a 'needs-focused' approach to the treatment of offenders, which might include a variety of strategies – medical, psychiatric, social work, educational – indistinguishable from welfare interventions in other contexts. The issues of 'safety' and 'community safety' as a focus of the criminal justice system can be seen in terms of a social welfare approach, as can the concern in recent criminal justice policy for the needs and welfare of victims. There are also connections between social work and youth justice, and the boundary between social work with young offenders and youth justice is a blurred one.

There is also an historical connection. The origins of the welfare state in the period of Liberal governments 1906–14 also saw the beginnings of significant developments in criminal justice: the introduction of borstals for young offenders, the introduction of juvenile courts and the beginnings of the probation service (Morris 1983: 167).

Finally, criminal justice policy can function as an alternative to welfare policy, and vice versa (Morris 2001: 363). Expenditure on social programmes and services may be regarded as an alternative to expenditure on law enforcement and criminal justice, given a particular interpretation of the roots of crime and criminality. The sociological interpretation of criminality sees it as arising out of poverty, deprivation, marginalization and exclusion. This implicitly points towards welfare solutions to the problem. International comparisons are illuminating here. The USA, for example, may be regarded as a society which chooses to prioritize law enforcement over social welfare as a solution to crime, disorder and social breakdown – prison as an alternative to social security. As is well known, the USA is a relatively punitive society in relation to law and order issues, choosing to incarcerate a much higher proportion of its population than any other country: around 2 million people are in prison in the USA. It is also one of the few countries which still retains, and uses, the death penalty. Its law and order budget is consequently much higher as a proportion of national income than that of the UK,

European countries or Japan. The USA is also a comparatively low spender on social policy programmes by comparison with these countries. We might therefore be tempted to observe that welfare spending and criminal justice spending are alternatives. (Japan is also a low spender on welfare as it happens, so the implication is not as clear as it might be.) One might infer that Americans simply prefer to spend their tax money on law and order rather than on social security, housing and health – an expression of 'American values' perhaps. Such an inference would be too hasty, but we have here an invitation to compare the criminal justice policies of different countries, and to try to arrive at explanations for the differences that we observe. This is the subject of our next section.

Comparing crime and criminal justice

> . . . understanding the international dimensions of punishment is both increasingly vital for the student of penology and inherently problematic.
>
> (Cavadino and Dignan 2000: 2)

In the previous section we noted some interesting differences between US and British (and other) criminal justice systems and policies. In this section we turn to consider a more systematic examination of inter-country differences. This will provide us with an opportunity for introducing the general topic of comparison and comparative study in social policy.

The question posed at the end of the previous section – why does a country such as the USA differ in its approach to criminal justice – gives us a way into the subject, but it is worth spending a little time to consider why comparison and comparative study have come to be regarded as indispensable in any credible analysis of social and public policy. Some researchers have gone so far as to suggest that 'all research is comparative' (Pickvance 1986, cited in Kennett 2001: 42; Nelken 2002: 184), or that comparative research is 'about everything' (Mabbett and Bolderson 1999: 34). There are a number of reasons for comparative study of any area of public policy.

One has to do with overcoming the parochialism and ethno- or Anglocentrism to which we in the UK are prone. Comparative study offers the student of criminal justice as well as other policy areas the opportunity of becoming more 'reflexive', learning to avoid the error of assuming that the Anglo-American approach to law is the norm.

A second reason for increasing interest in the comparative study of criminal justice, as well as other areas of public policy, has to do with what is called **'policy learning'**. Policy-makers have become more interested, in recent years, in examining the experiences, problems and policy ideas and solutions of other countries for the light that might be shed on their own policy concerns: for what can be learnt about 'what works' and what does not. There have been many examples of such 'policy learning'. The development of a rehabilitative approach to the treatment of offenders in the UK from the 1950s to the 1970s owes something to American influence, as does the decline of the rehabilitative ideal thereafter and its replacement by approaches based on 'justice' or 'deterrence'. The growth of more punitive attitudes and treatment of offenders from the 1980s onwards, and the willingness of political parties to exploit law and order issues for electoral purposes, might be seen as evidence of American cultural influence. The idea of 'zero tolerance' policing came from the USA at the end of the 1990s, a product of its alleged success in New York. It is interesting that most of the influence seems to be from the USA to the UK.

In this context, other countries may be viewed as providing experimental situations in which policy ideas and solutions can be tested and evaluated and from which lessons may be learned. Of course, some of the use made of foreign examples has less to do with a dispassionate and scientific evaluation of alternatives than with finding opportunities to boost and promote favoured ideas: 'It is ... one of the commonest tricks in the book when advocating or criticising any social policy to declare (whether accurately or otherwise but usually in the hope that one's opponents are insufficiently knowledgeable to contradict you) that they do things so much better/worse in Ruritania' (Cavadino and Dignan 2000: 2).

A third important rationale for comparative study is that it can be employed to test theories of social and institutional change, i.e. changes in policies and governing institutions. Here, the purpose is to identify and isolate causal factors in institutional change. Why do policies change, and change in particular directions? What explains the size of the USA's prison population, by comparison with Britain's – is it a difference of ideologies and values? Or is it socioeconomic 'modernization', bound to affect all countries as they develop and 'converge' on a single uniform approach to public policy?

The second strand of comparative analysis described above, policy learning, also invites questions: for example, how effective the US approach to imprisonment is in terms of the objectives of criminal justice policy. Is it something from which we can learn or, on the other hand, is it a model to avoid? Could, or should, Americans learn from Britain or from European countries about penal policy? This is particularly interesting in the light of the growth of a global human rights culture, explicitly committed to the idea of universality and, less explicitly, to policy convergence. The USA's policies on incarceration and the death penalty have in fact been criticized by international bodies such as the UN on human rights grounds (Ignatieff 2005; Peel 2005).

Another US difference from both the UK and European countries is, of course, the use of the death penalty. This was abolished in Britain in 1965, at roughly the same time that the USA imposed a moratorium on its use. This looked like a case of convergent evolution, but American policy was strikingly reversed in 1976 with a Supreme Court judgement which declared that the death penalty was, after all, legitimate. All other European countries have abolished the death penalty during the past three decades.

Comparison can of course be extended to cover all aspects of crime, criminal justice and law enforcement. Policy-makers in this country have, for example, been interested in borrowing US ideas about policing. The concept of 'zero tolerance' policing is an example, in this case copied by the Teesside force, under a charismatic and entrepreneurial Chief Constable, Ray Mallon. Other penal concepts and ideas – parole and electronic tagging for example – have been borrowed from foreign models.

The fact that 'penal ideas and practices are flitting around the globe like epidemics of Asian (or more often American) influenza' (Cavadino and Dignan 2000: 2) can be identified as an aspect of globalization, in terms of the flows of information and people, and the impact of multinational agencies such as intergovernmental bodies (Nelken 2002: 185). There is perhaps a tendency among criminologists to notice and highlight

American influence on UK policy, while downplaying other sources of influence. There has been a comparable tendency among social policy analysts (Annesley 2003). Attention has been drawn to the 'homogenising and converging influences of the European Union' on penal policy (Nelken 2002: 175).

However desirable and indispensable comparative study of criminal justice systems and policies may be, it must be noted that there are difficulties in doing it, as the quote from Cavadino and Dignan at the head of this section suggests. There are problems of data availability and comparability, if one relies, as many researchers in the field do, on quantitative methodological approaches and the use of official statistics. These problems recur across the whole field of public policy comparison and are not unique to criminal justice (Mabbett and Bolderson 1999: 34).

Countries differ in their legal systems, their criminal law and their legal and criminal justice concepts. Apart from the data generated by large-scale social surveys of criminal justice of the kind periodically undertaken by UN agencies, of which Kangaspunta *et al.* (1998) is an example, where an attempt has been made to produce standardized and comparable terms and variables, researchers must rely on data collected by the statistical services of each country. These are collected in the countries concerned for administrative reasons, not for the convenience of comparative researchers.

Comparison ' . . . does have to face special difficulties. These range from the technical, conceptual, and linguistic problems posed by the unreliability of statistics, lack of appropriate data, meaning of foreign terms, etc., to the complications of understanding the differences in other languages, practices and world views which make it difficult to know whether we are comparing like with like' (Nelken 2002: 184). Legal definitions of offences differ from country to country. 'Assault', for example, may be an independent category in some countries, while others may not consider an incident to be an assault unless it results in bodily injury (Kangaspunta *et al.* 1998: 3). There are also procedural differences between countries in the handling of offences. In some countries, for example, traffic offences are not considered to be offences, and are handled by a special police unit or some special procedure, and may not be recorded in statistics (Kangaspunta *et al.* 1998: 4). The statistical classification of crime differs from country to country. 'Theft', for example, may or may not include burglary, car theft or shoplifting.

Criminal justice policy in the Netherlands

In this section we turn to an examination of criminal justice policy in another member country of the EU, the Netherlands. This is of interest for a number of reasons. First, the Netherlands is a developed, capitalist country with a high standard of living, high-quality welfare services, a long tradition of liberal democratic government and a relatively open and tolerant culture. It is also characterized by a degree of pluralism and diversity in its social and demographic make up, based on both religious (Protestant and Catholic, and more recently Muslim) and ethnic differences, although its population size (15 million) is smaller than the UK. The criminal justice system and policy exhibit interesting differences from UK models, being based on different legal principles (Roman or civil law, rather than common law), and being rather more humane and 'progressive' in some respects. Finally, Dutch society has been subject to some of the same influences as has the

UK – globalization, for example – and criminal justice policy has shifted in ways which suggest a degree of convergence.

Cavadino and Dignan (2000), drawing heavily on work by Downes (1988), provide an illuminating discussion of Dutch criminal justice policy, in terms of a concept of 'penal crisis'. From being a 'beacon of tolerance' which it was in the 1960s, Dutch policy became increasingly harsh and the incarceration rate climbed, from a rate of 17 per 100,000 in 1975, to 67 per 100,000 in 1995. The severity of sentences increased and prison conditions deteriorated. Dutch penal mildness in the earlier period is ascribed to ideological factors, such as the corporatist and Christian Democratic nature of Dutch society – socially liberal, with generous welfare state provision. Dutch penal culture had 'Enlightenment' roots. Policy was 'inclusionary' and characterized by an emphasis on 'resocialization'. Prosecutions are frequently waived (35 per cent in 1996) and prison sentences tend to be shorter (Cavadino and Dignan 2000: 12–24).

In explaining the growth of a harsher penal regime in the 1980s and 1990s, the authors draw attention to general ideological and cultural changes associated with late modernity, such as the move towards a more individualized, less communitarian society. Church allegiance declined and there has been a growth of 'individualized anomie'. The Netherlands has been described by those deploring these trends as a 'victim of globalization'. Reference is made to the growth of 'American-style consumerist culture' (it is noted that the Dutch, as a multilingual nation, are open to penetration and persuasion by English-language media). There has been a growth of neo-liberal influence in public policy (although the welfare state remains relatively unscathed, despite some re-structuring) (Cavadino and Dignan 2000: 17–18). The result of all this has been a decline in Dutch tolerance of criminals and criminality. There has been a 'redrawing of the boundaries of community' and the development of a policy of 'bifurcation'.

It is suggested that recent developments in Dutch penal policy exhibit a good deal of English influence (more so than American). The Dutch Labour Party has consciously imitated Britain's 'New Labour'. Party politics has, however, played little part in the shift in Dutch attitudes. There has been a growth of top-down managerialism and increasing regulation and bureaucratization of the criminal justice system. 'In a country where a relatively small elite dictates penal policies, it may be that relatively rapid change is possible and even facilitated when that elite changes its mind and/or its personnel'. The Netherlands is a small country lacking the regional autonomy to be found in federal states such as the USA, Germany or Australia. In the Netherlands 'the mindset of this penal elite altered significantly over a relatively short time' (Cavadino and Dignan 2000: 21).

The claim that there is or was in the 1980s a 'penal crisis' in the Netherlands is rejected. There was no crisis of resources; the Dutch system is a relatively cheap one, because of its sparing use of prosecution and imprisonment (the 'waiting list' system, in which sentenced offenders were only imprisoned when a place in prison became available, helped here). Rather, it is or was a 'crisis of legitimacy', arising from popular perceptions of excessive lenience. To some extent the issue was related to the notably tolerant attitude of the Dutch towards drugs and the growing pressure from other countries such as the USA for a less relaxed attitude – an interesting example of global or international influence on domestic policy development (Cavadino and Dignan 2000:

22). Also influential was the growth of penal ideologies. Globalization in another sense has also played a part – that of transnational migration. There has been a decline in Dutch tolerance towards foreign migrants and a mental conflation of migrants with criminals.

The above brief discussion of Dutch policy is useful for a number of reasons, because it highlights a number of aspects of comparative analysis and its value. The authors are, to some extent, implicitly comparing Dutch policy with that of other countries, such as the UK, noting points of similarity and difference and convergence in policy, such as 'waiting lists' for imprisonment and diversion from prosecution and imprisonment. They are also attempting to explain these differences, similarities and convergences, drawing attention to penal ideologies; general social and political values in Dutch society and the character of party politics; the character of the Dutch state as a relatively small state, non-federal in nature and regionally undifferentiated, facilitating rapid shifts in elite thinking in public policy, such as criminal justice policy. They call attention to a degree of what looks like convergence in Dutch penal policy. This is a significant concept in comparative study, which points up, in particular, political and cultural factors from outside the country which have tended to move policy in particular directions. The objectives of this particular case study, and of comparative study in general therefore, include, among others, the identification of similarities and differences; the explanation of these, especially, perhaps, the latter; and describing and examining policy and institutional change and attempting to explain these. In addition, they involve, implicitly or explicitly, a degree of policy learning. The case study seems to imply that Dutch policies – the earlier ones – are recommendable and provide a positive model that other countries might emulate.

Measuring crime

The sociological or criminological mainstream view of crime and deviance is the so-called 'social constructionist' view. Crime is the product of processes which 'construct' particular behaviour as criminal, in line with, among other things, changes in social values (Pease 2002: 947). These processes take place via the medium of the criminal law on the one hand, which labels particular behaviour as deviant, and the criminal justice system on the other. Particular societies will view particular kinds of behaviour differently. A good comparative example of this is the labelling as criminal in the former Soviet Union and present-day Cuba of a variety of economic activities, such commercial buying and selling, or private ownership of property, which are perfectly legal in capitalist countries. A historical example of this, already cited, is domestic violence against women, which was arguably, to some extent, legitimate and permitted in earlier times, and is now regarded as criminal. Another historical example is provided by the operation of the Game Laws in the nineteenth-century English countryside. The autobiography of Joseph Arch, the founder of the agricultural workers' trade union in the 1870s, vividly depicts the struggles between rural labourers and the gentry over poaching (Arch 1986: Ch. 7).

Issues of definition and measurement loom large. A much-discussed issue is that of the 'real' incidence of crime, compared with the official recording of it. Crime statistics until the 1980s were generated first of all by what members of the public chose to report to the police, and by police practices in identifying and recording offences. The official recording of crime, therefore, is misleading as a guide to the social reality of crime, its volume, incidence and type. Since the early 1980s an alternative source of data on crime has been developed – the British Crime Survey (BCS). This is a large-scale, questionnaire-based survey of the population, conducted every two years, which seeks to measure the public's experience of crime. The BCS must be one of the largest of all such social surveys. Its data are potentially much more accurate than police figures, although not perfect. The BCS suggests that the real incidence of crime is about four times higher than that officially recorded. The number of respondents and the geographical coverage permit disaggregation of data on a local area basis. It is particularly useful in permitting us to view trends over time, a controversial and politically sensitive issue. Since the mid-1990s crime rates, as measured by the BCS, have fallen (Morris 2001: 361; Toynbee and Walker 2005: 215) (see Figure 4.1).

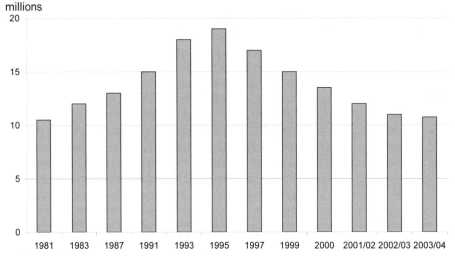

1 All incidents measured by the survey, whether or not they were recorded by the police.
Source: British Crime Survey, Home Office

Figure 4.1 British Crime Survey offences: England and Wales
Source: Office for National Statistics (2005b: 122).

The BCS figures must be regarded as a more accurate guide to the reality of crime by comparison with official figures. On the one hand, it appears to paint a bleaker picture of the incidence of crime – the figure is much higher than the official one – but on the other, it shows a recent fall in crime, which the official figures do not. Officially-recorded crime is subject to influences – people's changing willingness to report offences; an increase in numbers of police; changing police priorities and practices (for example, greater willingness to deal with domestic violence, rape and racial attacks, which may encourage people to report these things).

Something should be said at this point about the political salience of crime and crime figures. Crime and law and order, and what is supposed to be happening to them, have become one of the most popular topics for mass media reporting. There is a parallel here with health, and the state of the health services in Britain. It is worth observing that both these highly salient areas are also subject to extensive fictional and dramatic treatment by the broadcast media. Police dramas have always been staple television fare. Pseudo-documentary series like *Crimewatch* also testify to the public fascination with crime, deviance and law and order. Media scares about the incidence of crime – particularly the claim that crime is 'out of control' – tend to depend on the careless use of official figures rather than crime survey figures.

Governments tend to be on the defensive in relation to issues of law and order, and highly sensitive to them. This is perhaps particularly true of the present New Labour government, which has been subjected to a storm of criticism about the allegedly too lenient treatment of offenders by the courts. The issue of the relationship between crime, criminal justice, the media and politics will be explored in more detail in a later section.

The criminal justice process

It is useful to consider the working of the criminal justice system in terms of a *process* through which individuals move from one end to the other, or more accurately, are lost to the system at various stages. One can examine the various stages – arrest, trial, sentencing, imprisonment or other penalties. Figure 4.2 gives a schematic account of what happens to offenders as the system handles and processes them, taking them in at one end and disposing of them at various possible 'exit points'.

It is important to realize that offenders can exit the system at various points in the process, beginning with the actions of the police. Police *discretion* is in fact one of the most interesting and significant, as well as controversial, aspects of the system.

Discretion, or choice, on the part of front-line officials or 'service providers' is an inherent and unavoidable, and in some respects desirable, aspect of many areas of public policy and social services, including health care, social care, education and, to some extent, means-tested social security. It is intimately bound up with the exercise of professional judgement (in the present context, that of police officers), and with the 'rationing' of scarce resources (in this context 'rationing' simply means the allocation or distribution of some service, good or benefit by a professional or bureaucratic authority rather than by the market).

The so-called 'attrition rate' – the rate of loss of offenders to the system as they proceed through it – is a significant and revealing statistic. It is very high; only a tiny proportion of arrested offenders make it through all the stages – arrest, prosecution, trial, sentencing – to arrive in prison, or some alternative to prison. The police arrest around 2 million people a year (Home Office 2000: 27). At the stage of arrest, the police may choose to *take no further action*, to *caution* or warn a suspect, to *impose a fixed penalty* (in the case of motoring offences) or to bring a *charge* or *summons*. It is only the last of these which sets the offender on a path through the rest of the system. Charges are reviewed by the Crown Prosecution Service (CPS), which may decide that there is insufficient evidence for a successful prosecution and discontinue the case (Home Office 2000: 29). The

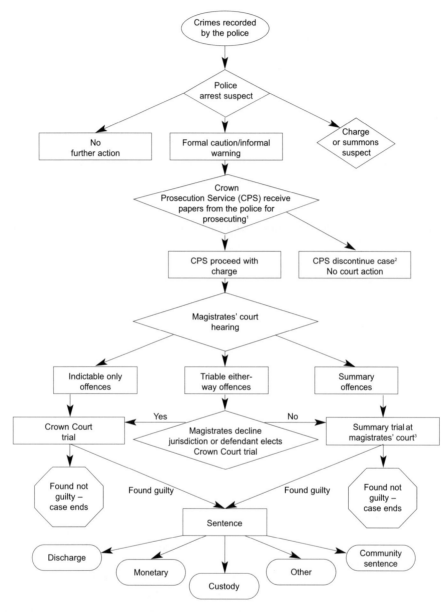

Figure 4.2 The prosecution process
1 Although the majority of prosecutions are handled by the CPS, other organizations can also bring prosecutions.
2 A case will be under continued review, and may be discontinued at any stage before the hearing at the magistrates' court or the prosecution may offer no evidence. In addition the charge may be altered up to the final decision of the court.
3 Magistrates may commit to the Crown Court for sentence.
Source: Home Office (2000: 4)

majority of offenders – over 90 per cent – are dealt with in magistrates' courts (Home Office 2000: 18).

Equality and discrimination

These processes are of particular interest in relation to issues of equality and discrimination. There has been much concern, for example, about the numbers of African-Caribbean offenders, and about police stop and search powers which appear to be biased against young African-Caribbean males. Some three-quarters of the 734,000 individuals stopped and searched in 2003–4 were white, yet whites make up over 90 per cent of the population (Office for National Statistics 2005b: 129). It appears, therefore, that non-whites are more likely to be stopped and searched than whites. This may be too hasty, however, and it is necessary to compare age-specific rates of stop and search for different ethnic groups to gain a more accurate picture. Such comparison reveals less of a bias.

Bias, it has been suggested, exists at other levels in the criminal justice system. Thus African-Caribbeans are more likely to be subject to imprisonment than whites or Asians. The findings of the Macpherson inquiry, which reported in 1999 on the murder of the black teenager Stephen Lawrence, suggested, controversially, that the police were less responsive to the policing needs of ethnic minorities than they should be (Lea 2003).

A further issue concerns the treatment of 'white collar' crime in comparison with that of working-class crime. It has been suggested that white collar crime is taken less seriously than blue collar offences such as theft, burglary and robbery. White collar crime includes, for example, fraud, embezzlement and tax evasion. There are also business or corporate crimes, for example, non-compliance with health and safety regulations which may endanger the life and health of workforces or consumers, the evasion of environmental and pollution controls, bribery and corruption. It has been suggested by criminologists of a Marxist persuasion that the criminal justice system is simply a tool for the social control of the working class, the weak and powerless. The 'crimes of the powerful' are overlooked, ignored or generally treated more leniently than are working-class crimes.

Another issue which has been highlighted in recent accounts of law and order is that of gender, the treatment of men and women offenders, and the particular situation of women as crime victims. Feminists have drawn attention to such issues as rape and domestic violence (Heidensohn 2002: 499–500). It has been argued that the criminal justice system has been reluctant to take these issues as seriously as they deserve and particular criticism has focused on police behaviour and the treatment of victims of rape and domestic violence. A related issue is that of children as victims. Paedophilia and physical abuse of children have been identified as especially male offences. Crime generally is perceived as a male activity. Women's participation rate is much lower, although it is increasing (Heidensohn 2002: 493–7).

What this suggests is that issues of fairness, justice, equal treatment and non-discrimination are live and important in the criminal justice system as elsewhere in public policy. The system is of course formally committed to justice in a more explicit way than most areas of public policy. Research seems to suggest that it falls short in various respects.

At this point we should note that a normative framework for the explicit consideration of these issues has been provided by the concept of human rights and the Human Rights Act 1998 (implemented in October 2000). The underlying principles of this legislation are not new. Britain has been a signatory of the European Convention on Human Rights, on which the law is based and whose provisions it incorporates, since 1951. Under its provisions Britons had a right of appeal to the European Court of Human Rights (ECHR) in Strasbourg. (The ECHR is an agency of the Council of Europe, and has nothing to do with the EU. The European Court of Justice, on the other hand, is an EU institution, charged with adjudicating on matters covered by EU law, and quite separate from the ECHR.) With the advent of the Human Rights Act, appellants may now appear before English courts, rather than having to mount a case at the ECHR and travel to Strasbourg to seek remedy, with a considerable saving in financial and time costs. All UK public agencies, and their actions, must conform to its provisions.

The contemporary politics of law and order

Analysts have argued that the 'landscape' of law and order policy has been transformed in the last three decades; a prevailing consensus, which was both social-scientific and political, about the nature of crime and crime control has dissipated, to be replaced by a new consensus.

The old consensus, it is suggested, was characterized by a view of crime as conceptually unproblematic, by a causal theory that understood crime as a 'presenting system of deep-seated social problems', and by the idea of crime control policy as the province of experts and expert knowledge (Loader and Sparks 2002: 84–5). This set of understandings has been undermined and transformed since the 1970s as the result of a number of factors.

First, postwar recorded crime rates have escalated, so that crime has moved from the margins of social life 'to become a routine part of modern consciousness'. This has also involved the discovery of hitherto hidden forms of criminality – domestic violence, sexual and physical abuse of children, racial violence, and environmental pollution (Loader and Sparks 2002: 85).

Second, there have been shifts in social and cultural relations attendant upon the advent of 'late' or 'post' modernity, involving changes in production and consumption, the family, urban ecology, the media and a 'democratization' of everyday life. These changes have contributed to an increase in opportunities and motivations for crime, as well as a greater concern about the performance and effectiveness of criminal justice agencies (Loader and Sparks 2002: 85).

Third, there have been changes in political ideology with the rise and governmental triumph of the so-called 'New Right' in the Anglophone countries. This, it is argued, has helped both to politicize issues of criminal justice and to undermine the sovereign state's claim to provide security to its citizens.

All these changes, it is argued, have heightened the profile of crime and criminal justice as issues and increased both public anxieties about them and public demands for order (Loader and Sparks 2002: 86). Another way of putting this is to say that there has been an apparent growth of *risk* (in this context, that of being a crime victim) accompanying the advent of a **'risk society'** (Loader and Sparks 2002: 92–5). So the contemporary state is expected to do *more* in the way of guaranteeing security, but paradoxically is trusted *less* in terms of being able to deliver. This is the context in which governments of the right and left have operated since the 1980s.

New Labour and criminal justice

In this section we shall explore some aspects of the current politics of criminal justice policy, focusing on the most recent phase of policy under the New Labour government first elected in 1997 and re-elected subsequently in 2001 and 2005.

'Tough on crime; tough on the causes of crime' is the celebrated slogan or soundbite which has come to stand for or symbolize New Labour criminal justice policy, first enunciated in a *New Statesman* article by Tony Blair when Shadow Home Secretary in 1993. Most subsequent attention, whether analysis, critique, dismissal or humorous put-down, has tended to focus on the first part of Blair's slogan rather than the second, yet it is arguable that the second part has been as important in the Blair 'project' as the first, and it is certainly that part of it that we, as students of social policy, should be interested in. How far have the Blair governments since 1997 observed these twin precepts, first put forward as part of Labour's 'modernizing' agenda in the 1990s?

Something must be said here about the emergence of Labour's law and order philosophy in the 1990s. The context for it was provided by more than a decade of Conservative rule, first under Margaret Thatcher as Prime Minister 1979–90, then under her successor John Major, 1990–7, and four general election defeats for the Labour Party, the last in 1992.

Criminal justice as an issue had been rising in the political agenda since the 1970s, becoming more salient for voters and political parties. It is striking how little law and order mattered as an election issue before the 1970s (Morris 1989): 'Compared with the contested party politics of the economy, foreign affairs, defence, health, housing and education, those of "law and order" are of remarkably recent origin: they emerged in the mid-1960s and came decisively to the fore in the 1979 election' (Downes and Morgan 2002: 286).

In the 1970s the Conservative Party recognized that law and order could be an election-winning issue for them. The Conservatives presented themselves as a party that was 'tough on crime' and more successful in the fight against it than the Labour Party. Politicians in general since the 1970s have come to believe, or assert, that crime can be affected by legislative measures or, as one observer put it, that governments can attempt to 'govern through crime' (Loader and Sparks 2002: 86, citing Simon 1997). The Conservatives were seen as the party which could, and did, spend more on the police, prisons and on administering 'short, sharp shocks' to young offenders. The growth of media interest in crime and law and order issues assisted the Conservatives in this; the print media have largely been dominated by owners sympathetic to the Conservatives.

The Labour Party in the 1970s and 1980s, on the other hand, was vulnerable to Conservative claims of being 'soft' on crime because of its link to four key constituencies – the trade union movement, the deprived working class and ethnic minorities, supporters of civil disobedience, and libertarian movements and causes (Downes and Morgan 2002: 299). The Labour Party (the Parliamentary Party, that is) was, for example, almost palpably embarrassed by the miners' strike of 1984–5.

In fact Conservative criminal justice policy between 1979 and the 1990s was rather less punitive than the received image might suggest or lead one to expect. Conservative Home Secretaries in the 1980s, particularly Douglas Hurd, 1984–88, pursued relatively 'liberal' policies regarding sentencing and the treatment of offenders, for example. There was some attempt to reduce prison numbers and to develop alternatives to prison. A notable piece of legislation was the Police and Criminal Evidence Act 1984, which, although attacked by the Labour opposition and civil libertarians at the time because of its alleged enhancement of police powers, did have the effect of circumscribing and making more uniform police discretion, particularly in relation to 'stop and search' procedures (Home Office 2000: 27); Labour eventually dropped its opposition to the measure (Downes and Morgan 2002: 290).

Conservative policy went into reverse after 1992, however, for two reasons: the disastrous collapse in public confidence in the government's economic competence after Britain's ejection from the Exchange Rate Mechanism of the European Monetary System (a precursor to the euro) in October 1992 ('Black Wednesday') and the resulting *de facto* devaluation of the pound; and Labour's shift in its law and order policy, under Tony Blair as Shadow Home Secretary, encapsulated in his 'tough on … ' slogan.

The boot was now on the other foot, and the Conservatives were being attacked for being too soft on law and order. The context for this was provided by rising crime rates from 1989 to 1993 as the Lawson boom of the late 1980s turned to bust, with economic recession and rising unemployment. Under Michael Howard as Home Secretary, with his own slogan 'prison works!', the Conservatives attempted to court popularity through a tougher line on law and order. Prison numbers grew rapidly between 1993 and 1997, a contrast with the position in the 1980s, when numbers fell. Blair's attempt to win back lost Labour ground on the law and order issue by shifting, or appearing to shift, Labour's position, had to some extent caused the Conservatives to shift position as well. Of course, this strategy yielded no electoral advantages for the Conservatives in the end – although it did them no harm either.

Since the Labour election victory of 1997 successive Home Secretaries have sought to implement the law and order strategy outlined by Blair in 1993. Jack Straw, David Blunkett, Charles Clarke and John Reid have pursued policies which the 'progressive consensus' has regarded as illiberal and in some respects merely a continuation of Conservative policies: 'almost all the measures that were either introduced or about to be implemented in the last days of Conservative rule have been continued or adopted by New Labour' (Morris 2001: 363).

In fact there was no detailed Labour blueprint for criminal justice policy in 1997 (by contrast with, for example, the Wilson government in 1964). Law and order was not the most salient issue for the electorate in 1997 or 2001 (most attention in Labour's 1997 manifesto focused on education and health) (Downes and Morgan 2002: 291). Law and order did not win the election for Labour in 1997, nor did it lose it for the Conservatives. There was however a lack of public confidence in the criminal justice system and the effectiveness of such components of it as the CPS, the youth justice system and the probation service. Public opinion surveys suggested that the public thought that the system favoured the interests of criminals rather than those of the public or victims (Toynbee and Walker 2005: 214).

Major early legislation included the Crime and Disorder Act 1998 and the Youth Justice and Criminal Justice Act 1999; these were at the heart of Labour's 'tough on crime' law and order agenda. They elaborated a comprehensive strategy for crime reduction and prevention based on statutory (i.e. compulsory) partnerships between police and local authorities (Home Office 2000: Ch. 7; Faulkner 2001). They included such measures as Anti-Social Behaviour Orders (ASBOs), 'neighbours from hell' provisions, minimum mandatory sentencing for repeat offences and electronic tagging of convicted offenders (Downes and Morgan 2002: 297).

It has been suggested by some critics, as we have seen, that Labour policy differs little from that of the Conservatives – 'New Labour/Blue Labour' has been the dismissive comment of some observers. Labour has been excessively sensitive, it has been suggested, to the wishes and interests of the 'tabloid voter' (Morris 2001: 363). Jack Straw (Home Secretary 1997–2001) continued with the 'prison works' strategy of Michael Howard. Another way of construing this phase of policy, on the other hand, is to see it as a return to a bipartisan consensus on law and order after its abandonment in the 1970s and 1980s. It is just that the grounds of the consensus have shifted 'rightwards'.

The second half of the Blair slogan – 'tough on the causes of crime' – has perhaps received less attention than it deserves. Arguably it was just as important in Blair's thinking and has proved to be important since 1997. It has obvious links with the concept of social exclusion, a major concept in New Labour social policy and an issue which has been highlighted across the whole field of social and public policy (Young 2002; Young and Matthews 2003). It also provides an obvious link with ('Old') Labour's traditional law and order thinking, in that it always involved an acknowledgement of the social roots of crime and disorder in poverty, inequality, marginalization or what is now fashionably identified by the catch-all, umbrella term 'exclusion'. Recognition of its centrality is symbolized by the creation of the Social Exclusion Unit (SEU) in 1997 and its placing, at the heart of the government machine, in the Cabinet Office. 'Tough on the causes of crime' might also be viewed as an approach to law and order of the kind which characterized both major political parties until the 1970s, when the consensus started to break down.

An assessment

Success or failure in criminal justice policy is hard to establish. Since the causes of criminality 'lie deep in society', as even the Conservatives were prepared to acknowledge in their 1987 election manifesto, dramatic short-term improvements in relevant variables are unlikely and difficult to bring about through legislation and overt policy change, even if it is in politicians' interests to claim otherwise. As we have already noted, crime rates, according to the BCS, have improved since 1995. There has been a 39 per cent fall in all crimes and a 24 per cent fall in violent crimes since that date (although a rise in violent crimes of 12 per cent in 2003–4). This includes a 5 per cent fall in violent attacks by people unknown to the victim. There have been some notable falls in particular types of offence. Thus domestic and 'acquaintance' violence has fallen by 50 per cent since 1997. One particular worry has concerned gun crime. There were restrictions on access to guns after the Dunblane massacre in 1996, and air rifles were banned in 2003. There was a doubling in firearms-related offences between 1997–8 and 2002–3, to over 10,000 – but gun crime constitutes only 0.3 per cent of all crime (Office for National Statistics 2005b: 124; Toynbee and Walker 2005: 217). Theft accounts for 78 per cent of all crime. Burglary fell by 39 per cent between 1995 and 2005, and car crime by 31 per cent. Some of this is due to 'target hardening' – improvements in home and car security. Improvements in home security have in fact been a focus of Labour policy.

In relation to drugs, there have been some reversals in Labour policy. Initial ambitions in 1997 have been scaled back, and the target promulgated in 1998 by the Labour-appointed 'drugs tsar' Keith Halliwell to cut drug use by 25 per cent by 2003 has been abandoned. A National Treatment Agency was established in 2001 and new drug-testing and treatment orders introduced. Some £500 million is now spent on these (Toynbee and Walker 2005: 220) and they have been regarded as progressive measures with some chance of success. Another issue similar to the drugs issue is that of alcohol, which is strongly implicated in much criminal behaviour. Over two-fifths of violent crime is alcohol-related. The issue of weekend 'binge drinking' by the young in town and city centres, to some extent a classic 'moral panic', has also gripped media and public imagination. Here we may observe a degree of inconsistency in Labour policy, because the government, consistent with a policy of prosperity-enhancing economic deregulation, has legislated to liberalize regulations on drinking hours, thus apparently increasing access to alcohol.

On the one hand, the 'prison works' philosophy still prevails. The prison population was 60,000 in 1997, 75,000 in 2004, and the Home Office is planning for a population of 109,000 by 2010. On the other hand, some observers have pointed to aspects of Labour policy to set against what appears to be an illiberal record: the Human Rights Act of 1998; the launch by Jack Straw in 1997 of the Macpherson inquiry into the murder of Stephen Lawrence and support for the resulting report of 1999; the introduction of the Youth Justice Board (YJB) and Youth Offending Teams (YOTs) (Home Office 2000: Ch. 5); the reduction in the homosexual age of consent; and the development of restorative justice for youth offending (Home Office 2000: 52; Downes and Morgan 2002).

Conclusion

Much of the improvement as has been noted since 1997 in crime statistics cannot be attributed to the government's criminal justice policy. Causes may include, for example, changes in demography (shrinkage in the 'at risk' age group – essentially young males – with the passing of the 'baby boom' generational cohort and subsequent decline in birth rates since the 1980s), and greater economic prosperity and growth in individual incomes as a result of the striking decline in UK unemployment since 1993, a period of uninterrupted economic growth. In the latter case, thanks are due at least as much to the Conservatives as Labour, since the economic policies – the achievement of macroeconomic stability through inflation targeting, and improvements in labour market efficiency and flexibility – that have yielded these results began with them.

Some credit – it is impossible to say how much – is no doubt also due to the Government's 'social inclusion' policies, such as Welfare to Work and the targeting of resources on poorer families, and the general attempt to arrest widening income inequality through these measures and higher, albeit 'stealthy', taxes on the better-off. In this sense the government has pursued a 'tough on causes' agenda as well as a 'tough on crime' agenda. This also testifies to the importance of the connection between crime policy and social policy more generally.

Key terms and concepts

Comparative analysis
Convergence
Deterrence
Due process
Human rights
Penal–welfare state
Policy learning
Rehabilitation
Risk society
Rule of Law

Suggestions for further reading

The *Oxford Handbook of Criminology* (Maguire *et al.* 2002) provides the most comprehensive single-volume discussion of criminal justice policy and practice, as well as of all other aspects of crime and criminality. For comparative discussion and description of criminal justice policy in various European countries, see the publications of HEUNI, a UN agency (e.g. Kangaspunta *et al.* 1998). These are available from the organization's website. For some historical background on English policy, see Morris (1989) and for updates on this see the same author's articles (Morris 1994, 2001). For a factual description of the English and Welsh criminal justice system, there is a useful Home Office publication, available from the website (Home Office 2000).

5 WHO GETS WHAT? SLICING THE WELFARE CAKE

Introduction: what are the benefits of the welfare system?

This chapter will discuss the key question of how the resources and services of the welfare system are shared out. In short, who gets what? As we saw in Chapter 2, important decisions about equality and need have to be taken by policy-makers, especially if social policies are aiming to reduce problems of poverty and social exclusion. Also, as Chapter 3 showed, these questions are not new. They have preoccupied governments and people since the early days of the Poor Law and the beginnings of organized social policy.

    The policy dilemmas or choices that face governments in deciding 'who gets what' can be summarized in two ways. First, there are choices to be made about *distribution* and possibly about *redistribution* of services, resources and money. And secondly there are choices to be made about *funding* the welfare system and deciding who will contribute and how much they will pay.

    With regard to the first set of choices, Lowi (1966; see also Blank and Burau 2004: 16) drew some helpful distinctions between 'regulatory', 'distributive' and 'redistributive' public policies. Lowi defined 'regulation' as the government's way of controlling, constraining or modifying the actions and behaviour of individuals and groups. 'Distribution' means providing some good or benefit to individuals collectively, through government action. 'Redistribution' means changing, by means of collective government action, the distribution of some good or benefit among individuals.

We are perhaps most familiar with distributive and redistributive policies in the shape of the NHS, and the education, social security and tax systems – major social programmes providing benefits in cash or kind, and the revenue-raising system which pays for them. Social policy is by no means to be identified exclusively with distributive or redistributive policies and politics, however. Regulation and control are also important, and these themes will receive further discussion in Chapter 6.

The second set of policy dilemmas – those of deciding how to *fund* the welfare system – are key to an understanding of social policy, because if firstly we are going to ask 'who benefits from the welfare system?' it is just as important to ask, 'who pays for it?' It is important to reflect upon how much has to be paid by each individual and by various groups, and how much of the nation's wealth is spent on welfare. These issues have implications for people's attitudes towards the welfare system, and towards groups that are particularly dependent upon welfare benefits and services – for instance, people seeking work, disabled people, older people or lone parents surviving on low incomes.

Directly or indirectly, therefore, the costs and benefits of the welfare system affect everyone. How far, and in what ways, people are affected will of course vary according to individual circumstances. Some people are totally dependent on welfare benefits for their incomes, while others receive no social security benefits and may make little or no use of public services.

A career-minded childless couple, for instance, may have little or no interest in a public service such as primary education. If they plan never to have children they may resent having to pay taxes to support services they never intend to use. However, when they go shopping, visit their doctor or work with colleagues, they are *indirectly* experiencing the results or benefits of the education system. They are relying on the schools to have taught certain skills (reading, writing, numeracy and perhaps some technical skills) to each of the people they come into contact with. The education system may do this well or badly, and its efficiency should be of as much concern to the childless couple as to anyone else. Even though they cannot be said to be benefiting directly from the education system as parents with school-age children, they are nevertheless receiving various indirect benefits.

The very rich could also be seen as a group that might question the value of publicly-provided welfare. Their children attend elite private schools, when in need of medical care they use private hospitals and they are sheltered by company welfare schemes that subsidize pensions and housing costs.

Such people do not directly use the state system of welfare, and may therefore gain little or nothing of direct benefit from it. They pay taxes that contribute to the running of state schools and hospitals, but if they do not use the public services they do not personally regain any of the money they have contributed towards them.

However, the rich also gain substantial indirect benefits from a public system of welfare. The doctor who treats a rich patient in a (private) hospital will probably have been trained at public expense. The roads upon which affluent people travel are publicly funded (except for a few private tolls on roads and crossing points). Those who own and control businesses depend on the welfare state being able to pick up the bill for health care for their employees. The public welfare system also helps to maintain the 'social fabric' and to prevent or minimize breakdowns of law and order. This is a function that benefits everyone, but particularly those who have most to lose. These benefits, termed 'external benefits' by economists, go beyond individual gains or payoffs.

Nor are the benefits of a fully developed welfare system necessarily restricted to externalities, as far as the rich are concerned. The well-off also derive *direct* benefits from the welfare system. Where social security pays out *universal benefits* (paid to everyone automatically, irrespective of means), the better-off do regain some of the money they have paid into the system: for instance, in the form of the state retirement pension. The amounts involved may be peanuts to the rich, but they symbolize principles of being included, and of citizenship, that were established when the welfare state was launched in the 1940s.

Should benefits and services be selective or universal?

Universal benefits, and the principle of citizenship that underpins them, are now increasingly questioned. There is an argument that benefits for all should be phased out in favour of targeting welfare benefits on the poor and those in greatest need. These benefits are termed *selective benefits* because they are provided selectively – that is, only to those people whose incomes have been assessed (means tested) and have been found to be below a certain level. However, as long as universal benefits and 'free' services remain (such as those provided by the NHS), middle-class and affluent people will be able to receive and use them even though they could afford to do without them or could pay for services out of their own pockets.

To those who support universal benefits, the drawback of providing 'free' services or cash benefits to everyone, including the better-off, is outweighed by the drawbacks of changing to a more selective, means-tested system. If higher income taxpayers feel excluded from the welfare state they have a strong incentive to avoid paying taxes, and some will go to great lengths to do so. Thus there is a danger that abandoning universal benefits and a common approach to paying for welfare and health services will quickly take us towards a more divided society.

Attachment to the old ideal of universal welfare is accompanied by fears of a return to widespread means testing. This is particularly the case in what used to be called the Labour Party's 'heartlands' – industrial areas of Britain, many of which are now in economic decline and have above-average rates of poverty. In these areas, as Routledge (1997: 17) comments, 'Means testing digs deep into Labour's psyche and prompts feelings of revulsion that are hard to shrug off'.

Frank Field, a leading thinker on social security, strongly opposes means testing but in the early years of Labour's first term in office advocated a radical restructuring of social security around a new system of social insurance. He objected to the present system because means testing encourages cheating and has not deterred claiming by people who are not entitled to benefits. He argued that, 'Welfare is therefore having the opposite effect from that for which it was devised. The welfare state was constructed as a means of extending full citizenship to the entire population, many of whom might otherwise remain outside society. Welfare fraud now acts as an expelling agent, encouraging people into criminal activity' (Field 1995: 27).

Despite the problems raised by means testing, however, Field and others recognize the flaws in the old system of universal social security benefits. These flaws have been identified by Toynbee (2000), for instance. Toynbee refers to state pensions as an example of social security where targeted, means-tested benefits are preferable to an extension of universal benefits. She argues that across-the-board increases in state pensions would represent a 'regressive, non-redistributive and unsocialist policy' based on 'a dead old idea of a national insurance principle that never actually delivered' (Toynbee 2000: 19). Part of the reason for Toynbee's, and the government's, dislike of universalism is perhaps the gradual reduction in the top rate of income tax since the 1970s. It is now 40 per cent. In the 1970s, when the top rate of income tax on earned incomes was set at 83 per cent (on unearned incomes it was 98 per cent), such universal cash benefits as the state retirement pension were effectively targeted at those with lower incomes and less was 'wasted' on the rich.

The problem with selectivity, or targeting, is that such an approach involves means testing and the evidence is that many pensioners will not undergo means tests to claim extra benefits due to them. Toynbee argues that much can be done – and is being done, by way of publicity campaigns – to inform older people of the additional benefits they can claim.

As the above examples show, opinion on the respective merits of universal and selective benefits continues to be sharply divided. The main arguments both for and against universalism and selectivism are summarized in Box 5.1.

It is difficult – and perhaps rather pointless – to try to conclude that either means-tested or universal benefits would be preferable throughout the social security system. Means testing might have fewer disadvantages if applied to some benefits (for example child benefit) rather than others (for example the state retirement pension).

Under New Labour, there has been a move away from universal benefits towards selective, or targeted, benefits. Universal benefits such as child benefit and the state retirement pension still exist, and have indeed been improved through regular uprating, but have been supplemented by new targeted benefits in the form of 'tax credits'. (Tax credits are discussed in more detail below. In fact these selective benefits are rather less new in principle than they appear. What is new is the use of the tax system to assess eligibility and pay the benefits and the high relative importance they have as part of the government's poverty, or 'social exclusion', reduction strategy.) The relative importance of the older universal benefits seems set to decline. Thus the pension credit is uprated each year in line with average earnings, but the state retirement pension is only uprated in line with general price increases. This means that the retirement pension is steadily shrinking as a proportion of average earnings, whereas the pension credit will be maintained as a constant proportion of average earnings.

Box 5.1 Arguments for and against selectivism and universalism

Selective benefits   *Universal benefits*

Arguments for

Income support and benefits only given to   Inclusive: high take-up among people in eli-
those who need them   gible groups (for example, parents)

Efficient: they allow more money to be tar-   Efficient: minimum of bureaucracy and ad-
geted on low-income families   ministration costs

Reduce demand for welfare and allow public   Promote citizenship and sense of social unity
spending to be reduced or contained

Arguments against

Means testing involves complex procedures   Lack fairness: benefits 'wasted' on the better-
and claim forms: low take-up likely; high ad-   off where taxes on earned incomes are low
ministration costs

Means testing may involve social disgrace and   Encourage welfare dependency and over-
stigma; low take-up likely   reliance on the state

If all benefits are related to income (means   Wasteful: even if people improve their income,
tested), a rise in income disqualifies people   they continue to receive universal benefits
from benefit, acting as a disincentive to work
(the poverty trap)

Gainers and losers: individuals and groups

To suggest that 'everyone benefits' from an extensive and expensive welfare system is to miss the point that some benefit much more than others do. In this chapter, we examine how there are 'gaining' and 'losing' groups in terms of how much people gain from, or lose out in paying for, the services and cash benefits of the welfare system.

The groups that stand out as either gaining or losing out in the welfare system are, first of all, income groups or – more broadly – social class groups. For instance, one way of picturing 'gainers' and 'losers' would be to think of three broad social class groups such as the rich, those on middling or average incomes, and the poor. More complicated (and accurate) divisions of social class can be constructed in order to understand inequalities between people, and the relative amounts they gain from the welfare system. Another way of looking at 'gaining' and 'losing' groups is to examine the effect of gender divisions. Do women get more out of the welfare system than men, or vice versa?

There are yet other social divisions and inequalities in the welfare system and in the wider society of which it is a part. For instance, there are divisions of age, race and ethnicity, sexual orientation, and inequalities between disabled and non-disabled people. A central question to be applied to all these social divisions is whether, or how far, the welfare system *redistributes* resources between groups. There are several possibilities.

1   The welfare system has a neutral role. It does not redistribute resources between groups to any significant degree, and its overall effect is to leave existing in-equalities largely untouched.

2   The welfare system has a 'Robin Hood' role, affecting the whole spectrum of society, redistributing from the rich or better-off groups to those on average incomes and to the poor.

3   The welfare system acts like the Sheriff of Nottingham, redistributing from the poorer to the better-off sections of society. For instance, poorer and average income groups may have to pay higher proportions of their incomes in tax and at the same time might fail to claim all the benefits they are entitled to, or underuse 'free' services.

4   There is also a possibility that the welfare system *partially* redistributes. Redis-tribution takes place, but within a limited range of groups. For instance, the poorest groups may take more out of the system than they are able to put into it, but the majority of people on middle incomes might be paying more than their fair share, while the rich escape with a relatively light tax burden. If this were the case, redistribution would be from the middle to the bottom, not from the top to the middle and bottom groups.

5   It is also likely that different parts of the welfare system will play different roles. For instance, the education system may play a 'Sheriff of Nottingham' role (if more is spent per head on middle-class children than those from lower or working-class backgrounds), while social security may be a 'Robin Hood'. Or, *within* a service such as education, there may be different effects. Primary edu-cation, for instance, may have the effect of transferring resources from the bet-ter-off to the less well-off (if more is spent on inner-city schools than schools in affluent suburbs), while higher education – which people from the poorest backgrounds hardly use – may achieve the opposite.

Three further points about the economics of welfare need to be borne in mind. The first two concern the nature of our contributions to the welfare system, *taxation* and *care*. The third relates to the importance of keeping a *perspective on the individual* as well as on groups in society, as far as 'gaining' and 'losing' from the welfare system is concerned.

Contributions: taxation

As mentioned at the outset, it is as important to consider how much people have to pay for welfare through the taxation system as it is to consider how much benefit they receive from the services they use. Glennerster provides helpful discussion of this issue (2003: Ch. 3).

First, *tax relief* may be as important as a social security benefit in protecting the interests of better-off people. For instance, tax relief on occupational and private pension contributions makes a substantial difference to the incomes and spending power of many in the middle classes. It represents a hidden form of welfare benefit and an example of 'fiscal welfare', as discussed by Titmuss (see Chapter 1).

Income tax and National Insurance contributions are *direct* taxes that by and large are *progressive*. For instance, in 2002 the Chancellor of the Exchequer, Gordon Brown, announced a rise of 1 per cent in the rate of National Insurance contributions to fund increases in government spending on the NHS. Only those in work pay National Insurance contributions so that older people in retirement, among a number of other groups, are a significant section of the community who have not had to make this additional contribution. The more someone earns, the more they will be paying for commonly-used services and benefits. In effect, a person who pays the top rate of tax and uses a 'free' NHS hospital service, for instance, has paid substantially more for that service than someone who has been paying a lower rate of tax. The net effect is to subsidize the hospital care of the lower earner and to transfer resources to that patient. However, the degree to which direct taxes are progressive varies. High rates of direct tax upon low-income wage earners will be unfair, as a relatively large proportion of their income will disappear in this way.

Indirect taxes, on the other hand, are nearly always *regressive*, though again there are exceptions, depending on the items that are taxed. Indirect taxes such as those on cigarettes and alcohol, and Value Added Tax (VAT) are placed on goods and services. They tend to be regressive because everyone, whether a high or low earner, must pay the same rate of tax. As a result, the better-off person loses a much lower proportion of their income through indirect taxes than the average or lower-income person. In Britain, the poorest households lose over a third of their disposable income by paying indirect taxes. The top fifth of households, on the other hand, lose only 16 per cent in indirect taxes – approximately half of what the poorest fifth pay, proportionately (Office for National Statistics 2000: 55).

If better-off people make extensive use of certain public services, such as NHS hospitals, and those services are increasingly paid for by indirect taxation, we may well find that poorer taxpayers are subsidizing the better-off. This pattern will become more pronounced the more taxation is shifted from the direct to the indirect type. One exception to this regressive effect occurs if heavy indirect taxes are levied on purchases of luxury items or very expensive goods such as large motor cars, yachts or diamonds. In this case, better-off people will pay more tax than the average and low-income groups, for whom the luxury items are unaffordable.

The effects of tax on people's incomes should not be considered in isolation. It is important to think about the way in which taxes *and* benefits (both cash benefits and 'benefits in kind', such as education and health services) together affect the final income of a household (see Figure 5.1 and Table 5.1).

Table 5.1 Direct and indirect taxes as percentages of gross income, 1998–9, in Great Britain (non-retired households grouped into five income bands)

	Bottom fifth	Second	Third	Fourth	Top fifth
All direct taxes	12.6	17.4	20.9	22.4	21.8
All indirect taxes	29.2	21.5	18.5	16.2	16.2
All taxes	41.9	38.9	39.4	38.7	38.1

Source: Office for National Statistics (2000), adapted from Table F, 55.

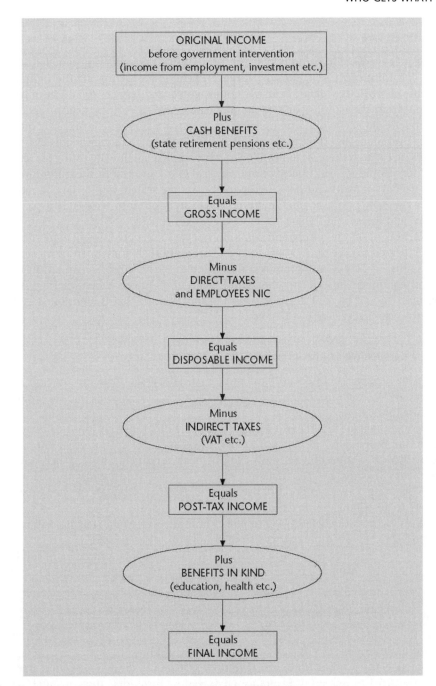

Figure 5.1 The effects of taxes and benefits on household income
(Reproduced by kind permission of the Office for National Statistics.)
Source: Economic Trends No. 494, December 1994: 9, Crown Copyright ©

Contributions: care

A second point to bear in mind is that contributions to the welfare system are not just made in the form of money, through taxation. Economics focuses on the more easily measurable or 'objective' data – flows of money, goods and services to and from people, and to and from the various parts of the welfare system such as the health service and social services. But contributions in kind, or in unpaid domestic work, can often be missed in these measures. Taking into account only how much money people either gain or contribute to the welfare system will give an incomplete picture. By caring for relatives or a partner, people are contributing time, physical effort and emotional commitment to meeting welfare needs that otherwise the public welfare system might have to meet.

If the time and effort devoted to informal care are taken into account, the picture of who gains and loses from the welfare system changes considerably. As Ungerson (1987) and other researchers on family and community care have noted, women are more frequently expected to care for relatives (other than spouses) than men, and they often do so from a sense of duty. The enormous contribution to the welfare system made by family carers and volunteers raises many moral and practical questions about whether, or how much, carers should be paid for their contributions, a point that is mentioned again in relation to community care in Chapter 11.

Keeping a perspective on the individual

Although we have begun by focusing on groups (social classes, men and women, and so on) as 'gainers' or 'losers' in the great welfare distribution game, it is important not to lose sight of the individual.

Thinking about an individual's life course sheds a different light on the distribution of welfare. An individual will switch from one category or group to another during their life. Individuals might become seriously ill or be made redundant, for instance, and thus find that they become net recipients of, rather than net contributors to, the welfare system. This perspective is important, because it shows that although the welfare system might fail to distribute resources or services fairly between various groups, it might nevertheless succeed in redistributing resources from the well to the sick, from those who are employed to the unemployed, and from younger to older people.

This type of thinking lay behind another of the fundamental principles of the 1940s welfare state – the insurance principle. From an individual's point of view, the welfare system was to be thought of as a huge savings bank. For most of a person's working career, the equivalent of perhaps only £60 in services and cash benefits would be regained for every £100 'lost' in taxation and National Insurance contributions. However, in time of need, the balance changes. Resources contributed during the 'productive' part of life are drawn upon to meet needs in a dependent phase of life.

In practice, the funding of the social security system and of welfare services does not work on the strict principles of insurance envisaged by Beveridge, the chief architect of the 1940s welfare system (see Chapter 3). Although the notion of a self-funded insurance scheme is a myth, however, the idea of an individual 'losing' or contributing and 'gaining' or receiving at different points of the life cycle is a valuable one. It helps to explain continued support for a publicly-funded welfare state and a willingness to tolerate taxation even when a majority are not net gainers from the system at any one point in time.

How large is the welfare cake?

Before we look at the way in which the welfare cake is sliced and at 'who gets what', we need to look briefly at the size of the cake itself and understand how welfare spending is connected to economic growth.

When an economy grows (that is, when the gross domestic product or GDP – all the goods and services produced in the country – is increasing), it is possible for government to spend larger amounts of money each year without raising the burden of taxation. If the economy stops growing or even shrinks, as in the 1991–2 recession in Britain, fewer goods and services are produced, less taxation can be gathered and the government must do one or more of the following things:

- borrow money to fund the shortfall in its tax revenues;
- increase taxes;
- reduce public spending.

In the long term, even a relatively slow-growing economy will create a significant increase in the resources available to government. For instance, a growth of 2 per cent per annum will increase the nation's wealth by a quarter over 12 years (that is, a real increase of between 24 and 26 per cent). Some industrial economies grow at a much faster rate than this. At 4 per cent growth per annum a country's wealth and income would grow by a half over the same period of 12 years.

If the population grows as quickly as the economy, however, the per capita (per head) wealth of the country will not increase and, if population growth outstrips economic growth, wealth per head will actually decline. In many parts of Africa, for instance, economic growth has been sluggish or non-existent and population growth rapid, so that standards of living in many African countries have declined to the level of the 1950s.

In ageing and low birthrate societies such as those in western Europe, on the other hand, economic growth has been relatively steady. But there have been increasing demands to fund social security payments and services for an increasing number of people outside the labour force: older people, rising numbers of unemployed people and younger people who remain in the education system for longer periods than before.

Table 5.2 shows how general public expenditure has risen over the past 40 years, whether we look at this as increases in the actual sums of money spent (billions of pounds) or as **real increases**. A real increase translates expenditure years ago into the value of money now, or recently, by allowing for inflation and devaluation.

The steepest rise in public expenditure took place between 1964 and 1976. From the late 1970s on, the rate of increase dropped, but nevertheless real increases in public spending continued at a steady rate under Mrs Thatcher's administrations in the 1980s. By 1997, at the end of John Major's Conservative administration, government was spending, in real terms, around 60 per cent more than in 1970–1, when Edward Heath became Prime Minister.

Table 5.2 Total managed expenditure

Year	Cash £ billion	Real terms £ billion	Percentage of GDP
1970–1	22.6	222.9	42.7
1980–1	111.8	295.6	47.3
1990–1	225.3	325.2	40.0
1996–7	314.1	373.9	40.6
2000–1	364.1	397.4	37.9
2003–4	455.2	455.2	40.8
2004–5	484.1	474.7	41.2
2007–8	580.0	526.1	42.1

Real terms figures are the cash figures adjusted to 2003–4 price levels using GDP deflators.
Source: HM Treasury (2005), adapted from Table 3.1.

Thus we are now spending far more actual money on roads, law and order, education, social security, health services and other things than in the 1960s. But note in Table 5.2 how spending *as a proportion of the nation's wealth* (GDP) was reduced by the end of Mrs Thatcher's term of office in 1990, from its 1980 high point of 47.3 per cent. The 2000–1 figure (below 40 per cent) shows how successful the New Labour government of Tony Blair was in controlling public spending during their first term. The most recent figure, for 2004–5, shows that the Labour government elected in 1997 has succeeded in increasing public spending as a share of a growing economy. The planned spending figures for 2007–8 show that spending as a proportion of GDP will continue to increase. The table conceals as much as it reveals however, because only a few years are selected. There were actually considerable fluctuations in spending as a share of GDP in the 1980s and 1990s; spending reached a high of 48.5 per cent of GDP in 1982–3 and another little high of 44.2 per cent in 1992–3, both times during a period of Conservative government. These were both years of recession in the British economy, with low levels of growth and high levels of unemployment. In these circumstances the public spending share will naturally rise.

Thus largely as a result of economic growth (but also including some gains from the sell-off or privatization of state-run services and assets), British governments have managed to fund much of the real increase without devoting a greater share of the nation's wealth to public spending. The economic cake has grown, but the slice given to government spending has stabilized at a little over or under 40 per cent of GDP. However, to highlight the connection between economic growth and government spending, note how 38 per cent of the nation's wealth in 2000–1 translates into £397 billion in real terms. This was £72 billion more than in 1990–1, when a higher proportion of the nation's wealth (40 per cent) represented only £325 billion (see Table 5.2).

General government expenditure covers a wide variety of items and services. Some substantial government priorities lie outside the field of welfare or social policy, as traditionally defined: for instance, defence, trade and industry, agriculture, forestry, fisheries and food.

Table 5.3 gives an idea of the government's spending priorities and how the money is divided between 'social' expenditure (social security, health, education and so on) and other services. These priorities are not set in stone, and it is important to remember that the *proportions* of public money devoted to some areas have been declining in recent years (for instance, defence, housing), while they have been rising in others (for example, social security).

The Labour government elected in 1997 spent proportionately *less* on the traditional areas of social welfare between the time it took office and the end of the century. The proportions of Britain's national wealth spent on education and social security declined slightly after Labour took over from the Conservatives, while health spending stayed at the same percentage. Significant economic growth in the late 1990s meant, however, that real increases in spending on education, health and other services were achieved even though the proportion of GDP devoted to these services was held at a steady level.

Table 5.3 Total expenditure on services by function as a percentage of GDP[1], 1990–1 to 2004–5 based on cash accruals

Function	1990–1 outturn	1996–7 outturn	2000–1 outturn	2004–5 estimated outturn
Defence	3.9	2.8	2.6	2.4
Public order and safety	2.0	2.1	2.1	2.5
Employment policies	0.4	0.4	0.4	0.3
Transport	1.6	1.3	0.9	1.6
Housing and community amenities	1.0	0.6	0.5	0.6
Health	4.8	5.5	5.6	7.0
Education and training	5.0	4.9	4.8	5.6
Of which: education	*4.8*	*4.7*	*4.6*	*5.4*
Social protection	12.0	14.5	13.3	13.9
Total expenditure on services			36.4	39.8
Total managed expenditure	**40.0**	**40.6**	**37.9**	**41.2**

1 For years 1987–8 to 2003–4 using GDP consistent with the latest figures from the Office for National Statistics (published 23 March 2005). For 2004–5, GDP is consistent with the March 2005 *Financial Statement and Budget Report*.
2 Includes allowance for shortfall and departmental unallocated provision.

Source: HM Treasury (2005) Table 3.4.

Social security: who benefits?

There are basically two kinds of social security benefit: non-contributory benefits and grants (which people qualify for on grounds of need or because they fall into a particular category, such as parents or children) and contributory benefits, which are based on the principle of insurance. People are eligible for these if they have paid into – contributed towards – the benefits system through National Insurance (or have had credits paid on their behalf by the government or employer).

Non-contributory benefits

Non-contributory benefits are either income-related (conditional on a means test of some kind) or non-income-related – that is, paid irrespective of the level of income a person has. Among the latter, the more important in terms of expenditure are child benefit, attendance allowance and disability living allowance, although other non-income-related benefits include war pension, severe disablement allowance, industrial injuries disablement benefit and disability working allowance. None of these benefits are taxable.

By far the biggest item of expenditure of all non-contributory benefits is the income-related (that is, means tested) income support, which is taxable. This is the benefit upon which many poorer families and individuals rely. It is the descendant of a long line of means-tested assistance to the poor, beginning with 'outdoor relief' under the Poor Law (see Chapter 3). When the Poor Law system was abolished, National Assistance was introduced in 1946 as a safety net for people in poverty not adequately covered by the contributory benefits scheme. National Assistance was in turn replaced by supplementary benefit, which established a set of rights to a wide range of benefits until income support was introduced in 1986.

People who are out of work and whose incomes are below a specified level receive the jobseeker's allowance, which replaced income support for unemployed people in 1996. However, in general, help will be given only as long as recipients of the jobseeker's allowance meet certain conditions – chiefly, a requirement to be available for full-time work (at least 40 hours per week) and to be actively seeking work.

Other income-related benefits include housing benefit, Council Tax benefit and child tax credit and working tax credit, which between them replaced working families tax credit in 2003, and pension credit, which replaced the minimum income guarantee in the same year.

Tax credits

Tax credits represent an interesting new approach to the provision of cash benefits. They are income-related benefits, and therefore means tested, and therefore selective, or targeted benefits. Instead of being assessed and paid out by a conventional social security agency, however, they are administered by the tax authorities now, with the recent amalgamation of the Department of Inland Revenue with Customs and Excise, called H.M. Revenue and Customs (HMRC). There are now three tax credits – the child tax credit, the working tax credit and the childcare tax credit. They are designed to encourage people to take paid work rather than remain on benefits; they act as a form of supplementation of wages. The child tax credit is, in addition, a weapon in the government's attack on child and family poverty. Tax credit claimants complete a fairly lengthy and complex claim form. Income is calculated over the year and the credits payable are assessed on the basis of the year's income. There may appear to be advantages in having a single agency for handling taxation and benefit payment, but flaws in the current management of the scheme as it affects children have come to light since 2005 and the system has been subject to serious criticism. There have been problems of under- and over-payment resulting from the difficulty of tracking changes in people's financial circumstances as their incomes fluctuate, and hardship has been caused to some needy families as HMRC has clawed back overpayments. Tax credits represent a significant shift in the direction of targeted benefits and away from universal benefits. To provide financial support to families with children, for example, the government could simply have chosen to steeply raise rates of child benefit, the universal system of child support that has existed in some form or another since the 1940s, rather than introduce a new system of tax credits (it should be noted that the principle of targeted child support goes back to the family income supplement introduced by the Conservative Heath government in 1971, although this was not a tax credit). Child benefit is a simple benefit to administer and has a virtually 100 per cent take-up rate. The government has not done this, although child benefit rates have been increased since 1997. At present, therefore, we have a somewhat anomalous dual system of child support.

The pension credit, so-called, is not really a tax credit in the same way as the others, but a means-tested benefit for retirement pensioners like, but more generous than, income support. It replaced the minimum income guarantee in 2003 and is a revamped version of the means-tested supplementation that has always been available for recipients of the state retirement pension whose overall incomes were low enough to qualify. It is administered not by HMRC but by the Department for Work and Pensions (DWP).

Contributory benefits

Among contributory benefits, the lion's share goes towards the huge retirement pensions bill. Incapacity benefit also takes a sizeable slice of the social security budget. Other contributory benefits include the jobseeker's allowance, which – rather confusingly – was introduced as both a contributory and non-contributory benefit (and is now administered by the DWP). This is because it replaced the previous unemployment benefit, a contributory National Insurance scheme, in 1996, as well as replacing non-contributory income support for unemployed people. However, compared to the very large amounts spent on retirement pensions and incapacity benefits, the jobseeker's allowance and other contributory benefits, such as widows' benefit and maternity allowance, take relatively small slices of the social security budget.

Who benefits?

Who benefits from all this expenditure on contributory and non-contributory benefits, representing an estimated £105 billion in 2003 (DWP 2004: 4)? If we examine this question in relation to the main recipient groups, we find that older people (see 'Objective 3: combat poverty and promote security and independence for today's and tomorrow's pensioners' – see Table 5.4) are the largest single category. People aged 65 and over represent less than a seventh of the population of the UK, but in 2003–4 they received close to 60 per cent of all benefit expenditure. Note the anomalous-looking dip in expenditure on children ('objective 1: ensure the best start for all children and end child poverty in 20 years' – Table 5.4) in 2003–4; this is because responsibility for child support was transferred to the Inland Revenue, with the introduction of the child tax credit in 2003. This is a change in budget headings rather than a reduction in the volume of resources going to children. Older people and other recipient groups can be ranked, as shown in Table 5.4.

Table 5.4 Benefit expenditure, £ millions, cash

Year	Total benefit spending	Objective 1	Objective 2	Objective 3	Objective 4
1991–2	**66,303**	7,804	21,297	32,829	4,373
1996–7	**92,212**	10,615	30,415	41,829	9,354
2001–2	**106,685**	12,279	27,562	54,493	12,351
2003–4*	**105,434**	3,847	28,214	60,309	13,064

Objective 1: ensure the best start for all children and end child poverty in 20 years; Objective 2: promote work as the best form of welfare for people of working age, whilst protecting the position of those in greatest need; Objective 3: combat poverty and promote security and independence for today's and tomorrow's pensioners; Objective 4: improve rights and opportunities for disabled people in a fair and inclusive society.

* 2003–4 estimated amounts

Source: DWP (2004: 4).

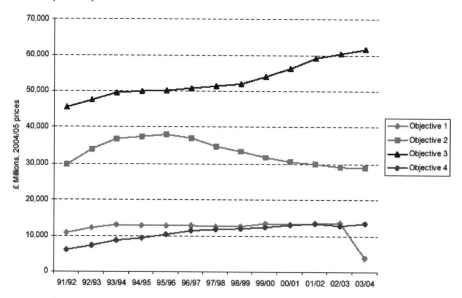

Figure 5.2 Benefit expenditure in real terms: Total benefit expenditure 1991/2 to 2003/4
Source: DWP (2004: 4).

While older people are the largest single group of social security beneficiaries, it is interesting to note how the pattern of benefit expenditure changed between 1991–2 and the early years of the present century (see Table 5.4). In 1991–2, disabled people received an eighth, in cash terms, of the total that elderly people received. By 2003–4, however, expenditure on benefits for disabled people had increased relative to those for elderly people, from around an eighth to between a quarter and a fifth of the size of the share spent on older people's benefits. Note that the data in the table is expressed in terms of cash expenditure, unadjusted for inflation, whereas that in the graph (see Figure 5.2), which presents the same information over the same time period, it is expressed in 'real' terms, that is, adjusted for general inflation in the economy over the period. The price baseline chosen is that for 2004–5. This increase is not simply a reflection of an increase in the number of people who are either disabled or have a long-term illness. It shows, rather, how the social security system has – despite criticisms of it – allowed for a considerable increase in benefit expenditure on sick and disabled people.

By contrast, benefit spending on unemployed people was much higher in the early 1990s, as a proportion of the total. In 1991–2, when the unemployment rate was high, the total benefit received by unemployed people was around two-thirds of the total amount received by older people, in cash terms. By 2003–4, however, the proportion taken by unemployed people had dwindled to about a half of older people's benefits in cash terms. Thus one of the major changes in social security priorities in recent years can be summed up as a shift of spending from supporting unemployed people towards supporting disabled people.

In more general terms, government figures show that 'households in the bottom half of the income distribution tend to be net gainers from the tax and benefit systems while those in the top half pay more in tax than they receive as benefits' (Office for National Statistics 2005b: 15). Thus, as this report points out, 'Taken as a whole, government intervention leads to income being shared more equally between households'. So the social security and taxation systems do act more like a 'Robin Hood' than a 'Sheriff of Nottingham'.

One way of looking at how far incomes are evened out by the tax and benefit system is to consider how much each group's income is modified by it. For instance, before taxes and benefits in cash and kind are taken into account, the 'original income' of the richest fifth of households is 17 times the income of the poorest fifth. After benefits and taxes are taken into account, the 'final income' of the richest fifth is only four times that of the poorest fifth (Office for National Statistics 2005b, Table 4).

Note that the effect of indirect taxation is to modify slightly the redistributive effect, resulting in a lessening of the poorer groups' shares of 'final income'.

Figure 5.3 illustrates the overall effects of taxes and benefits on household incomes. This ranks the population in bands called quintiles (fifths) in terms of income, from highest to lowest, and employs the concepts of 'original' and 'final' income to demonstrate the impact of taxes and benefits. Figure 5.3 shows a clear redistributive effect, taking into account direct and indirect taxes, cash benefits and benefits in kind (such as health services and education).

This is even more apparent if redistribution is looked at from the point of view of *lifetime* earnings and contributions rather than from a single point in time. Reporting on income data for individuals over their complete lives, Hills shows that the 'lifetime poorest' receive 'somewhat more' than the 'lifetime richest' (2004: 197). These estimates include benefits in kind, such as the NHS and education, as well as social security.

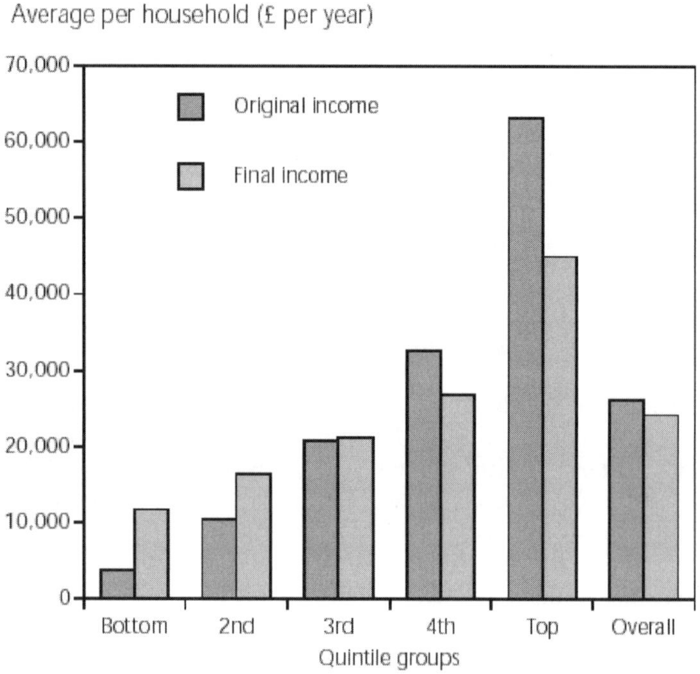

Average per household (£ per year)

Figure. 5.3 Original income and final income by quintile groups for *all* households, 2003–4
Source: Office for National Statistics (2005b: 15).

However, ' ... most benefits are self-financed over people's lifetimes, rather than being paid for by others. Nearly three-quarters of what the welfare state was doing in the late 1980s and early 1990s was like a "savings bank"; only a quarter was "Robin Hood" redistribution between different people' (Hills 2004: 197).

Hills shows that 'regardless of lifetime income, gross benefits from the state look much the same – around £200,000 per person (at 2001 prices), but also shows a clear redistributive effect, in that more of the receipts of higher income groups are 'self-financed'. What this means is that the better-off are paying more for the benefits they receive; the less well-off pay less – i.e., a higher proportion of their benefits involves some redistribution from the better-off (Hills 2004: 196).

Again, this broad picture of 'who benefits' from social security and other forms of welfare provision must be qualified by a number of things. For instance, gender makes a difference in that, 'on average, women are net lifetime beneficiaries from the system, men net lifetime payers for it' (Hills 1997: 21; 2004: 197). The question of how much an individual gains or loses over a lifetime is also affected by the generation or 'age cohort' they were born into. Those now in middle age will have to fund existing benefits and services throughout their lives – including, for instance, retirement pensions for those who are now old. But if the welfare system contracts in the future, withdrawing or effectively lowering the real value of pensions and social security benefits, they will not gain as much in their lifetimes as earlier generations or cohorts did.

These assessments of the redistributive effects of state welfare spending and taxation need to be placed in context. Inequalities of wealth and income grew between the 1970s and the 1990s in the UK, and there are persisting inequalities in relation to health, educational achievement and so on. These result from a variety of causes, including growing inequalities in incomes from work and the growth of unemployment since the 1970s as well as other effects which can be attributed to globalization. The system obviously does not equalize in the sense of eliminating all inequalities. What can be said is that inequalities would be greater without the tax and benefit system. New Labour's tax and spend policies have probably done something to slow down the rate of increase in inequalities, if not eliminating it altogether.

Poverty and social exclusion

The sums spent on social security in Britain each year are so vast as to be almost unimaginable. For instance, in 2003–4, the cost of social security as a whole, including tax credits, amounted to a colossal £138 billion of government expenditure (Dornan 2006: 83).

However, these sums translate into small amounts for the individual or the family. For example, in 2005 the basic state pension was only £82.05 per week for a single person (£131.20 for a couple). In that year the more generous pension credit, the 'top up' means-tested income guarantee below which no pensioner's income will fall, was £109.45 for a single person and £167.05 for a pensioner couple. Only two-thirds of eligible pensioners claim pension credit however, ignorance being largely responsible for the lack of take-up among the remainder (Toynbee and Walker 2005: 65).

Significant increases in pensions and benefits for older people who are on low incomes have taken place in recent years. However, even these increases do not alter the fact that, when divided up between millions of pensioners and other benefit recipients, the huge amounts of money collected and distributed as social security become relatively small weekly sums for the individual household.

This provides the most basic answer to the question 'why does poverty persist in a society with a well-developed welfare system?' The sums paid to benefit recipients are simply too low to lift them out of poverty. However, to leave our discussion at this point would be highly unsatisfactory. In the first place, showing that social security benefits are 'too low' does not address the question of *why* – if they are too low – this is the case, or the question of *how* this state of affairs has come about.

Second, there are other causes of poverty than apparently meagre levels of state benefit. Some argue that many of those in poverty have brought their fates upon their own heads, that benefit levels are adequate enough and that the poor cannot manage their incomes very well. Others argue the opposite – that the poor are caught in poverty not through their own faults but as a result of economic forces they cannot control, for instance, a decline in job opportunities for people without educational qualifications or skills.

The question of why poverty persists therefore demands a fuller answer. The causes of poverty are complex, and there are many different faces of poverty. As some commentators have pointed out, 'There is genuine uncertainty about how poverty might be measured and about whether, indeed, it is possible to measure a single state called poverty' (Johnson *et al.* 2000: 112).

To begin to understand poverty, it is helpful to disentangle various concepts and ideas about the subject. This will then enable us to look in greater depth at the causes of both poverty and social exclusion, and at the role of social policy in dealing (or not dealing) with these problems.

- As a first step, it is important to separate – but also see the connections between – *inequality* and *poverty*.
- Second, the relationship between inequality and poverty helps to clarify the idea of *relative poverty* (that is, the theory that poverty in a highly unequal society can only be defined relative to what other people, or the majority, have). Definitions of poverty as 'relative' can be contrasted with the concept of *absolute poverty*.
- Third, poverty and social exclusion are overlapping states – that is, many people in poverty are 'socially excluded'. However, it is useful to separate these concepts. Not *everyone* who is poor is socially excluded, and some of the socially excluded are not poor.

Poverty and inequality

Inequality can be defined in various ways. One way of measuring the degree of inequality is to compare differences in income and wealth between the top, middle and bottom sections of society. The greater the difference between the top and bottom, the greater the degree of inequality.

Some have argued that poverty does not automatically increase as inequality increases. Thinkers on the political right such as Hayek (1944), Friedman (1962), Joseph and Sumption (1979) and Scruton (1984) have all suggested that inequalities are a natural and desirable characteristic of a free, capitalist society (see Chapter 2). If the better-off have incentives to increase their incomes and to amass wealth, so this argument runs, then the resultant economic growth and prosperity will benefit everyone, including those on the lowest incomes. According to this theory, there can be a society in which there are wide disparities in income and wealth, but in which those on the lowest rungs of the ladder live modestly, but not in poverty-stricken conditions.

One not-so-charming expression to illustrate this view is to call it a 'horse-and-sparrows' theory of reducing poverty. The more oats that are stuffed into the horse at one end (that is, the faster the economy grows and the more the rich benefit from this), the more horse droppings will come out of the other, for the little sparrows (the poor) to pick over.

Much the same idea prevailed during the 1960s and the 1970s in the developing world. Economists and development planners then thought that the best way to help the poor in developing countries would be to stimulate economic growth – and therefore employment and general prosperity – by giving aid to capitalist firms and business people, not directly to the poor themselves.

There are major flaws with this approach and not much evidence that the horse-and-sparrow mechanism actually works. Far from a trickle-down effect, whereby wealth amassed by people at the top of society permeates the lower levels to create general prosperity, most observers of trends in inequality have noted the opposite. Increases in inequality and rises in the incomes of the better-off are usually accompanied by stagnating or even falling real incomes among the low-income groups, as Douthwaite (1992) and others have shown.

This seems to have been the experience in Britain in the 1980s and 1990s. Substantial economic growth benefited the rich, but not the poor. For instance, according to the government's own research (DSS 1994), the incomes of the poorest tenth of the population *fell* in real terms by 17 per cent between 1979, when Mrs Thatcher's Conservative government came into power, and the early 1990s. Over the same period, the incomes of the richest tenth rose by 62 per cent. And taking the population as a whole, the income of the better-off half rose by 50 per cent in real terms, while the income of the poorer half rose by only 10 per cent. The same government statistics showed that nearly a third of all children were living in poverty by 1991 – a total of 4.1 million.

The legacy of two decades of Conservative government (between 1979 and 1997) was therefore, according to Denny (2000: 2), to leave Britain 'with the worst poverty record in the developed world'. Referring to international statistics of poverty, Denny shows that poverty affected 20 per cent of the British population a year, on average, between 1991 and 1996. But in other European countries, the equivalent figures were much lower: for instance, 10 per cent in Germany, 7.4 per cent in Sweden and 6.1 per cent in the Netherlands. Britain also 'performed worse than the United States on every count – average poverty rates, long-term poverty rates and the proportion who had experienced poverty at some point over the six years' (Denny 2000: 2). These latter findings are surprising, given that the USA has a less comprehensive safety net of benefits than exists in Britain, and they underline the inadequacy of Britain's welfare system in preventing poverty.

More recent evidence on both inequality and poverty in Britain shows that, in the late 1990s, 'the disposable incomes of the poorest and richest decile groups were still edging apart' (Gordon *et al.* 2000: 8). The authors of this report by the Joseph Rowntree Foundation conclude that 'Evidence of the arrest or reversal of the divergent trend, while eagerly awaited, is not yet showing up in published survey data' (p. 8). At the end of the twentieth century there were still over 14 million people in the UK living in poverty, defined in the report as having to live on incomes that are below half the average. The total of children living in poor households had risen to 4.5 million in 1998–9 – an increase from 1.4 million in 1979. Meanwhile, the incomes of the richest tenth continued to grow.

The policies of the present government, however, do appear to have had a measurable impact on poverty, and especially child poverty, according to recent research. The impact on inequality generally is more ambiguous (Hills 2004; Hills and Stewart 2005; Stewart 2005). The government appears to be making some progress towards the objective enunciated in 1999 by Blair of eliminating child poverty in a generation. As one commentator noted, ' . . . by the start of the twenty-first century there was a commitment to tackle poverty and disadvantage that had not been seen since the 1960s, if not the 1940s, and a raft of specific policy initiatives aimed at particular aspects of the problem'

(Glennerster *et al.* 2004: 101). This may be regarded as encouraging, or, on the other hand, as disappointing by those who feel that, in relation to the scale of the problem, the policy response is inadequate and that much more could have been done.

Relative and absolute poverty

However, in making any statement about poverty in the UK such as the one above, we have to accept certain assumptions and conventions about the way poverty is defined. Does the UK really have one of the worst records in the developed world in failing to prevent poverty? How widespread is poverty in the UK, in fact? To answer questions such as this we have to remember that, as mentioned at the outset, poverty is not a single, identifiable 'thing'. There are two commonly accepted ways of defining it, and these view poverty either as a *relative*, or as an *absolute*, fixed measure.

One way of seeing poverty as relative is to say that people who have incomes below half the national average are poor. The incomes of the poorer groups are defined *relative to* average incomes, or incomes in society as a whole. There are several disadvantages with this kind of relative measure. It might be comparatively easy to work out, but it is a fairly arbitrary one. Why 50 per cent of the national average income – why not define poverty as having an income of less than 60 per cent, or 40 per cent, or 33 per cent of the average? Also, as Gordon *et al.* (2000) point out, a single statistical measure such as this, while convenient, is not 'based on independent criteria of deprivation or disadvantage; it does not relate to the needs of individuals, or to any agreed definition of what it is to be poor' (pp. 8–9).

Thus estimates of people's incomes that calculate whether they are getting 60, 50 or only 40 per cent of the average person's income are arguably providing us with information about *inequality* and *low income* rather than poverty. We cannot be certain that everyone whose income is below 50 per cent of the average is actually poor. At the same time, there might be some poverty among people whose incomes are above 50 per cent of the average. Householders who are buying their own homes, for instance, might be earning wages that are well above average but, because of having to make steep mortgage repayments, find that they cannot easily afford household essentials.

Johnson *et al.* (2000: 116) also show how calculating poverty by the half-average measure can be very misleading 'because it is very sensitive to changes in income levels among the richest people'. As they point out, incomes of the richest 10 per cent of the UK population increased very quickly in the late 1980s. This had the effect of significantly raising average incomes, so that 'measured "poverty" grew dramatically in the late 1980s, when unemployment was relatively low, but earnings growth at the top end was high'.

Similar problems of using the half-average measure of poverty also occur if benefit payments give people incomes that one year are just above the half-average figure, then the next year just below. Not much change will have occurred in the incomes of less well-off groups, but suddenly many more people will be recorded as living in poverty. As Johnson *et al.* conclude, the half-average measure is therefore purely arbitrary for this reason also, and 'can result in very large numbers of people being recorded as in poverty' (2000: 116).

Therefore, though poverty seems to be more common in Britain than in other comparable countries, the arbitrariness of the half-average indicator and other measures has the effect of throwing a cloud of uncertainty over the picture.

In order to better understand both the extent and nature of poverty in Britain, a number of researchers have spent a great deal of time and effort in trying to refine definitions of relative poverty. For example, in 1979 Townsend published *Poverty in the United Kingdom*, a huge book (longer than *War and Peace*, as one commentator observed). It did more than any other study in recent decades to stimulate debate about poverty and how social policies can address it. The breakthrough in poverty research that Townsend made was to build upon earlier ideas that it is not just lack of money or bare necessities that define poverty, but the lack of things that are widely *perceived* as necessary by society.

Thus Townsend developed a sociological definition of poverty, suggesting that it is an obstacle to people being able to take part in activities (such as watching television) that are customary in that society. He argued that it is possible to be objective about the things that are commonly regarded as necessities (for example, a television set), and thus objectively to define poverty as being deprived of those things. Townsend constructed a 'deprivation index' from a list of 60 items that he and his colleagues regarded as key indicators of a standard of living that would avoid poverty. The index included a wide range of amenities and activities relating to health, diet, social support, heating and lighting, housing conditions, clothing and so on. This list was then tested in surveys of the public to ascertain its validity. As Alcock (1997: 80) points out, the indicators included items such as 'the lack of a refrigerator, no holiday away from home in the last twelve months and the lack of a cooked breakfast most days of the week, all of which correlated highly with low income'. However, it is important to note that Townsend's overall measure of relative poverty was based on a *combination* of the deprivation index and incomes of households, not on income alone or simply on a measure of deprivation from commonly accepted necessities.

Townsend's masterpiece soon became the subject of controversy. Some argued that its definition of relative poverty was too generous. *Poverty in the United Kingdom* suggested that about 25 per cent of British households were poor, compared with the 7 per cent counted as poor according to official calculations (which equated poverty with being in receipt of means-tested supplementary benefits). Townsend's figure was regarded as an overestimate by many commentators. Official estimates of poverty might have been too low, but they raised the question of whether Townsend's estimate was too high.

Other questions about Townsend's influential study were raised by David Piachaud (1981), who did not question the concepts of relative poverty developed by Townsend but queried the validity of the deprivation index. Piachaud argued that much of the variation in deprivation scores reported in the study were 'merely due to diversity in styles of living wholly unrelated to poverty' (p. 420). For instance, questions about whether the children of the family had had other children to play or to tea in the past four weeks, or whether the family had eaten a roast Sunday dinner, were more to do with lifestyle than with deprivation. Piachaud therefore concluded that, though people on low incomes would tend to score high on the deprivation index, there would also have been 'considerable numbers' of people on low incomes who would not be identified as deprived, as well as 'many with high incomes who score high on the deprivation index' (p. 420).

These criticisms seem to have had a constructive outcome. Townsend and other social policy researchers went on to further improve the methods by which it is possible to identify the items that a majority of the population consider necessary, and thus – by implication – to discover what proportion of the population is deprived of these things. Major poverty surveys were conducted in Britain in the 1980s and 1990s (see Mack and Lansley 1985; Gordon and Pantazis 1997) and this research was built upon and extended by the most recent poverty study by the Joseph Rowntree Foundation (Gordon *et al.* 2000; Pantazis *et al.* 2006).

This latter study used items identified by a large-scale survey of the general public as necessities, rather than items identified solely by poverty experts or academics. You might like to consider whether you agree that the following items are necessary to avoid poverty and deprivation. These are a selection from Table 12 of the study (see Gordon *et al.* 2000: 44). Only *some* of these items were rated by a clear majority of respondents as necessities. Can you guess which ones? (The results of the survey are listed near the end of this chapter.)

- damp-free home
- beds and bedding for everyone
- mobile phone
- attending weddings, funerals
- refrigerator
- warm, waterproof coat
- home computer
- television set
- toys (for example, dolls, teddies)
- celebrations on special occasions
- a meal in a restaurant/pub monthly
- three meals a day for children; two meals a day for adults
- freezer
- fresh fruit and vegetables daily
- hobby or leisure activity
- telephone
- washing machine
- car

The conclusions of this study confirm the earlier findings of the steady growth of poverty in Britain and the comparatively large numbers of people involved. In line with other studies based solely on income measures, this study found that poverty affects a quarter of British households. However, the authors add that 'the welfare state provides an effective "safety net" which prevents people from sinking too deeply into poverty. For many households, the experience of poverty is extremely unpleasant but relatively brief' (Gordon *et al.* 2000: 53).

Such problems remind us that poverty is a complex, multidimensional phenomenon affecting different groups of people in different ways, and having different causes. Thus we can identify specific kinds of poverty in terms of the groups affected – for instance, child poverty, 'pensioner' poverty, urban or inner-city deprivation. Types of poverty can also be identified in terms of inability to afford certain things, such as fuel poverty, housing poverty or water poverty (which, in a developed society such as the UK, means being unable to afford a plentiful supply of water from a metered supply).

Given this complexity, together with nagging doubts about the reliability of relative measures of poverty, it is not surprising that absolute measures of poverty hold a certain attraction. Does not a single 'absolute' line of income, below which people or households can be counted as being in poverty, offer a much more scientific and objective measure than apparently wishy-washy relative definitions? Governments in other countries, such as the USA, clearly think so. The US federal government establishes a 'poverty line' of minimum income and regularly updates it. From this, numbers of households and individual people living in poverty, below the line, can be calculated. This information is used not only by federal and state governments to evaluate their anti-poverty policies, but also by critics of government policy and NGOs working to reduce poverty.

The UK has no such official poverty line. However, there is one commonly used 'absolute' definition of poverty, in addition to relative definitions such as the half-average income measure discussed above. This is the definition of poverty as *having an income that is below the level at which means-tested benefits are payable*.

This 'absolute' measure is not particularly objective or scientific, however, because it reflects the government's *idea* of minimum income, or how much money the government of the day thinks it necessary to give individuals and families in poverty to live on. Yet there can be many people with incomes that are just above the official minimum level, but who are actually in poverty. Older people reliant on state retirement pensions are a case in point, as mentioned earlier (see Toynbee 2000).

In the UK, social security benefits have been set at a rather cheese-paring level since the earliest days of the welfare state. As we saw in Chapter 3, Beveridge calculated a national minimum income that was based on the poverty surveys of the 1930s and beforehand, conducted by Seebohm Rowntree. These surveys employed an absolute definition of poverty that converted the cost of a range of essential items in a weekly household budget (basic foodstuffs, heating and lighting, rent – but no 'luxuries' to speak of) into a total amount that a typical family could subsist upon. And as the experience of the 1950s and 1960s showed, when poverty was 'rediscovered' in the welfare state, typical levels of social security benefit had simply been set too low to lift people out of poverty.

Thus absolute definitions of poverty suffer from the same problem of arbitrariness that relative measures do. Who decides where the poverty line, or level of minimum income, should be set? Whose interests are considered when the calculation is made – those of the poor, or those of governments wishing to hold down social security expenditure?

The latter question implies that official interests always win out, and that by setting the minimum income and means-testing levels rather low, governments seek to underestimate true levels of poverty. However, an absolute measure based on receipt of state benefits can have the opposite effect. If governments extend eligibility for means-tested state benefits or take active steps to encourage take-up of existing benefits, this can have the perverse effect of simultaneously improving many people's incomes yet defining more people than before as being poor – because they are receiving means-tested benefits!

In summary, absolute measures of poverty – whether based on minimum income required, on whether a person or a family is receiving means-tested benefits, or on more complex indicators of income – cannot provide a problem-free, scientific alternative to relative definitions. As Burden (2000: 43–4) points out, an absolute measure has the attraction of providing an obvious and precise measure of poverty that can be debated publicly and can act as a clear guide to policy-makers wishing to address problems of low income. As he suggests, though, it is an arbitrary measure that can distort the picture of poverty rather than clarify it. An absolute measure also tends to focus attention on the poor as a separate group. This distracts attention from the broad pattern of inequality, and the idea that growing poverty in one section of society could be related to growing affluence in another.

Social exclusion

The concept of social exclusion, on the other hand, helps to highlight the idea that poverty and deprivation in one part of society are linked in some ways to what is happening in the rest of society. If social exclusion exists on a large scale, this might point to a failure of government to develop 'inclusive' policies that relieve deprivation and create opportunities for people to climb out of poverty.

But what is 'social exclusion' and how does it compare with definitions of poverty? As Alcock (1997: 92) notes, the term social exclusion began to enter social policy debates from the mid-1980s onwards. It became a highly fashionable term once the Labour government of 1997 was elected. The phrase peppers every official report and document on poverty and the social issues connected with it, such as poor health and education standards, crime, housing, employment and economic regeneration.

Social exclusion can often appear as a substitute term for 'poverty'. This is partly because governments tend not to like to admit to the persistence of poverty. Poverty reminds governments that they might not have been as effective as they would like to portray themselves. Discussion of poverty certainly does not sit well with a New Labour government that wishes to be seen as a progressive, reforming administration. For similar reasons, the previous Conservative administrations led by Thatcher and Major preferred to discuss 'low income' or 'low income groups' rather than 'poverty' or 'the poor'.

Thus governments sometimes use euphemisms and polite words to mask appalling social conditions in some sections of the community, and their slowness in tackling these problems. However, there is a case for employing the term 'social exclusion' as a genuinely useful and valuable way of understanding how the nature of poverty, deprivation and inequality have been changing in recent years.

Perhaps this is best understood by contrasting the core concepts of 'poverty' and 'social exclusion'. As mentioned at the outset, though, these are two *overlapping* concepts. This means that much of what is implied by the term 'poverty' also applies to 'social exclusion', and vice versa.

- First, concepts of poverty tend to focus on lack of *material resources* (chiefly money income, but also including other things such as lack of adequate housing). Social exclusion, on the other hand, focuses on the *relationship* (or lack of it) between the excluded individual, family or community and the rest of society. The 'socially excluded' have been pushed out by the rest of the community and therefore find it hard to take up opportunities to improve their situation. Material poverty and social exclusion often go hand in hand, therefore, but separating the two concepts allows us to recognize how some people might be socially excluded even when they are *not* poor or living on particularly low incomes. For instance, black people and disabled people experience high poverty rates, but some people in these groups are not poor. Nevertheless, they might experience social exclusion in the form of racism or discrimination and restriction of opportunities. However, as indicated above, these distinctions are blurred. Relative definitions of poverty – such as those used by Townsend and his colleagues – refer to poverty as being deprived not only of material resources, but also of opportunities to play a full part in society. They are, in effect, 'socially excluded' (see Townsend 1979; Gordon *et al.* 2000).

- Second, concepts of social exclusion tend to focus on lack of educational and employment opportunities. Being socially excluded is usually taken to mean being excluded from the labour market or being unemployed. Consequently, much of government policy to reduce social exclusion rests upon efforts to get people into a job, education or some kind of 'mainstream' activity in the community. This does not mean that social exclusion is *always* associated with unemployment, only that it tends to be seen this way. Poverty, on the other hand, is a concept that can be applied as easily to people in work on 'poverty wages' (the working poor) as to people who are unemployed or excluded from the labour market for other reasons (such as older people).

- Third, the remedies for poverty and social exclusion tend to emphasize different strategies or policies. Again there is overlap, but anti-poverty strategies have tended to stress the importance of bringing about *greater equality of incomes* and other material resources. If a whole community is poor, for instance, there might be a government strategy to put extra resources into that community, such as better-equipped schools, improved infrastructure, leisure facilities and so on. At a nationwide level, poverty could be tackled by raising levels of social security benefits to raise the incomes of poorer people. Policies to combat social exclusion, on the other hand, have tended to stress *creating more opportunities* for poorer people so that they can improve their incomes themselves. Government handouts and across-the-board increases in social security benefits are seen as a form of 'passive welfare' that might stifle initiative and not help poorer people in the long run. In practice, however, these are differences of emphasis rather than clear-cut differences. Many anti-poverty programmes in the UK – and particularly in the USA – have included efforts to stimulate enterprise, retraining and community involvement as well as trying to redistribute resources or improve income levels. At the same time, the government's policies to combat social exclusion have not just emphasized work, training and the theme of self-reliance or encouraging people to seize opportunities. They have also included putting substantial resources into poorer and socially excluded areas to improve facilities and services (for example, nurseries).

In summary, though the concepts of poverty and social exclusion overlap, there seems to be some merit in using the term social exclusion to identify new problems of deprivation and disadvantage. For instance Lawson (1995) refers to the way that 'new poverty' has increased as a result of economic restructuring and changes in the job market. New kinds of social and economic insecurity have come about, leading to the exclusion of 'an increasingly vulnerable minority', for whom 'the prospects are a life more or less detached from the broader economic and social experiences of mainstream society' (p. 5).

People in poverty have commonly experienced social rejection and found their social status devalued, especially in a materialistic and competitive society. However, the point being made by authors such as Lawson is that two newer kinds of change are happening in the 'postmodern' world (see Chapter 13). The first is a widening of opportunity and significantly improving standards of living for the 'broad middle mass' of society. As a result, traditional class barriers and allegiances are weakening, together with other social divisions such as those of gender and race. But as these fragmenting processes occur and living standards improve for the affluent majority, this majority is less and less able to understand or identify with the minority who are effectively excluded from taking up the same opportunities. The second kind of change, therefore, is a fragmentation of 'the poor' into increasingly isolated and vulnerable groups – for instance, older people on very low incomes, young unemployed people, certain groups of mentally ill and disabled people, young lone parents, and some sections of 'racial' and ethnic minority communities.

Therefore, although both poverty and social exclusion appear to have increased significantly in the UK in the 1980s and 1990s, poverty is far from being a 'mass' experience. Large numbers of people are affected, but poverty is not a shared experience or a common pattern of life as it might have been, for instance, in the days of high unemployment and economic depression in the 1930s. The challenge for governments in the twenty-first century will be to find ways of changing social policies to make them more flexible and able to meet the increasingly diverse needs of the fragmented groups that are both poor and socially excluded.

Conclusions

This chapter has discussed 'who gets what' from the welfare system. The focus has largely been upon economic benefits and costs. This is not to deny the importance of the social and political costs and benefits of having a well-developed welfare system. For instance, commentators on the right claim that an 'over-generous' or open-handed welfare system creates social costs or problems such as welfare dependency and laziness – or, more politely, 'work disincentives'. Supporters of a comprehensive welfare system, whether on the left or the right, would point to social benefits such as greater social stability and perhaps less crime.

These latter questions, important though they are, were not the main subject of this chapter. Discussion of the social effects of the welfare system – especially the connections between social policy, social control and poverty – is continued in the next chapter.

However, restricting our gaze to cash or money benefits can give a rather narrow view of equality. As mentioned at the outset, conventional economics might miss the important contributions of labour or care provided 'free' by carers or family members.

In addition, as Powell (1995) reminds us, when earlier social theorists such as Tawney (1964) and Marshall (1970) defined equality in social policy, 'they appeared to be talking about equality of status, entitlement, universality and citizenship rather than the more demanding forms of distributive justice' (Powell 1995: 170). In other words, it would be a mistake to judge the welfare system solely according to the way in which it distributes cash benefits or other calculable outcomes, such as length and quality of medical treatments, or the number of educational qualifications gained.

There is something over and above these rather narrowly defined outcomes: a principle of equality that transcends class and other inequalities. The politicians and planners who established the welfare system after the Second World War were inspired by this idea of equality. 'Equality of entitlement' is a principle that one will be treated equally as a citizen when in need of a service, whatever one's earnings or station in life.

As we have seen in this chapter, the impact of the welfare system as a whole upon top-, middle- and bottom-income groups is mixed. With regard to services in kind, there is considerable evidence that the NHS gives more to people at the lower end of the income scale than it takes from them (Wilkin *et al.* 1987; O'Donnell and Propper 1991). As Hills (1997: 16) remarks, 'benefits in kind are less concentrated on the poor than cash benefits, but households at the bottom of the distribution scale still receive more than those at the top (particularly from the NHS)'.

The impact of education (and especially unequal take-up of higher education) and some aspects of housing policy, on the other hand, do appear to be less 'pro-poor'. Hills's survey suggests that overall it is households on *middle* incomes that gain most from services in kind such as education and health, whereas top-income households gain relatively little from such public services.

Social security, by far the most significant 'gatherer and distributor' of resources in the welfare system, funnels a net flow of money from better-off to poorer income groups. However, because of wider social and economic inequalities, this vital role of social security might be obscured. For one thing, tax reforms have lightened the burden of those on the highest incomes, while relatively high taxes have been levied on poorer groups, especially through increases in indirect taxation. As a result, British society through the 1980s and 1990s moved decisively towards a 'two-thirds affluent, one-third poor' division.

People in poverty – one-parent families, older people, unemployed people – would have been even poorer without the welfare and social security system. Each pruning exercise, or restriction of the rate of increase in benefits (such as the freezing of child benefit levels between 1988 and 1992) made the poor worse off than they had been before. But as we have seen in this chapter, the social security system continued to have a mildly redistributive effect in favour of the poor, even in the 1980s and 1990s. The social security system could not prevent rising levels of poverty, but it continued to be a 'Robin Hood' – albeit a rather old and arthritic Robin Hood. How far has the change of government from Conservative to Labour in 1997 had a detectable impact on problems of poverty, and on the future of the welfare system as a whole? Answers to these questions, and the performance of the Labour government in a number of social policy fields, are discussed in Chapter 13.

We need to bear in mind that there is a range of explanations for rises and falls in rates of poverty. Government actions alone do not determine the rate of poverty. It cannot be controlled like a tap, as if economic and social policies can either quickly increase poverty, or reduce it to a trickle in months. It is true that the sudden and rapid rise in poverty in the 1980s did seem to show the clear effect of Conservative policies. However, it is also true that underlying economic and social changes were encouraging the trends in inequality and poverty. These changes included change in the employment market leading to declining demand for unskilled and semi-skilled labour, which in turn leads to higher unemployment or lower wages for people in low-income social groups. Globalization can also have an effect, tending to depress wages because employers in other countries can produce goods more competitively.

Therefore the Labour government elected in 1997 would have needed to swim strongly against a tide of rising income inequality in order to have made a significant and early impact on poverty. The evidence, however, is that the government put its economic objectives before those of social policy. As shown above, public spending as a proportion of GDP fell under the Labour government between 1997 and 2000 to its lowest levels since the early 1960s. To establish its credentials as a pro-business party, Labour stead-fastly refused to make any significant increases in spending on health, education or social security during its first term of office.

However, as the election of 2001 approached, the government announced very large spending increases to be implemented in the health service, education and various anti-poverty programmes through to 2004. According to opinion supportive of the government, this 'long term spending boost to social policy' was 'historic' and accounts for 'the largest sustained increase in social policy spending ever envisaged' (*The Guardian* 2001: 19).

However, some scepticism about the likely impact of these spending increases is needed. First, the delay in releasing public money to revive the UK's cash-starved social and health services created severe problems in terms of finding sufficient staff and management resources to begin to implement planned improvements. A shortage of expertise and personnel to set up new anti-poverty initiatives, and to improve existing services in social services, health and education, had been created.

Much of the planned increase in public expenditure was earmarked either, on the one hand, for health and education services, or on the other for a wide range of special schemes and initiatives to deal with child poverty, to aid working families on low in-comes, and to encourage training and education among 'excluded' groups. Social security spending was, therefore, selectively increased to benefit particular groups, notably families with children, and pensioners. Rather than there being across-the-board improvements, benefit increases have been increasingly targeted.

As shown in this chapter, it is social security that does more than any other arm of the welfare system to redistribute resources in favour of the poor. In its second term in office, New Labour did plan to significantly reduce 'pensioner poverty' through its pension credit scheme, introduced in 2003, a successor to the minimum income guar-antee, whereby means-tested additional benefits can be claimed by those on low incomes in old age. This was indexed to earnings rather than price increases, and to that extent the 'relative deprivation' of pensioners should not increase. But this commitment – while welcome to many older people – will still leave Britain's public spending on pensions well below the European average. Also, despite a Royal Commission's recommendations to fund long-term nursing and personal care for older people, the government turned its back on the personal care element of these proposals. It was concerned about the long-term impact on government finances (though in Scotland a decision to fund personal care universally was approved by the Scottish Parliament in 2001 – see Chapter 12). As a result, some older and chronically ill people will continue to experience severe financial hardship in trying to pay for expensive nursing and personal care.

These latter examples show that, while there are likely to be significant reductions in poverty and social exclusion in the coming years, there will also be considerable numbers of missing guests at the feast, particularly among Britain's growing population of older people. The virtues of large increases in public expenditure on social welfare are being rediscovered after two decades of government attempts to rein it in. However, the signs are that policies will attempt to construct a much more flexible, targeted and means-tested welfare system rather than try to revive the goal of creating a more equal society through a traditional welfare state of universalistic services and benefits.

Perception of necessities

In the section on relative and absolute poverty earlier in the chapter, items from Table 12 in the study by Gordon *et al.* (2000) were listed. These were items that the authors of the study asked members of the public to rate as necessities. In the above text, however, we left out the percentages of the public that consider each item to be a necessity. You might like to compare your own estimations of which items are necessary with the results of Gordon *et al.*'s survey, shown in Table 5.5. The percentages show the proportions of the general public deeming each item a necessity in 1999, and in a previous survey in 1983 (where included).

Table 5.5 Rating of necessities

Item	1999	1983
Damp-free home	94	96
Beds and bedding for everyone	95	97
Mobile phone	8	—
Attending weddings, funerals	81	—
Refrigerator	89	77
Warm, waterproof coat	87	87
Home computer	11	—
Television set	58	51
Toys (for example dolls, teddies)	84	71
Celebrations on special occasions	83	69
A meal in a restaurant/pub monthly	27	—
Three meals a day for children; two meals a day for adults	91	82
Freezer	55	—

Fresh fruit and vegetables daily	87	—
Hobby or leisure activity	79	64
Telephone	72	43
Washing machine	77	67
Car	36	22

Source: extracts from Gordon *et al.* (2000), Table 12, p. 44.

Key terms and concepts

disposable income
economic growth
external benefits
gross domestic product (GDP)
income:
   original income
   gross income
poverty:
   absolute
   relative
real increases (for example, in spending, wages or benefits)
redistribution

social security benefits:
   contributory
   non-contributory
   income-related
   non-income-related
   selective
   universal
targeting
taxation:
   direct
   indirect
   progressive
   regressive

Suggestions for further reading

Among several textbooks on the economics of welfare, Barr's *The Economics of the Welfare State* (4th edn, 2005) is perhaps the best in terms of combining in-depth economic analysis with a comprehensive coverage of the welfare system. Howard Glennerster's *Understanding the Finance of Welfare: What Welfare Costs and How to Pay for It* (2003) is a readable and also an authoritative introduction.

For an overview of the main themes in social security, Michael Hill's *Social Security Policy in Britain* (1990) and Pete Alcock's *Understanding Poverty* (2nd edn, 1997) are very helpful. If you are writing an essay or project that involves reference to the social security system, you would find the annual publication *Work and Pensions Statistics* by the DWP extremely useful. This source gives a breakdown of public spending on all the main social security benefits. It also provides helpful explanations of the purposes of each benefit, the rules governing eligibility and so on.

A study for the Joseph Rowntree Foundation, John Hills's *The Future of Welfare* (1997) (2nd edn), provides a valuable corrective to doom-laden and apocalyptic notions that the ageing society and growing demand for health and welfare services will make the current welfare system unaffordable. The Rowntree Foundation's importance in studies of poverty is also illustrated in the report edited by Pantazis *et al.*, *Poverty and Social Exclusion in Britain: The Millennium Survey* (2006), which updates Gordon *et al.*'s *Poverty and Social*

Exclusion in Britain (2000). This report gives not only fascinating insights into public attitudes towards poverty, but also much useful information about the nature and extent of poverty in Britain. The latter is available as a free download from the Joseph Rowntree Foundation's website. Another useful publication is Glennerster *et al.*'s *One Hundred Years of Poverty and Policy* (2004), also available from the website. There is also a useful House of Commons Library research paper on poverty measures and concepts, *Poverty: Measures and Targets*, research paper 04/23 (2004). This can be downloaded from the House of Commons website.

6   SOCIAL POLICY, POLITICS AND SOCIAL CONTROL

Introduction: social control and the rise of welfare

Chapter 5 focused on economic issues and 'who gets what?' from the welfare system. But that topic has social and political implications in that 'who gets what?' is also a way of looking at social inequality and the impact of government policy on social divisions. This chapter builds on these issues by continuing the debate about what impact social policy has on society. It focuses on the central question of how far social policies play a political function in terms of maintaining the social order and buttressing government power.

Did the gradual building up of a system of government-organized welfare in the twentieth century increase the state's control over us? Did it erode liberty and personal freedoms? In return for a certain amount of security, did the welfare state destroy both self-reliance and willingness to look after others? Or are such ideas misleading, and could the opposite be true – that only when there is generous state provision of education, health care and world class social services can people be genuinely free and able to fulfil their potential to develop themselves and help others?

This chapter addresses these questions and explores the debate about the connections between social policy on the one hand, and questions of social control, coercion and freedom on the other. Such questions might seem unnecessary, however, to anyone who takes it for granted that social welfare is unequivocally 'a good thing'. Surely, if education, health and welfare services successfully meet most people's needs and alleviate social problems, the more that is provided the better?

There is a case to be answered, however. Sometimes the welfare system does become more concerned with controlling us than with meeting our needs or respecting our rights as independent citizens. Commentators on both the political left and right have suggested that a bureaucratic state can, in the name of providing help, become paternalistic and insensitive.

But was this the main reason for the development of social policy and welfare services in the nineteenth and twentieth centuries? Was the state's growing concern with public welfare – for instance, public health, the welfare and education of children, better housing and so on – really motivated by a need to manage and control the population? If this theory is correct, it means that the actual welfare of the population was always secondary to governmental aims of maintaining order and political control. It also implies that, once political and social order can be maintained by other means than providing welfare – for instance, by cultivating consumerism or materialism – governments will be less and less interested in supporting the continued improvement and extension of the welfare state.

Before jumping to these conclusions, however, it is important to look at what history tells us about the development of welfare states. Historical experience suggests that the rise of welfare can be explained only by reference to a wide range of factors, not just attempts by the state to extend social control.

Industrialization in the nineteenth and early twentieth centuries certainly did pose problems of social conflict and disorder. Sometimes governments saw the expansion of welfare benefits and improvements in living conditions for the working classes as ways of dampening down these conflicts, mainly by giving concessions or 'buying off' the strongest and more militant groups. However, the reasons for the development of welfare were complex and included a number of influences, as suggested below.

- *Industrialization* occurred at different times, at varying speeds and in different ways in different countries, but broadly speaking the development of industrial society can be seen as perhaps the most important stimulus to the development of social welfare. However, different national governments responded in their own particular ways, according to the political and cultural traditions of each country, to the new needs of the industrial age – for instance, needs for more housing, sanitation and better education – and some highly industrialized societies (notably the USA and Japan) never developed western European-style welfare states.
- *War* between countries – at least preparation for military conflict – was sometimes as important a stimulus to improve social welfare as conflict and protest within countries. Governments began to see the connections between health, education and literacy and the building up of effective military strength.
- *Religious activity* and competition between different churches or denominations was sometimes as important as political conflict in promoting the growth of education, hospitals and charitable efforts to care for the poor. For instance, the role of charity and charitable institutions was particularly significant in Britain and the USA. And in the Netherlands, one reason for the high level of educational and welfare development was the determination of both Protestant and Catholic communities to develop their own systems of social support and welfare.

- *Economic efficiency* can also be seen as an important factor in the development of social policy. Governments and employers began to realize that public spending on health care, social insurance, education and other benefits resulted in a more productive and efficient labour force.
- *Public demand* for better public services and more education led governments that were reluctant to develop social policies to consider doing so. Note that this explanation is not quite the same as the theory that governments decided to prevent general social disorder or political unrest through the cynical use of welfare improvements or concessions. Public demand for more social welfare was a reflection of the development of *democracy*. Once elected parliaments were in place, welfare and social policy began to develop to unprecedented levels, and this was more an unexpected, 'bottom-up' type of development than a result of 'top-down' policies imposed by paternalistic governments.

Thus welfare systems developed for a variety of reasons in each European country and in North America (see Jones 1985: 34–77 for a useful summary of the evidence). This variety of influences also meant that the *scale* of welfare provision, and how far it was considered proper for the state to intervene in people's lives, varied considerably from country to country.

Clearly, some explanations for the development of welfare during the industrial age fit some countries better than others. Economic development and the modernization of society in Britain during the nineteenth century were certainly strong influences (see Chapter 3). However, Jones (1985) concludes that political and social control factors, while by no means being the only ones, did play a leading part in stimulating the early development of social policy and welfare provision:

> There exists no discernible link between the level of economic development (indices of industrialization and urbanization) and the first introduction of social insurance measures designed to meet the needs of . . . the sick . . . the old, and the unemployed. It [was], if anything, the less developed of European societies which [proved] to be the most prompt in introducing social insurance . . . [There was] a tendency for traditional, patriarchal regimes to embark promptly – even prematurely – upon preventive social policy measures.
>
> (Jones 1985: 52)

Other observers of the development of welfare have also established this early connection between social policy and political control. A famous study entitled *Regulating the Poor: The Functions of Public Welfare*, by Piven and Cloward (1971), showed that federal spending by the US government on social welfare tended to increase where there had been civil unrest and inner-city riots. On the other hand, Piven and Cloward argued, growing restrictiveness in providing welfare and the introduction of stricter forms of means test can be used by government as ways of not only gaining electoral support among the comfortable majority but also controlling or 'regulating' the poor. Social policies, in their view, have contributed to a process of marginalization of the poor.

Hillyard and Percy-Smith (1988) have argued in their book *The Coercive State* that a wide variety of social policies, including social security and health service reform, illustrate a trend in Britain towards a more controlling and less democratic form of government than before. This is taking place, they suggest, despite a 'liberal rhetoric' or widespread assumption that government is based on democracy and that the actions of the state are legitimate. However, they are careful to point out that the growing power of the state is a complex phenomenon. It cannot be reduced to a single trend or example, because government – and people's experience of it – is multifaceted: 'In short, the state in its various roles may at different times, in different situations and for different people, be seen as benevolent protector or provider, impartial arbiter between competing interests, a minor irritant, or alternatively, as obstructive, intrusive, oppressive and coercive' (Hillyard and Percy-Smith 1988: 14).

Social policy and regulation

The term social control has negative connotations and is often identified with coercion, limitation of individual freedom, or disempowerment. This is, however, too narrow a view. All social policy is 'social control' and who says 'social policy' is effectively saying 'social control'. In its most general sense, social control simply means some kind of collective regulation of individual or group behaviour or actions. Social control is not merely inescapable, it is arguably highly desirable. A society of any degree of size, complexity, internal differentiation and division of labour is inconceivable without some kind of social control. Any society which is sufficiently differentiated to possess some system of governance – that is, a state – is necessarily involved in social control of a formal kind. (Social control may of course be informal, as in the exercise of discipline over children within the family – see concluding section.)

A broader, more ideologically neutral concept which is roughly synonymous with that of social control is 'regulation'. In the previous chapter we noted Lowi's suggestion that a distinction could be made between regulatory, distributive and redistributive public policies and politics, or more accurately, perhaps, regulatory, distributive and redistributive aspects of such policies (see Lowi 1966; Blank and Burau 2004).

What aspects of social control or regulation would most of us, apart, perhaps, from a few anarchists, welcome and find highly desirable? The criminal law is one aspect of regulation or social control, as are many other areas of law. Law in general is clearly an instrument of social control – a device through which governments promote control of or over society. Legislation and regulations governing public, or preventive, health – clean water, sewerage, the collection and disposal of human wastes, communicable disease control, environmental standards, regulations governing food standards and purity, and workplace health and safety; legislation which restricts maximum hours of work; housing standards; the minimum wage; regulations governing public house opening hours; the National Curriculum; anti-discrimination legislation in relation to race, gender, age and disability; the law relating to the treatment of children; regulations governing the compulsory detention of the mentally ill – all these are examples of collective interference with individual freedom.

At a certain level, therefore, all politics and public policy are really regulatory, because distributive and redistributive policies can themselves be regarded as forms of regulation. Governments interfere with the freedom of individuals and free markets in all kinds of ways. The existence of the NHS providing 'free' health care at the point of use, for example, is an interference with free markets in health care and a form of market regulation.

Too much control – or not enough?

Rather than social control being seen as the problem, there is mounting concern that, as welfare systems retract and social inequalities grow, increasing disorder will result. The problem could be a *lack* of social control. Gray (1995: 12), for instance, argues: 'What is less obvious is the role played by the new inequality in weakening the ties of community. Inequality has divided us, most palpably, in cities, where it has enforced a brutal segregation according to income and access to jobs. It has promoted an erosion of relationships of trust affecting most aspects of social life, alongside a precipitous collapse of public trust in institutions'.

This represents an important change in thinking, because it shows that 'social control', though it has many negative connotations, also has a positive side. This becomes clearer if we use other words than social control or social order. Notice how Gray uses the words 'ties of community' and 'institutions' in the extract. If we put the words 'social control' in place of 'the ties of community' in the passage quoted above, and substitute 'the social order' for 'institutions', the meaning is more or less the same. Social control can lead to a social order that enhances welfare, security and trust. The difference between an ordered and a disordered society can mean the difference between being free to walk alone at night without fear of intimidation or violence, or not. It will also affect whether or not we have to pay a steep price for individual security (insurance premiums, alarm systems, house security and so on).

Note that these examples illustrate a contradiction. A social order which is rule-bound, in which there is effective law enforcement and where everyone is expected to conform also brings certain freedoms: chiefly, freedom from worries about crime or, more positively, a sense of belonging to a structured community.

One particular welfare system illustrates this contradiction very well: the city-state of Singapore. In Singapore, which is virtually a one-party state, the government represses free thought and political opposition. The mass media, the universities and any potential sources of dissidence are tightly controlled. There are strict penalties for infringing rules governing everyday life, from personal dress and hairstyles to throwing litter. Yet Singapore is one of the few large modern cities in today's world in which women can walk freely without serious worries of being attacked, and where street crime and burglary are still relatively uncommon.

The key to understanding social control in Singapore is not just effective law enforcement and political repression, and an economy in which work is plentiful – in fact there have been threats to Singapore's strong economy in recent years – but also its social policies. Singapore has a comprehensive system of health and education services that buttress the social order and enhance social consensus, making the existing paternalism seem more acceptable than a nakedly repressive regime.

Does this mean that, in western market economies, social disorder and violent crime

(Paton Walsh 2001) are attributable to cutbacks in the growth of welfare provision? Unfortunately, the answer may not be straightforward. Whether social policy maintains order or causes change is much debated. Depending on one's political viewpoint, the relationship between social policy and social stability can be seen in different ways.

- First, factors other than changes in social policy or cutbacks in welfare could be causing upheaval. For instance, social and geographical mobility; the break-up of old neighbourhoods, communities and extended family ties; the decline of stable employment opportunities (especially affecting young men); and changes in culture and social norms reflect, among other things, more individualistic approaches to life and greater tolerance of self-seeking or violent behaviour.
- Second, there is, on the other hand, an argument that 'over-generous' or open-handed social security policies have brought about increasing social disorder. Arguing from the political right, Murray (1994) suggested that in the period between the 1950s and 1980s social security benefits were both substantially increased in real terms and made easier to obtain. According to this argument, increasingly liberal welfare systems undermined work disciplines and subsidized the lifestyles of an underclass that are socially deviant and rejecting of authority. Family structures were undermined by welfare, which made single parenthood both more financially feasible and more morally acceptable.
- Third, social welfare might be achieving the opposite of what Murray (1994) suggests. If social controls are weakening, it might not be social policies that are bringing this about. Rather, social policies, despite many governments' attempts to curb the growth of the welfare system, are doing the opposite. They provide some (crumbling) social cement and some protection from the divisive effects of economic and cultural change.

Bearing these different perspectives in mind, we examine in this chapter *whether* or *how far* social policies have played, and might continue to play, a central role in buttressing the social order. The relationship between social policy and social control will be discussed in three main ways:

- at a political level;
- at an individual level;
- at a local or urban community level (in the concluding section of this chapter).

Social policy and the political order

Social welfare and political control in historical perspective

One of the best known examples of the political uses of social policy is provided by the history of welfare in Germany. In the late nineteenth century, Otto von Bismarck, the German Chancellor, introduced the first comprehensive national scheme of social insurance in the world. Thus Germany led the field in social insurance at the time, and

Germany's insurance scheme had an important influence on social policy in other countries, including Britain. The leading Liberal politician, David Lloyd George, visited Germany and was impressed not only by the social benefits of the scheme but also by the political credit gained by the government. By 1911, the Liberal government had introduced the first social insurance scheme to Britain in the form of a National Insurance Act (Part I dealt with insurance against loss of earnings through sickness, Part II with unemployment insurance).

The German government's reforms brought in compulsory insurance for sickness, industrial injury and old age pensions during the 1880s. These policies were developed before the vote was gained by the working classes and at a time when the government was trying to contain the pressures and demands of a rising trade union and labour movement.

Jones (1985: 50) is not alone in seeing early social insurance in Germany as very much a top-down set of reforms, and 'a means whereby an existing ruling elite endeavours to shore up and legitimize its position in the face of threatened ... upheaval.' But this was not the whole story. As mentioned in the introduction, social welfare development occurred for a variety of reasons. In Germany, social insurance was provided at a comparatively early stage, partly because of long-standing traditions of paternalistically looking after workers and giving them some social protection (Spicker 1993: 136).

This protective, paternalistic attitude could itself be seen as a form of social control and of trying to preserve a traditional, semi-feudal order. However, Spicker (1993) argues that it also represented a genuine recognition of workers' rights and needs. To see the German reforms solely as a matter of veiled repression would be wrong. There were other autocratic regimes in the nineteenth century where nothing like the apparently progressive social insurance schemes in Germany was ever conceded to the workers.

Twentieth-century Britain: social welfare in the political order

Another point to remember is that while governments might try to use social policies to establish political control, this does not mean that they always succeed. Sometimes new social policies have an effect that is far from stabilizing.

In Britain, Lloyd George's social insurance reforms of 1911 initially led to more conflict and disorder than consensus and acceptance of government control (Lloyd 1993: 34–5). Opposition came from employers who resented having to pay towards employees' insurance cover. There was also some rather frivolous opposition among well-to-do employers, who played up outrage at the idea of having to lick insurance stamps to record weekly contributions for their domestic servants. More significantly, private insurance companies opposed the government scheme, fearing a loss of business, while even trade unions were sceptical about it. Better-paid manual workers' unions had already set up their own 'sick clubs' or medical insurance schemes, and resented the idea of government takeover or control. Finally, many doctors opposed compulsory health insurance because they feared growing state regulation of the work of the medical profession. This latter objection proved to be rather short-sighted, as many people could not afford medical treatment and, until the introduction of the NHS later on, some doctors found it hard to make a living. Earlier introduction of a full health insurance scheme in Britain would have swelled patient numbers and meant more business for doctors.

The willingness of Lloyd George and the Liberal government to struggle against all this opposition was significant. Despite the end result in 1911 being a rather modest and limited insurance scheme that only covered certain sections of low-paid workers, the reform showed that Lloyd George and the Liberals were strongly motivated to challenge many established interests.

Why were they prepared to do this, and to take considerable political risks in introducing the National Insurance Act? There is no doubt that political factors played their part. Liberal leaders were hoping to steal the thunder of a growing Labour Party movement by pushing ahead with social legislation. But there were reasons other than trying to retain electoral support. Lloyd George's motives were, at least in part, genuinely to help low-paid workers. There was a challenging, radical side to Lloyd George's campaign, and therefore it is hard to see the social policies of this time simply as a device to maintain party political control, or the status quo.

However, while social and economic reforms can cause controversy and disrupt the political order rather than cement it, at least in the short term, there is an argument that over a longer period social policies do have the effect of stabilizing society and reducing political conflict. What is the evidence for this?

In Britain, there have been three major 'leaps' in welfare development: the Liberal reforms of 1906–14, the Labour government's welfare state programmes from 1946 to 1951 and the Conservative social reforms that began in 1979 but accelerated from the mid-1980s to the early 1990s (see Chapter 3).

Mrs Thatcher's new broom approach to social policy – while it was intended to win popular support as well as representing a hard-headed approach to government spending – received a very mixed reception and in the short term seemed to provoke conflict rather than develop a new consensus (Deakin 1994).

Labour's 1940s reforms, which introduced a comprehensive welfare state in the exceptionally consensual and socially disciplined atmosphere of the immediate postwar years, could be seen as an attempt to prevent the 1930s world of economic depression and social division from returning. It was, in this way, a response to a *potential* rather than an *actual* threat of crisis and social disorder (Hennessy 1992). However, even these comprehensive and inclusive reforms stimulated as much political conflict and tension as stability. A consensus on the continuation of a welfare state existed between the two main political parties between 1945 and the mid-1970s. A loose social contract between government, trade unions and employers emerged in the 1960s and 1970s, but there were always divisions on *how* social policy should be developed (for instance, with regard to education policy and comprehensive schools).

Marxist or 'political economy' views of the social order (see Chapter 7 for a discussion of this perspective) suggest that, although governments have proved willing to invest in large-scale welfare systems in order to stabilize the inherent tensions and inequalities of capitalist society, this will eventually lead to greater instability. This is mainly because welfare spending exacts too high a tax on private employers and may begin to make capitalist firms in high welfare-spending countries uncompetitive.

At the same time, welfare capitalism cannot really do without an advanced welfare system. A welfare state:

- helps to regulate the labour market by absorbing the shocks of economic re-structuring and redundancy;
- mitigates the effects of political crisis and questioning of 'the system' by giving capitalism a human face or an appearance of fairness and equal opportunity;
- meets the needs of a capitalist economy for a labour force that is kept in reasonable health and is sufficiently well educated to keep up with new work technologies.

Although Marxist explanations such as these have given some insight into past connections between social policy, the political order and capitalism, more recent social policy trends in the UK and elsewhere cast doubt on their relevance today. A capitalist economy's need for a well-maintained traditional welfare state might not be as great as suggested.

The UK's experience shows that governments can dispense with the 'social contract' approach to social welfare that had developed in the 1970s, based on agreements between government, trade unions and employers. When she came to power, Mrs Thatcher made short shrift of anything smacking of old Labourite social consensus. The 'Thatcher experiment' also demonstrated that previously unthinkable levels of unemployment could be allowed to occur, together with relatively radical reforms and pruning of the welfare system. Despite these threats to political and social stability, governments could not only survive but even prosper electorally.

Britain and other examples

However, this conclusion could be based on too short-term a view. We do not yet know whether the social policy changes introduced by former Conservative administrations have indeed unleashed unmanageable political and social tensions and, if so, whether new forms of social policy will be needed to help to restore the political and social order.

Despite some social policy innovations and anti-poverty measures (see Chapter 5), New Labour's first term in office (1997–2001) revealed a cautious approach. Social inequalities continued to widen (Dilnot 2001), violent crime increased (Paton Walsh 2001) and, as Islam and Mathiason (2001: 1) point out, 'Investment in hospitals, schools and transport infrastructure sunk to its lowest sustained level since the Second World War during Labour's [first] four years in power'.

Interestingly, the general election campaigns of 2001 and 2005 focused on the various political parties' commitment to restoring public services, particularly in health and education. The tide of public opinion might be swinging towards wider acceptance of the need for better public services, and for more direct taxation to pay for them. However, in broad outline the second and third Labour government's agenda for public services and social welfare showed more similarity with the market-style reforms of previous Conservative administrations than a determination to introduce clearly pro-welfare and pro-public sector policies (see Chapter 13 for further discussion of this point).

Arguably, both general discontent with government and specific dissatisfactions with health services, education and other public services are more likely to increase as a result of following this kind of policy. However, much depends on other factors. The state of the economy and the public's sense of satisfaction with their incomes play a key part, as do constantly rising expectations of what the education, health and social services should be able to deliver.

One way of assessing future prospects in the UK is to consider the impact of welfare reforms in other countries, though comparisons are always difficult because distinctive and different political conditions affect outcomes. However, one particularly telling example is provided by New Zealand's experience of radical cutbacks to its welfare state in the 1990s.

New Zealand had built up an advanced welfare state that was in many ways the forerunner of the British model, and 'by 1938, New Zealand had the most comprehensive social security system in the world' (Walker 1994: 17). However, two governments (first a Labour government, then a National Party (conservative) government) brought in drastic social policy changes. These included selling off the entire stock of public housing, together with cuts in housing benefit. A new tax was introduced to claw back the retirement pension from all but low-income pensioners. The reforms also included the ending of 'free' health care and the introduction of new means tests for access to health services, plus reductions in unemployment, single parent and widows' benefits of between 10 and 25 per cent.

However, the New Zealand example demonstrated that welfare cutbacks and restructuring can go a very long way before there are anything like completely unmanageable political tensions or conflicts. The 'cementing' role of social policies in maintaining the political order, though important, might not be absolutely crucial. Other ways of maintaining political order – in particular, a greater reliance on policing and the criminal justice system – might to some extent replace the role of social welfare, as discussed in Chapter 4.

Finally, though, we should remember that the relationship between social policy and the political order varies greatly between countries. In France in 1995–6, for instance, a great deal of political instability (including nationwide strikes and protests) was triggered by proposals to trim the country's huge social security budget and introduce welfare reforms. And more recently, in 2006, proposals by the French government to deregulate the job market for young people, and to remove laws protecting security of employment for people aged under 25, triggered widespread civil unrest, riots and destruction of property in many French towns and cities. The French example of political conflict and disorder *before* welfare cutbacks or proposed changes in regulatory policies have taken place is very different from the New Zealand case, where these things happened after cutbacks began to bite.

Social control and individual freedom

So far we have considered social policy and social control at what might be called a political or institutional level – that is, the ways in which social order and control might be affected by government and by changes in welfare institutions. We have seen that both the introduction of social insurance (as in Germany at the end of the nineteenth century) and severely pruning the welfare state (as in New Zealand) can have important consequences for the social order.

However, changes in policy and their impact are an individual matter as well as being changes that are played out on the wider political stage. Social control involves a relationship between individual human beings and the various social and political institutions that make up the individual's world. But what does 'social control' in this sense actually mean? Perhaps two definitions might help:

- social control that is *directly* coercive, such that an individual's autonomy or freedom is deliberately and obviously suppressed;
- social control that is *subtly* oppressive and which encourages people to fit into accepted social roles, or suppresses their individuality in less obvious ways.

Social welfare and coercion

Those who are in a controlling position in the field of welfare – for instance, professionals and practitioners in health and welfare services – might tell service users that what is being done for them is 'in their own interests'. However, an objective appraisal might reveal that control operates to benefit the service provider or the administrator of a policy more than the user of services.

Not surprisingly, most of the criticisms of directly coercive control occurred when long-stay care in mental hospitals and other kinds of residential institution was much more common than it is today. Ken Kesey's fictional *One Flew Over the Cuckoo's Nest* (1962) – later dramatized and made into a feature film starring Jack Nicholson – and a study by Erving Goffman of institutional care, *Asylums* (1991), had a telling effect upon attitudes among professionals as well as the general public towards 'over-control' in long-stay institutions.

Kesey and Goffman both tried to show not only that patients in mental hospitals are restricted in their freedoms, losing civil liberties and their rights as citizens, but also that institutional control seeks to change behaviour and identity in a malign way, disabling individuals and making them more dependent than before.

The 'liberal critique' of social control in institutions helped to pave the way for the development of community care policies and the widespread closure of long-stay facilities (see Chapter 11). Despite the development of community care, however, abuses of power and 'over-control' in residential settings still occur.

Nor is the directly coercive approach restricted to health services or personal social services. Since the early 1990s there has been a renewed interest in government in finding new ways to deter undeserving claimants and to prevent social security fraud. In the USA, for instance, welfare reforms introduced by Bill Clinton's administration consolidated tougher approaches to welfare claimants that had begun earlier on. President Clinton's reforms introduced strict time limits to the receipt of benefits, after which all government help is withdrawn.

In the UK nothing quite as strict as this has yet been introduced. However, the trend in Britain is also towards a more directly controlling approach in benefits policy that began in the early 1990s (Dean 1991: 180; Spicker 1993: 108). It was further developed by the Labour government re-elected in 2001, which introduced a Welfare Reform Act designed to detect and curb welfare fraud. Labour's policies were an attempt to show greater willingness to suspend benefits where fraud is suspected and greater likelihood of pro-secution in cases of benefit 'fiddles'. The tougher approach has also been revealed in policies since the early 1990s to lower the value of benefits in order to encourage clai-mants to find work. And it can be seen in the policy of making receipt of benefits conditional upon taking up employment training; and, in the USA, the introduction of workfare policies. As Spicker (1993) observes, the prospect of 'workfare work' (together with the possibility of parents having to place their children in sub-standard child care facilities while at work) becomes a deterrent against claiming.

Welfare reform in the USA is an important example to consider because US social policies have been an influential model for British politicians and decision-makers. Both Conservative politicians before 1997 and Labour politicians since have been keen about learning from US experiments to try to change the behaviour and attitude of welfare recipients. The underlying ideas, language and terminology of American reforms can be seen in UK social security and welfare reforms.

It is not true to say, though, that by adopting an American philosophy British welfare reforms are bound to introduce new ways of controlling claimants that are always directly coercive or never in the claimants' interests. US evidence on the impact of welfare reforms is mixed. For instance, Horowitz (1995), studying a federal government-sponsored project to assist teenage mothers, found that some professional helpers relied heavily on a coercive, controlling approach. In seeing their task as 'making responsible citizens' out of people who are over-dependent on welfare, these workers demanded submission to authority from the teenage mothers. They wanted to see what the professional workers defined as 'changed attitudes'. The results of this type of interven-tion were, in some cases, the opposite of what was required. Welfare dependency was increased while self-esteem and independence were reduced. Other professional workers, however, genuinely fostered a more independent outlook among teenage mothers and helped them to make their own decisions.

The point about this study is not just that the attitudes or approach of welfare workers or employment advisers varies, affecting the degree or nature of social control in welfare and employment schemes. It is also that *policy* and the underlying aims of the project are a crucial determinant. In the US and British cases, moral concerns about single parenthood and fears about the welfare system creating dependency, strongly voiced by right-of-centre New Labour politicians as well as traditional conservatives, have helped to create a social climate in which a more directly coercive approach to control is encouraged.

This is not to say that social security fraud and undeserved claiming should be ignored. There is a substantial amount of unjustified claiming. This results not only in a loss of resources that could be better used elsewhere but also in an undesirable degree of welfare dependency among claimants, as well as general cynicism and disillusion with the welfare system. Nor is it sufficiently convincing to make the point that losses from the public purse through dishonest tax evasion are greater than social security fraud, therefore the latter is excusable. Two wrongs do not make a right, even if the tax evasion wrong is of a much bigger size.

A more relevant point, perhaps, is that while a degree of control and a fair system for checking eligibility are clearly needed, the recent policy shift towards a tougher stance on social security carries with it dangers of excessive or punitive control. It could represent the growth of a kind of 'policing' of personal and family life that is unacceptable in a free society.

One way in which this 'policing' and additional supervision of people's lives has been justified is in relation to the underclass debate mentioned earlier (see the section on citizenship in Chapter 2). Murray (1994) and others on the political right drew attention to the supposed threat posed to the social order by the emergence of an underclass, and the need to take a more restrictive approach to the provision of social benefits, housing and other forms of welfare to people in poverty. However, since the late 1980s – when conservative opinion was preoccupied by worries about the underclass – there has been disagreement about whether such a group exists. Even if it does, it is not certain that social welfare plays the role in trapping people in an underclass that Murray suggests.

However, assuming that there is an underclass, there has also been debate about the causes of underclass formation. Is an underclass created by cultural causes (the values and lifestyle of a criminal, 'work-shy' group who reject society) or structural factors (lack of opportunity, and people being excluded from the labour force as a result of economic change and high unemployment in run-down areas)?

For commentators and politicians on the political right, the former idea – that the underclass is a way of life that can be altered – is a more attractive explanation for welfare dependency and a reason for 'getting tough' on social security. It is interesting to see how far New Labour thinking has combined both types of explanation in their policies on social security and welfare dependency, though the terms 'social exclusion' and 'the socially excluded' (see Chapter 5) have become the preferred ones; the term 'underclass' is now rarely used.

Labour's New Deal policies and other initiatives on employment were based partly on a structural explanation of problems – there is a lack of opportunities, so work and training opportunities must be provided. But there is also a strong government commitment to right-of-centre cultural explanations – the attitudes and outlook of those claiming benefit need to be changed, and claimants must be re-educated. In Chapter 8, the question of how far government policies in these areas of employment and social security are directly controlling or coercive in this way, will be further discussed.

What can be concluded here, though, is that there has been a clear trend since the early 1990s towards increasing regulation and restriction of welfare benefits. Despite Labour government policy to lessen dependence on the state and to reduce the state's role in our lives, social policy is steadily increasing the importance of means testing and selectivity of benefits (see Chapter 5). It is this, more than anything else, that is likely to result in greater need for control.

Social policies and indirect control: the examples of age and other social divisions

As well as direct forms of control we also need to consider the ways in which social policies and social welfare might be thought to have *indirectly* controlling effects. To illustrate this, the examples of age divisions in social policy will be discussed. Other examples, such as the indirect ways in which social policies might maintain gender divisions, or disadvantage disabled people, are also important.

One way of detecting the impact of the more subtle or indirect forms of social control is to observe the impact of *ideas* and *beliefs* on particular groups. For instance, Thompson (1998) outlines the various ways in which prevalent stereotypes and myths oppress disabled and older people. They are often seen as incapable of participating fully in decision-making or in shaping policy. Welfare practitioners and professionals are prone to think of older and/or disabled people as dependent, needy and as victims of tragic circumstances (the decline of health in old age, or the 'tragedy' of disability).

These dominant assumptions can subtly (and sometimes not so subtly) reinforce the idea that it is only younger and non-disabled people who can legitimately take decisions on behalf of, or make policy about, the welfare of older and disabled people. Often, these ideas are so powerful and such common currency that many people who themselves are older and/or disabled will share them, or at least be reluctant or unable to challenge them.

The term oppression is helpful in understanding this. As Thompson (1998: 10) suggests, oppression can include any action or degrading treatment that denies people their citizenship and human dignity. It can take the form of obvious coercion, such as mental cruelty or physical abuse. However, the kinds of oppression we are about to look at are not so obvious, and often are all the harder to challenge because they might exist in an atmosphere of cooperation between those who provide health and welfare services and those who are provided for.

This is illustrated very well by the example of state pensions for older people. The state retirement pension is a key example of the way a welfare benefit can become a form of social control.

When the first state pension was introduced in Britain in 1908, it was very popular. Millions of older people saw it as a liberation from worries about the Poor Law and 'going on the parish'. Yet the first state pension was not a large amount and was restricted to people over the age of 70. As average life expectancy for most people was *below* 70 years in the early twentieth century, and many would die before they qualified for it, the state pension was not quite the generous innovation it might have seemed to begin with! In an age of individualism and of expecting people to fend for themselves, however, it was seen as a generous policy for the state to commit itself to giving a regular – if very small – income to older people.

Also, the first state pension was seen very much as a *gift* – because it was a *non-contributory* benefit (see Chapter 5) at that stage. Any older person who qualified (they had to be means tested and on a low income) received the pension without having had to make insurance contributions earlier on.

Thus we can see in this early example of social policy the contradictory effects of welfare. The first pension was both liberating and oppressive. It was liberating because it provided a small income and a little independence for every old person who qualified for it. It was oppressive and controlling, however, in that it was a form of welfare provided as a gift for which people were expected to feel grateful. It was not at that stage a benefit which people had earned through insurance contributions. Above all, it began the trend towards marking out old age as a distinct phase of 'retirement', in which people would increasingly be expected to adopt a passive, dependent role in society.

At the time the first pension was introduced, about two-thirds of men aged 65 were still in paid employment (and only a small minority of women, young or old, were in full-time paid work). Admittedly, much of this work was a necessity. Without a pension to look forward to, many men had to carry on working – possibly until they died – simply to make ends meet, and despite increasing infirmity. Nevertheless, the positive side of this was that 'retirement' did not really exist then in the same way that it does now. Old age was seen as a distinct – if typically short – period of life, but it involved roles at work and in the family and community.

In the 1930s, the proportion of men still in work after their 65th birthday had fallen to a third. By the 1950s – following the Beveridge-inspired reform in 1946 of the con-tribution-based state retirement pension – first introduced in 1925 – the proportion had shrunk yet further, to just a few per cent of 65-year-olds. As Phillipson (1982) has argued, this represents the *social construction* of a phase of life. Old age is not simply a 'natural' stage in which the ways we behave or the ways we are seen by others are determined by the physiological or biological processes of ageing. Later life, according to Phillipson and others (see, for instance, Johnson and Slater 1993), is also a social experience very much influenced by social expectations and economic pressures.

This can also be illustrated by the further development of the pensions system. By 1946, when a National Insurance Act implemented Beveridge's reform of the state re-tirement pension (see Chapter 3), pensionable ages were set at 60 for women and 65 for men (they had been the same for both men and women – 65 – until 1940). That mo-mentous step from 'middle aged' to 'old' and from 'employed' (or employable) to 'retired' was based on a rather arbitrary, socially defined dividing line. Not only that, but also a more significant condition was introduced. From 1946 on, older people could not get the state pension unless they 'retired' and gave up work. This institutionalized the idea of old age as a 'pensioned off' and workless phase of life (Walker 1990: 59). The notion of older people being excluded from work (with its connotations of being made valueless) became an entrenched idea. It has remained as a defining characteristic of the status of older people even though the retirement condition was abolished in 1989.

In this way social policy has indirectly been an instrument of social control and, according to Phillipson (1982), an integral part of a capitalist market economy's con-struction of the 'redundant' status of old age and 'retirement'.

Similar patterns can be observed in other areas of welfare. As with the state pension, being entitled to certain 'special' benefits and services that are targeted towards a parti-cular group is a mixed blessing. On the one hand, such welfare benefits are genuinely helpful and needed. People need pensions, and they need a range of social services. They can be in the form of free or subsidized transport (for example, bus passes), specially designed accommodation (for example, sheltered housing), or domiciliary and com-munity services (for example, 'meals on wheels', day centres). They also include cash benefits such as special one-off allowances for older people, which echo the gift-like nature of the first state pension.

On the other hand, the more that the welfare system creates 'special' services and benefits for older people the more likely it is to assist in the process of marking out later life as an 'unfortunate', needy or dependent phase of life. The 'concessions' that are provided to people when they reach retirement age are a subject of humour. Jibes such as 'Have you collected your bus pass yet?' illustrate the rather pointed ways in which people remind each other of age divisions. They also illustrate the way in which a stereotype of *welfarism* can be applied to older people and to the status of old age.

Welfarism does not only devalue the status of older people. As Thompson (1998) points out, it can also be the basis of patronizing attitudes towards disabled people and other marginalized groups such as people with mental health problems. In all these cases, being dependent on welfare is seen as the defining characteristic of such social groups.

A number of shocking revelations of the maltreatment and routine abuse of older people in hospitals and other situations have been made (see, for instance, Laurance 2001). These cases show that the distinction between 'indirect' and 'direct' social control can be rather artificial. In practice, the connections between prejudice and action, or discrimination, are close. The neglect and abuse of older people in the health and social care system are reflections not only of economic or staffing crises in an over-stretched health service, but also of an underlying culture that has given us a set of negative perceptions of older people.

Therefore, as we have seen, social policy and welfare services have a dual impact. On the one hand, welfare services and benefits are – despite their limitations – often protective and helpful. On the other, they mark out certain groups such as older people as 'special' or marginal. This reinforces a dependent, devalued status. A similar dual impact of social policy has been observed in relation to gender divisions, and in particular with regard to women's independence and social position.

The development of a welfare state undoubtedly helped women in many ways – for instance through the introduction of general benefits such as the retirement pension and unemployment benefits, and special benefits such as widows' pensions, maternity benefit and child benefit (see Chapter 5). At the same time, however, the way in which these benefits were introduced in the 1940s helped to reinforce a dependent status for many women. By building on certain assumptions about marriage and the family role of women, social policies also reinforced a traditional 'breadwinner' role for men and a domestic role for women.

Consequently, there has been much criticism of sexist bias in social security. The system worked on the assumption that women would be economically dependent on men and that they would play a less important role than men in the job market (see, for example, Lewis 1983; Dale and Foster 1986; Pascall 1986; Hallett 1995).

The Beveridge committee's plan for social security assumed that most married women would not continue in full-time paid work. Married women were allowed to opt out of the full-time workers' scheme (single women were on the same footing as men as long as they contributed to the insurance scheme). The married women's option was phased out only in 1978. Up to 1978, therefore, the majority of women did not build up a pension equal to that of men in full-time jobs and they did not have the same rights to unemployment and sickness benefits. Even after 1978, married women paying reduced insurance contributions could continue to do so, with the result that in 1989, 20 per cent of married women were still on a lower rate of contribution – and consequently would qualify for lower rates of benefit than men (Callender 1992: 134).

Early social security policy therefore assumed that it was right for married women's security to be determined by their husbands' contribution records. Married women could not claim important benefits as independent citizens in their own right. Thus many women were categorized in terms of 'marriage, motherhood and family'. The status of 'widows, divorced and deserted women, and cohabiting and single women' was to be defined as 'deviant' in social security regulations (Colwill 1994: 56).

The social security system has gradually been reformed so that traditional distinctions like the married women's option have disappeared. However, some gender distinctions have only recently been removed, or still remain. One example is the state widows' benefit – there is no equivalent benefit for widowers. And there is still evidence that the social security system is built upon 'a male model of employment patterns requiring full time and continuous employment' (Wyn 1991: 108).

Successive tightening of entitlement rules has meant that women are more likely than before to find it harder to claim jobseeker's allowance, for instance. This 'increases women's economic reliance on their partners' (Callender 1992: 135). One way the benefits system can do this is by requiring claimants to demonstrate that they are immediately available for work and that they are willing to accept full-time work offers. Women – and a small but growing number of men – who wish to take on family responsibilities and combine these with part-time paid work often find these requirements difficult to meet. This can result in withdrawal of benefit and greater dependence on partners or other family members (see Callender 1992: 134–7 for additional examples).

Despite the evidence that the social security system can be oppressive, however, there is another side to the story. Income support and benefits of other kinds, though providing only a basic income, may nevertheless give a degree of independence to some women's lives. This 'modicum of independence', suggests Wyn (1991: 109), might 'enable women to get out of dangerous relationships with men'. So while life on social security can hardly be said to be liberating in the full sense, it might give a degree of freedom to women wanting to set up their own households or control their own resources.

Taken to an extreme, this is the argument put forward by Murray (1994) and others on the political right – that social security policy has been a key element in weakening traditional family norms and in creating the acceptability of single parenthood. However, this argument does not have to be pushed to the extreme to show that the effects of social security benefits on people's lives are contradictory. They have mixed effects. As we have seen, social security rules bring disincentives and controlling effects. The take-up of benefits by lone parents has increased very significantly since 1990 (see Chapter 5), but the low levels of income on benefit are hardly conducive to a free or liberating lifestyle.

Nevertheless it is true that without social security, a certain amount of freedom would be lost. If there are decisions to freeze or reduce a benefit – such as the Labour government's decision in 1997 to remove the lone-parent premium on income support for new claimants – then those who defend women's rights and women's freedoms are among the first to object.

Britain's relatively ungenerous welfare system does not provide as good an example of the effects of social security and other policies on gender roles as some other west European countries where provision in areas such as maternity benefit, child and family policy is much more extensive. For example, Sweden, though it has undergone welfare reforms and has slightly reduced the scale of some welfare benefits and services, is still one of the most generous and comprehensive examples of a welfare system that is designed to help women. This is especially so in the case of policies which are meant to ease women's re-entry to work and support them in the task of balancing family and paid work responsibilities (Summerskill and Hinsliff 2001).

Interestingly, Swedish women's participation in the labour force is much higher than in Britain. In Sweden, almost 90 per cent of women of working age are in paid employment, compared with just over 60 per cent of British women. On the other hand, the apparently liberating family and child care policies in Sweden seem to have subtly confirmed traditional gender roles. A lot of Swedish women continue to work 'long' part-time hours (over 20 hours per week) rather than full time, whereas – because of traditional gender roles – relatively few fathers work part-time or share parental leave equally with mothers. Given the persistence of these values and of gender roles, it is not surprising that the generosity of the welfare system gives little incentive to women to work full-time and perhaps pursue a career to higher positions.

In this way a generous and enlightened welfare system can be seen to be subtly reinforcing the social order and its established gender divisions. But this is not an argument for reducing support for parents who work. Nor does the Swedish example prove that social policies that strongly support women will *inevitably* reinforce traditional gender roles. Swedish policies provide many positive outcomes for women – the opportunity to enjoy a protected standard of living while being involved with childrearing and paid work. The point is rather that social policies that try to bridge the worlds of work and family seem to have a mixture of effects, both liberating and controlling.

Conclusions: can social policies bring benign control?

Social policies have brought benefits to people and even a measure of liberation. However, critics of the welfare system on the political right have argued that welfare – especially social security – can become too controlling and can easily interfere in people's lives in negative ways. To radical critics of welfare on the left, the traditional welfare state was shot through with sexist assumptions about the roles of men and women, and continues to foster ageist definitions of older people and patronizing attitudes towards disabled people as dependent and redundant.

In trying to reach your own conclusions about the role of social policy in the social order, you might find it helpful to review the main strands in the argument outlined at the beginning of this chapter. The welfare system can be seen either as maintaining and supporting the social order and accepted means of social control, or as undermining and weakening the foundations of existing society. But it is quite likely that different parts of the welfare system play different roles and have different effects from each other. In total, the welfare system probably performs *both* functions – simultaneously supporting some parts of the social fabric but causing change and a weakening of traditional social bonds in other respects.

First, the point has been made in this chapter that it might not be fair to view social control in an entirely negative light. There are some positive definitions of social control that deserve exploration. A view of the social order as something that can genuinely help individuals to develop, or that will encourage the social integration of individuals and minority groups, suggests that social control can be benign.

The educational process can be used as an illustration. Learning to read, for instance, involves mastering the rules and conventions of language in written form – the shapes of the different letters, how words are spelt, the rules of grammar and punctuation. The parent who reads with the child and points out these rules and understandings is in a way exercising 'social control', though usually in an enjoyable and flexible way. Nevertheless, in pointing out where the child has misread a word, or by gently correcting mistakes and guiding the young reader back to the text, the parent is controlling the situation and the child's learning. Of course, this may be done well or badly. With too much control and too little enjoyment, the young child may well reject the parent's help.

Later, at school, the same principles apply. To make progress, children need a certain amount of control. The tasks they work on must be sufficiently exciting and interesting, but the classroom environment must also be relatively calm and secure. Equally, the school itself will need to be well run. Thus social control exists at a number of levels: individual, group and institutional.

Presented in this unproblematic way, social control *can* be seen to be working in the individual's best interests even though individuals – for instance, young children – may not realize the benefits of being controlled. Control that leads to independence of the individual is genuinely liberating. The child is guided into reading, but eventually becomes an independent reader who is free to explore a wider world of books or the internet.

The problem with this definition, however, is that social control is not always completely in the best interests of the person being controlled. There is the question – raised at the very beginning of this chapter – of whether the welfare system, being part of government and the state, is more concerned with controlling us than with our welfare (for instance, by restricting demand for good quality services by telling us what we 'really' need). Control involves paternalism and, in its most paternalistic forms, will make it difficult for individuals to exercise their rights.

A number of examples and trends in social policy illustrate these problems. As discussed in this chapter, there has been a noticeable change in British social policy – beginning with the Conservative administration before 1997 but still being pursued vigorously by Labour – towards a 'tougher', more restrictive approach towards welfare claimants. Also, the emphasis of social security policy is now much more upon the goal of getting claimants into paid work, where this is feasible (see Chapter 8 for further discussion of employment policy). As pointed out above, this can be seen as a positive goal and being encouraged into work will often be in the interests of people, but it has increased the danger of creating a society in which 'the state knows best what's good for you'.

In this respect, one view of New Labour politics is that it has returned to the paternalism of the 1940s (see Chapter 13). At that time, paternalism and the belief that 'the state knows best' held sway, and welfare rights were not much discussed. In other respects, though, there are signs that some recent legislation will protect rights and freedoms and will perhaps increase individual citizens' ability to challenge government institutions that become too controlling. For example, Wadham and Mountfield predicted that the Human Rights Act 1998 would 'have a momentous impact on our legal system' and 'will make an awareness of and respect for human rights an integral part of our culture' (1999: xi). The Act that was passed by the Labour government in 1998 made the European Convention on Human Rights (an agreement about respecting rights drawn up by European countries in 1951) part of domestic law in every country in the United Kingdom – England, Wales, Scotland and Northern Ireland. As the UK has never had a Bill of Rights for the modern age, and as there have never before been positive guarantees of human rights in a written constitution, this Act is already creating controversy, especially in cases where offenders serving custodial sentences have claimed that their human rights have been infringed.

Although much of the Act deals with civil and political rights (for instance, Article 6 deals with the right to a fair trial), there are significant social policy and welfare implications. For instance, the rights of people with mental health problems is likely to be a growing issue in which the Act plays a key part.

However, it is worth noting that in at least one social policy area, the right to education, the Act defines freedoms in the negative sense rather than as positive obligations upon government. As Wadham and Mountfield show, the UK government was anxious to phrase the right to education negatively ('No person shall be denied the right to education') rather than using the more positive wording of the original European Convention ('Every person has the right to education'). Therefore this social right (to education) will be accepted by British courts 'only so far as it is compatible with ... the avoidance of unreasonable public expenditure' (Wadham and Mountfield 1999: 122).

In addition to the Act there have been other significant steps in advancing human rights by introducing legislation that helps people to challenge unfair discrimination or to win access to services or facilities that they have a right to use. For instance the Disability Discrimination Act 1995 is seen by Casserley (2000) and others as 'a significant milestone', though 'not the fully comprehensive civil rights legislation that disabled people campaigned for' (Casserley 2000: 139). One of the main drawbacks of the Act is that it is based on a 'medical model' of disability (see Chapter 9 for further discussion of the medical model). Applying medical evidence to the meaning and impact of disability has led to a number of significant difficulties in interpreting the Act in employment disputes, according to Casserley (2000: 140).

Despite their limitations, the Human Rights Act and the Disability Discrimination Act provide positive and potentially very helpful means for people to challenge 'the coercive state' discussed by Hillyard and Percy-Smith (1988). Also, as Stainton (1994) points out with reference to the needs of people with learning difficulties, there are ways – even without relying upon anti-discrimination legislation – to give more respect, choice and freedom to users of welfare services. This can be achieved by decentralizing services, encouraging more flexible ways of funding services, and by encouraging the participation of service users in designing and running them. An example of the second means – funding of services – is the growing use of direct payments to disabled individuals to enable them to purchase care. This is, interestingly, a *de facto* voucher system, of a kind long argued for by the neo-liberal right, precisely as a means of empowering consumers of social services (see Chapter 11).

Therefore the prospects for 'benign' social control and for greater openness, freedom and democratic participation in providing and running welfare services are mixed. On the one hand, we are witnessing – especially in the field of social security and employment – a tendency towards more 'top-down' control and paternalism. In other respects the advent of the Human Rights Act and other equality legislation could possibly act as a counterbalancing influence to 'the enormous growth of the power of public and quasi-public bodies over the lives of individuals' (Wadham and Mountfield 1999: 4).

This suggests that we will need to keep an open mind about the success or otherwise of governments in being able to respect the issues raised by the Human Rights Act – personal freedoms, dignity, self-determination. It is likely that the question of how far social policies are either liberating or oppressive will only be resolved with any certainty by studies of specific policies or the particular social groups or individuals affected by those policies. Far-reaching 'radical' criticisms of the nature of society, social control and 'the oppressive welfare system' might not be as helpful, because – as we have seen in this chapter – the relationship between social policy and social control is complicated and contradictory.

Key terms and concepts

coercion
marginalization
oppression
social consensus
social contract
social control
stigmatization
underclass
welfare capitalism
welfare dependency
welfarism
workfare

Suggestions for further reading

Though written over three decades ago in an American context, Piven and Cloward's *Regulating the Poor* (1971) is a classic study of the link between welfare and social control. It still deserves to be read, especially with hindsight and as a way of understanding the subsequent assault on the welfare system by conservative politicians in the USA and Britain in the 1980s.

Hillyard and Percy-Smith's *The Coercive State* (1988) is a useful book to complement Piven and Cloward's earlier study, though the main thesis and contents are quite different. Hillyard and Percy-Smith's book surveys a wide range of policy areas (including examples such as the 1988 reform of the NHS) to show that in many respects the welfare state has become much less democratic and accountable over the years.

Hartley Dean's *Social Security and Social Control* (1991) is a rather specialized study of social security tribunals, though there are plenty of general observations and in-depth discussion of some of the themes mentioned in this chapter. As an alternative, Pete Alcock's *Understanding Poverty* (1997) provides a readable and succinct overview of social security policy which also has much to say about the nature of social control. A longer historical view of poverty and social control can be found in Tony Novak's *Poverty and the State* (1988).

A large number of books by feminist authors trace the connection between gender divisions, social policy and social control. See, for instance, Lewis (1983), Dale and Foster (1986) or Hallett (1995). Rapid change in social security and other policy means, however, that some of the observations in these books are outdated. However, Caroline Glendinning's and Jane Millar's *Women and Poverty in Britain: The 1990s* (1992) provides a factual and thoughtful account.

For a discussion of the relationship between the status of older people, social policy and the context of a capitalist economy, Chris Phillipson's *Capitalism and the Construction of Old Age* (1982) is a readable and thought-provoking book that is still worth reading. Finally, as far as the topic of social control, social policy and disabled people is concerned, there is no better overview than that provided by Robert Drake in his *Understanding Disability Policies* (1999). For further understanding of social control and disability, and how disabled people have been affected by changes in social policy and the law, a book edited by Jeremy Cooper – *Law, Rights and Disability* (2000) – has brought together a useful collection of studies on the Disability Discrimination Act and other civil rights and policy issues.

7 WHO MAKES POLICY? THE EXAMPLE OF EDUCATION

Introduction: power and democracy

In Chapter 6 we explored a general question – how far is social policy an agent of social control? In this chapter we continue the theme of power and control. This is because social policies are always the result of the exercise of power in some way. Government might introduce policies without much consultation with those outside the narrow circle of elite politicians and their advisers (in which case we may refer to policies that are imposed from the 'top down'). Or policies might be the result of a lengthy political process that sometimes involves a lot of conflict among politicians and various pressure groups outside government. In the case of policy on abortion, for instance, there is long-standing conflict between, on the one hand, 'pro-life' groups that strongly believe in restricting the number of abortions as far as possible, and on the other, a number of other groups supporting policies that give women access to abortion services when these are seen as necessary or justifiable.

However, not all policy-making is surrounded by intense controversy or conflict between different groups in society. First, 'top-down' or imposed social policies might be widely accepted without opposition either because they are seen as beneficial or good policies in themselves or, in a 'paternalistic' welfare state (see Chapter 5), because it does not occur to most people that they should, or could, be able to participate in the decisions made about their welfare. Much of the legislation and policy-making that created the British welfare state in the 1940s could be seen this way (see Chapter 2). Second, new social policies might emerge from a democratic process of discussion, or consultation between government and people, without highly divisive conflict. As a rule, though, democratic involvement in policy-making entails heated debate, disagreements between groups who see things differently from each other, and eventually some trade-offs or compromises.

Where policy-making is less democratic, governments are able to develop policies that suit their own interests before those of the general public or the people who are going to be most affected by the new policies. Thus it is highly important to be sceptical about *why* any given social policy has been introduced, and how far the power of central government will be enhanced or reduced by it. This is because some policies are made not only for the 'official' reasons that are stated by government – for instance, to improve social welfare or educational services in some way – but also because they have been designed to promote the power of government (and the political party that runs it). For instance, as will be discussed later in this chapter, a series of reforms to education in England and Wales have much reduced the power of local authorities over schools and, in various ways, strengthened the ability of central government and the governing political party to control the education system.

Thus it is crucial to make a distinction between the two roles, or 'faces' of a policy. One role of a social policy is to try to make an improvement in human welfare or to develop services (which it might or might not do very effectively). The other role – often as equally important as the first, at least to those who draft policies – is to enhance the power of the political leader, government department or minister responsible for the policy. In extreme cases, where the political motivations of government and rival political parties become increasingly blatant, the policy in question will come to be seen as a 'political football'. In other words, it will have become more important for a government or for an opposition party to score points over their rival, or to try to switch the direction of policy to suit their particular ideology, than it is to have thought about the pros and cons of the policy itself. Housing policy (see the conclusion of Chapter 10), for example, has been described as a 'policy football'.

In summary, then, there are two introductory points to make about the relationship between social policy, power and the role of government.

- First, there is a distinction to be made between policies that are, on the one hand, drawn up and imposed by government without much discussion or democratic input and, on the other, policies that have been shaped by a more democratic process of negotiation between interest groups, or of participation and 'grass roots' involvement.
- Second, there is the question of how far policies are developed in the public interest. In education, for instance, will a new policy actually benefit children's learning or respond to parents' wishes for a better education system? Or is the new policy designed primarily to promote the power and reputation of a governing party (thus enhancing its prospects for re-election) or the 'government machine' as a whole (civil servants and advisers, as well as politicians)?

This chapter will use education policy as an example to examine both these points. Therefore you should have gained, by the end of this chapter, some knowledge of recent developments in the education service. However, the chapter is not intended to give a comprehensive overview of education policy in the UK. Key developments in education will be referred to as *illustrations* of the way policies and decisions are made, in order to examine how democratic the policy-making process is. Another point to bear in mind is that devolution of important areas of decision-making from the Westminster (UK) Parliament particularly affects education. The changes in education that affect Northern Ireland, Scotland (which has long had its own distinctive education service) and Wales are dealt with separately in Chapter 12.

Government and state

In education, as with all major public services, government and state play leading roles in shaping the system. However, what is meant by 'government' and 'state' is not always obvious, and first some basic definitions are needed.

Government involves an intricate web of relationships among:

- a Prime Minister and his or her ministers in Cabinet, who with their political advisers form the core of central government policy-making in the UK.
- senior civil servants and government ministers who, in their various departments, work out the details of important policy changes.
- Parliament and the government of the day. The UK government at Westminster must manage legislation in the House of Commons and House of Lords. It must deal with challenges to its policies from opposition MPs and sometimes from MPs in the government's own party. Government must also respond to select committees (small cross-party committees of MPs that are appointed for the lifetime of a Parliament to scrutinize government legislation and to investigate important policy questions).

The *state* includes:

- Public servants: for example, teachers, and Department for Education and Skills (DfES) civil servants who administer and implement policy.
- Local government (elected councillors and local government officials) and other local bodies (for example, school governing bodies).
- Quangos (quasi-autonomous non-governmental organizations), which are set up by central government (for example, by the DfES) to supervise and/or fund a particular function or task. For instance, the Office for Standards in Education (Ofsted) is headed by a Chief Inspector of Schools and is responsible for supervising arrangements for assessing the quality of schools and teachers.

Government shapes policy, but what actually happens on the ground is often determined by the effectiveness of civil servants at the national level, or by the amount of cooperation with central government departments shown by local officials or by professionals such as teachers.

Government and state are sometimes partners and sometimes rivals in creating and implementing policies. However, they are far from being the sole influences on policy. Many other things constrain the hands of government and state: for instance, the *economic cost* of a policy and the public money available, the *political acceptability* of a policy and the legacy of *previous policy decisions*. Even a government strongly committed to change will often find it extremely difficult to alter existing policies or the ways in which policies have been decided in the past.

Key interest groups (for example, business interests or parents' lobby groups) might also have enough power either to block a policy or to amend it, or to put new issues on the *policy agenda*. This last term refers to the way in which some issues gain leading importance in national life while others do not, or slip off the agenda after a period of being in the limelight. There are differences of opinion as to what is of pressing importance. Therefore, it would be wrong to think of the policy agenda as a single list of priorities that everyone agrees upon. However, it is a useful concept. It helps to understand which issues the government wishes to place at the top of the agenda and which at the bottom, while pressure groups such as parents' representatives may have different priorities.

Models of power – understanding how decisions are made

In order to make sense of what has been happening in education, or in any area of social policy, it is helpful to compare different views or models of how policies develop. No single model or theory will perfectly account for every policy and its outcome. To understand the policy process satisfactorily we need to combine a number of models.

The democratic pluralist model

The **democratic pluralist model** is probably the closest to popular and 'common sense' views of how government *should* act and how policies *should* be made in a democratic society. However, partly as a result of widespread publicity about leading politicians' alleged manipulation of evidence put before Parliament (for instance, before and after the second war in Iraq), and about abuses of power and privilege by politicians, many people's trust in the idea that decisions are made democratically, or that politicians are accountable to the people, has been eroded. This loss of belief in democracy has been demonstrated by decreasing turnout at general elections. For instance in the election of 2005 the lowest turnout since 1919 was registered, and less than half of young voters (aged 18–25) bothered to vote.

While public disillusion with politics and politicians is growing in the UK, however, this does not mean that the democratic model, or view of how politics works, is completely worthless or outdated. Arguably, there is at least *some* democratic input into the policy-making process in Britain, and politicians are held accountable to the democratic will to some degree.

However, it is impossible to resolve the argument about 'how much' democracy we have, or how democratic policy-making is, without defining democracy itself. For instance, if we were to define a democracy as a community in which everyone had an exactly equal say, and in which power was shared absolutely equally between all individuals, then no large-scale societies or political groups would qualify as 'democratic'. This ideal does not, and cannot, exist in its purest form.

Thus a realistic definition of democracy does not necessarily entail complete equality of power or an equal say in policy-making. This point was made by Dahl (1961) in a classic study of how politicians and other power-holders operated in an American city. He concluded that there are clear inequalities in democratic politics – certain business interests and pressure groups are much more powerful than others, for instance. However, a political system can be regarded as sufficiently democratic as long as electors and democratic parties have the final say.

Similarly, in British politics, some individuals and groups are clearly more articulate and better resourced than others, and for a variety of reasons will have more say over policy than poorer and marginalized groups. In a *parliamentary democracy* the people's representatives (MPs) are supposed to be able to speak from their own point of view and according to their own consciences. MPs are not supposed to be delegates who simply report or mirror the opinions of their constituents. In any case, constituents' views are often difficult to summarize, as opinion on many key issues is sharply divided.

In practice, MPs are often more constrained by party discipline than by their own consciences or views. Their behaviour in the House of Commons usually reflects the instructions of party leaders and 'party whips' (MPs who act as organizers to make sure that their fellow members follow the 'party line' and vote accordingly). However, when a governing party is divided over certain key issues these constraints might be loosened. At these times it is possible for opposition and dissent to grow within the governing party's own ranks. This will lead to a fuller, more democratic debate about the contentious policies being fought over. Also, the democratic model holds that general elections guarantee the accountability of governments to the public. A government that persistently ignores the wishes of the people can expect to be thrown out of office when the next general election is held.

Finally, the democratic pluralist model suggests that governments are held in check because power is widely diffused in society beyond government and Parliament. For instance, decisions about education will not be made by government acting alone. According to the democratic model, a plurality of groups or a number of voices will have their say. These may include bodies such as business leaders and associations (the Institute of Directors and the Confederation of British Industry are two leading examples), teachers' associations and unions, parents' lobby groups, and religious organizations.

A government that ignores powerful vested interests and pressure groups will, according to this model of power, quickly lose its authority and be forced to back down on policy decisions. This suggests a picture of policy-making as a constant contest between government and major social institutions and groups. Government might initially set the agenda, but must constantly respond to demands from the social groups and economic influences that surround it.

The elite control model

The **elite control model** suggests that elite groups of various kinds combine to run all the major government institutions, with relatively little accountability to anyone outside their own exclusive ranks. 'Democratic' institutions exist: for example, relatively unfettered mass media, elections, parliaments and individual rights to express oneself. However, as a result of a combination of skill, experience and monopolizing key leadership positions, it is always members of elites who have the decisive influence or the authoritative voice in these supposedly democratic institutions.

Elites are rather different from each other in terms of what they do and what their first priorities will be. There may be some conflicts of interest among civil service, political, military, business and professional elites. However, a theory of elite control suggests that top-ranking members of leading professional, governmental and business organizations will tend to be drawn from the same social backgrounds, to have gone to the same elite schools and universities, and to share a similar culture. Bonds of family and kinship will also tend to tie them together. Even if some have risen into the elite from non-elite backgrounds, they will have been safely incorporated into the exclusive club. Thus, despite their differences, members of elites will tend to pull together to make sure that they retain overall control of policy decisions.

This model would suggest that the blueprint of the 1940s welfare state was the work of a government elite. A tiny influential group worked out what would be in the best interests of the masses and proceeded, in the postwar period, to implement their wartime plans. Barnett (1986) contends that this civil service elite of 'Whitehall mandarins' was both high-minded and left-leaning in its aims and political values.

Whether or not Barnett is right about the way in which the welfare state was created (for further comment, see Deakin 1994: 36), this example raises the interesting point that elite control need not necessarily result in policies that are fashioned according to the narrow self-interest of the elite itself. The NHS, for instance, is largely the product of conflict and power struggles between a political and a medical elite (see Klein 1995). There was relatively little input from Parliament, which endorsed the NHS Bill with little amendment, or from any other broad-based democratic institutions. Yet the NHS remains one of the most popular institutions: a socialist-inspired health service brought into being by elites.

The political economy model

The **political economy model** rests on rather different assumptions from the first two. Basically, both the democratic pluralist and elite control models pose the question, 'which groups are in control?' Are policies shaped primarily by democratic institutions and groups or are they determined by elites?

A political economy perspective, on the other hand, draws more attention to the underlying economic system and how the political system interacts with it. The economic systems that prevail in almost every country in the world are now openly capitalist market economies of one kind or another. Even China, though retaining a one-party communist political structure, has become the fastest-growing capitalist or market economy in the world.

Thus the basic idea of a political economy perspective is that social policy will tend to be shaped by the needs or demands of a market economy. This includes education policy. The political economy view of power asks in what ways government spending on education is influenced by the needs and demands of business and industry. For instance, the drive to cut employers' costs by reducing the burden of taxation might influence government to restrain public spending on all public services, including education. But this factor could be balanced by some employers' pressure on government to increase education spending, especially in areas such as improving literacy and numeracy or the use of new technologies, in order to lift the levels of skills and productivity of the school-leavers or university graduates they wish to recruit.

Although a political economy perspective emphasizes the needs of the capitalist system as a whole, it also has implications, like the first two models, for the question of who controls or dominates policy-making.

In many respects, the political economy model comes close to the theory of elite control. As it suggests that most major policy decisions are subject to the backing of 'big business' or capitalist interests, it is a short step to saying that government and civil service elites interlock with business elites (leaders of City and financial institutions, and of manufacturing, retail and other commercial organizations). Evidence of this is provided partly by recent governments' reliance on business leaders to head new developments in education policy, such as their increasingly important role in funding and running the city academy programme (see further discussion below).

The political economy model can be equated with Marxist views of a class-structured society in which a ruling class controls policy and makes most, if not all, the big decisions. The way in which this control is actually exercised is a matter of debate among Marxists, who disagree with each other about how directly or openly government and state are manipulated by ruling class interests (Ham and Hill 1993: 35).

Despite these differences, however, Marxist perspectives share a common view that it is the underlying political–economic system that shapes policy, rather than the particular elite groups, political parties or leaders that happen to be in power at a given time. There may be shifts of power within the ruling class, they argue, but the system as a whole will tend to perpetuate gross inequalities of wealth and power. These inequalities will have an increasingly international dimension as the globalization of trade and capitalism concentrates wealth in fewer and fewer hands, and in huge international business corporations. This in turn creates the potential for growing conflict between the haves and have-nots – between those who control policy and the mass of people who have to deal with the consequences of government decisions that tend to favour the rich and powerful.

The background: education and Conservative policies of the 1980s and 1990s

In this section the development of education policy before New Labour came to power in 1997 will be discussed. The aim, as stated at the beginning of the chapter, is not to summarize every change in education but to analyse the *process* of change – in particular, how and why certain decisions were made, and what this tells us about the democratic nature (or otherwise) of decision-making in Britain. You may find it helpful to reflect on the three models of power, outlined in the previous section, as explanations of the way in which education policy developed in the 1980s and, in particular, at the turning point of a landmark in policy, the 1988 Education Act.

In 1987, a Conservative government was elected to power for a third term in office under the leadership of Mrs Thatcher. Some changes in education policy had already been introduced in the period 1979–86 by Mrs Thatcher's previous administrations (for instance, a 1980 Education Act strengthened parents' rights to preferred places for their children in state schools). However, Mrs Thatcher's third term in office represented a long-awaited chance to bring radical organizational changes to all the main welfare state services, including education.

A common element in Mrs Thatcher's government's strategy for overhauling the public services was the introduction of an *internal market*. As far as schools were concerned, this meant a new approach that would result in competition among local state schools to attract and retain pupils. The theory was that with greater freedom to choose between different schools in the locality, parents would 'reward' what they saw as the better schools by trying to get their children enrolled in them. Meanwhile the schools with a poorer record would experience falling enrolment. They would thus be confronted with a strong incentive to improve the educational performance of their children in order to make themselves more attractive to parents.

As 'money follows the pupil' – that is, each school receives a set amount per year for each student it enrols – the aim was therefore to develop a *market-like* system of state education to reward the better-achieving schools with more money, and thus more teachers and resources. At the same time, the discipline of the market – as demonstrated by declining student numbers and less money every year – would force the poorer schools to improve their performance.

Whether an internal market in education would work in the way just outlined was (and still is) hotly contested. Some of the drawbacks of introducing market-like competition in education are discussed later in this chapter, and they have implications for the wider question of whether internal markets achieve the desired effects in *any* public services such as the NHS and social services.

However, at this point it is sufficient to note that Mrs Thatcher's government in 1987 was about to press ahead with some gradual, but in the end very significant and far-reaching changes to the way education and other public services were going to be run. Their strategy for change included not only the introduction of internal markets in public services, but also:

- challenges to the traditional power and status of professional groups such as teachers;
- weakening the power of local authorities;
- setting up quangos or central government agencies to regulate and inspect services;
- emphasizing 'consumer choice' rather than democratic accountability in the public services.

The 1988 Education Act

This Act was a very significant landmark. It introduced many important reforms to schools in England and Wales, and it paved the way for the development of the internal market in education referred to in the previous section. The 1988 Act set the policy agenda in education for the 1990s – not only for Major's Conservative governments (1990–2 and 1992–7) but also for the incoming Labour government in 1997.

A significant sign of the lasting impact of the 1988 Act can be seen in the fact that, during its first term in office, the Labour government retained all the significant changes made by the Conservatives. In particular, Labour retained the internal market system that has made each primary and secondary school responsible for its own budget and has encouraged competition between schools.

The main features of the 1988 reforms were:

1   The removal of many of the powers of local education authorities (LEAs) over the running of schools, and handing over of most of the responsibilities of school management to head teachers and school governing bodies. This was a new policy of *local management of schools* (LMS). It applied to all secondary schools and most primary schools (over a certain size). As a measure designed to develop the internal market in education, every state school was now required to manage its own budget and plan its own development, including staffing. The money to run each individual school was still to be funnelled through the LEA, but the school itself would take most of the decisions on how to spend it.

2   In addition, the Education Reform Act 1988 sought to strengthen the voice of education consumers (parents and employers) in the running of schools. School governing bodies were to have elected parent governors and nominated teacher representatives, as well as other members representing the local authority and local businesses or community organizations.

3   The introduction of a National Curriculum and SATs for all children at the ages of 7, 11 and 14.

4   The creation of a new category of grant-maintained schools – basically, independent state schools. These were to be funded directly by central government rather than via the LEA. This funding formula gave an incentive to schools to opt out of LEAs. The Act stipulated that parents had to be balloted about any proposals for a change to grant-maintained status, and that a majority of those who voted had to be in favour for the change to be agreed by the Secretary of State for Education.

5   Drawing on a US policy experiment ('magnet schools'), the Act launched proposals for a new range of specialist schools such as city technology colleges that were to be jointly funded by government and business. This new kind of secondary education was to be provided in the best-equipped and best-staffed environment possible.

The lessons of the 1988 education reforms: how policy was made

The 1988 reforms were extremely important in terms of what was to change in the classroom, how children and older students were going to be tested and what they would learn. At the same time the reforms were important not only because of the scale of the change but also the *way* in which the new policy was introduced.

Central government appeared to be taking to itself many additional powers to run state education, and this provoked a great deal of controversy, especially among educationalists and the teaching profession. But it had also done so in a way that had apparently involved little consultation with the general public and little involvement with the teaching profession or with local authorities.

This is not to deny that the case for some educational reform was strong. The argument for a National Curriculum, for example, had been accepted in educational circles well before 1988. Also, significantly higher numbers of British young people were leaving school with few or no qualifications compared with most other European countries. This had already led to demands from employers and other groups for testing and for setting national standards of school attainment in literacy and numeracy. And in the teaching profession there was pressure for devolved management from local authorities to schools.

The significance of the 1988 education reforms therefore lies less in the basic ideas, which were not particularly original, but more in the ways those ideas were interpreted and put into practice. There were three main features of the education reform process – first, the speed with which changes were introduced; second, the lack of consultation or consideration of alternatives; third, the degree to which the reforms centralized power.

There was little warning before the general election in 1987 that the sorts of changes outlined above were going to be unleashed in the education service. Broad proposals for change were released by the government shortly beforehand, but not with enough detail to spell out the full implications. Thus a democratic model of power – a view of policy-making that is based on ideas of consultation and participation from all sides – offers little insight into the origins of the education reforms of 1988, or the early stages of the policy.

Nor is there much evidence to support a 'business power' or political economy explanation for the reforms. Mrs Thatcher's government may have professed an understanding of the needs of business and enjoyed close attachments with business leaders, but the specific ideas on how to reorganize education came from a small political elite, not from sustained discussions between government and industry or business groups.

Business interests perhaps worked more as a background explanation of the forces influencing government at the time. As discussed above, some business opinion laments the relatively low standards attained by British school-leavers and the way this reduces Britain's productivity and competitive edge. Therefore the education reforms of 1988 would have been regarded favourably both by business and government if they looked like policies that could raise standards with relatively little increase in expenditure.

The strongest interpretation, however, is that the political elite leading government was motivated first and foremost by ideology. Many of Mrs Thatcher's policies began in this way. There was a tendency to push innovations from the top downwards, although in many cases this was tempered by political pragmatism and caution. In the case of education, it was the lack of consultation with education representatives outside government that underlined the impression of policy-making by a tight circle of top people in government: the Prime Minister and her policy advisory group, and selected Cabinet ministers. No Green Paper or consultative document was issued to air the government's broad plans for the education system. The 'elite control' model seems to be particularly powerful as an explanation of the genesis of this important policy.

One element of the reforms – the idea of allowing secondary schools to opt out of the local education system – was a particularly good example of the way policy was created at the very top level of government. This policy was created 'on the hoof'. Mrs Thatcher suddenly launched the idea in the 1987 general election campaign 'to the surprise of her colleagues'. She predicted, in a stirring speech, that 'opting out would be as successful as council house sales in liberating families from socialism' (Carvel and MacLeod 1995: 15).

The education reforms were very quickly drafted after the general election by Kenneth Baker, the Education Secretary, and by top civil servants. The late Nicholas Ridley, a former government minister, is quoted as saying that they were 'hammered out in ... no more than a month' (Gilmour 1992: 167). It was these quickly drafted plans that became law shortly afterwards.

The government at that time enjoyed a large majority in the House of Commons. When a government has a small majority, as under John Major's leadership up to 1997, it is more likely that proposed legislation will be subjected to scrutiny and amendment. This is especially the case if the government is divided and if its supporting MPs must be placated with concessions or changes to a Bill. Proposed legislation for the UK must go through a series of stages in Parliament at Westminster before it becomes law and government policy (see Figure 7.1).

In the case of the Education Reform Bill, however, the government's original plans as set out in the White Paper (see Step 4 in Figure 7.1) survived virtually intact to the final stage of legislation (see Step 12). This occurred despite widespread concern that the Education Reform Act 1988 gave too many new powers to central government and, in so doing, raised serious constitutional issues. However, the British system allows a Prime Minister with a safe majority to push a legislative programme through Parliament, using it more or less as a rubber stamp.

As in Mrs Thatcher's day, Mr Blair's Labour government won a huge majority in Parliament as a result of its second landslide victory in 2001, and again an impressively large majority, if not a landslide, in 2005. Not surprisingly, therefore, parallels have been drawn between New Labour and Mrs Thatcher's government in their approach to Parliament, and the danger of an authoritarian style developing.

In other democratic systems (for example, in the USA), there are more checks and balances between different legislatures (Senate and Congress). The role of the President in both the USA and in France is a very powerful one. But, unlike the British Prime Minister, a US or French President may be forced to govern with a majority or near majority of representatives from opposition parties.

Both of these examples – and many other western countries – have written constitutions. In most cases this gives a more significant role than in the UK to supreme courts, whose role is to test whether a government's actions and policies are lawful within the constitution. In the USA, Supreme Court decisions can effectively amend or block government policies.

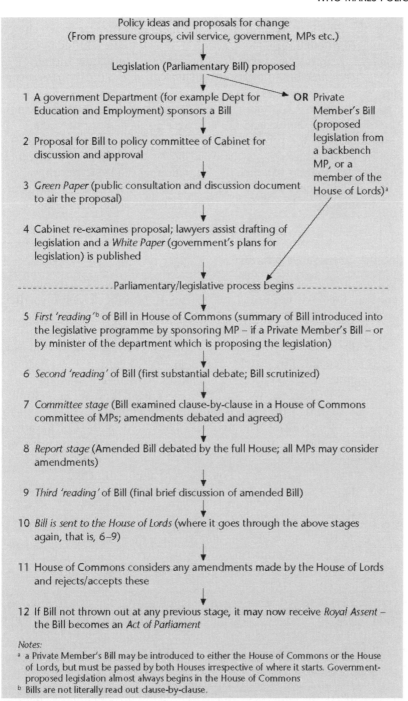

Policy ideas and proposals for change
(From pressure groups, civil service, government, MPs etc.)

↓

Legislation (Parliamentary Bill) proposed

↓

1 A government Department (for example Dept for →   **OR** Private
   Education and Employment) sponsors a Bill   Member's Bill
                                                        (proposed
↓   legislation from
2 Proposal for Bill to policy committee of Cabinet for   a backbench
   discussion and approval   MP, or a
                                                        member of the
↓   House of Lords)[a]
3 *Green Paper* (public consultation and discussion document
   to air the proposal)

↓

4 Cabinet re-examines proposal; lawyers assist drafting of
   legislation and a *White Paper* (government's plans for
   legislation) is published

↓

------------------Parliamentary/legislative process begins------------------

↓

5 *First 'reading'*[b] of Bill in House of Commons (summary of Bill introduced into
   the legislative programme by sponsoring MP – if a Private Member's Bill – or
   by minister of the department which is proposing the legislation)

↓

6 *Second 'reading'* of Bill (first substantial debate; Bill scrutinized)

↓

7 *Committee stage* (Bill examined clause-by-clause in a House of Commons
   committee of MPs; amendments debated and agreed)

↓

8 *Report stage* (Amended Bill debated by the full House; all MPs may consider
   amendments)

↓

9 *Third 'reading'* of Bill (final brief discussion of amended Bill)

↓

10 *Bill is sent to the House of Lords* (where it goes through the above stages
   again, that is, 6–9)

↓

11 House of Commons considers any amendments made by the House of Lords
   and rejects/accepts these

↓

12 If Bill not thrown out at any previous stage, it may now receive *Royal Assent* –
   the Bill becomes an *Act of Parliament*

Notes:
[a] a Private Member's Bill may be introduced to either the House of Commons or the House
     of Lords, but must be passed by both Houses irrespective of where it starts. Government-
     proposed legislation almost always begins in the House of Commons
[b] Bills are not literally read out clause-by-clause.

Figure 7.1   Policy-making and the legislative process at Westminster

In contrast, the 1988 legislation on education highlights the way in which policies can be steam-rollered through Parliament, however hotly they are debated by opposition MPs. The House of Lords may also find flaws in proposed legislation and seek amendments, but the second chamber's powers are circumscribed and it cannot permanently veto legislation or insist on changes.

It is for these reasons that Gilmour (1992: 187) argues that the British system is best described as a 'plebiscitary democracy' rather than a parliamentary democracy. A plebiscite is a one-off vote of the people, as in a referendum or general election. Having made one key decision, the electorate hands all power to a ruling elite. In education policy, as we have seen, the way in which the legislation for the 1988 reforms was created and pushed through Parliament seems to bear out Gilmour's criticisms. But what does the development of education policy *since* the 1988 Act tell us about the nature of policy-making in Britain?

Implementing the Conservative reforms

A policy is not just a piece of legislation or a static list of written objectives and guidelines. As stated at the very beginning of this book, policies *develop* once the implementation process starts. Although the initial stage – the creation of a policy – is interesting, it is the further development of a policy in the 'real' world that makes the study of social policy particularly fascinating. Policies are living things – and a policy becomes what is implemented in practice as well as what is written down in formal or legal terms. Sometimes social policies are successful. This means that they actually achieve what they were designed for, or at the very least they are successfully implemented in a way that fits with the government's initial plan or vision. Sometimes, though, policies are less successful. The troubles experienced by the Conservative government in trying to implement the 1988 Act illustrate this. In this case the power of central government was challenged by professional groups (teachers), and by other groups and interests at the local level and outside central government.

For instance, despite the strengthening grip of central government on education policy after the 1988 Education Act, significant numbers of teachers began to resist certain aspects of the National Curriculum. Implementing the new curriculum and testing procedures proved to be far more difficult and complex than the Department for Education (DFE) had anticipated. Another factor was teachers' morale, which had already been steadily eroded by a relative decline in their pay and working conditions. As a result, teachers began to refuse to set SATs. The boycott spread widely in 1993 and, as Ranson and Travers (1994: 224) observed, what began as a protest over ill-prepared tests 'became a general dispute about the national curriculum, testing, and . . . using information from the tests to create national league tables of school performance'. This example is particularly illustrative because it modifies the 'elite control' view of policy-making. In this case, the teachers were not able to create a new policy but they were able as a professional pressure group to challenge and obstruct government power.

A second example of the limits of central government power to impose change from the top can be found in the slow progress of the secondary school 'opt out' policy. In the first few years, only a handful of schools in England and Wales applied to opt out. In

Scotland the policy did not take off at all. By 1995, the total of grant-maintained schools (those that had opted out of their LEA) was still little over a thousand. Far from quickening, the rate at which schools applied for grant-maintained status or held ballots on the issue declined sharply after 1993. However, the relative success of LMS may in part account for the reluctance of school heads and governors to opt out, as they now enjoyed considerable management autonomy within a local authority framework.

Also, we must remember that, though the schools 'opt out' policy progressed at a snail's pace, the Conservative government was successful in pushing through the main framework of the 1988 Act. An internal market was introduced into every level or sector of education, the National Curriculum was implemented, SATs became an institutional part of the education process in England, if not Scotland and Wales, and far-reaching reforms in the funding and inspection of education were carried out. These were the foundations of the new education policies that Labour inherited in 1997.

Centralizing control: Labour and education policy

After its first election victory in 1997, the Labour government announced that 'education, education, education' was to be at the top of its policy agenda. The decision to announce that education would be a priority reflects the strong emphasis in New Labour ideology on providing opportunities for individuals to better themselves. This ideology carries with it the assumption that it is more important to equalize *opportunity* – the chance to do well and to enjoy individual success – than it is to equalize *outcomes* such as incomes, standards of living or levels of education. Thus the reverse side of this coin is that New Labour philosophy accepts that marked inequalities in achievement and outcomes are inevitable. This is a contrast to the more socialist or social democratic ideas of 'Old Labour'. New Labour is guided by the belief that lack of resources does not itself explain failure. As Toynbee and Walker (2001: 47) suggested, New Labour's ideology stressed the point that 'it is not so much resources as attitudes and organization that explained poor school performance'.

Thus the Labour approach to education, while branching off in some new directions, reflects a degree of continuity with 1980s education policy in a number of ways. First, there is a similar emphasis on policies to create different kinds of secondary school and to justify the gradual break-up of the comprehensive school system – a process that has come to be known by the ugly term 'de-comprehensivization'. Second, there has been a similar emphasis on the belief that individual effort, merit and striving can overcome social disadvantage. But above all, it is the determination of a strongly interventionist central government to impose its agenda, and to centralize control of the education system, that stands out as a strong similarity between the Thatcherite and New Labour approaches to policy.

Before we look at a summary of the key changes Labour has made, though, it is important to recognize what the government has not done in education. Policy-making includes 'non-decisions' – that is, decisions not to act – as well as decisions to do certain things.

So first, what did Labour not do in its first term in government?

- It did not dismantle the education reforms made in 1988. As mentioned, this meant that the internal market and the idea of competition between state schools were retained.
- It did not aim for a return to the 1970s Labour policy of developing a common or comprehensive secondary school for everyone.
- It did not significantly increase government expenditure on education in its first term, 1997–2001 (see above, and Toynbee and Walker 2001: 48). However, in its second term in office (2001–5), the government did increase education spending in real terms by 5.4 per cent annually. This impressive increase in spending on education marked a significant departure from previous government policy, which had allowed relatively small increases.
- It did not abolish grammar schools and other forms of selection in other types of school.

The above policies (apart from the significant rise in education spending) are examples of New Labour's decisions not to implement 'Old Labour' policies on education, which would have put much more emphasis on trying to strengthen the comprehensive school system. But what policies did New Labour follow instead? The following is not a complete list, but represents some of the key decisions and changes brought about by New Labour during the three terms in government that it has enjoyed so far.

- A variety of policies have been implemented to improve teaching standards in schools. For instance, the Schools Standards and Framework Act 1998 brought in new government powers to tackle 'failing' schools. Where local authorities did not seem to be able to improve matters, the government could impose central supervision. Failing schools and LEAs with poor school attainment results can be 'named and shamed' by the DfES. Ofsted – a schools watchdog inherited from the Conservative government – has continued to play a key role in setting tough targets for schools to achieve. In some areas where education is judged to be failing, local authority management of schools can be handed over completely to private sector companies.
- In October 2005 the government published plans to turn all local authority secondary schools in England into independent trust schools. This policy, if implemented, will mean that English secondary schools will continue to be 'state schools', but as independent trusts they would be able to appoint their own governing bodies, take charge of their own assets and, within certain guidelines, set their own admissions policies. Before the 2005 plans were announced by the Minister for Education and Skills, Ruth Kelly, the government had already put in place policies to develop specialist secondary schools and to expand the number of 'faith' schools, which are schools run by single-faith religious bodies or charities. Taken together, all these education reforms became a centrepiece of New Labour's – and Tony Blair's – push for radical reform in all the public services. In education, the intention was to break up (in England) the existing sector of state comprehensive schools into a much more diverse system. Critics fear that this would entrench a two-tier system of secondary schools, with

better-funded, successful and selective specialist schools in the top tier, and unpopular and under-resourced comprehensive schools in the lower tier (see below for further discussion of recent education reforms).

- A related policy development, and an equally important part of the government's strategy for more specialized schools, is the development of city academies. These are secondary schools that are intended to replace existing schools in urban areas where there is social disadvantage and low educational achievement. The government intends to build 200 city academies by 2010 (see discussion in the next section).

- A daily 'literacy hour' has been instituted in primary schools in England and, from September 2000, a daily 'numeracy hour' was also announced. These initiatives represent a Labour version of the former Conservative government's 'back to basics' campaign in education, which emphasized the learning of basic skills in a traditional way. Whatever their merits (and literacy and numeracy scores have continued to improve among primary-age children during Labour's period in office), the literacy and numeracy hours represent another extension of central control over schools and the teaching profession.

- In higher education, the government rejected an advisory body's recommendation of a 'graduate tax' to fund student maintenance and tuition fees. It abolished free tuition and passed the Teaching and Higher Education Act that requires students (in England – see Chapter 12) to pay tuition fees, and has further developed the previous administration's policy of funding student maintenance through student loans.

As mentioned, the above list represents only the highlights of Labour's education policy. However, it is possible even from a relatively brief list to make out its main contours. First, Labour's policy has continued to centralize power in many ways. Most of the examples of policy in the list show central government placing a much heavier, more interventionist hand on local affairs than used to be the case. Even where central government seems to be delegating management to local schools or trusts, the effect is likely to reduce at the community level the role of locally elected representatives and parents in running schools. This can be seen, for instance, in the policy to develop 'city academies'.

City academies

New Labour's programme to develop this new type of secondary school was, at the time of writing, a controversial issue. As mentioned above, central government had planned to stimulate the development of 200 city academies by 2010, though by the end of 2005 only 17 had been opened. These new schools cost twice as much to build, on average, as a comprehensive school of similar size (Curtis 2005). Central government meets almost all the cost of building each new academy (approximately £25m) while the individual sponsor or sponsoring organization that undertakes to run the school contributes £2m. In return, the sponsors of academies are given almost complete management and financial control over their institutions. They are free to choose almost all of the academy's governors and the senior management team. They enjoy a lot of influence over the ethos of the school (this might be a Christian ethos, for instance), the curriculum and teaching methods. Sponsors who have so far come forward to run city academies include a mixture of wealthy businessmen, some of whom own groups of private schools in the UK and in other countries, philanthropists and voluntary sector organizations, and evangelical Christian groups (Taylor 2005).

The city academy programme shows how central government wished to step into local areas to create independent state schools. The academies cannot charge fees, but in many other respects are intended to model themselves on independent private schools. They are state schools but stand outside the main system of secondary schools. In this respect they also stand outside the local system for ensuring democratic accountability: the locally elected councils and their LEAs. Thus parents cannot take a complaint about a city academy to their local council, and there is no guarantee that the academy's governors will represent local interests and concerns. For instance, Taylor (2006a) provides evidence of parental frustration and anger over the allegedly high-handed and 'Dickensian-style' discipline of a particular academy. Furthermore, the Freedom of Information Act (2000) does not apply to city academies because they are independent trusts that exist outside local and central government (though, at the time of writing, this matter was under review by government). This meant that a large amount of public money was handed over to the sponsors of city academies without members of the public being given the same rights to scrutinize their accounts, or the way they are being run, as would apply to a public body or a local authority school.

However, city academies are subject to inspection by Ofsted and must meet the required standards of quality in education that are demanded of all schools by central government. Also, by 2005 the city programme as a whole had been evaluated by other bodies: for instance in 2005 a review carried out for the government by the firm PricewaterhouseCooper (PWC) found that some city academies were proving to be popular with the pupils attending them, though bullying remained a significant problem, as did reliance on unsuitable buildings in some (Curtis 2005).

It is important to remember that the initial aim of the city academy programme was to replace schools that were performing very poorly in socially deprived inner-city areas, so it would have been surprising if some of the new academies had not encountered significant problems at the start. However, neither the PWC review of city academies nor other investigations of the programme found convincing evidence that the first batch had made a significant difference to examination results or to broader measures of educational achievement. There is evidence that some academies have been diverting their students from studying GCSE subjects to the vocational GNVQ, in order to boost their standing in school league tables (Taylor 2006b).

A highly critical study conducted for England's Local Authorities Association concluded that the city academy programme was 'hugely expensive' and 'unproven' in terms of transforming failed schools (Smithers 2005). Similarly, a Parliamentary Select Committee in 2005 found that while patchy educational improvement could be detected in city academies, progress in low-achieving, inner-city schools *not* in the city academy programme had been significantly *greater*.

The lesson to be drawn from this seemed to be clear: while educational opportunities and achievement can perhaps be lifted by heavy investment and dramatic improvements in a few selected academies, a more general and better rate of improvement can be sustained by spreading the extra resources more widely across inner-city schools. However, doing this would have meant channelling the extra resources through local authorities for them to spend on existing local schools, and this would have been contrary to the main thrust of New Labour's approach to education policy, which seems to have preferred to set up initiatives from the centre and has been distrustful of local authorities. In 2005, for instance, Tony Blair criticized local authorities' efforts to create equity in education, arguing that they had resulted in 'deadening uniformity' and had promoted a 'levelling-down mentality' (White and Taylor 2005).

In sum, city academies, though they are run by their sponsors as independent trusts, are the creatures of central government. They are part of a wider, central government strategy to greatly reduce the role of the local authorities in education, and to make almost all secondary schools (in England) city academies or specialist schools.

Restructuring secondary education: radical reform or piecemeal change?

This brings us to what might become the most fundamental reform in English education since the 1988 Education Act. This potentially large-scale change is contained in the proposed reforms to secondary schools outlined in a controversial White Paper on education that caused divisions among government ministers and Labour MPs, and was hotly debated among educationists, teachers' unions and political commentators in 2005. The subsequent Education Bill passed through the legislative process (see Figure 7.1) in 2006, again with a great deal of debate in the House of Commons and real uncertainty as to whether it would be passed at each stage or 'reading'.

The Education Bill of 2006 was important as a 'test case' of how radical the New Labour project tried to be, and to what lengths the government was prepared to go to reform the public services generally. There is no doubt that the Prime Minister saw it this way. In various 'back me or sack me' speeches (Wintour 2005), Tony Blair made it clear that he saw school reform as pivotal, and as a model for a much wider shake-up of public services in which 'contestability' (or competition) between a diversity of service providers would become even more important than it was in the Thatcher era.

However, while the Labour government has claimed to be a very active, interventionist government intent on introducing sweeping reforms from the centre, before 2006 the overall impression given was one of *piecemeal reform* – that is, an approach that introduces change bit by bit, or in small steps. Labour education policy before 2005 did not seem to be directed by one 'big idea' or one major piece of legislation, such as the previous government's Education Reform Act 1988.

In education there were some minor departures from Conservative policy such as the abolition of the assisted places scheme – a programme developed by the last Conservative administration to subsidize private school places for children of ability who could not afford them. However, as shown in the summary of reforms after 1997 listed earlier, Labour worked to gradually extend, rather than to reverse, the internal market-oriented reforms of the education and welfare system introduced by Mrs Thatcher's government in the 1980s.

Did the proposals for secondary education in 2006 mark a decisive shift from this gradual approach? To answer this question we need to consider the main points of the reforms that were first published in October 2005.

- For every secondary school in England, and eventually for every primary school, to become independent trusts backed by businesses, charities, faith groups, or groups of parents and community organizations. Schools would receive state funding from the centre, but each school's backers would also play a role in providing resources and support.
- Each school, like the existing city academies, would be able to appoint their own governing body, which would own the assets of the school trust. These independent school trusts could acquire other schools to form groups.
- Each school trust could set its own admissions policy, though policy on selection would have to respect guidelines on fairness.
- 'Failing' schools would be given 12 months to improve their performance; if they did not do this, there would be a competition for new providers or trusts to take over the school.
- LEAs would be stripped of most of their existing powers to distribute education funding to LEA schools; they would no longer be 'providers' of education but would act more as 'champions' of pupils' and parents' interests (for instance, in disputes over admissions policy).

As can be seen from these key points, the aims of these reforms were certainly radical and far-reaching in terms of their *scale* if not their *content*. In terms of content, the proposal to turn secondary schools into self-administered trusts, largely independent of local authorities, was not a new or 'radical' idea. Labour's independent trust schools idea bore a striking resemblance to the Conservatives' 'grant-maintained' schools that had been introduced after their 1988 reforms. But if implemented in full, Labour's proposals would go further than any previous education reforms in completely breaking up the long-standing local authority-based system of providing education that has formed the main framework for state schools for over a hundred years. They would also completely dismantle the comprehensive system of secondary education in England that was established in the 1960s and 1970s. In its place there would be a diverse non-system of city academies, trust schools and faith schools, each one establishing its distinctive ethos and approach. The aim is for parents to have choices about where their children would attend school after the age of 11. They would all be expected to apply to a number of schools rather than automatically sending their child to the local comprehensive.

The scale of the proposed changes was demonstrated by the strong reactions they provoked in Labour MPs as well as in opposition politicians, teachers' unions and others in the world of education. Perhaps the most notable and significant reaction was that of the Deputy Prime Minister, John Prescott, who made his disquiet about the education reforms known in Cabinet meetings. Prescott's questioning of government policy was unprecedented. Since becoming Deputy Prime Minister in 1994, he had been a loyal supporter of all of Tony Blair's policies, so to part company with the Prime Minister on the issue of education reform was highly significant. Furthermore, Prescott made public his reservations about the proposed education reforms: 'Since I was an 11-plus failure, since I do believe that produced a 'first-class/second class' education system, I fear this is a framework that may do the same. I'm somewhat critical of it. That's why I expressed my view in the Cabinet about it' (interviewed by Crosland 2005).

John Prescott was not alone among Labour MPs in his critical attitude to the proposed reforms. At least 70 Labour MPs openly declared that they would vote against the Education White Paper, including prominent 'middle of the road' politicians such as Estelle Morris (a former Minister for Education) and John Denham.

As Toynbee suggested, the proposed Education White Paper began to look like turning into the government Bill 'that shows power draining away from Labour' (Toynbee 2005: 27). However, this threat to the government's authority occurred not only because of the strength of opposition to the proposed education reforms from within Labour ranks, but also because of significant changes in the political landscape. First, David Cameron (elected to the leadership of the Conservative Party in late 2005) backed the main points of Labour's proposed education reforms by promising the opposition Conservatives' support for them in Parliament. Cameron claimed that the plan for independent trust schools was basically a Conservative idea. This move was made primarily to try to embarrass the Prime Minister and to deepen the divide between Blair and his own party. The position of a Prime Minister who has to rely on the votes of the opposition party in the House of Commons, rather than the support of his own party, is an untenable one. Second, Tony Blair himself had announced, shortly after the 2005 general election, that he would resign from his position as Prime Minister at an unspecified date before the next general election. The effect of this announcement was to further weaken the authority of the government, as backbench MPs are more likely to challenge a leader who they know will not be exercising power for much longer.

However, the fast-changing political situation does not wholly explain the openness of the conflict within Labour about the education reforms. Opposition from Labour MPs to Tony Blair's earlier reforms – for example, on tuition fees and funding higher education students – had also been strikingly evident in the previous Parliament. These rebellions took place even though the government was then more secure – Labour enjoyed a very large majority of MPs in Parliament at that time. Therefore the controversy surrounding the most recent education reforms can only be fully understood as a reflection of a clash of politicians' deeply held convictions.

On the one hand, critics of the government's proposals to turn all English secondary schools into independent trusts agreed with the points raised by John Prescott: that such a reform would be likely to have the effect of exaggerating differences between 'good' and 'bad' schools. The education system in England is becoming increasingly fragmented and divisive, according to a number of commentators (see, for instance, Gillborn and Youdell 2000; Wragg 2005a). The introduction of greater numbers of independent state schools would be likely to exacerbate these divisions, according to the critics' argument, and to increase dissatisfaction among parents who would find it more, not less, difficult to obtain places for their children in 'good' schools.

On the other hand, those who supported New Labour's proposals argued that the existing comprehensive system of secondary education was already socially divisive, especially in terms of social class. As social class background is closely related to educational achievement, it is the school *intake* that largely determines the academic level of a school rather than school *type*. Children of middle and upper social class backgrounds tend, for a variety of reasons, to perform better in school than those who come from less affluent backgrounds. Therefore, as comprehensive schools tend to recruit children from local catchments that are often socially divided into 'middle-class' and 'working-class' neighbourhoods, comprehensive schools will reflect these divisions and become predominantly 'middle-class' or 'working-class' schools. Supporters of the proposed education reforms claim that a more flexible, diverse system would allow parents and pupils a wider choice of schools, and that this would begin to break down the social class and other social divisions between schools. For instance, to enable poorer parents and their children to take advantage of a greater diversity of schools, the government proposed to subsidize transport costs between home and any of the three nearest secondary schools so that poorer families would not be at a disadvantage compared with affluent families with cars.

Against this, opponents of the 2005 Education White Paper expressed strong concerns about the likely impact of selective admissions policies in the new breed of independent state school. According to this argument, the problem of restrictive or selective admissions is already evident in existing semi-independent state schools. For instance, in addition to city academies, New Labour has developed specialist schools, faith schools and foundation schools. These are former comprehensive schools that specialize in particular subject areas or already have a degree of independence from the local authority. Such schools often become a popular parental choice and, as they do, begin to find ways of selecting the pupils they want and of 'screening out' the unwanted. Officially, specialist schools are permitted to select only 10 per cent of their pupils by 'aptitude' rather than 'ability', but a wide variety of sources suggest that in practice a lot more selection takes place in subtle or hidden ways (see, for instance, Gillborn and Youdell 2000; Revell 2005).

In the initial plans, the government had proposed a voluntary system for fair admissions to secondary schools which would be based on a 'banding' of 11-year-olds into top, middle and bottom levels of ability. Each school would then be expected, but not compelled, to take its fair share of children from each band. However, as a result of opposition by backbench Labour MPs to significant parts of the Education Bill, the government was forced – at the third reading stage – to agree to an amendment on admissions policy. Trust schools will be legally compelled to act in accordance with a strengthened admissions code, and not merely to take note of the code.

At the second reading, earlier in 2006, the government had already conceded other amendments, including legislation making it illegal for independent trust schools to interview parents and children as part of any selection process. In 2006 it was also agreed that local authorities could continue to be able to set up their own community (comprehensive) schools – a significant concession.

This example of policy-making shows how, when the Prime Minister and his government cannot have everything their own way in Parliament, the eventual 'shape' and content of government policy is much more likely to be the result of compromise than in political circumstances when 'top-down' policies can be more readily imposed. In early 2006 the political situation was a fascinating one because there was a more even balance of power between backbench Labour MPs and the government, and between the governing party and the opposition, than had been the case in the previous two Labour administrations. The Labour government suffered significant blows to its authority as a result of opposition from its own backbench MPs to its education reforms. Some Labour MPs voted against the proposed legislation, while others abstained. The controversial bill easily passed both its second and third readings in the House of Commons, but on both occasions this was only because a large majority of Conservative MPs voted for the government's legislation.

As we have seen, in order to win support of at least some Labour MPs, the government was forced to make a number of important amendments to its proposals for education reform. The Bill of 2006 had by that stage come to resemble a torn and much-patched garment compared with the sweeping robe of reforms to secondary education that had originally been proposed by the Prime Minister. The contrast between the rough Parliamentary ride experienced by Labour's 2006 Education Bill and the relatively smooth progress of the Conservatives' Education Bill in 1988 is also striking. Labour's Bill is therefore likely to become another example of 'piecemeal' policy change (Wintour *et al.* 2005), even though the Prime Minister had staked his reputation on making at least some radical changes before stepping down.

Policies for the future?

So far we have briefly examined a number of recent policies on education to show that there are several key features or themes in the way that policies have been made under Labour. One unifying theme, as mentioned earlier, is a strong determination to run education (in England) from the centre, by the DfES and its supporting agencies and quangos, rather than reviving the more decentralized form of educational administration through the local authorities that used to prevail. A second theme is that most of Labour's education policies have been more 'right wing' than 'left wing', if by these terms we mean that they seem to resemble the right-wing Conservative policies of the 1980s much more than those of (left wing) 'Old Labour'.

The right-wing nature of many New Labour policies on education is illustrated, for instance, in the reforms of student loans and the financing of higher education, in the policy of bringing in private companies to run 'failing' state schools and LEAs, and in wanting to replace (in England) the old-style comprehensive school system with a more diverse system. It was also shown in a government proposal, in 2005, to extend school hours from 8 a.m. to 6 p.m. This proposal was to extend the availability of child care (on school premises) rather than the school day itself. But as Williams (2005: 21) points out, 'it is never adequately explained why it will be cheaper for a government to buy these hours in than to bankroll their provision by state institutions'. As this example shows, New Labour adopted the strategy of privatization (in this case, the provision of child care and supervision in schools by voluntary and private bodies) so unquestioningly that it was not even raised as an option in the development of policy. Privatization, a 'right-wing' strategy that used to be seen as highly questionable and of debatable benefits, came to be accepted by Blair's government as 'common sense'.

This does not mean that the Labour approach to education completely lacked left-wing, or pro-poor, policies. The recent expansion of, and subsidies towards, preschool child care and nursery facilities, for example, show that the government has genuinely attempted to improve opportunities among social groups that have hitherto been seriously disadvantaged. Similarly, in higher education, the introduction of another government watchdog, the Office for Fair Access (Offa) to monitor the numbers of students from state schools and from low-income home backgrounds in every university, together with penalties for universities that do not recruit a sufficiently diverse range of students, shows some commitment to 'left-wing' goals of equality. The point, however, is that these latter policies were somewhat overshadowed by the more dominant right-wing policies to push ahead with the development of an internal market in education, and with a more competitive, selective approach to schooling than would have prevailed if the comprehensive secondary education system had been maintained.

Comprehensive education was very much associated with social democratic solutions to problems of educational inequality in the 1960s and 1970s, the days of 'Old Labour' government (1964–70 and 1974–9). Despite initial opposition from the Conservatives and from the general public in many local areas, comprehensive schools in England, Wales and Scotland (but not Northern Ireland) were eventually accepted as the main form of secondary education. Therefore any change to this system, which of necessity will involve an increasing amount of selection of pupils by schools, would be regarded as an important and fundamental one, carrying with it a degree of political risk and uncertainty for Labour.

If Labour's plans for a transformation of secondary and further education into a more diverse, less comprehensive system are fully realized by 2015, then this would represent a large-scale, far-reaching change. In the long run, a 'piecemeal' approach to making changes is not necessarily the same as making only small-scale or modest changes. Over a longer period, perhaps a decade or more, a series of relatively minor changes and innovations can amount to a fundamental change. At the same time, such change can 'creep up' on the public if it is introduced through *inexplicit policies*, or policies that do not openly state what the wider strategy of government is.

This brings us back to the question of how policies are formed and developed. In the concluding section we will examine which of the three models of power ('democratic', 'elite control' and 'political economy' models) throws most light on the way government makes policy.

Conclusions

Recent education policy provides an intriguing example of how policies are implemented in Britain and of who makes the key decisions in the first place. As we have seen, what sense we make of the education reforms of 1988 and subsequent policy on education under Labour depends on our views about democracy and the role of government.

First, the idea that policy-making is a democratic process would appear to have little value as an explanation of the origin of the education policies that have been discussed, whether these are the policies introduced as a result of the 1988 Education Act, or more recent Labour policies such as the development of city academies and independent trust schools. All the specific proposals for change in education, and in many other policy areas, seem to come from the Prime Minister at the time, and her or his closest advisers and ministers (Gilmour 1992; Deakin 1994; Woodward 2006).

This point about the way the key decisions are often made at the very top of government (rather than emerging from democratic discussion in Parliament, or as a result of consultation with experts and the general public) also applies to 'non-decisions'. These are, as pointed out earlier, crucial decisions not to take a particular course of action. In education, a striking example of the exercise of Prime Ministerial power (not discussed above because it has become a 'dead' issue) was the fate of a radical plan to transform the content and assessment of education for students aged 14–19: the Tomlinson Report of October 2004.

Sir Mike Tomlinson, a former Chief Inspector of Schools and a respected educationist, had been asked to head a committee to examine how the education system for 14–19–year-olds could be modernized. He produced a plan which met with broad approval in the educational world, including the top universities such as Oxford and Cambridge. Hodgson and Spours referred to Tomlinson's suggestions as 'a carefully constructed consensus for a unified and inclusive diploma ... built up over months of consultation' (2005: 4). But, as soon as the report was published, Tony Blair made it clear that whatever was agreed about the radical proposals for the new diploma in England, the 'gold standard' A-level examination would not be scrapped (Smithers *et al.* 2004). This announcement effectively scuppered the Tomlinson proposals immediately, because retaining A-levels under the umbrella of the new diploma would have undermined the status of any other qualification, and especially vocational (work-related) courses.

The Prime Minister's decision to stop the Tomlinson proposals in their tracks was therefore a very clear example of the degree to which power has been centralized within government in Britain. In this case, the Prime Minister intervened over the heads of the DfES (who had broadly accepted the Tomlinson plan) and of his own ministers, Charles Clarke (then Secretary of State for Education) and David Miliband (then the Schools Minister). In a despondent reflection on the extraordinary dominance of the Prime Minister's office and of political advisers in contemporary government, Wragg concluded that there seemed to be 'no point in having a structure for education, because the Number 10 policy unit decides everything' (2005b: 7).

Does this example, and the other examples of 'top-down' policy-making made earlier, completely invalidate the idea of democratic influences on policy? There are two dangers in reaching this conclusion. The first is that a democratic model does not rule out the idea that power is concentrated in government. It would be naive to expect every policy to reflect grassroots opinion or consultation with pressure groups. As Dahl (1961) concluded, a pluralistic democracy in the real world works on the principle that central and local government are in control. The point is that, in a democracy, government is accountable to the people at election time, and also (especially in the USA) to the courts.

Thus, a different conclusion would be that Thatcher's, Blair's or any other Prime Minister's government has only been acting as any government does in a parliamentary democracy. Government may run ahead of the public will in education matters, but it was open to the electorate to reject a Conservative government and its education policies

– which it did in 1997 – and to reject a Labour government and its policies in 2001 and 2005, which it did not.

Does this mean that a democratic model provides an accurate view of policy-making in Britain after all? Unfortunately, neither is this the case. Such a conclusion would also be unsatisfactory.

A democratic model, although it does allow for the idea of government playing a lead role, nevertheless portrays political leaders and institutions as relatively open to 'outside' or pressure group influences *during the process of policy-making*. According to Dahl (1961), interest groups should be able to influence government decisions *before* they are finalized. However, the education reforms of the 1980s were introduced with little or no consultation. As will be recalled, only the vaguest references to the education reforms were made in the 1987 election campaign, and when government put forward its proposals in 1988 it did so without going through a consultative (Green Paper) stage. Similarly, there were only the vaguest hints during the 2001 election campaign of the government's firm intention to expand the roles of specialist secondary schools and of the private sector in education. This occurred again at the next general election, when Labour only mentioned their long-term plan to 'de-comprehensivize' secondary education, and to replace the standard comprehensive school with a more diverse system of independent school trusts, in veiled terms that did not spell out the alternatives to the public. Finally, the decision to reject the Tomlinson proposals for the reform of 14–19 education was reached without any consultation with the teaching profession or with education pressure groups.

The tendency of governments not to disclose before elections what they are intending to do lends weight to wider concerns about the health of democratic institutions in Britain today (see, for instance, Hutton 1995; Rawnsley 2001). These concerns throw additional doubts upon the value of a democratic model as a way of really understanding how decisions are made. In education, we have seen how control by democratically elected local councils has been eroded in a number of fields. Key functions (funding, running schools and colleges, delivering local education services such as transport) have been taken over by centralized bodies and unelected quangos, by school governing bodies that meet in private, and by private sector companies. Quangos do not necessarily lack competence or commitment to education. The main worry about their role, as Meikle (1994) concludes, is about the selection of quango board members, who are 'responsible for either huge budgets or huge powers [and] are there through patronage'.

In sum, there is a strong argument that the trend towards ever more centralized government, combined with the weakening of local democracy, has put increasing amounts of power into the hands of a small political elite of decision-makers. This has been particularly noticeable when one political party is dominant in the House of Commons (as with the Conservative Party in the 1980s and with Labour between 1997 and 2005) and when the Prime Minister can be relatively unconcerned about opposition from other political parties or from rebels in the ranks of the governing party. Despite this, however, it would be wrong to jettison the democratic explanation of policy development altogether. MPs, even those who belong to the governing party, have the right and the freedom to oppose legislation proposed by the government, as the case of the near-defeat of the Labour government in the parliamentary debate on higher education student funding and tuition fees showed, and as the heated debates about Labour's Education Bill in 2005 and 2006 also showed.

In addition, even if the government has a free hand to decide *what* is to be done, *whether* it is done, and *how*, are rather different matters. As we saw at the implementation stage of certain policies discussed in this chapter (for instance, opposition by teachers to aspects of the National Curriculum), a pluralist – if not fully democratic – model can help to explain how policies are modified and adapted after they have been launched, or legislation passed.

On balance, then, a reliable or accurate picture of policy-making depends on the simultaneous use of two or three theories of power and politics, rather than exclusive reliance upon one. An emphasis on the power of elites might be particularly relevant for analysis of the 'corridors of power' and the early stages of policy formation. But it might be necessary to incorporate ideas about pluralistic politics and democratic influences when looking at the local level or at how policies are received at the grassroots.

The third, political economy model of power, as discussed earlier, points to the underlying economic and political influences on policy as a way of analysing why particular policies were adopted and others were not. There are contradictory pressures to hold down taxes on business and to limit social spending by government (as demonstrated in the ever-tightening grip of central government on LEA finances and spending) and yet also to develop a more productive workforce through better training and *more* spending on certain types of education.

As we have seen in this chapter, the winning side in this tug-of-war was initially the pressure to keep down public expenditure, including spending on education. The proportion of Britain's resources devoted to education changed very little during the 1990s, and even fell slightly during Labour's first term in office, 1997–2001. However, during its second term in office, 2001–5, the other side of the tug-of-war gained a lot of ground, as government spending on education (and on related services and facilities, such as child care and preschool or nursery provision) increased significantly. Part of the impetus for this impressive financial commitment to education is undoubtedly a genuine drive, on the part of a Labour government, to widen opportunities for children and to improve the quality of educational services. A political economy perspective reminds us, however, that an additional reason for the extra spending on education can be found in the 'business case' for it. For the UK to remain a competitive economy in global markets, it is imperative that the education system be able to produce a sufficiently well educated and adaptable workforce. As the Tomlinson inquiry and many other reports have shown, there are strong reasons to question whether the UK's education system has received enough investment over the past few decades, and whether it is sufficiently good at retaining enough young people in the kinds of education and training that help to boost productivity.

Thus, as mentioned in the earlier section on the Conservatives' education reforms of 1988, the political economy view of power might be better in helping us to interpret the general direction of policy, such as trends in government spending on a service such as education, rather than in understanding specific policy changes. For instance, the whole idea of developing an internal market in state education seemed to be inspired by a strong belief among politicians in the value of incorporating business methods and competition into the state sector. But the specific policy to do this did not result from a clear set of demands from business leaders or those representing financial interests.

The importance of political leaders' beliefs about what ought to be done illustrates another way in which the political economy perspective is useful. It can help to show us how changes in a capitalist or market economy change ideas and the expectations we have of government and the public services. The Conservatives' education reforms show how we have gradually become accustomed to certain ideas about privatization, the introduction of an internal market in public services and competition between service providers. Arguably, it is now seen as more 'natural' and 'common sense' than before the 1980s' reforms for there to be competition between schools for students and funding, or that getting private sector bodies to run schools is likely to provide the best administrative solution – even though there is often evidence against this, as the example of city academies shows.

As the business of running schools becomes less and less obviously a public service, people will be more likely to turn to their school's governing body, or the local consortium or company running education in their area, than government. It is for this reason that central governments in the future might not be as damaged in elections or lose as much popularity as might be expected as a result of crises or failures in the nation's schools.

However, we cannot explain any of these problems or the education reforms discussed in this chapter unless we recognize the importance of elite control in UK policy-making. The reasons for the elite's ability to formulate and direct policy are a matter of debate, but it is likely that Britain's traditional class divisions in education play a large part. Political elites, whether of the left or right, are reluctant to bring change to a selective and elitist system that suits them very well. Adopting the Tomlinson proposals for a unified diploma that would have combined academic and vocational education, for instance, would have confronted the political elite with the possibility of *their* children, and the children of middle-class parents (if state educated) being drawn into courses on social care, plumbing or tourism. As it was, the government's rejection of Tomlinson's unified diploma for 14–19-year-olds in a White Paper in 2005 (DfES 2005) kept the academic and vocational routes 'safely' apart.

Thus, compared with the view that policy-making is basically democratic in Britain, an elite control model seems to better explain the formation of education policy. Despite differences in matters of detail, and a more impressive commitment to public spending on schools, Labour's policies on education closely resemble those of the preceding Conservative government. This bears out the contention that, while the UK is a parliamentary democracy, any change of government at election time largely has the effect of exchanging one political elite for another that has broadly similar aims and interests.

Key terms and concepts

democratic pluralist model of power
elite control model of power
implementation
parliamentary democracy
political economy model of power

quangos

policy agenda

Suggestions for further reading

Chris Ham and Michael Hill's *The Policy Process in the Modern Capitalist State* (1993) re-mains one of the best and more readable texts on the nature of policy-making and models of power. An elegant and succinct view of the nature of power in modern society has been written by Steven Lukes: *Power: A Radical View* (2nd edn, 2005). Though written primarily for a sociological and political science audience, it has many applications in social policy. For a wry and insightful view of the exercise of power inside Mrs Thatcher's government, Sir Ian Gilmour's *Dancing with Dogma* (1992) is well worth reading. It is especially interesting as an example of an 'old guard' Tory's view of Mrs Thatcher's policies and politics. Having looked at power in the past, it is possible to get a similarly insightful and fascinating view of the inside workings of government by reading Andrew Rawnsley's *Servants of the People: The Inside Story of New Labour* (2000). A textbook on politics, such as *The New British Politics* (1998), by Ian Budge and colleagues is also useful as a source book to provide detailed information about the way government and the political system work in the UK.

For reading about education policy, you can find no better book than Sally Tom-linson's *Education in a Post-welfare Society* (2001). This provides an overview that is both extremely informative and readable. Her book includes thorough discussions of key policy issues such as education and equity (class, gender and 'race'), education and the economy, and New Labour's record on education. It also includes a succinct discussion of the development of education policy in England and Wales since 1944, though for a fuller history Brian Simon's *Education and the Social Order, 1940–1990* (1990) provides an excellent overview of the rise of comprehensive education and much more besides.

8 WORK AND WELFARE

Introduction

Work is, will be, or has been a central part of most people's lives. The kinds of work we do, how much we earn and where we work play a very important part in defining who we are. Not surprisingly, therefore, work strongly affects a person's welfare. Work might be deeply satisfying, or stressful, or mundane and boring. It strongly influences our psychological welfare in various ways. The amount of money earned and the amount of time spent earning it constrain the choices we can make. At a personal level, the quality of the food we eat, whether we can easily take part in leisure and sporting activities, enjoy the holidays we want, and have a satisfactory home are all likely to be strongly influenced by the jobs we have. Similarly, health, education and social security are all affected by work and income, and by changes in employment patterns.

Historical connections between work and human welfare are deeply rooted. Concerns about well-being at work can be traced back to the nineteenth century or even before that. For instance, the Factory Acts that were passed in 1833, 1844 and 1847 limited the hours per day that children could be expected to work (Fraser 1984). The aim was to protect children from being exploited under the harshest conditions in factories and other hazardous workplaces. Eventually, child labour was abolished as elementary schooling became commonplace.

Another example of the historical relationship between work and welfare can be seen in the development of trade unions in the pre-welfare state era. As unions and workers' associations grew in importance, many established a wide range of benefits and services for their members. These included social facilities and leisure activities, holiday schemes, insurance against the cost of sickness or funeral expenses and other welfare benefits. Trade unions and professional associations retain an important function in managing occupational pensions, and in negotiating a wide range of concessions and benefits for their members – for instance, in health, vehicle and travel insurance.

Work: an object of social *and* economic policy

Given the historical connections between work and welfare, it is surprising to realize that, traditionally, social policy as an academic subject seemed to downplay employment policy or ignore it altogether. Most university courses in social policy used to focus on the 'five great social services' (see Chapter 1) – education, health, housing, personal social services and social security. Employment policy was often left in the shade. Similarly, the first edition of this book did not contain a separate chapter on work – an omission remedied in the second edition.

There is now a lot of interest in employment policy and its connections with social welfare, especially in relation to certain groups in society such as school-leavers and the section of young people who have difficulty finding worthwhile jobs. The Labour government's approach to employment policy and its various 'welfare to work' programmes have undoubtedly stimulated interest in this field. New Labour has placed work centre stage in social, as well as economic, policy.

However, it remains the case that there is still something of a mental divide between the world of employment – often associated with the realities of making a living, of commerce and the private sector – and the world of social policy and welfare. The latter is more often associated with care, protection and with the problems of people who cannot work.

The conceptual divide between economic policy – including employment policy – on the one hand, and social policy on the other, can be traced back to the development of the welfare state after the Second World War. Unlike other European countries, the British approach to planning the economy and the welfare system ran on two rather separate tracks.

Beveridge's plans in the 1940s for a universal system of social security assumed that there would have to be full employment after the Second World War. It was seen as essential to have as high a number of (male) workers in jobs and contributing to the system as possible, to keep it solvent. This was part of a Keynesian strategy that involved managing public spending in ways that would maintain full employment and economic growth. However, despite the postwar recognition that the success of the welfare state rested on the economy, and vice versa, not as much was done in Britain as in other welfare states to dovetail economic and social policy.

In France, Germany, Sweden and other countries, a more *corporatist* approach (see Chapter 3) led to planning the economy and the welfare system together. The main link between the two was work. Thus in a country such as Germany or Sweden, wages were never thought of in isolation from social benefits, even in the private sector of employment. Negotiations between employers, unions and government led to agreements on pay, the amount of tax and insurance contributions to be levied by government, and the level or value of social benefits (for example, child benefits or family benefits). Sometimes unions were willing to moderate their wage demands if government did not increase taxes, or if social benefits could be raised.

In the UK, this idea of a firm social contract between employers, employees and government never developed to the degree that it did in most of the major north European countries. Employment policy, wages policy and economic development were seen mainly as 'economics' issues in the UK and as separate from 'welfare' issues.

There were attempts by the Labour government of the 1970s (1974–9) to encourage trade unions, the major employers and government to work together to reach agreements on wages, prices, taxation and social benefits. However, the lack of a corporatist tradition and the conflict-ridden state of industrial relations in Britain meant that none of these agreements held.

Arguably, Labour lost the general election in 1979 mainly because it was perceived as a government that had failed in its attempt to manage industrial relations, or to weld together any lasting agreements between trade unions and employers. Mrs Thatcher, who led the Conservative government that replaced Labour in 1979, abhorred any policy that smacked of government 'interference' in the labour market, or of any attempt to engineer agreements on wages, prices and social security through a corporatist approach. Consequently the 1980s were the decade in which the Conservative government dismantled Labour's mechanisms for bringing trade unions, employers and government together to discuss economic and social policy. Trade union power and influence were cut down drastically. Government firmly turned its back on consensus politics and on policies to integrate economic and social policy.

Now that old-style corporatism is also being dismantled in Europe, it is very unlikely that the UK will ever develop such integrated policies for managing the economy, employment and social benefits. The trend begun by Mrs Thatcher is now in the opposite direction, towards the deregulation of employment conditions and wage bargaining between employers and employees that is free of government influence or control. However, there is still a considerable gulf between the employment policies followed by countries such as France, Germany and Sweden, and employment policies in the UK.

Does work equal welfare?

First it is necessary to explore in a little more depth the connections between work and welfare. While it is one thing to safeguard welfare *at* work (for example, through health and safety regulations) or *after* working life (for example, through the provision of pensions), it is another to claim that *work itself* is beneficial and enhances human welfare. Clearly, everything depends on the work in question. Heavy manual work for a pittance in degrading or hazardous conditions is one thing; well-paid work in a bright, pleasant office is another. However, even though work varies widely and different working conditions have different welfare implications, some claim that work generally has positive effects on people.

- Being in work generally means that people's *incomes* are higher than they would be if they were unemployed or dependent on someone else. It has been shown that incomes have a very direct effect on health and education. Rates of illness and illiteracy are much higher in areas where unemployment and poverty are common. Children are more likely to thrive and to develop to their full potential in households that have good, or at least adequate, incomes.

- Employment promotes *social inclusion*. Unemployed people are more likely than those in employment to be socially isolated and excluded. On the other hand, being at work tends to get people involved in friendships and community life. Traditionally, getting a job after leaving school was a very important transition that marked maturation from adolescence to adulthood. Nowadays, even though average rates of unemployment have fallen, young people – and young men in particular – are unlikely to be able to progress from school to work in the uncomplicated way that most people used to do. As they are unable to acquire the badge of adulthood through getting a job in the traditional way, some feel alienated from society (Robertson Elliot 1996). Similarly, many older workers have been excluded from employment since the 1950s (see Chapter 6).

- There is also an argument that work promotes *psychological well-being*. This can come from two main sources. First, work brings social contacts and involvement, and through these we find and develop our identities. A second source of psychological welfare could be the work itself. This is most likely to happen when the work is intrinsically satisfying, skilled, challenging or worthwhile. However, it could also occur even when there are some strongly negative aspects to the work if the individual draws some satisfaction from being able to hold down a difficult job or overcome its hardships.

In reality, most people find that work has a mixture of positive and negative effects on their lives. What are the negative effects of work on welfare?

- *Is work always good for us, either in terms of income or other benefits?* There are some important exceptions to the principle that getting a job or staying in employment is always beneficial. First, there is a growing group of people aged 50 and above who are choosing to leave full-time employment, suggesting that when it is possible to make a choice, some people expect their welfare and general satisfaction with life to be better when not employed. Second, poverty is not restricted to people out of work. Having a job does not guarantee a higher income than being unemployed, despite the introduction of a minimum wage.

- *Work does not necessarily promote social inclusion.* In fact, the opposite might occur if a dual labour market develops. This means that there are broadly two types or 'sectors' of work available. First, getting a job in the formal employment sector does not always require a lot of educational qualifications or a high level of skills, but there is a formal selection process. Second, there are jobs in the 'informal' sector, in which the work is more often available on a casual or temporary basis than in the formal sector. Typically, jobs in this sector are low-paid and often mean working irregular hours, or during evenings, nights and early mornings.

Employers might do little or nothing to safeguard the welfare, pension or health rights of employees. Disproportionate numbers of women, disabled workers, black and ethnic minority workers and other disadvantaged groups are found in temporary, part-time and insecure employment of this type. A dual labour market therefore acts as a mechanism for *excluding*, rather than including, some groups. There is a debate about how far a dual labour market has been developing in the UK in recent years – a debate that centres on whether it is desirable for the UK to be a low-wage economy in which casualization and deregulation of employment are to be encouraged. There is further discussion of this issue in the next section.

- *Work can cause unhappiness, alienation and psychological stress.* There are several major causes of these kinds of problems. Work remains an alienating, dehumanizing experience for significant groups of people. As a result of constant changes in the technologies of mass production, much work has been deskilled and reduced to a series of fragmented, monotonous tasks. Work can also make us ill from accidents, pollution, absorption of hazardous chemicals and other substances, noise and repetitive strain.

- *For some, problems arise from overwork as much as the work itself.* Workers in the UK on average have to spend significantly more hours at work each week and have fewer holidays than their counterparts in western European countries. Also, job insecurity – the real or perceived threat of redundancy – adds to feelings of dissatisfaction and stress. Finally, conflicts between the demands of work and home – particularly those experienced by lone parents, or by those caring for ill and frail relatives – can exacerbate levels of stress. One illustration of this is the debate that was sparked about the government drive to encourage lone parents into employment, as part of their 'welfare to work' strategy. There are concerns about whether the welfare of babies and young children is put at risk if alternative child care and nursery facilities are not provided at an adequate standard.

Employment policy options

As suggested earlier, most people find that work brings a mixture of positive and negative influences on their welfare. For instance, an employee might find that they are in a work group that is both supportive and fun to be with, and that the work itself is fairly interesting. In the same job they might suffer from repetitive strain injury and discover that their leave entitlement is less than they anticipated.

However, the fact that the impact of work on human welfare varies considerably from individual to individual should not blind us to some of the broader patterns and inequalities in employment that exist. This applies particularly to the 'stark contrasts' that have been observed in both the amount of unemployment and the quality of jobs available in different parts of the UK (see Bennett 2000: 678–9). Similarly, in a review of the Labour government's record in improving pay, working conditions and the availability of work, Toynbee and Walker conclude that, while access to employment and wage levels became fairer in some respects between 1997 and 2001, significant problems remain. These were particularly evident in continuing difficulties in providing enough child care to enable parents, particularly mothers, to get to work, and other gender-related issues such as the persistence of basic inequalities in men's and women's pay (Toynbee and Walker 2001: 30).

Thus persistent inequalities and problems in the workplace pose two policy questions for government.

First, if work has mixed effects on people's welfare and in some cases might have strongly negative effects, should employment policy concentrate on simply getting as many people as possible into jobs as quickly as possible? This kind of strategy would focus on stimulating *demand* for workers. It is the kind of policy that makes it easy for employers to hire workers. For instance, employers can be given a government subsidy for every unemployed worker who is taken onto the payroll. Another aim would be to reduce the amount of regulations governing pay and conditions that employers have to abide by. The main goal of this sort of policy is to reduce the number of people officially counted as unemployed, and not to look too closely at the sorts of work that people are more or less firmly pushed into.

A second approach to employment policy rests more on improving people's prospects of employment by enhancing and upgrading their skills and general employability. This kind of policy concentrates on what has been termed the 'supply side' of the labour market – that is, the supply of labour and the quality of the people (as demonstrated by their skills and capabilities) available for work. In this approach there is more emphasis on people's long-term employability and success in staying in work than on the short-term goal of getting them any job as quickly as possible.

Before looking at the kinds of employment policy that the government introduced during its 1997–2001 term in office, however, we need to see the government's efforts in the context of the labour market – that is, the basic characteristics of working patterns and the labour force in the UK. Only then can we fully assess the value of recent employment policies, and how far they represent worthwhile efforts by government.

The context: work and unemployment in the UK

In the year 2004 almost 30 million people, about half of the UK's population, were economically active. In other words, they could be counted as members of the labour force in the sense that they were either in paid employment or available for work (Office for National Statistics 2005b, Table 4.2: 47). This labour force was made up of 13.6 million women and 16.2 million men. Of the total of 29.8 million economically active persons, 1.4 million were unemployed, of which 0.8 million were men and 0.6 million were women (Office for National Statistics 2005b, Table 4.2: 47). This was the lowest rate of unemployment since the late 1970s (Office for National Statistics 2005b: 5).

Since the middle of the twentieth century there have been very significant changes in the composition of the labour force, as well as in the nature of work itself and the main types of jobs that are available. The main changes have been in the *age and gender composition* of the labour force. For instance, in the past almost all men used to work right up to the standard retirement age of 65. In 1971 over 95 per cent of men aged between 60 and 64 were economically active but now this situation has been reversed, with a large majority of older men being outside the workforce. In fact the economic activity rate among all men has been in decline since the 1970s. This is explained partly by increases in the numbers of men taking early retirement after the age of 45, and by an increase in the number claiming that either disability or long-term illness prevents them from working.

Although the percentage of men who are economically active has been falling the *total* of men in work increased slightly, from 16 million to 16.2 million, between 1971 and 2004. Population growth and an increase in numbers of men of working age explain this.

Over the same period the total of women who are economically active increased dramatically, from only 10 million to 13.6 million. It has been estimated that 1 million extra women will become economically active by 2011 (Office for National Statistics 2001: 77).

These very marked increases can be explained only by the long-term trend for women to take up paid employment, either full-time or part-time (over 16 hours per week). In the 1950s and before that, a large majority of women were engaged in domestic work in their own homes, and relatively few combined this with part-time paid work.

More recently (2004), 84 per cent of working-age men and 73 per cent of women were economically active in the UK (Office for National Statistics 2005b: 46). Thus women are closing the gap in economic activity rates between themselves and men. The situation has not reached the near-equal rate of men and women in paid work that prevails in Sweden and other Scandinavian countries, however, the proportion of working-age British women in paid employment is 10 per cent higher than the EU average of 55.1 per cent (this percentage refers to the recently-expanded EU of 25 countries; for the 'old' 15-country EU, the percentage is 56.1) (Office for National Statistics 2005b: 51).

The rise in British women's rate of participation in the workforce is impressive but, to put it in context, we must note that many more women than men work part-time. As can be seen in Table 8.1, over three-quarters of economically active men in the UK work full-time, but only just over a half of women do so. On the other hand, 40 per cent of women are part-time workers, but only 8 per cent of men. Significantly, the proportion of men who are self-employed is double that of male part-timers, while few women work independently on a self-employed basis.

Table 8.1   Employment status by sex in the UK, 2004 (percentages)

Employment status	Males	Females	All
Full-time employees	74	52	64
Part-time employees	8	40	23
Self-employed	18	8	13
Others (e.g. training)	1	1	1
All in employment	100	100	100
N (millions)	15.4	13.0	28.4

Note: Of economically active people in work Percentages have been rounded to the nearest whole number, so do not sum to 100.
Source: Office for National Statistics (2005b), adapted from Table 4.2.

These gender differences in rates of full-time and part-time work partly explain other gender inequalities in the workforce. As many more women than men are in part-time work, it is not surprising that their total earnings are considerably less than men's. Also, the discrimination against part-time workers that can occur when opportunities for promotion or training are considered means that women are more likely than men to be held back in their career development.

However, not all of the gender inequalities in pay and promotion can be explained by women's much greater involvement in part-time paid work. There are also significant differences in the types of work that men and women tend to do. While many men work in the service sector of the economy (which includes jobs in catering, hotels and leisure services, welfare and care services, retail, and clerical and administrative jobs), a higher proportion of women do so. Conversely, significantly more men than women work in construction, transport and manufacturing.

Traditionally, service sector jobs have been more often part-time, less valued and lower paid than jobs in manufacturing and related areas of the economy. The tendency for men to be in jobs that are seen as suitable for them, and for women to be steered towards traditionally 'feminized' occupations, has tended to underpin and maintain pay inequalities between men and women. Discrimination against women employees, whether or not they are working alongside men, is also a strong factor in holding down women's pay. As Toynbee and Walker (2001: 30) point out, the gap between men's and women's pay remains wide, 'with an average of £326.50 a week for women and £442.41 for men which, allowing for the difference in hours, meant a 19 per cent pay gap'. This gap narrowed only slightly under the Labour governments of 1997 to 2005.

Toynbee and Walker go on to suggest that this pay gap will probably continue to narrow in the future, but only slowly and more as a result of market forces than government attempts to equalize pay between men and women. This is a significant point because the labour market is far from static and, whatever happens to pay inequality there will undoubtedly be further changes to the working roles of men and women. For one thing, the number of jobs in manufacturing is in long-term decline. Men have found it increasingly difficult to get work in occupations that they used to rely on. An increasing proportion of men will have to take jobs in the service sector and, like women, may have to adapt to working 'flexible hours' or in part-time jobs.

This brings us to another facet of change in employment, because there has been an increase not only in part-time and flexible working but also in the number of *temporary jobs*. As will be recalled, this has raised concerns about whether a dual labour market is developing in the UK, and whether this is going to lead to a lot more job insecurity and casualization of work contracts in the future. For instance, there has been concern in recent years about the practice of imposing 'zero hours contracts' on employees – a kind of piecework whereby the worker is paid only if there is work to be done in a given time period or part of the working day.

The evidence on the spread of casual work contracts and job insecurity in the UK is mixed. On the one hand, a study by the Citizens' Advice Bureau (1998) found that 'flexible' working does lead to casualization, zero hours contracts, job insecurity and worsening working conditions for a growing number of people. Another study by Worrall and Cooper (1998), for the Institute of Management, found that managers are the section of the workforce who often have to cope with the heaviest demands and pressures in the modern workplace. They report low morale and long working hours among many in management as more flexible working practices are introduced.

On the other hand, the proportion of all employees in temporary jobs is small, rising from only 5 per cent in the 1980s to 7 per cent in the 1990s (Sly and Stillwell 1997). Also, research by the Centre for Economic Policy Research shows that 'the average time people typically hold jobs has hardly changed in twenty years' (reported by Bennett 1998: 406). Therefore, in some respects the UK's workforce remains a relatively stable one. Change is more evident in working practices and growing expectations of employers that their employees will work longer and more flexible hours. And as James (1998) suggests, depression and mental stress are on the increase in Britain only partly because of an objective increase in workload. Subjective attitudes to what are perceived to be the growing pressures of work are also significant – in particular, the stress of trying to combine the emotional demands of parenting with the completely different emotional commitments expected at work (James 1998: 149).

The story of unemployment

Any understanding of work and policies to stimulate employment would be incomplete without some knowledge of *un*employment. At the time of writing, unemployment had been declining in the UK for a considerable period, though in 2006 it began to rise again even though the total in work also continued to grow. These mixed trends reflected slower growth and layoffs in some sectors of the economy (particularly in manufacturing and farming) while other sectors (retail and service industry sectors) continued to grow and to provide more jobs. In the future, the ups and downs of the labour market are bound to increase unemployment in some areas while there are still employment opportunities in others. We can put these trends into context by looking at waves of unemployment in the past.

Perhaps one of the best known periods of high unemployment in the UK and other countries was that of the Great Depression of the 1930s. It was during the early 1930s in particular that existing unemployment insurance schemes struggled to provide enough benefits to the millions of people who had been thrown out of work. For this reason Pierson (1991: 116) and other commentators believe that the 1930s became a seedbed for the development of the welfare state after the Second World War. Political leaders expressed a common wish never to return to the days of high unemployment and poverty that were experienced in the 1930s. As mentioned earlier, Beveridge insisted that full employment would have to be a central plank in the development of an adequately funded system of social security and health care.

Whether as a result of government policy or the inevitable upswing in economic activity that came with postwar reconstruction, full employment – at least, for men – became a reality during the three decades that followed the end of the Second World War in 1945. This was the so-called 'golden age' of the welfare state. Among all those who were counted as economically active, unemployment stayed below 3 per cent of the labour force until 1975.

From the mid-1970s on, however, the rate of unemployment began to rise. Between

1976 and 1986, it rose from 5 to almost 12 per cent of the workforce. The steepest rise took place in the early 1980s, during Mrs Thatcher's first period in office. Her government abandoned the economic strategies used by previous Labour and Conservative governments to assist struggling industries and to use public spending to stimulate employment. As a result, unemployment soared and government expenditure on unemployment and social security benefits also rose very substantially.

At the time, there was concern not only about what seemed to be a reckless economic strategy but also about the impact of high unemployment on the 'social fabric' of the UK. For instance, by the end of the 1970s, unemployment in Northern Ireland had risen to what then seemed an astronomical 9 per cent of the labour force – three times the typical rate in the UK before 1975. It was said at the time that, if unemployment in the rest of the UK were to reach such a high level, there would almost certainly be some kind of profound social crisis. Within two years, however, a 9 per cent rate of unemployment had become the *lowest* rate to be found in any of the UK's regions – the South-East of England.

Thus the steep rise in unemployment in the 1980s did not result in the predicted 'melt down' of the social order. For the reasons discussed in Chapter 6, social policy – in particular, unemployment benefit, other social benefits and temporary employment schemes – succeeded in buffering society and government from the full impact of unemployment.

However, even though complete social breakdown was avoided, unemployment and associated changes in the labour force did bring momentous social change. The 1980s are associated with the first great shake-outs of labour to take place since the 1930s, and with the sharp decline of traditional heavy industries and coal-mining as large-scale employers. The Conservative government of the 1980s decided to tough out the inevitable confrontations with the trade unions. In the ensuing struggles between organized labour and government, the threat of unemployment played a key role. Grudgingly, the trade unions had to accept government-imposed reforms of labour relations and new controls on strikes.

It would be wrong to conclude, however, that Mrs Thatcher's government was unconcerned about the political implications of high unemployment. Considerable government effort was devoted to reducing the official rate of unemployment. Critics argued that much of this was an exercise in recategorizing unemployed people as economically inactive so that they would no longer appear in the official statistics as unemployed. However, the Conservative government of the 1980s did make vigorous efforts to develop job creation and training schemes, particularly to reduce the unemployment rate among young people. This was in one way surprising, because the government was also strongly committed to a policy of non-intervention or laissez-faire in the job market.

As can be seen from Table 8.2, unemployment rose in the early 1990s, reflecting the effects of the recession of 1991–2. But since 1994 unemployment declined steadily, with a particularly substantial reduction in the last three years of Major's Conservative government. Blair's periods in office saw continued falls in unemployment, though none of these were quite as substantial as in the years 1994–7.

Table 8.2 Unemployment rates by gender, 1988–2000 (percentages)

Gender	1988	1991	1994	1997	2000	2004
Men	12.1	9.2	11.4	8.1	6.1	4.9
Women	8.3	7.2	7.3	5.7	4.8	4.4

Source: For 1988, Central Statistical Office (1989: 79); for other years, Office for National Statistics (2001), Table 4.21 and Office for National Statistics (2005), Table 4.2.

In sum, a historical perspective shows that the ability of government to manage employment, to link work to welfare issues or reduce unemployment is very dependent on the health of the economy and the business cycle. This point should be borne in mind in the next section, which reviews the impact of various government policies on employment and unemployment.

Current employment policy

As mentioned at the beginning of the chapter, the Labour government since 1997 has made work the centrepiece of its policies on social welfare. The government has tried, with varying degrees of success, to break down the division between policies on welfare and social security on the one hand, and employment on the other. In attempting to 'get people off welfare and into work', it has been developing an *active labour market policy*. This amounts to a set of government strategies to actively intervene in the job market. Government aims to forge partnerships with employers, not only to stimulate the creation of more jobs but also to encourage more efficient employment of workers, using detailed measures to match individual people to jobs.

Adopting an active labour market policy means that the government has committed itself to the principle that no one who is able to work should be left out of the labour market. The aim is to improve people's welfare through employment. Government policy is to try to ensure that both individuals and families are better off financially, and can obtain benefits (notably tax credits) through being employed, rather than by obtaining benefits through being unemployed.

Although Britain's recent active labour market policies do not yet match those of Sweden and other Scandinavian countries, they do represent a step towards a system in which it is assumed that almost everyone's 'gateway' to social benefits and full citizenship is through getting a job. In Sweden, for instance, strong efforts are made to integrate into the workforce as many disabled people as possible, so that benefits for disabled people can be channelled through employment. Likewise, parental benefits – for instance, an insurance scheme that pays for parental leave from work – are obtained through employment.

Under Labour, Britain's active labour market policies have developed in two directions: first, various New Deal schemes have been introduced in order to reduce unemployment and improve the skills and general employability of workers, and especially of young people. Second, a variety of policies to *improve the conditions and welfare of people already in work* have been implemented.

The New Deal

Before the general election in 1997, Labour had announced plans for a new policy to deal with the problem of unemployment among young people. These plans became the 'New Deal' – a scheme that, to begin with, was funded from a £5 billion windfall tax on privatized utility companies (Toynbee and Walker 2001: 13). The New Deal for Young People (NDYP) began full operation in 1998 and has been supplemented by other employment schemes – New Deals for the long-term unemployed, for lone parents, for disabled people and for workers over 50 years of age.

A large number of young people have now experienced the New Deal. Between January 1998 and June 2004, almost 419,000 (39 per cent) of those leaving the NDYP went into sustained, unsubsidized employment (Office for National Statistics 2005b: 58).

In implementing its New Deal philosophy, the government was trying to bring about the active labour market approach to employment policy mentioned above. As Hasluck (2000: 370) points out, the New Deal was supposed to be different in trying to offer 'help that is tailored to the needs of individual job-seekers'.

First, the NDYP requires 18–24-year-olds who are claiming jobseeker's allowance to see an employment adviser, who over a period of four months assesses them and helps them to find work. If this is not successful, those who wish to continue claiming benefits are required to take one of four 'options'. These are:

- a voluntary job (with some cash benefits);
- education for up to a year;
- work with/on an environmental improvement project;
- a subsidized job.

Introducing the New Deal, Gordon Brown, the Chancellor of the Exchequer, explained that there would be no 'fifth option' of 'staying at home in bed watching television' (Vickerstaff 2003: 151) – a statement that revealed a complete lack of awareness in government circles of the pleasures of daytime TV.

The NDYP represents both the 'caring' and 'controlling' strands of welfare discussed in Chapter 6. Claimants who refuse to take a job that is available, or refuse training, face having their benefit stopped for 14 days, rising to a month if they continue to turn down all of the four options listed above. Also, unemployed people can now be required to take basic lessons in literacy and numeracy, in how to present themselves and how to dress appropriately for job interviews.

These requirements in the New Deal programme and in the rules governing the jobseeker's allowance raise important arguments for and against compulsion in employment policy. On one side, any attempt by the state to compel people to change their personal behaviour and appearance can be seen as a dangerous infringement of personal freedom, even if as a result people are 'encouraged' into jobs. But on the other side, there is practical evidence that the more coercive approach of the New Deal works better than previous policies with people who are demotivated and have been unemployed long term. Hasluck (2000: 372), for instance, points to evidence that there is a relatively positive view of the NDYP among young people who are involved in it.

There are other fundamental questions to ask about the New Deal – in particular, whether it has actually helped many people to obtain work or created many jobs. There is little doubt among economists that 14 (at the time of writing) unbroken years of economic growth after 1992 are the main reason for the steady fall in unemployment, rather than government employment schemes such as the New Deal (see, for instance, Elliott 2000).

Also, a lot of expenditure on NDYP schemes might have been wasted. This might be partly because spending on training or subsidizing work for some young people has been unnecessary – there is a widespread consensus that about a half would have found jobs anyway. Or waste can occur because New Deal training and other schemes to improve employability are not effective. Despite spending between perhaps £4000 and £6000 on each young 'New Dealer', as many as 40 per cent of NDYP graduates have not found permanent work (Toynbee and Walker 2005: 61).

The problem of trying to find solutions for people who have been unemployed long term has been a particularly intractable one. While the NDYP can be seen as having some success in cutting the numbers of long-term young unemployed (Finn 2003: 123–4), the other New Deal schemes for long-term unemployed people, lone parents, disabled people and those over 50 seem to have had a much less noticeable impact. Hasluck (2000: 371), for instance, noted that the New Deal for long-term unemployed people 'has yet to establish similar support and good will' among employers and people looking for work, compared with NDYP. Hasluck also comments on the New Deal for lone parents. Research on this scheme (entry to which is voluntary – a crucial difference from the NDYP) finds that, while the New Deal helped single mothers with advice and general support, it was of 'little particular help in the process of obtaining specific job vacancies' (Hasluck 2000: 372), at least to begin with. Single parents often find it difficult to obtain work because they lack skills and qualifications, while older workers and disabled people can find it difficult to obtain permanent work because of discrimination in the job market. The New Deal 50 Plus nevertheless found employment for 110,000 older workers, while that for lone parents helped to place 260,000 between 1998 and 2004 (Toynbee and Walker 2005: 61).

Despite the persistence of pockets of high rates of unemployment in some areas and the problems faced by a core of long-term unemployed people, it would be wrong to conclude that New Deal policies have been a failure or an irrelevance. A lot of unemployment would have disappeared 'naturally' as a result of economic growth, but there is still evidence that the NDYP helped many young unemployed people into jobs more quickly than would have been the case otherwise. Also, there is an argument that active labour market policies such as the New Deal help people to find more *suitable* jobs than they would otherwise have done. Finally, as far as the argument about the cost of subsidizing jobs is concerned, this point seemed to be voiced more often when the New Deal was being launched than it is today. More recent evidence shows that the New Deal is almost paying for itself. As Riley and Young (2001) show, bringing even a relatively small number of long-term unemployed people back into the workforce tends to hold down wage levels, thus creating extra jobs and boosting economic growth. Since 2005, the entry into the UK's job market of hundreds of thousands of young immigrant workers from the new member states of the EU, such as Poland, seems to be having similar effects of adding to Britain's economic growth rate while holding down wages.

In sum, therefore, the impact of the New Deal on employment seems to have been modest but significant. Whether or not a New Deal policy had been introduced, the overall size of the labour force would not have been much different from what it is today. However, one of the principal aims of the New Deal has been to reduce social exclusion as well as to promote sustained employment. Arguably, the New Deal schemes have been helpful to social groups that often experience the most difficulty in obtaining work – and the NDYP seems to have been particularly helpful in assisting a sizeable number of young people to obtain their first job. There have also been more subtle effects in the economy and society as a whole, as employability has become the norm and the principle has been established that as many people who can work will be helped by government to do so.

Other policies – the welfare of people in work

While the New Deal represented new ways of getting people into jobs, recent employment policy has also concentrated on the welfare and incomes of people who are already in paid work. The main employment policies that have developed in this direction are as follows.

Employment relations

An Employment Relations Act was passed in 2000. This legislation was enacted partly to satisfy the requirements of EU law following the British government decision to sign up to EU social legislation in 1997. It establishes new rules governing the recognition of trade unions and of employee rights (such as the right to be consulted by large employers about major decisions concerning the future of the firm or business). It also reflects a requirement by the EU to regulate working time. It is now illegal for employers to require their employees to work for more than 48 hours per week – though a number of occupations are exempt and professional and senior management employees can also be exempted through voluntary agreements to work longer hours. Another important element in this legislation was the introduction of new 'family-friendly' rights concerning parental or family leave from work. For instance, for the first time fathers have been given the right to take (unpaid) parental leave following the birth of a child. Family leave includes the right of parents of young children to take time off for family emergencies. Statutory maternity leave has been increased from 14 to 18 weeks, and the qualifying period (the time that the mother has to be in work before being able to claim this right) has been reduced from two years to one.

Tax credits

Various kinds of tax credit have been introduced in order to raise the incomes of people who are in work but on low incomes. These are an important part of the government's 'welfare to work' policy and the drive to eliminate the 'poverty trap'. The most important of the tax credits was the working families tax credit (WFTC), launched in 2000 to replace family credit, a social security benefit that had been inherited and continued by the former Conservative government. WFTC was an interesting and significant development because it was managed by the Inland Revenue, as part of the tax system, not as a benefit to people in work from the DWP. It represents the growing importance of the Treasury in shaping social policy in the UK.

By 2001 WFTC was supplementing the incomes of approximately 1.5 million families, paying on average an extra £24 per week more than such families would have obtained from family credit (Toynbee and Walker 2001: 21). Other kinds of tax credits have also been introduced. For instance, there is a child care tax credit to help working parents on low incomes to meet these costs. Up to 70 per cent of the costs can be reimbursed this way and the government has promised to raise this proportion to 80 per cent in 2006 (Toynbee and Walker 2005: 57). WFTC was replaced in 2003 by child tax credit and working tax credit for working people on low incomes – the former being much more important. These tax credits are effectively targeted, means-tested benefits paid through HMRC and designed to 'make work pay'. Child tax credit in particular has been an important means of channelling resources towards families with children and is a component of the government's strategy for tackling child poverty. The government has also introduced a disabled person's tax credit, which helps employed people who become disabled and is intended to encourage such people to stay in work.

Minimum wage

A minimum wage was introduced in 1999. Labour's announcement of its minimum wage policy met with a great deal of controversy, with objections both from the trade unions and business. Trade unions and other groups representing the low paid argued that the minimum was set too low (it was introduced at only £3.60 an hour for the full rate). There is also evidence that the former Wages Councils, local bodies that used to adjudicate on wage levels and wage disputes, were a better system for raising and maintaining the pay of low-income workers than a national minimum wage.

The rate has, however, been steadily increased since its introduction. By October 2005 the adult rate was £5.05 per hour, and the youth rate £4.25, an increase in the adult rate since introduction of around 40 per cent.

Business leaders strongly opposed the introduction of a minimum wage because of the cost to employers and their argument that wage increases for the lowest paid would price some people out of jobs. In a buoyant job market and a period of economic growth, however, this proved not to be the case – there is no evidence that introducing the minimum wage led to higher unemployment. On the contrary, in periods of economic growth, raising the lowest paid people's incomes to a minimum level leads to increases in spending, more economic activity and thus more employment. After initial opposition, the Conservative Party now accepts the minimum wage and has included it as a policy in its own programme.

Part-time workers

The government has also introduced legislation to protect the interests of part-time workers. As with the Employment Relations Act 2000 and the introduction of more 'family-friendly' employment policies, this policy represents the influence of EU social legislation. The UK government must implement the EU's part-time working directive, which means that part-time workers will be entitled (on a pro-rata basis) to the same rights to holidays, parental leave, sick leave, pensions and other social benefits as full-time workers. The UK has a relatively high proportion of part-time workers, compared with most European countries except, for instance, the Netherlands. Therefore, this measure will have a considerable impact in the future. It will add considerably to employers' costs, but promises to lend stability and security to a workforce that, as discussed earlier, has experienced some problems of job insecurity and 'casualization'.

Conclusions – in whose interests is employment policy?

When New Labour won the general election in 1997, opinion was divided as to whether it would be weakened by the same divided loyalties that previous Labour governments in 1964–70 and 1974–9 had experienced in employment policy – namely, the conflict between party loyalty to the trade unions and the pressure on government to meet the demands of business and employers.

As the name of the party suggests, 'Labour' was formed to defend and promote the interests of working people. In practice and in government though, Labour's relationships with the trade unions have often proved to be uneasy. In the 1960s and 1970s, Labour's attempts to control union demands for higher wages and to establish a legal framework for strikes and disputes were only partially successful. And failure to establish a settlement with the unions over an agreed wages and employment policy badly affected Labour's electoral fortunes, not only in 1979, when Callaghan's government was defeated by the Conservatives, but also in subsequent elections in 1983 and 1987.

Since its election to power in 1997 and re-election in 2001, there has been no mistaking New Labour's stance on its relationship with the unions and with business. Under Blair's leadership the Labour Party has made it very clear that it wishes to sever many of its historical links with the unions. Reform of the Labour Party constitution and the introduction of a 'one member, one vote' system for electing the leadership removed much of the direct, block vote influence trade unions had had on party policy and the selection of a new party leader. New Labour depends much less on financial support from trade unions as it did in the past, and controversially the Labour Party received large donations and loans from business firms and individual millionaires to bankroll its expensive election campaign in 2005.

Looking at these signs of political change it would be dangerously easy to conclude that New Labour has become a pro-business party in much the same way as the preceding Conservative administration was. Has Labour's employment policy been designed primarily with the welfare of employers in mind rather than that of the workers and unemployed people?

This question assumes that employers' and employees' interests *must* be in conflict with one another. But can pro-welfare employment policies – in some respects at least – be beneficial to both sides of industry, and do they necessarily favour one side's interests at the expense of the other? That employment policy can serve both the interests of labour and business would certainly be New Labour's claim. It is an argument that the government once put forward, in 1997, as a 'Third Way' between what is seen as old-fashioned socialism on the one hand and, on the other, the pro-business, individualistic market liberalism of the political right.

The evidence needs to be weighed carefully to judge whose interests are being served by recent employment policy. First, as Bevan (2000) shows, there are grounds for accepting the argument that 'family-friendly' employment policies of the kind Labour has introduced (for instance, limits on working time, parental leave, incentives to employers to improve child care facilities) are also in the interests of business. There is not always a conflict here, despite some costs to business, because 'family-friendly' policies do not only benefit employees, they also lift productivity because employees are more satisfied, and better able to work productively, when conflicts between the demands of work and family are reduced. Also, business firms are more likely to retain valued and skilled workers with children, and to attract productive workers with family commitments when they implement 'family-friendly' policies.

Second, as the example of the minimum wage shows, there is not necessarily a conflict of interest between having this policy and making profits or sustaining economic growth. The USA, a country devoted to free-market capitalism and minimal state control of business, nevertheless has a minimum wage policy. For the reasons discussed previously, a minimum wage tends to increase employment opportunities and general economic growth rather than acting as a burden on business.

Third, there are more general signs that the government's employment and economic policies have benefited both business and the majority of people in work in Britain. Not only have Labour policies apparently delivered full or near-full employment, but also the average wage has exceeded £20,000 for the first time. Increases in prosperity led to higher consumption and sales and thus greater market opportunities for business. To this can be added the effect of the WFTC and other tax credits and benefits in lifting the incomes of low earners. There is thus a strong case for concluding that New Labour has successfully followed employment and economic policies that have benefited the workforce as a whole, as well as business interests.

But if the question 'who has benefited more from government policies?' is considered from the employer's point of view, there is an understandable feeling that bearing the cost of Labour's employment and social security policies has been far from painless. Seen from this perspective, the answer would be that employees have gained a lot more than employers, and sometimes at employers' expense. As an illustration of this point of view, consider the following letter from a firm of consultant accountants to a small business:

19 September 2000

Dear Sir/Madam

What else do you have to do to run your payroll?
Over the last 12 months, in addition to actually running your basic payroll, you have had to add on the following responsibilities:

Minimum wage legislation (twice!)
Holiday entitlement legislation
Working time directive legislation
Working family tax credits

Disabled persons' tax credits
Parental leave
Emergency time off for dependants
Changes to maternity leave
Student loan deductions

As if all of this wasn't enough, from next year you also have to provide your staff with an approved pension scheme. At your expense.

> (The letter continues with advice on how to deal with the above obligations, and advertises the services of the consultants' company)

This illustration could give the wrong impression because it concentrates on the 'problems' and extra costs that changes in government policy have caused, rather than any of the advantages in recent employment policy. However, the letter is a rather telling reminder of the burden that has been placed on the shoulders of employers in recent years, both in administering new policies and paying for some of them.

Despite the impression among UK employers that they have had to adjust to a more complex, tightly-regulated set of policies than before, the government has made great play of its goal to create a relatively lightly regulated, flexible labour market in the UK. It has drawn contrasts between its own employment policies and those of most of the countries in western Europe. As mentioned above, countries such as France, Germany and Sweden have retained – despite some changes towards flexible employment policies – a more tightly regulated approach to labour relations. Comparisons between different countries' employment policies and their impact on employees' welfare can be misleading, however. While British workers' job security might not be protected by legislation as fully as workers in other European countries, we have seen in this chapter that job insecurity in the UK is not as widespread as is often believed.

On the other hand, if unemployment and job security are taken out of the picture, there is little doubt that some key aspects of workers' welfare are less well looked after in the UK than in other leading European countries. As mentioned earlier, British employees work longer hours, have fewer holiday entitlements, a lower minimum wage (compared to France), fewer training opportunities, less paid parental leave and poor child care facilities for children of working parents, compared to the European norm.

The employment prospects and welfare of disabled people are particularly poorly protected in the UK. According to a report by Burchardt (2000), not only do disabled people in the UK find it more difficult to find employment in the first place – even when qualified for the job – but also they are much more likely than other workers to lose their jobs within a year of starting. Employed disabled people are likely to have significantly lower earnings than their non-disabled peers, even when comparisons take account of age, qualifications and occupation.

Burchardt (2000) suggests that, though disabled employees face particular problems of discrimination and poor protection of their interests at work, their problems are shared with other groups in society that face economic exclusion. The position of disabled workers is representative of wider problems of inequality and discrimination in the labour market.

In sum, therefore, the UK has not witnessed the kind of economic and employment policies since 1997 that would have led to significant change in the labour market. Most observers of the New Deal and the other employment policies that Labour have implemented agree that they have led to modest improvements: declining unemployment, more training opportunities and better working conditions. However, much of the change, especially the decline in unemployment, has occurred because of economic growth rather than because of specific government employment policies.

Labour's aims in employment policy – though more sympathetic to workers' rights and welfare than the preceding Conservative administration's – are to steer the UK away from the much tighter regulation of working conditions and workers' rights that exists in other leading European states. In that respect recent employment policy in the UK tilts more towards employers' interests than employees' and reflects Labour's overt aim to be a pro-business government. Where employers' and employees' interests in improving employment conditions seem to coincide, there have been small but significant steps towards improved welfare at work.

Key terms and concepts

active labour market policy
business cycle
casualization
deregulation
disposable income
dual labour market
economic activity and the economically active
full employment
Keynesian strategy/policy
recession
social exclusion

Suggestions for further reading

For an overview and assessment of employment policies introduced by New Labour between 2001 and 2005, Polly Toynbee's and David Walker's *Better or Worse? Has Labour Delivered?* (2005) is a useful book to start with (see Chapter 2 especially). It summarizes the main objectives of the government's 'welfare to work' strategy and offers realistic, brief and trenchant comments on the government's successes and failures in employment policy.

Sarah Vickerstaff's excellent contribution to *Social Policy* (2003), edited by John Baldock and colleagues also provides an overview of employment policy and welfare – see her chapter on 'Work and welfare'.

Government publications must always be read sceptically because they are intended to show government efforts in the best light rather than give an objective account.

However, a publication by the Department of Social Security (DSS), *Opportunity for All* (2000) is worth consulting because it presents the full range of government initiatives in a particularly clear way. It not only lists and summarizes policies on employment and widening opportunities for people of working age, but also puts these alongside other policies that affect other groups (for example, the new deal for lone parents). A summary version of this publication can be accessed on the internet at www.dss.gov.uk (and, by the time you are reading this, *Opportunity for All* will have been succeeded by a current annual report).

Finally, to gain further insights into wider and more academic debates about employment policy, a book edited by John Philpott, *Working for Full Employment* (1997), is relevant because it includes chapters that discuss employment strategies in western Europe and the USA. This book is helpful in putting UK employment policies in context, and in extending the discussion of contrasts between British and other European countries' approaches to work and welfare that were introduced in this chapter.

9 ARE PROFESSIONALS GOOD FOR YOU? THE EXAMPLE OF HEALTH POLICY AND HEALTH PROFESSIONALS

Introduction
Health, illness, modern medicine and health policy
  The health professions: too much power?
A crisis of confidence in the medical profession
  Flaws in service delivery
Medical and nursing professions in the development of the NHS
  The advantages and limitations of the NHS
The health professions and health service reform
  The NHS and the medical profession in a new era of uncertainty
Conclusions
Key terms and concepts
Suggestions for further reading

Introduction

Consider some personal situations in which you have been treated by a health professional such as a doctor, dentist, nurse or an expert with particular skills such as a physiotherapist. For example, think about reclining in a dentist's chair. The dentist is hovering above, ready to administer a local anaesthetic. Although anticipation of pain might be uppermost in your mind, there may be some other thoughts: how effective will this course of treatment be? How much will it cost, and who will be paying? If you have to bear most of the cost, is this fair and can you afford it?

Although you may be concentrating on how to get through the next 15 minutes, other thoughts may flit across your mind: what are your impressions of the equipment or 'technology' used by the dentist? Who paid for it? How considerate or friendly is the dentist, and how good are they at finding out what you need? When and where did the dentist receive training, and do you have confidence that they will not hit a sensitive nerve?

The more we reflect on personal experiences such as this, whether with a dentist, a nurse, a doctor or a therapist, the more we come to realize that what happens – the outcome of the course of treatment – is not simply the result of an individual professional treating an individual patient. Individual outcomes are also affected by broader factors, such as the following.

- *Government policy*: for instance, how much treatment and what kinds of treatment, if any, will be provided 'free' at the point of use for patients? How does this affect our willingness to use health services?
- *Technology*: what have advances in the 'tools' available (medical equipment and techniques, drugs and other therapies) done to change our experience of medical treatment, of going into hospital or going to the dentist's?
- *The 'market' in health care*: is demand for health care and for particular treatments – whether through the NHS or on a private basis – high or low? Are doctors, nurses, radiographers or speech therapists in short supply? How difficult was it for you to obtain an appointment with the practitioner, and were you placed on a waiting list?
- *The professions*: are medical professionals and practitioners such as dentists able to dictate the level or quality of treatment given to patients? Are they able to insist on certain professional standards of treatment, or are they sometimes forced to provide cheaper, short-term remedies?

These are just four major types of background influences on the relationship between the medical professional and the user of health services. They show that professionals alone do not determine outcomes. Professionals themselves operate in a world of constraints, costs and opportunities. However, this chapter, in addressing the fundamental question 'Are professionals good for you?' will focus on the role of the professional as a key actor in social policy. The examples in this chapter are taken from the field of health, but some of the lessons about professional power and influence that we may learn from them can be applied to other parts of the welfare system. For instance, in the personal social services, probation, housing and planning, education and training, similar questions can be asked about how much trust should be placed in professionals and practitioners. How much freedom of action and responsibility should they be given to make policy, or to provide services as they see fit?

Health, illness, modern medicine and health policy

The wider social and economic influences on what happens to us in the doctor's surgery or the hospital are reflected in government policy. What the government can afford by way of health services, the rising cost of drugs, what the public expects from health services, developments in medical technology and many other factors all contribute to the shaping of health policy. This in turn will constrain what an individual doctor, dentist or nurse can offer.

However, health policy is not solely something to do with medical experts or health services. Of course, medical treatment may enhance health. Unless a decaying tooth is filled it may be lost, leading to other problems and poorer dental health. Sometimes, however, treatment may actually make no difference or, even worse, may adversely affect health. *Iatrogenic diseases* are those that result from medical intervention or from medical complications following treatment.

In general, health and illness is decided by many factors other than individual treatment. Dental health, for example, is much affected by diet and lifestyle (for example, how much sugary food we eat, and how often) and by preventive health policies such as fluoridization of water supplies, something which has had a very marked effect on reducing the incidence of tooth decay in children.

In sum, 'health policy' can be defined in two ways – either as:

- government efforts and policy to improve health through the health services and medical treatment; or as
- any government activity that affects health and illness, not just the activities of the Department of Health (DoH), the NHS, health professionals or other health services.

The second, broader definition of health policy shows that it is related to many other policies: for instance, taxation of sales of tobacco, or the effectiveness of regulations on air and water pollution, the safety of food and of the working environment.

Health, illness and poverty in developing countries clearly illustrate how health and illness are often more influenced by policies in other fields than health services. Agricultural and food policies, for instance, may have a much greater impact than health care on children's life expectancy if they succeed in stimulating the production and distribution of nutritious local foods. Similarly, economic or agricultural policies to increase the production of cash crops can have the effect of raising the cost of locally produced foods and thus threaten balanced diets and the health of children in the poorest families.

Another example of the connections between environment and health can be seen in research on inequalities in health. For example, a study by Phillimore *et al.* (1994) of mortality rates in northern England showed an *increase* in death rates in the poorest communities. This is an alarming trend because, although there are persistent health inequalities between better-off and poorer sections of society, it was thought that the health of poorer groups was improving, albeit more slowly than among the better-off. The research by Phillimore *et al.* shows that widening material inequalities – and, in particular, the effects of poverty, poor nutrition and unemployment on middle-aged men – are the primary cause of increasing health inequality. Higher rates of illness and death in some sections of the population are clearly linked to environmental factors and, faced with these problems, the impact of health services and modern medicine is limited.

This is perhaps even more the case because concerns about health and the role of health services often neglect the less visible or glamorous preventive and environmental services. *Curative* services and the work of doctors, nurses and other specialists in front-line medicine succeed in gaining a lot more public attention than *preventive* services, as illustrated by strong interest in medical dramas such as the American series *ER* or the BBC's *Casualty*. However, the chief role of curative health services is to deal with illness or injury that has already occurred. Curative services play an insignificant role in improving general health. Arguably the contribution of the less glamorous, behind-the-scenes preventive services can be much greater, though even here their contribution can be overestimated; social and environmental factors are the main determinants of health and illness.

Going back to the dentist's chair, for instance, perhaps a more pertinent question to ask than 'will this treatment work?' would be, 'why am I here at all?' or 'why have preventive services not worked, in my case?' Seen in this light, the assumption that health services and health professionals play a major part in making people healthy must be seriously questioned. However, the work of health professionals is important and can contribute to improving quality of life when people have fallen ill.

In relation to more serious illnesses, there have been remarkable improvements in medical treatment. Advances in keyhole surgery and in anaesthesia, to give just two examples, have enabled operations to be performed on very old patients, for whom some treatments (under general anaesthetic) would formerly have been too risky.

Modern health services therefore face a set of priorities and needs which are entirely different from those of 100 or even 50 years ago. Acute illnesses or life-threatening (mainly infectious) diseases have been replaced by long-term or chronic illnesses or conditions as the more prevalent forms of illness: examples are rheumatoid arthritis, multiple sclerosis, diabetes, asthma and various forms of mental illness. Death is now often preceded by relatively long periods of disability. Medical services and treatments may assist with the control and management of symptoms, but they can rarely cure these diseases.

The health professions: too much power?

A number of sociologists and other critics of the medical profession have put forward the idea that it does indeed have too much power over policy and patients. But to justify this argument, somewhat different explanations have been put forward. Feminists suggest that the rise of the medical profession has provided a vehicle for medically-trained men to exercise power over women. For example, Donnison (1988) shows how professional men began to gain control of midwifery from the eighteenth century onwards.

Another kind of explanation has been put forward by Illich (1990), who argues that modern medicine has actively 'colonized' areas of our lives that formerly were not medicalized or subject to the scrutiny and control of the medical profession. In Illich's eyes, the medical profession has become an exploitative and disabling influence on society. It has sought to capitalize on patients' vulnerability by making them ever more dependent on medical solutions for their ills (in the form of drug-based treatments, surgery and hospitalization) when, according to Illich, the solutions lie more in a basic change to healthier ways of life and patterns of consumption.

One problem with Illich's view is that it puts a lot of emphasis on the medical profession's own actions and its ability to colonize or dominate health policy. But we do not have to put all the blame on the shoulders of doctors to conclude that much of what doctors are expected to do is inappropriate to our needs. As Kennedy (1980: 641) put it, 'We have all been willing participants in the creation of a myth' of modern medicine, 'because it seems to serve our interests to believe that illness can be vanquished and death postponed until further notice'.

Thus the medicalization of social problems – the tendency to seek medical solutions to socially-influenced ills such as depression or sadness, unemployment and redundancy, poverty and isolation – could be part of society's response to deeper or more fundamental changes.

De Swaan (1989) suggests that the medical profession does not so much set out to dominate society as fill a void by responding to a growing demand for the medicalization of people's problems. He gives other examples of the ways in which decisions and policies have become increasingly 'medical' in recent decades. For instance, medicalization can be observed in decisions about offenders and whether they should be 'treated' rather than punished or simply kept in prison. It can also be seen in the use of medical advice in assessing the income support needs of disabled people and in the increasing use of medical checks in employment, recruitment and the world of mortgage and life insurance (de Swaan 1989: 1167).

Another illustration of the medicalization of the social world is suicide and self-harm. Self-harm is committed by many thousands of people each year. It includes not only those who end their lives but also those who disable themselves, sometimes permanently, as a result of drug overdoses or other actions. However, some think that the government's confidence in the medical profession's ability to deal effectively with these problems is misplaced. As Taylor and Field (1997: 147–8) suggest, in the case of suicide and self-harm the influence of a medical approach to these problems may be more likely to make them worse than better.

These examples illustrate the limitations of modern medicine. However, a balanced view must recognize that the influential role of doctors is partly the product of social demands and pressures. These include consumer demand for medical solutions to personal and social problems, for new medical treatments and the development of medical technology.

If the medical profession were all-powerful, the status and role of doctors would be broadly similar in every society. However, as de Swaan (1989) suggests, the position of the medical profession varies considerably in relation to the health services of different countries, together with the amount of power or influence it has over health policy.

In fact, the status and power of the medical profession also varies over time. This can be demonstrated by the changing role of doctors in Britain's health service. In recent years there has been a lot of upheaval and reorganization in the NHS and this has significantly affected the status and role of doctors and how much control they have been able to exercise over health services. The roles of the nursing profession and of other health care practitioners and professionals have also been much affected, not only in relation to their work with doctors but also in terms of their general position in the NHS and in the wider society.

In the remainder of this chapter, we shall look first at how and why a crisis in the role of the medical profession has developed in recent years, and how public confidence in the competence and ability of doctors to provide adequate standards of medical care has been badly dented. Second, we shall look at key aspects of current health policy and at recent health service reforms to examine how far they are likely to succeed in addressing the crisis in health care. Is current health policy likely to generate greater confidence in health services and health professionals?

A crisis of confidence in the medical profession

There are several important signs of a growing crisis of confidence in Britain's medical profession and in the ability of the NHS to provide effective health care treatment. One of these is a steep rise in the number of dissatisfied patients who claim to have been harmed by faulty medical practice and a corresponding rise in the cost of settling claims of medical negligence. As one observer reports, the cost to the NHS of medical negligence claims had already reached £3.9 billion by 2001 (Sherman 2001: 4), an amount that had doubled since 1998, and the NHS currently faces an even higher number of outstanding claims.

However, as the same observer points out, not all the increase in willingness to take legal action against the medical profession is a result of an objective decline in professional standards. Perhaps just as many mistakes in medical practice were made in the past. In more recent times, several factors have lessened a traditional reluctance in Britain to challenge medical opinion and practice. These factors include the exploration of medical errors and dilemmas in 'popular television series [such as] *ER*, medical diagnoses on the internet and a climate where complaints against all public services are encouraged' (Sherman 2001: 4).

But it is important to stress that the current crisis of confidence in medical expertise has not been caused simply by the spread of increasingly well informed and disillusioned public perceptions of doctors or greater willingness to challenge medical authority. It seems as though the traditions of secrecy and professional autonomy that used to hide the true scale of medical error are being removed (Boseley 2000a; Gibbs 2000). A more objective picture can now be seen – a picture that can be pieced together by various public inquiries and reports that have followed in the wake of tragic cases of professional incompetence and wrongdoing.

The following examples illustrate a number of disturbing questions about the safety and effectiveness of medical treatment. These examples of medical error and malpractice also show how further doubts have arisen about the ability of the medical profession to regulate itself. Self-regulation is of key importance to any professional group that wants to maintain a high level of status and professional authority. But as these examples show, trust in the medical profession to manage itself has been dealt a severe blow.

- *The Shipman case:* Harold Shipman, a general practitioner (GP) working in Hyde, near Manchester, was found guilty of murdering 15 of his women patients. It is suspected that many more – possibly as many as 250 – patients have been killed by Shipman. One of the most important lessons to be learned from this case has been that there was no central checking system or established procedure for analysing the unusual pattern of sudden deaths that took place for years in Shipman's practice. If such a central checking system had been in place this doctor's lethal activities would have been detected much earlier than they were. As it was, lack of effective regulation by the medical authorities was a contributory factor in the large number of fatalities. Dr Shipman worked as a single-handed GP, thereby eluding detection much longer than might have been possible in a group practice, and this underlines the need for careful monitoring of the work of independent practitioners. However, another unfortunate consequence of the Shipman case, discussed widely in the medical profession in 2006, has been the reluctance of some GPs to prescribe pain-killing drugs to patients who desperately need large and frequent doses of them. The GPs' caution and their withholding of these drugs can be explained by their worry that they might be accused of murder.

- *The Elwood case:* James Elwood was a consultant at the Swindon and Marlborough NHS Trust when, in 1999, staff at the hospital where he worked decided to review 400 of the cervical smear tests that he had analysed and taken treatment decisions about. This first check showed a serious mismatch between the test results and the problems being presented by patients at the outpatient gynaecology clinic. As a result, a much wider investigation of Elwood's work was carried out, involving 10,358 cases at hospitals in different parts of southern England (Gibbs 2000). This revealed serious concerns about a pattern of misdiagnosis in Elwood's medical career. Some patients had received unnecessary treatment for cervical and other forms of cancer while others were shocked to discover that they still needed cancer checks – and in some cases urgent treatment – when they thought they were clear of the disease. Some medical opinion suggested that Elwood's diagnosis errors were no worse than average and had led to clinically serious consequences in less than 1 per cent of his patients (Boseley 2000a). However, this example is important because it shows not just that one doctor's actions might have been harmful, but also the failure of the professional system to systematically check the work of individual practitioners.

- *Heart surgery at Bristol Royal Infirmary:* government concern to make the medical profession more accountable had already been growing for several years before the two cases described above. There had been particular concern after the publication of an inquiry into the deaths of babies in Bristol Royal Infirmary between 1984 and 1995 following heart surgery. It was found that the two surgeons who carried out this work had continued even though they should have known that the survival rate of the babies they operated on was significantly worse than at other hospitals (Kennedy 2001).

- *Inadequate regulation of locum doctors:* this was brought to public attention by the tragic death in 1998 of Darren Denholm, a 10-year-old boy who died during what should have been a routine tooth extraction. Dr Evans-Appiah, a locum doctor who had trained overseas and was registered as a dental anaesthetist, administered a general anaesthetic but made serious mistakes in doing so – and as a result caused the death of the patient. He was found guilty of 17 charges of malpractice in October 2000 (Boseley 2000b). Incredibly, however, Dr Evans-Appiah was allowed to continue working after the death of Darren Denholm. Three weeks after his death, this doctor bungled the administration of an anaesthetic to a woman about to have a caesarian section to deliver her baby. She suffered intense pain when the anaesthetic failed to work during the operation. This example illustrates not just individual failure to meet professional standards but also a failure of the NHS to adequately regulate the work of a large number of locum doctors, upon whom the health service is heavily reliant in certain areas.

- *Ageism in medical practitioners' and nurses' attitudes to patients:* this is a rather different point from those made above. However, it has also dented public confidence in doctors and other health care workers. Older people (aged over 65) represent less than a fifth of the population but make up over half of all hospital patients. Therefore the discovery of widespread ageism in the health service has extremely important implications. Age discrimination in health services has been known about for some time and a recent survey has confirmed that younger patients are twice as likely as older ones to be given the best available treatment (Browne 2000).

When considering the significance of the above examples of medical error, malpractice and discrimination, it is important to remember that most medical treatments are carried out satisfactorily. More than this, many contrasting examples of medicine and nursing could be found to demonstrate high levels of care and professional commitment. For every rare case of a doctor or nurse who is allowed to continue killing or at least risking the lives of patients over a long period of time there are many more who are dedicated and professional – but who make an occasional mistake. One of the main problems of health policy has been to discover a way of safely monitoring the work of medical professionals without excessive central control and regulation, and without further undermining the professional credibility of medical staff.

Flaws in service delivery

A key problem in this respect is deciding how far the professional doctor or nurse has been personally responsible for flaws in health care and how far problems have resulted from shortcomings in the health service.

For instance, health care trusts differ in their willingness to pay for expensive drugs and to provide them free to their patients. Boseley (2001) reports on a case that illustrates these area differences – that of a woman aged 79 who faced losing expensive treatments for Alzheimer's disease when she moved house to live near her daughter. Such cases have been termed examples of 'postcode prescribing'. They are continuing to occur despite the setting up of a national body, the National Institute for Health and Clinical Excellence (NICE), which is designed to regulate the treatments that are available free of charge under the NHS and to bring equality of treatment between different areas (see further discussion of the role of NICE below). Controversy arose more recently over NICE's decision to restrict the use of such drugs for treating Alzheimer's to those with a moderate form of the condition (Jack and Timmins 2006). Another much-publicized recent case was that of Anne-Marie Rogers, a sufferer from breast cancer, who failed initially, and then succeeded, in her attempt to use the courts to force her local primary care trust (PCT) to fund the prescription of the anti-cancer drug Herceptin (Tait 2006). The PCT's refusal to allow prescription of the drug was a clear case of 'postcode rationing' in that funding for the drug was available in more than a dozen other areas (Jack 2006; Tait 2006).

Problems continue because health authorities and trusts control their own budgets and have different spending priorities. A consultant might wish to prescribe a certain drug or treatment but knows that the health trust will not pay for it. Medical professionals might be involved in the decisions made at local level about which treatments should be provided to patients, but nevertheless might not have as free a hand to prescribe expensive or unusual treatments as many patients and members of the public assume they have. Consequently, some of the current crisis of confidence affecting the health care professions originates not so much in the failings of the professions themselves as in local variations in the NHS system for deciding which treatments are to be 'free'. Also, there is a general pressure on the NHS to limit spending on expensive treatments.

A similar point can be made about public concern over waiting lists. Waiting times become a problem for doctors, nurses and other health care workers because they are the front-line staff who must explain to anxious or angry patients why delays in treatment are occurring. They also have to take hard decisions about which patients should have priority in the queue. As a result, the waiting list and waiting times have become another factor that can undermine the status and respect generally accorded to the medical and nursing professions. While many discontented patients might continue to respect hard-pressed medical staff and blame a faulty health care system for delays in treatment, some might not – the individual consultant or doctor will be blamed for the delay. For instance this can occur because of delays some patients have experienced in obtaining a first appointment with a consultant (patients who have not been seen by a consultant are not officially on a waiting list). The number of patients experiencing such delays (waiting for more than three months to see a specialist) increased from 247,488 in 1997 to almost 400,000 by the end of the year 2000 (Carvel 2001: 4). Delays in waiting for outpatient treatment also increased rapidly during the same period. The total of people on out-patient waiting lists more than doubled, though it was successfully brought down to near-1997 levels as the 2001 general election approached. Since then, as a result of in-creased spending on measures to reduce waiting times and lists, the situation has sig-nificantly improved in England, though in Wales's devolved NHS there was a marked lag in improvement between 2001 and 2005.

In 2004 the DoH established a new target for maximum hospital waiting times of 18 weeks, to be reached by 2008. The average wait should, however, be only 9 or 10 weeks. It was intended that the 'clock' for waiting times should start ticking from the date of a GP's referral of a patient to hospital, not when the hospital consultant put the patient on the list (Toynbee and Walker 2005: 12).

In addition to dealing with disquiet or discontent about variations in treatments available and delays in obtaining treatment, medical professionals must also cope with other strains in the NHS. For instance, there have been mounting concerns about dirty hospitals (the government set up a task force in 2001 to try to reduce the problems of infection and other health risks resulting from poor hygiene in hospitals). The problem of hospital cross-infection with the MRSA 'superbug' has continued to plague the NHS and the DoH. There has also been public concern about second-rate dental treatment for NHS patients and about breaches of confidentiality when medical records of patients have been released inadvertently by administrative or medical staff.

Thus there are many concerns about the poor quality of health services in the UK. As we have seen, some of these concerns are being expressed because of objectively poor standards of care – for instance, waiting times, discrimination against older patients, dirty hospitals. Rising concern can also be explained by subjective factors or changing public attitudes. There are rising public expectations of what the health service should be able to provide, and greater public awareness of what the latest medical treatments can achieve. Conversely, people are also increasingly aware of the limitations and flaws in modern medical practice. Either way, medical professionals are increasingly exposed to challenges to the traditional basis upon which their status and authority depended.

Medical and nursing professions in the development of the NHS

To understand professional power and its influence on health policy more fully, we need to consider how the health professions – and especially doctors – were incorporated into the NHS in the first place. Understanding the choices that were made in the 1940s about the kind of health service Britain was to have throws light on the choices and dilemmas facing us today about what kind of health service we want.

The introduction of the NHS after the Second World War represented one of the more radical and socialist policies in the Labour government's welfare state programme. The NHS Bill put before Parliament in 1946 proposed sweeping changes, but it also entrenched medical professional power in various ways. With the NHS, Britain was given a health service in which the GP was to act as a gatekeeper to specialist care or hospital treatment. The patient firstly had to convince the GP that they were a 'suitable case' for further treatment before accessing other services.

Also, the NHS contract hammered out between the medical profession and the government in 1948, when the health service began to operate, was to make GPs *independent contractors* to the NHS, not *salaried employees* of the health service. This deal was struck mainly to protect the professional independence of family doctors. Therefore Britain developed a health service in which a key role – acting as gatekeeper to other services – was to be played by professionals who saw themselves as a somewhat independent and separate group. Britain did not develop an integrated service of salaried doctors in which GPs, specialist doctors, the hospitals and community or preventive health services worked closely together.

The advantages and limitations of the NHS

However, the NHS became a justifiably popular institution. The concept of free health care for everyone enshrined certain values of equality, fairness and compassion. Thus the NHS became a defining characteristic of the British way of life, much as the BBC and other national institutions did in postwar society. More than one commentator described the NHS as 'the sacred cow of British politics'. Others, such as the former Labour Secretary of State Barbara Castle, have described the NHS as a 'church'; the implication of this sort of label is that the system has value over and above the value of the medical care provided and the reductions in illness and disease that result. In the words of Rudolf Klein, ' ... the NHS was seen to have a moral, as well as a scientific, mission' (1993: 137).

The advantages of a health service designed like the NHS can be summarized in the following ways:

- easy access to services;
- universal coverage;
- equality and economy;
- avoiding the commercialization of health care;
- professionalism.

Despite the positive aspects of the NHS, the British public has always had worries about its performance in relation to specific issues such as waiting lists. However, until recently public opinion in the UK has tended to endorse and approve the original design. Other countries' health services were usually compared unfavourably with Britain's NHS, especially on the point of the main virtue of the NHS – 'free' health care for everyone, whatever their status, provided according to need.

In the last few years, though, growing concern about the effectiveness and safety of treatment provided by consultants and medical professionals, as discussed above, has fed deeper unease about the drawbacks of having the kind of health service that Britain introduced in 1948. The limitations of the 'NHS design' for health services can be summarized as follows.

- Queuing for, and rationing of, medical services. Access to 'free' services might be a good thing but, unless medical facilities and staffing are increased to keep up with demand, it leads to the formation of long waiting lists. Medical professionals often have to take hard decisions about which patients are to be given priority, and are thus accused of 'rationing' medical services.
- The universally available family doctor service can act more like a barrier slowing access to other services than as a link promptly facilitating access to specialist services.
- The quality and effectiveness of the NHS is patchy. Survival rates after treatment for cancer, for instance, vary widely from one district to another. In practice there is often a two-tier health service, with world-class treatments and highly effective specialists in some areas and second-rate treatment in others.
- Until recently, the UK has managed to spend significantly less of its national income on health services than comparable countries have. As already mentioned, economy and cost containment are advantages of the NHS system. However, this is also a drawback. As discussed earlier in the chapter, the strains of running a health service with a minimum of resources are now glaringly obvious, especially as evidenced by delays in obtaining treatment, and poorer outcomes after treatment when compared with outcomes in other European countries.

The role of the medical profession in the NHS, though it has brought some advantages, has also brought serious drawbacks in the way the health service has been run.

In 1948 the government gave the medical profession a very free hand and a lot of power to run the health service. In particular, consultants were given the largest say in deciding on how medical services should develop in the hospitals, and they took the key policy decisions about spending priorities. While this brought some benefits to the NHS and encouraged the development of leading medical research in certain specialisms, it also distorted the development of health services. Often, facilities were developed more in line with consultants' professional interests and the more glamorous, high prestige areas of medicine (for example, heart surgery) than with health care needs in the surrounding community. Public health services and geriatric medicine, for instance, tended to be neglected. Also, giving the doctors a great deal of power and responsibility in running the health service added to the problem of lack of accountability in the NHS, and has fostered an atmosphere in which the medical profession can be seen as acting in a high-handed or arrogant way.

The health professions and health service reform

Concern about the limitations of the NHS is not new and in one way or another has been expressed ever since the NHS was brought into being (Klein 2006). Because both the medical profession and the NHS have traditionally enjoyed a lot of public respect, however, governments have been wary of introducing any fundamental changes. Even Mrs Thatcher's Conservative government, inspired by the 'radical' ideas of the pro-market, anti-welfare state right, did not dare to attempt a root and branch reform of health services in Britain.

On the other hand, a succession of important reforms to the structure of the NHS have been introduced since 1974. The pace of change and reform has quickened since the late 1980s, reflecting government concern about public dissatisfaction with the health service and questions about the effectiveness of the medical profession. Recent change in the health service prompts the question of whether the power of the health professions is as strong as it was.

For instance, a key reform was introduced at the end of Mrs Thatcher's period in office – the NHS and Community Care Act 1990. Well before this major change was introduced, policy thinking had been shaped by an influential report (DHSS 1983) on the need for management reform in the NHS. Sir Roy Griffiths – an independent adviser to the government and chief executive of Sainsbury's supermarkets – wrote this report (not to be confused with Griffiths's later report on community care – see Griffiths 1988).

Sir Roy's 1983 report paved the way for a great deal of internal change in the structure of the NHS during the 1980s. It introduced the concept of the *general manager* – a powerful role which Griffiths had envisaged as leading and controlling the competing interests of the various professional groups in the health service (doctors, nurses and the various therapeutic professions).

Doctors were to face further changes in the way in which hospitals and the health system as a whole were to be run. The most important change was the introduction of an *internal market* into the NHS – the main purpose of the NHS and Community Care Act 1990.

As a result of this legislation, the existing administrative structure of the NHS was broken up. Rather than the DoH funding each health authority according to a complicated formula based on health needs in the area and patients' use of services, a market system of funding meant that money was supposed to 'follow the patient'. Just as with other public services that were subjected to market reforms by the Thatcher and Major governments, the health service was divided into groups of 'purchasers' and 'providers' of health services. Health service providers (for instance, hospital trusts) were expected to compete to provide their services, with the aim of increasing efficiency and awareness of the costs and benefits of NHS services.

The internal market system introduced into the NHS by the Conservatives was formally scrapped as a result of Labour government reforms after 1997. In some respects, however, New Labour has subsequently shifted its position on the NHS, at least in England, if not in the rest of the UK, in ways which can be seen as a return to aspects of the regime established by the Conservatives after 1991. There may appear to be little point in examining the details of the Conservative reforms or the degree to which they actually succeeded in meeting their aims. The verdict of evaluative research is a mixed one (Le Grand *et al*. 1998; Ham 2004: 44–7). The Conservative reforms were inherently hard to evaluate for various reasons, not least because the plans were modified in the process of implementation and afterwards. Also, the effects of the reforms are hard to disentangle from the effects of other policy changes occurring at the same time. It is worth bearing in mind the view of observers like Rudolf Klein that, in relation to NHS reform, 'implementation is all' (Klein 1998: v).

In many respects the Conservative 'blueprint' was watered-down. By 1996 and the last Conservative White Paper on the NHS, not much apparently remained of the original conception of a market-driven, competitive system in which the preferences of the health care consumer/patient shaped developments (DoH 1996; Ham 2004: 50–52). It has been argued that professional medical power was not seriously dented by the management and market reforms of the 1990s, even though doctors have had to cope with a great deal of change.

This is because, it has been suggested, some doctors came to have more, not less, power over their patients as a result of the internal market. There was, for example, the danger of 'cream-skimming' by some GPs – that is, deterring the more costly, chronically ill patients from registering with their practices and attracting the healthier, less costly ones (Robinson and Le Grand 1994), and although the internal market was meant to give consumer choice to the patient, in practice it was usually the GP or specialist doctor who chose which hospital or treatment the patient was to be referred to. Thus money tended to follow the choices made by doctors, on their patients' behalf, rather than following the patient as an independent consumer. Increasing numbers of doctors became experienced in the new style of management (Hunter 1992). Instead of being frozen out of vital decisions by non-medical managers, many began to adopt new strategies to protect their professional dominance.

The conclusion of one observer, reflecting other findings, is, however, that 'the change in behaviour and culture was nevertheless tangible ... the separation of purchaser and provider responsibilities altered the organizational politics of the NHS leading to changes in the balance of power both within the medical profession and between doctors and managers' (Ham 2004: 46–7).

The NHS and the medical profession in a new era of uncertainty

One of New Labour's main objectives when elected in 1997 was to make significant improvements to British people's health. In line with this objective, the health services were to be rebuilt. The government put forward its plans in a White Paper, *The New NHS: Modern, Dependable* (DoH 1997). At the same time, though, the government was also determined to restrain public expenditure to the targets outlined by the previous Conservative administration. This meant, in effect, that – as with education policy – the government's health objectives in its first years in office were addressed without a significant injection of extra money.

The emphasis was on achieving change through yet further reorganization and re-direction of resources within the NHS, rather than on improving the facilities, staffing and resources available to the health service that were inherited from the Conservatives. In fact, however, the NHS (like education) was relatively generously treated during the first term of the Blair government in comparison with the rest of the public sector, receiving higher than average annual increases in funding by comparison with other services, and by comparison with the later years of the Major Government: 4.8 per cent per year, compared with a historical average of 3 per cent (Ham 2004: 61–2; Glennerster 2005: 286).

Qualitative improvements in NHS funding have taken place since 2000, and the government has sought to increase significantly the amount of public money to be spent on health services. In January 2000 the Prime Minister promised, in a television interview, to increase the rate of spending on the NHS to bring it up to the level of the EU average. Implementation of the promise began in the March 2000 Budget with NHS spending increases of £2 billion above those set out in the 1998 Comprehensive Spending Review and a commitment to increase funding by a third in real terms in five years.

The government's commitment to health and the NHS therefore appears to be strong. Some of this commitment has been stimulated by the apparent failure of New Labour in its 1997–2001 term in office to improve NHS performance significantly. The government was stung by comparisons on health spending between the UK and other western European countries, which in the majority of cases show that Britain has been spending significantly less per head on health services. Having made strong public commitments to improving health services, the government felt it had to meet its promises or suffer increasingly damaging electoral consequences. Also, there is a genuine impulse in government circles to change the priorities of health policy by, for instance, bringing greater attention to connections between the environment and health, and reducing some of the stark inequality in disease between poorer and better-off groups in society.

In its second and third terms in office, tracking the twists and turns of New Labour's approach to reforming the NHS has in some respects been hard. Quite apart from the complexities brought about by greater devolution within the UK, NHS policy in England has undergone a number of changes of direction and emphasis. However, taking a broader view, Labour's policies on the NHS do not seem to have changed fundamentally from its policy during the 1997–2001 term. The emphasis on quality and performance has continued. While it was true that significantly more money was channelled into the

NHS, the government tried to follow a policy of releasing extra money only if certain conditions were met, and improvements in performance achieved. As in education, the government plans to extend and expand various ways of testing the quality and performance of health services. The aim is to develop a more 'patient-centred' NHS (see below), but to do this by making the NHS more accountable to a range of inspectorates and quangos that are charged with the task of monitoring health care standards.

Clearly, the strengthening of procedures to make doctors, nurses and other health service groups more accountable to bodies that supervise and stand outside the NHS will have important implications for the issues of professional power, competence and freedom to run health services, as discussed earlier.

To understand this, we need to review briefly what the main aims of current health policy are. Following the publication of a White Paper on 'the New NHS' in 1997, and various other consultation documents, wide-ranging health reforms were discussed in Parliament, leading to the passing of a Health Act in 1999. This Act, together with other legislation, brought about certain key changes in the NHS and its relationship with professional groups.

- The internal market in the NHS, introduced by the Conservatives during the 1990s to stimulate competition between a variety of health service providers was, formally at least, replaced by a policy of encouraging cooperation and partnership between health services, and between the NHS, social services and other care providers.
- A degree of purchaser–provider separation was, however, retained, as was the Conservative emphasis on the development of primary care, via GP fundholding. New Labour clearly recognized that purchaser–provider separation and the creation of primary care commissioning had brought some benefits. Labour built on and expanded the Conservative experiment by, in effect, making all GPs 'fundholders'. To achieve this, the 1997 White Paper proposed the establishment of *primary care groups* (PCGs). These organizations were to oversee the delivery of primary health care to the local community (mainly through the GP service), but also 'commissioned' other services (mainly in hospitals) for local patients. Thus PCGs not only directed resources to primary care itself, but also controlled some of the resources available to NHS trusts (hospitals and community health services) and other health service organizations. In 2001 PCGs were established in every area of England and controlled two-thirds of the £20 billion NHS budget in that year (see Chapter 12 for an outline of the different ways of administering the NHS in Northern Ireland, Scotland and Wales).
- The Health Act 1999 had envisaged the possibility of converting PCGs into PCTs. The government proposed an acceleration of the process of conversion of PCGs into PCTs. This was a product of an initiative, an implementation follow-up to the NHS Plan of 2000, entitled *Shifting the Balance of Power* (DoH 2001). The government aimed to give PCTs control of 75 per cent of the NHS budget by 2004.
- The government have committed themselves more firmly than ever to the idea of a 'patient-led' NHS, to the expansion of patient choice and, in principle, to a

greater devolution of decision-making responsibility to lower levels in the system. The creation of PCTs and, more recently so-called 'foundation hospitals' – practically a return to the original Conservative trust idea – bear witness to this. On the other hand, all this is taking place in a context of a commitment to central regulation, enshrined in the 1997 White Paper's principle of a return to a 'national' service, embodied in National Service Frameworks for particular conditions and treatments, and the work of NICE, referred to below. There are clear differences of view within the government about the degree of devolution, independence and the extent of market freedom within the NHS, between on the one hand the Prime Minister and a succession of secretaries of state since the departure of Frank Dobson in 2001, and Gordon Brown and the Treasury on the other. The former were committed to greater devolution, provider pluralism and choice, the latter to the retention of a more centralized, public model and central control (Brown 2003).

- Recent policies are beginning to change doctors' contracts with the NHS. The government is aware of the limitations of the capitation system for funding GPs, for instance. In its place, the government is introducing what it sees as 'modern' contracts for GPs and hospital doctors. These contracts are 'quality-based' and make payment to doctors more conditional upon reaching certain performance targets. Consultants will also be able to receive substantial increases in pay, but must raise their 'productivity' – for instance, numbers of successfully completed operations – in order to do so. GPs will have to meet specified improvements in preventive care and the quality of their services to patients.

- There will be more central regulation and inspection of the health service. Standards of health care and health service delivery will be monitored by NICE, which, among other things, decides which drugs and new treatments are to be available to patients 'free' on the NHS. Another regulatory body, the Commission for Health Improvement (CHI) (after various re-namings now known as the Healthcare Commission) was set up to inspect standards of hospital and primary health care. The role of the Healthcare Commission is intended to be like that of Ofsted's role in providing league tables of schools and colleges (see Chapter 7). For example, the Commission publishes patient survival rates after various hospital treatments and operations, thus creating hospital performance league tables.

Conclusions

As mentioned at the start of this chapter, professionals – though given enormous responsibility in many situations – themselves operate in a world of constraints and uncertainties. In addition to the ethical and moral choices professionals are called on to make, there are the constraints of government health policy, the cost and feasibility of providing services, and so on.

Therefore, while health professionals can easily become too dominant or may be expected to have the final say in resolving a dilemma, it would be wrong to portray the medical profession as an all-powerful group which always acts in a single-minded, unified and self-interested way. The medical profession is not a homogeneous group. Also, the other health professions (for example, nursing and the various therapies, such as physiotherapy) have always been divided in their attitudes towards health policy, as shown by the history of the NHS and in arguments between them and doctors about recent health reforms.

Another point to be underlined is that, despite the attention drawn to the shortcomings and flaws of health professionals in this chapter, there are many altruistic, caring and public-spirited professionals. Nor is it true to say that professional interests are always narrow, or self-seeking, or against the public interest. Often, the professional approach benefits the patient, and the interests of the professional and the patient coincide (for instance, in raising standards of post-operative care, or investment in medical research that leads to treatment breakthroughs).

However, in promoting a curative approach to medicine which downplays the economic, social and environmental causes of disease, the professional tradition in medicine inevitably draws doctors and other health professionals into supporting a health system that does relatively little to improve health. If all health practitioners were suddenly removed from society, and if every hospital and doctor's surgery were to be closed, their absence would hardly be noticed in terms of the amount of illness or the death rate. What *would* be noticed, of course, is a great deal more pain, discomfort and uncertainty. The health professions and health services play a very important role in managing illness, but a much less effective role in creating or maintaining health.

Despite the limitations of modern medicine, government policies to improve health still place a lot of emphasis on the role of the medical and nursing professions, and much of the debate about health policy focuses on the health of the NHS rather than upon health itself. This comment is not entirely fair, as government policy has recently tried to put more emphasis on public health than on curative services. The recent drive to improve public health began under the previous Conservative administration, and was continued in 1998 with the publication of *Our Healthier Nation* (DoH 1998b), a public health Green Paper that outlined Labour's strategy. Labour has put more emphasis than before on the need to improve the health of low-income groups and to reduce the sharp health inequalities in British society, which necessarily involves a consideration of the environmental and social determinants of health and illness.

Notwithstanding the government's concerns about the ways that social inequalities are linked to poor health, however, it is still true to say that the bulk of investment in 'health' is still in mopping up illness, and in trying to improve the performance of the NHS in this respect. This is particularly the case in health because of the size and dominance of the NHS. Changing the direction of the NHS, and of health policy in general, has sometimes been compared to steering a 'super-tanker' – drastic actions might be taken on the bridge and in the engine room, but with apparently little effect until some time later.

Thus it is never easy to reach firm conclusions about either the future of the NHS or the long-term effects of changing government policy on the role of the health professions. What signs are there, if any, that the Labour government's agenda of reforming the health service have eroded the traditional power and status of professional groups?

One possible threat to traditional medical authority can perhaps be seen in the introduction of NHS Direct, a telephone advice service to the general public, and such innovations as new-style one-stop medical centres sponsored by Boots the Chemists and other private companies which are beginning to challenge GPs' control of patients' access to health services. And the development of PCGs as the main structure for administering the health service has imposed a burden of extra work on doctors. They are now expected to take on this extra administrative work, but without the financial rewards of the GP fundholding system that had been introduced by the previous Conservative government and was scrapped by Labour.

On the other hand, there are reasons to doubt whether current health reforms will substantially reduce professional control over health services. And even if they do, neither is it clear that the result will be a 'patient-centred NHS' along the lines envisaged by the government.

One reason for caution in interpreting the likely results of the government's NHS reforms is that the government committed itself firmly to the existing method of funding the NHS – that is, mainly from income tax and partly from National Insurance contributions (significantly increased in the Budget of 2002 – see Chapter 5). More radical solutions might have involved a completely new way of funding health care – for instance through social insurance or hypothecated taxation and funding of the NHS, or by extending the role of private insurance and out-of-pocket fees for consulting a GP or using other health services. Either of these types of reforms would have put the relationship between patients and doctors on a new footing and would have brought the British system more in line with that of other European countries. As already mentioned, these countries – for instance, France – spend significantly higher proportions of the national wealth on health. Patients tend to have more choice in their treatment and the ways in which they are cared for.

Another strong brake on change is the government's very dependence on the medical profession to carry out the improvements it wishes. There are severe limits on the reforms that can be implemented without doctors' cooperation and, just as the government's plans to introduce the NHS in 1948 depended on winning over the doctors, so do New Labour's plans for health service reform and improvements in health services.

As pointed out at the beginning of this chapter, professional power and status depend to some extent on the 'scarcity value' of an occupational group. By and large, doctors have retained their monopoly and control over health services, despite the encroachment of new procedures to assess and monitor their work. Any shortage of doctors not only threatens the government's current plans to expand the health service but also is likely to protect at least some of their traditional status and power.

The government cannot afford to alienate the doctors too much, and it is desperately trying to boost the numbers of medical students and reduce the number of working doctors who leave the profession every year. A growing number of GPs, especially women in their late twenties and thirties, now want to reduce their working week to part-time hours to meet child-rearing or family responsibilities.

Specialists and consultants will also be in short supply. According to Sir Peter Morris (President of the Royal College of Surgeons), for instance, 'By all the best predictions we can make, there will be a shortfall of 2,000 surgeons by 2009. New students will eventually provide the numbers needed, but you're looking at 12 to 15 years down the line' (Riddell 2001: 21).

Thus for this and the other reasons mentioned above, the medical profession is likely to retain much of its power over health services and health policy. As Leathard (2000: 248) suggests, none of the recent health reforms give much impetus to improving the *democratic* accountability of the NHS. There is little evidence in today's NHS of a fundamental shift in the balance of power towards the patient. There are signs that patients are becoming more questioning and are prepared to be more critical of doctors than they used to be. But despite such apparent readiness to challenge traditional professional attitudes, the policy-making and administrative machinery is simply not in place to give patients an effective voice at the *policy level* of the NHS.

Whether professionals are good for us – the initial question – is therefore decided upon mainly by the non-elected quangos that scrutinize the quality of health services and by the medical profession itself, rather than by the people who use health services or their representatives.

Key terms and concepts

acute illnesses	internal market
chronic illnesses	medicalization
curative medicine	outcomes
hypothecated taxation	preventive health policies/services
iatrogenic disease	

Suggestions for further reading

Ian Kennedy's *The Unmasking of Medicine* (2nd edn, 1983), though now rather dated, still offers one of the best critiques of the dominant role of the medical profession in health services and in thinking about medical and ethical issues.

Similarly, Thomas McKeown's *The Role of Medicine* (2nd edn, 1979) remains a classic historical study of the changing nature of disease and the limited role of medicine.

There are now a great many general texts on health policy, the health services and related areas such as the sociology of nursing and other health professions. One of the best is Steve Taylor's and David Field's *Sociology of Health and Health Care* (1997 – a 4th edn is forthcoming in 2007). This book provides a succinct and stimulating policy-related overview of key health issues. It is written for both the general reader and nursing students. The best general book on UK health policy is still Chris Ham's *Health Policy in Britain*, now in its 5th edn (2004). Other useful texts are Robert Baggott's *Health and Health Care in Britain* (3rd edn, 2004) and Audrey Leathard's *Health Care Provision* (2nd edn, 2000). To understand recent health policy against the historical development of the NHS, Rudolf Klein's *The New Politics of the NHS* (5th edn, 2006) is outstanding. This is one of the few indispensable books about the NHS.

Radical critiques of the medical profession can be found in a wide range of books, but the following offer fascinating historical evidence as well: Jane Lewis's *Politics of Motherhood: Child and Maternal Welfare in England, 1900–1939* (1980) and Jean Donnison's *Midwives and Medical Men* (2nd edn, 1988). On a different tack, Ivan Illich's *Limits to Medicine – Medical Nemesis* (1990) is also worth looking at, but needs to be taken with a pinch of salt.

10 UTOPIAS AND IDEALS: HOUSING POLICY AND THE ENVIRONMENT

Introduction
Housing policy: definitions and significance
Housing utopias and ideals
    From philanthropy and self-help to social engineering
    The triumph of market ideals: housing policy in the 1980s and 1990s
Housing under New Labour – a forgotten dream?
Conclusions: housing and the environment in a postmodern society
Key terms and concepts
Suggestions for further reading

Introduction

Of all human needs, shelter is one of the most fundamental. But housing is also important because it can give the sense of security that stems from bonding with 'home'. Satisfactory homes help personal development and also help people to develop roots: a fusion of personal identity with place, neighbourhood and family. Establishing a home of one's own can also give a sense of responsibility and achievement. Not least, the economic investments that people make in their homes represent important goals of status and success. But these are not necessarily selfish: many people are motivated to own and improve their properties in order to pass them on to their descendants.

Given the deep significance of the home in the human psyche it is not surprising that government policies on housing are subject to a lot of commentary and criticism. The same can be said of any policies that affect people's ability to purchase a home. Indirectly, there are important housing implications, for instance, in the government's ability to manage the economy. This will affect economic growth and employment prospects in particular regions, which in turn might affect the chances of young people being able to find well-paid jobs and to purchase homes of their own. Similarly, economic policies have effects on interest rates (which are set by the Bank of England, independently of government), which in turn determine the cost of borrowing and therefore of mortgages to purchase houses. Another example of 'non-housing' policies which nevertheless affect housing are policies on the 'green belt' around urban areas, and whether house building should be allowed in environmentally protected or 'green' areas.

Yet despite the strong importance attached to housing, it is also an example of welfare and human needs that for decades government has been tiptoeing away from. As will be explained in this chapter, the notion that government should be directly involved in building housing on a large scale, renting it out and controlling the housing market in various ways was once widely taken for granted – not only by Labour, but also by Conservative governments. This was especially the case in the mid-twentieth century. The 'welfare settlement' established at that time included an assumption that the state would play a growing part in providing and managing housing, and the welfare state promised a society in which everyone had a right to good quality homes whether or not they wanted to purchase them. In the general elections of the 1950s and 1960s, the Conservative Party was as anxious to boast about its record in building record numbers of council houses, when in government, as Labour was.

However, housing is now – and always has been to a considerable degree – an area of welfare in which the *market* is far and away the most important means of settling who gets what, or how needs are to be met. The other four of the five great social services (health, social security, education and personal social services) are increasingly being run on market lines. However, they are still basically public services and most people's needs for education, health care, social security and so on are still being met from public funds and not solely according to what they can personally afford, as is mostly the case with housing. Therefore, a focus on housing provides an important test of how well or badly the market serves people's needs. It is also an example of welfare in which, if anything goes wrong, government is going to be held less and less accountable. Eventually, if present policies prevail, individuals with housing problems, even if they are renting social housing, will no more think of taking their difficulties to a representative of local or central government than they would if they had experienced problems with faulty electrical goods or a flight cancellation.

The dominance of the market in housing suggests that there is little scope in this area of welfare for dreams and ideals – surely, if the market decides almost everything, money considerations override all others? As will be discussed in this chapter, the history of housing in Britain suggests that this point is only partly true. In the past many idealistic plans of housing philanthropists or state planners to provide better housing for ordinary people were 'anti-market' attempts to break the chains of market forces, and to make 'ideal homes' affordable. However, pro-market housing policy can also be inspired by dreams and ideals. For instance, Mrs Thatcher's housing policies in the 1980s were strongly affected by the aspiration of home ownership for virtually everyone, and the dream – shattered by the property crash of the early 1990s – of a housing market in which everyone would gain and no one would lose.

In this chapter we shall examine these and other kinds of housing utopias and ideals, together with the inevitable disillusion and reassessment that follows them. In some cases, housing ideals are connected to wider visions, involving dreams of ideal communities and environments. Although space will not permit detailed examinations of these broader ideas, it is important to see housing in its context. Social planners in the past, and those who want to develop new kinds of housing today, link policies for better housing with policies for better (for example, 'greener' or more sustainable) environments and communities.

Before returning to these broader questions near the end of the chapter, however, we need to examine definitions of housing policy in more detail.

Housing policy: definitions and significance

'Housing policy' refers to a wide range of government action. It covers any government actions, legislation or economic policies that have a direct or indirect effect on housing. These might include policies affecting supply of housing, house prices, tax policies affecting house purchase, housing standards and patterns of tenure.

However, definitions in themselves do not indicate *why* housing is of special significance in the study of social policy. Three main reasons may be identified. First, as mentioned above, housing illustrates an area of welfare in which the market is supreme. Studying housing therefore allows us to see what the strengths and weaknesses of the market are, in terms of meeting people's needs. Second, housing is an area of special interest because it highlights the complex nature of *needs* and how need could be defined. 'Having a roof over your head' is an attractively simple but insufficient definition of housing needs. To define either housing or being homeless properly, we have to use concepts of *quality* and *autonomy*.

Thus, if someone has a roof over their head but lives in a severely overcrowded dwelling which is hazardous to health, arguably they are not adequately housed and are therefore homeless. Similarly, there is an argument that adults who have virtually no independence or autonomy in their dwelling are homeless: for instance, if such a person does not have any say in when they can use the space or rooms in the dwelling. People living in hostels, residential institutions or 'bed and breakfast' accommodation might fit into this category, and could therefore be regarded as homeless.

Thus, official statistics on homelessness should be treated with caution, because it is in any government's interests to use narrow definitions of homelessness and to present it as a manageable problem that they are dealing with effectively. Official definitions of homelessness are likely to concentrate on categories of people who live on the streets or sleep rough more than upon the larger group without adequate homes.

A third reason for exploring housing as a key area of social policy is that it is intimately connected with a wide range of other welfare issues such as health. According to historians of public health (see, for instance, McKeown 1979), housing policy, along with other environmental improvements such as the introduction of effective sanitation, did more to improve health and life expectancy in the nineteenth and early twentieth centuries than anything achieved in medicine or health services. Poor housing conditions are still with us, however, and the effects of damp, poorly-heated homes on health can still be observed.

In terms of social division, local housing policies might either be able to prevent the development of 'sink' housing estates, where people on low incomes and experiencing high rates of joblessness are concentrated, or they might have few resources to be able to prevent them developing. For similar reasons, local housing policies might contribute to either a heightening or a lessening of racial tensions. In 2001, for instance, there were serious outbreaks of violence and property damage in northern English towns such as Oldham and Burnley. Tensions between the local white and Asian communities were exacerbated by their effective segregation into different territories and areas of housing; conflict and street fighting erupted when each side thought that the other was invading 'their' territory.

A relevant study of housing in Bradford found that 'the Pakistani and Bangladeshi communities, although forming close on one-fifth of the city's population, occupy only 2.24 per cent of council housing and 8.4 per cent of other housing lets' (Wainwright 2001: 6). The high rate of owner-occupation among the Asian communities is partly an expression of preference – there is a history of many in the Pakistani community, for instance, preferring to buy houses rather than rent. However, there is also a fear factor – few families in the minority communities wish to move into the predominantly white council housing estates in Bradford. Local housing policies have not succeeded in combating racism in council housing allocation, nor have local authorities been able to reduce the minority communities' fears of racial abuse, vandalism and crime – the reason 'repeatedly given for Asian families turning down offers of empty houses on "bad reputation" estates' (Wainwright 2001: 6).

This is not to say that housing policy alone could solve every problem of poor health, racial conflict or social deprivation, but it is true that, more than in any other area of social policy, decisions made in housing policy have a directly territorial impact. Visible, spatial inequalities can be either lessened or accentuated, as illustrated by the gulf between run-down council estates and spruce, security-conscious housing developments for the affluent.

Housing utopias and ideals

First, to put recent changes in perspective, it helps to look at how housing has been the subject of utopian plans and ideals for a long time. Therefore, in this section we consider the main landmarks in the development of housing policy. Three broad phases of 'housing dreams' and ideals can be discerned in recent British history.

First, the nineteenth-century period, in which 'model housing' schemes were like beacons in a sea of squalid, overcrowded accommodation for the masses. Most of these schemes were the result of industrial paternalism – enlightened employers building good quality housing for their workers – but some were associated with charity and with efforts to provide 'decent' accommodation for people in poverty.

Second, the period after the First World War and up to the 1960s, in which housing ideals were much affected by concepts of social engineering. The idea of planned new towns and 'garden cities', for instance, predates the First World War, but became influential in housing policy and the design of suburban housing in the 1920s and 1930s. In addition to planning ideal communities in the physical or environmental sense, this phase of idealism encouraged socialistic ideas about housing, including the ideal of mixing together people of different social classes. In practice, examples of such social engineering were few and far between. However, this 'middle period' in housing policy was one in which the idea of local councils as providers of housing (through rented council housing) was strongly endorsed by Conservative as well as Labour governments – as mentioned at the outset.

Third, the period after 1970, in which the market and home ownership have become even more central to housing policy than before. Mrs Thatcher's governments of the 1980s were chiefly responsible for widening the base of home ownership in Britain, but the percentage of people in council housing had already reached a plateau before 1979 (see Figure 10.1) and the percentage in private rented accommodation was in steep decline. The policy of selling council houses to tenants had existed before Mrs Thatcher came to office. Usually only a few thousand dwellings were sold by local authorities in England and Wales each year, though nearly 46,000 were sold in 1972 (under a Conservative government) and over 30,000 in 1978 (under Labour). However, these proved to be relatively small totals compared with the 201,015 sold in 1982, the year Mrs Thatcher's council house sales policy gained momentum (Forrest and Murie 1988: 110).

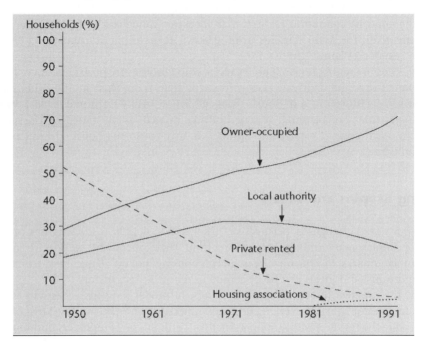

Figure 10.1 Housing tenure in Great Britain, 1950–1991 (adapted from Balchin 1995: 6)

From philanthropy and self-help to social engineering

Although housing standards were generally very poor in the Victorian period, housing did gradually improve as the nineteenth century progressed and as large numbers of working people became better off than before. Further, although much housing was squalid, conditions and types of housing varied.

In both rural and urban areas, there were isolated but significant attempts by employers, philanthropic organizations and the growing number of 'respectable' working-class families to improve housing. Each of these groups had somewhat different housing ideals and aims (see Box 10.1), though they shared a common determination to bring about greater security of tenure and a healthier environment with better sanitation.

Victorian philanthropy, industrial paternalism and workers' self-help failed to provide enough low-cost homes for the mass of working people by the time the First

World War broke out in 1914. Also, only a small number of council houses were built before 1914. However, local authority housing was to become the main solution for trying to reduce the housing shortage between the wars, when 900,000 council homes were built.

The period from the end of the First World War in 1918 to the 1970s can be regarded as the heyday of state intervention in housing. Even though market forces continued to dominate the housing sector, and home ownership increased dramatically during this period, there was widespread agreement that the market alone could not satisfactorily provide enough housing of acceptable quality.

More than this, there was a revolution in ideas about housing and the environment. Individualistic British notions of laissez-faire and letting people find their own housing solutions remained strong, but they were challenged by new ideas about architecture and planning. These ideas suggested that, in an ideal world, the state could plan everyone's housing needs and design an environment in which social divisions could be minimized.

Such ideas came from a variety of sources. Before the First World War, Ebenezer Howard – a radical liberal thinker who advocated a new kind of urban living – developed the concept of the garden city. He had worked in Chicago in its pre-skyscraper days and had been impressed by the idea of a decentralized city in a spacious landscape. Howard believed that new towns could be built in the countryside of Britain; people could collectively own common facilities such as schools and workshops, for which they would pay a common rent, and they would be free to build their own houses in planned green spaces.

Similarly, after the Second World War, the idea of building new towns and outer suburbs in green open spaces continued to have a strong effect on British planning and housing policy. In the 1950s and 1960s, a succession of new towns appeared in England and Scotland. These, along with 'outer ring' housing estates, were usually part of a policy of clearing away inner-city sub-standard housing and 'decanting' people to environments which were seen by planners as infinitely better than those they were uprooted from.

The major task of slum clearance and rehousing fell to governments after the Second World War. Between 1945 and the end of the 1960s, the twin ideals of state intervention in housing and government planning of the environment reached full bloom. The percentage of households in public rented (council house) homes rose from 12 to 31 between 1945 and 1971, while the percentage in private rented accommodation plummeted from 62 to 17 over the same period (Malpass and Murie 1994: 73). However, owner-occupation rose from a quarter to a half of all households, and this represented a flowering of the private housing market as well, albeit greatly helped by government intervention through tax relief to mortgage payers.

Box 10.1 Octavia Hill (1838–1912)

Octavia Hill can be seen as one of the key founders of modern social work, as well as a pioneer of housing policy and management. The daughter of a middle-class but not particularly well-off family, she concentrated on trying to find housing solutions for slum-dwellers and the very poor. This involved social casework and developing a relationship with families as well as finding them housing.

She hit upon the idea of developing an organization to *manage* rented properties that could be let to 'deserving' poor people in need of accommodation. Property owners handed over management responsibility to Octavia Hill's scheme, which guaranteed them a fair financial return and which was staffed by middle-class women volunteers who collected rents and supervised tenants and properties.

Owners could be assured that their properties would be well looked after, thus encouraging them to let to people from the poorest backgrounds. Otherwise, landlords were reluctant to let rooms to the poor. Usually, high rents were charged for inferior accommodation and, as a result, tenants at the bottom end of the rented accommodation market tended to 'flit' or default on rent.

After the opening of Paradise Place in Marylebone in 1865, Octavia Hill's housing scheme spread to include a large number of properties in London. Although it only ever reached a minority of people in need, it was an imaginative breakthrough in providing basic accommodation for poor families. However, her scheme was far from being 'pro-poor'. Its philosophy was governed by rather authoritarian ideas about how the behaviour of the poor could be improved. Tenants were expected to follow the advice of their social superiors, the volunteer women who called to collect rents and to instruct them how to conduct their lives.

Hill's philosophy did not challenge the economic principles of the housing market. She opposed the idea of using charity to help poor people with their rents, or of subsidizing the cost of housing in other ways. Octavia Hill was against the early experiments with subsidized council housing in London in the 1890s, for example (Malpass 1984: 35).

If Hill's philosophy meant that a poor family had to struggle to pay rent for a single room (and, according to Hill's standards, one room per family was usually 'adequate'), then this was quite proper in a market system and the only way to develop independence in the poor. On the other hand, Hill wanted a fair housing market with legislation to guarantee basic standards. She successfully lobbied Parliament to improve housing: for example, through the Artisans' and Labourers' Dwellings Improvement Act 1875. However, Hill's views of the causes of poverty remained fundamentally individualistic and moralistic, and these perspectives were clearly evident in the stance she took as a member of the Royal Commission on the Poor Laws (1905–9).

The Conservative governments of the 1950s continued the council house building programme and were especially active in this respect between 1951 and 1954, but after 1955 they put a higher priority on encouraging private builders to meet general housing need. Gradually, local authority council housing came to be seen as the sector in which poorer households would be *re*housed, and which was to carry the burden of slum clearance in the 1950s and 1960s. As Malpass and Murie (1994) point out, the official standards governing council houses were lowered after 1953, and council housing began to be seen as of significantly lower status and as having less appeal than privately built homes.

This was also the case during the period of Labour government in 1964–70, when owner-occupation was endorsed as the favoured form of housing tenure for the majority. However, Labour began a crash programme of public sector house-building, rehousing and slum clearance for the inner cities. Tower blocks and large housing estates were thrown together with great haste, while long-standing urban communities in inner cities were bulldozed to make way for new roads, open spaces and shopping centres.

The pace of public sector house-building at this time, combined with local government corruption in some areas and the patchy implementation of quality controls, meant that many problems were laid down for the future. Many of today's problems of leaking roofs, inadequate ventilation and corroding concrete date from the 1960s' and 1970s' rush to build cheap public sector housing. Poor building standards were matched by ill-conceived designs for housing estates. In many cases, either warren-like 'concrete jungles' were built, or bleak wastelands that are poorly serviced with shops and other community facilities.

The triumph of market ideals: housing policy in the 1980s and 1990s

The 1980s saw the tide turning against the ideas of social engineering and planning that had come to dominate housing policy. In practice both Conservative and Labour governments *before* 1979 had increasingly looked to the private market as the main supplier of housing, despite differences of emphasis between the parties. But it was the housing policies of Mrs Thatcher's government after 1979 that marked a decisive change in policy ideals and assumptions. Planning restrictions on the sale of land would be eased. No longer would council housing remain as a major player on the scene. This kind of housing would be increasingly residualized (see Box 10.2).

Mrs Thatcher's housing policies went with the grain of public attitudes and aspirations (Cole and Furbey 1994), which in Britain – and particularly in England – favour owner-occupied housing for the reasons mentioned at the beginning of this chapter.

However, the housing policies of Mrs Thatcher's government included a lot more than encouraging owner-occupation through council house sales. Other pro-market changes were brought in, such as the decontrol of rented accommodation. For instance, the Housing Act 1980 introduced shorthold tenancies (giving landlords the right to evict tenants after a contracted period of between one and five years) and 'fair rents', a new procedure through which former rent controls were abolished and landlords could more easily charge higher rents than before. The aim of these policies was to stimulate the private rented sector by offering greater incentives to landlords. But there was also continuity, as in the policy (popular with people buying their homes) of continuing to give tax relief on mortgage repayments.

Box 10.2 Residualization

This is a useful concept in social policy. It refers to a process whereby public services are increasingly used by a 'residual' or excluded minority of poorer people, rather than by the community as a whole. Two-tier services or facilities develop, with the better-off majority using private sector services (including housing) which they or their employers pay for. Poorer families and individuals are left with public welfare services which, because the middle-class and better-off working-class families no longer use them, tend to become run-down, poorly funded and socially stigmatized. If council accommodation is becoming a residual category of housing, for example, this would mean that a certain stigma would be attached to living on a council estate – it would be a sign of social exclusion and downward social mobility.

Above all, though, it is the 'right to buy' legislation that Mrs Thatcher's administration is most remembered for in the field of housing. The Housing Act 1980 gave both council tenants and some housing association tenants the right to buy their homes. As far as council tenants were concerned, this law gave substantial government discounts on the price of homes as an incentive to buy. These were discounts of between a third and a half of the property's market value, depending on the tenant's length of tenure. Local authorities were required to provide mortgages of 100 per cent for buyers.

Another Housing Act, in 1985, extended the powers of central government to force local authorities to sell council accommodation to tenants. Similarly, the Housing and Planning Act 1986 forced the pace of council house sales by increasing discounts to buyers and by making it easier for whole blocks of housing estates to be sold off (see Malpass and Murie 1994: 106).

The Housing Act 1988 sought to break up further what was seen by Conservatives as a 'municipal monopoly' of council estates. This Act not only gave individual tenants the right to choose another landlord, such as a housing association, but also introduced a policy of large-scale voluntary transfers (LSVTs) of council estates from local authorities to housing associations or even to private landlords. These policies were attempts to privatize 'problem' council estates – those which were particularly run down and where very low market prices for accommodation made it difficult to purchase or sell, under the former 'right to buy' legislation.

The 1988 Act also introduced housing action trusts (HATs) – another device to try to renovate social housing in deprived areas and at the same time to prise council estates from local authority control. HATs were set up in selected areas. The housing estates affected were to be run by management boards, which included central government appointees, elected tenant representatives and local government representation. In return, each trust would receive substantial sums of central government money to improve the housing and the local environment.

The concept of HATs and the separation of council estates from their local authorities has been paralleled in education by that of state schools being able to opt out of local authority control, thereby receiving extra central government cash for improvements. As Balchin (1995) explains, after an uncertain start HATs had been established in four urban areas by 1992. The local authorities concerned soon realized the advantages to them of receiving large amounts of central government money to help to renovate very poor council housing. Tenants of HATs would not have to be paid housing benefit by the local authority but would instead receive it directly from central government – another saving to the local authority.

The 'right to buy' legislation and the other policies to transform large council housing estates were aimed at stimulating market solutions to Britain's housing needs. As such, they have been contrasted with the former mentality of social engineering and state planning which had held sway over housing policy. However, in some ways Mrs Thatcher's policies were also examples of social engineering, if by this we mean a paternalistic use of the state to bring about changes on people's behalf that are seen as beneficial for them. It was not as though Mrs Thatcher's government simply relaxed local authority control over housing and let the market run free in the private rented or owner-occupied sectors. Rather, pro-market ideals and solutions had to be brought about – engineered – by all kinds of government incentives such as discounts to council house purchasers.

The most immediate achievement of this state-directed and state-subsidized market was an explosion of sales of council houses and housing association homes, which rose from under 50,000 in 1979 to 120,000 in 1981 and to almost a quarter of a million in 1982 (Malpass and Murie 1994: 117). After the initial 'gold rush', sales declined sharply but they revived markedly again after the Housing Act 1988, reaching the 200,000 mark in 1989–90. The proportion of local authority rented properties in Great Britain (i.e. UK minus Northern Ireland) declined from 30 per cent to 19 per cent of the total housing stock between 1979 and 1997 (Ford 2003: 144, Table 8.1).

Selling off government-owned assets (that is council housing) on a large scale, promoting goals of individual ownership and gain, and enlarging the role of the market, were all hallmarks of the 'Thatcherite' approach. In retrospect, housing policy in the 1980s now stands out as the area of social policy in which these ideals or goals had their most marked effect. Accompanying this trend was an increase in the overall proportion of owner-occupied dwellings, from 56 per cent in 1970 to 67 per cent in 1997 (Ford 2003: 144, Table 8.1).

By the early 1990s, however, the housing market was in serious crisis. It suffered from an economic hangover, following the 'wild party' of property speculation and booming house prices in the 1980s. House prices fell steeply and, at the same time, interest rates set by building societies for first mortgages rocketed from about 9.5 to almost 15 per cent in 1990. This represented a crippling increase for some first-time buyers, especially as tax relief on repayments was being pared down and many had taken out large mortgages to buy houses at inflated prices.

Whether or not governments are wholly responsible for bringing about such outcomes in the housing market, the effects of the 1980s boom and of government housing policy in the 1980s show very mixed results from the pro-market and privatization dreams of that period. Some notable problems in housing in the early and mid-1990s were as follows.

- A rising rate of house repossession, as a growing number of householders experienced mortgage repayment difficulties.
- A cutback in the number of new houses being built, as the construction industry faced an uncertain future.
- The spread of negative equity, another sign of market failure that was almost unheard of before the 1990s. Negative equity occurs when house values fall so steeply that house-buyers face having to pay back a loan or mortgage that is greater than the current market value of the property. In 1992, over a fifth of British households were affected by negative equity to some degree, so that for a while the market was 'to an extent, ceasing to work' (Balchin 1995: 214).
- Disappointing performance of the private rented sector. Though various items of legislation were brought in to add flexibility to rental agreements and to reduce restrictions on private landlords, these policies did not result in a revival of the private rented sector. In 1994, for instance, there were only 2.5 million privately rented dwellings in the UK (a slight decrease from 1981), whereas there were 16 million owner-occupied dwellings – a third more than in 1981 (CSO 1996: 176). By 2003 there were 18 million owner-occupied dwellings (Office for National

Statistics 2005b: 137). Renting from housing associations, though increasing by a tenth every year, is still less common than private renting.

- An increase in homelessness. A number of social trends combined to increase homelessness: high rates of divorce, separation, family conflict and break-up. Arguably there would have been a rise in homelessness in the 1990s whatever kind of government had been in power or whatever housing policies had been implemented. However, a range of policies introduced in the 1980s do seem to have contributed to the rise in homelessness and the number of people living in temporary accommodation. For instance, the reduction of social security benefits to people aged under 25, the removal of benefits from 16- and 17-year-olds (unless participating in a youth training scheme) and the failure of the private rented sector to meet the needs of low-income families were all contributory factors. Above all, the drastic reduction in the amount of low-cost council housing seems to have had the most significant effect in that it took away opportunities for young people and others facing family difficulties to find affordable accommodation.

This brings us to the more general question of what the outcomes were of Mrs Thatcher's policy of council house sales. By 1994, the number of dwellings rented from local authorities had fallen to its lowest level since 1963 – about one in five of the then 23.7 million dwellings in Great Britain (CSO 1996: 176). However, this shows not only the enormous impact of the Conservative government's housing sell-off policy but also that the rented public housing sector did not completely disappear. Despite the haemorrhage of sales, it remains a substantial sector, accounting for almost 5 million homes. Such a large sector is bound to include wage earners and younger households, not just a residual minority of older people, or unemployed people and those dependent on social benefits.

Although people who live in local authority housing cannot be portrayed as a 'housing underclass' or as a completely residualized group, however, there has undeniably been a *trend* towards residualization as a result of selling off council accommodation. Between 1983 and 1990 the proportion of 'economically inactive' people in Britain increased from 32 to 38 per cent. But among council house heads of household the proportion was already much higher (50 per cent in 1983) and increased at a faster rate to 61 per cent in 1991 (GHS 1983: Table 6.9, 1992: Table 3.31). In other words, during the period of maximum council house sales, the people 'left behind' in council accommodation were increasingly those out of work or older people. Over the same period, the proportion of skilled manual people as householders in council accommodation fell from 24 to 15 per cent, another indicator of residualization. Council housing is now only rarely the type of home occupied by skilled, higher paid working-class people.

Opponents of the council house sales policy pointed to what they saw as the negative consequences – for instance, the cost to the public purse from sales which, far from saving public expenditure, have added to it (Balchin 1995: 166). The cost of giving tax relief to first-time buyers with mortgages cancelled out the gains from house sales and from cutting back council house building. Further, it should not be forgotten that large subsidies had to be given out to make purchases feasible for low-income families.

In terms of the social effects, critics of council house sales point to the 'creaming off' of better council houses by purchasers. It is mainly the more popular two-storey houses with gardens that have sold well, and this makes it increasingly likely that poorer families with young children must be housed in the unsuitable accommodation that is left, often in high-rise blocks. Communities also face break-up, according to the critics, because families who have purchased their homes trade up for a better house elsewhere and leave the neighbourhood.

But whether selling council housing inevitably has these effects is a matter of debate. Much seems to depend on the type of area and community in question. For instance, an interesting study of council housing and the African-Caribbean community by Peach and Byron (1994) showed that black tenants often experienced racial discrimination in the allocation of council accommodation. They were more often given flats rather than houses or accommodation on the least-favoured floors or parts of tower blocks, compared to white tenants. Despite this unequal treatment, however, the research showed that a surprisingly high number of African-Caribbean council tenants were interested in the right to buy. Furthermore, those who had bought their council homes were found to have improved their position in the community and their well-being. In other words, the right to buy policy had not excluded the African-Caribbean community or led to further residualization of black tenants in council-owned accommodation.

An important exception to this finding was that single Caribbean women with dependent children *were* more likely to be in inappropriate, council-rented accommodation. For this group, the option of purchasing their home was likely to be unrealistic or difficult. However, the authors conclude that, for this community as a whole, householders who purchase their flat or house are more likely to stay in the neighbourhood and to seek improvements in the local area. Rather than contributing to the break-up of community life and rapid turnover of residents, the right to buy policy in this example showed that it had helped to stabilize the local community.

This finding about one minority community could have implications for everyone living in council estates. 'Since it is the more economically able and entrepreneurial who buy', Peach and Byron (1994: 381) suggest, 'it could be argued that the act of purchase ties them to the locality more strongly'. As they also point out, the opposite has been found to be the case in 'housing projects' (social housing) in the USA, where all tenants must be receiving welfare payments to qualify for housing. The experience here has been that, as no accommodation is sold, anyone who 'makes good' and improves their income is automatically ineligible for housing and has to leave.

The African-Caribbean example is important because it shows the dangers of generalizing about the longer-term effects of 1980s and early 1990s housing privatization. While there are clear trends towards residualization, or the concentration of poor, socially excluded and unemployed people in rented council accommodation, this is far from being a universal phenomenon.

Housing under New Labour – a forgotten dream?

Dreams and utopias, it will be recalled, are the underlying theme of this chapter. Until recent times, housing policy seemed to be directed by large-scale plans and strong ideological preferences – 'dreams' of a better way to live, and hopes of solving Britain's housing shortage. 'Old' Labour in the 1960s realized ambitious plans to tear down old inner-city housing and build modern, publicly-owned tower blocks and whole new towns to replace it. And in 1979, Mrs Thatcher's radically different housing policy – to sell council homes on a large scale – was widely trumpeted and quickly implemented.

By contrast, housing under New Labour since 1997 seems to have become a low-profile public issue. As Kemp (1999) points out, Labour's 'silence' about housing policy in 1997 was striking, and 'Apart from a few specific manifesto commitments . . . it was not at all clear what Labour's housing policy objectives would be, nor what instruments it would use to pursue them' (p. 134). A housing Green Paper appeared in 2000, followed in the same year by a *Housing Policy Statement, The Way Forward for Housing*, a rather slow rate of policy formation by comparison with health and education, for example (DETR 2000a; DETR/DSS 2000).

Toynbee and Walker (2001) agree, citing as evidence Labour's avoidance of the issue of the large numbers of new homes that will be needed in the UK in the next two decades. Projections based on 1998 suggested that there will be an extra 4.3 million households in Britain by 2021 (Toynbee and Walker 2001: 197). As housing need in the South-East of England is growing particularly fast, as many as 50,000 new homes every year might be needed in this region, or an extra million in England by 2021. The Barker report, commissioned by the Treasury in 2004, demonstrated the lack of investment in British housing and the existence of what is in effect a housing shortage. It has been pointed out that the low level of investment in new housing presupposes a lifetime for dwellings of 1000 years (Toynbee and Walker 2005: 134, 260).

As with all projections, these estimates are controversial and debatable. However, the significant point is that the government has shied away from the issue rather than devised a plan or opened up a public debate. As Toynbee and Walker (2001: 197) put it, 'Where once Labour ministers would have relished regional plans and dreamed of new towns to cope with such patterns of change, the Blairites merely shivered'.

To say that New Labour's approach to housing and to related environmental issues seems to have been low key is not to say that the government has *no* policy at all. Nor is it to suggest that large-scale plans and dreams of solutions to Britain's housing problems are always 'a good thing'. As shown above, the ambitious plans contained in previous governments' housing policies have gone sour in various ways.

It has been suggested that 'the approach and philosophy that now inform housing policy are a clear continuation of the principle and practice of previous Conservative Governments' (Ford 2003: 146). New Labour's modest policies seem to have two strands.

First, there is a mainly laissez-faire approach to housing for the majority of the population. Provision of new housing is being left largely to private developers and companies, and the government is seeking only to steer housing development, at arm's length, to so-called 'brownfield' sites (land formerly used for industrial or other urban uses such as housing, but now vacant or derelict). As mentioned at the outset, Labour is no longer a party or a government of large-scale planning and, as far as housing is concerned, the policy is to follow the 'market model' developed by Mrs Thatcher's government. This policy will mean that housing will be seen less and less as a government responsibility, and that government will be reluctant to direct or plan private development too closely. Home ownership is regarded as the preferred and dominant tenure. Some degree of control and regulation there may be, but the emphasis is on achieving 'sustainable' home ownership for the majority of households. 'Sustainability' here means trying to reduce the insecurities that accompany the spread of debt-incurring house purchase to lower-income groups, in the context of a more flexible labour market through, for example, encouraging the development of different types of mortgage products and of mortgage protection insurance (Ford 2003: 150–1).

In relation to public or social housing, the focus of the Green Paper was here, too, on a continuation of the Conservative policy of transfer. Transfers may be to registered social landlords, Private Finance Initiative (PFI) schemes, or local housing companies (LHCs), and it was proposed that transfers should amount to 200,000 per year, a much higher rate than was achieved under the Conservatives (Ford 2003: 153–4). The Green Paper was also concerned with increasing responsiveness and widening choice and access, moving away from the traditional bureaucratic housing allocation procedures of local authorities. In relation to rents and assistance with housing costs, New Labour has attempted to reform social sector rents to make them fairer and more affordable, and to resolve inherited dilemmas over the marketization of rents and the linked issue of extent of assistance via housing benefit (Ford 2003: 156–7). Of course, some of these policies have simply created tensions and dilemmas of their own, or continued old ones.

Second, some effort and extra public money has been devoted to community regeneration. The government has made a particular point of trying to connect housing policy to its other policies to improve the quality of life in poorer neighbourhoods and socially excluded communities. A bewildering variety of local initiatives and community development projects have been launched in order to coordinate housing improvement with other efforts to upgrade public services such as education and health care, and to reduce crime and vandalism. This kind of approach is not entirely new. Various kinds of community regeneration projects were initiated by the previous Conservative administration in cities such as Liverpool. However, it is the strong emphasis of New Labour on this kind of policy that makes the government's housing and environment policy a distinctive departure from previous governments. As Kemp (1999: 135) explains, New Labour seems to be preoccupied above all else with 'rundown council estates' and its 'housing policy is to be focused not so much on housing objectives as ensuring that housing plays its part in combating "social exclusion" and in contributing to urban regeneration'. The most recent initiative, in 2003, was John Prescott's Sustainable Communities Plan. This envisaged, perhaps surprisingly in the light of Labour's professed social exclusion goals, higher levels of new household formation and housing growth in the South East than in the rest of the country. Some intellectual support for this approach was provided by the Barker report, referred to above. It seemed like an acknowledgement of the power of market forces to determine appropriate development goals and the associated development of communities (Toynbee and Walker 2005: 261–4).

As far as the first strand of policy is concerned, following a market approach to housing has been relatively trouble-free for the government to date. This is because the housing market recovered from its early 1990s crisis and the problems that ensued. At the time of writing, interest rates have declined to their lowest levels since the 1960s. Unemployment has also declined to a low level and, as the real incomes of the majority have risen steadily since the mid-1990s, all these favourable economic trends have stimulated house purchases and home ownership. House prices rose by 60 per cent between 1995 and 2000, but because of the reduction of interest and mortgage rates this has not led to the scale of debt problems and repayment difficulties seen in the early 1990s. In fact the government was confident enough to abolish mortgage interest tax relief altogether in 2000, as mentioned above. And for those who had already purchased homes before 1995, the housing boom has led to a substantial appreciation in the value of their property.

For some, however, the market has not worked well. While the 'affordability crisis' of the early 1990s in housing was mainly among people who could not afford to keep up repayments on their mortgages, in the early years of the twenty-first century it is becoming a problem of those who cannot afford to buy a house to begin with. The problem is particularly acute in London. Consequently, the capital is experiencing severe problems in attracting or retaining public sector workers on average incomes (cleaners, nurses, police officers, teachers, transport workers) who cannot afford the available housing. Similar problems are occurring in other parts of South-East England, as well as in rural areas and exclusive city areas outside this region.

These problems show that supply of low-cost housing is a vital part of any housing policy aiming to meet the needs of the population as a whole. As Toynbee and Walker (2001: 179) point out, about a third of the new homes to be built in the South East to meet the huge anticipated rise in demand for housing will need to be affordable – that is, 'built by councils or social landlords'. The lesson of history is that the market alone cannot be relied on to meet such needs very well.

However, Labour's main strategy, as Kemp (1999) explains, is to accept that market forces and owner-occupation are now the dominant ways in which housing is provided and distributed. For instance, the government has not rescinded the Conservatives' right to buy legislation, nor the discounts and incentives available to people buying social rented properties.

Nor will there be a return, under New Labour, to policies that favour the idea of continuing with local authorities as the main providers of social housing. Government policy is to continue to transfer council housing stock to registered social landlords (RSLs) – that is, non-profit-making housing associations. What is now called the 'social sector' of housing declined from 7 million homes in 1981 to 5 million in 2003 (Office for National Statistics 2005b: 137). To some extent, this change partly explains the negative trends in homelessness referred to below. In some cities and conurbations, notably in Scotland where there is a large stock of council accommodation, municipal authorities are 'working overtime', according to Hetherington (1998: 9), 'to transfer their housing to associations and trusts'. By 2005 RSLs are set to overtake local authorities as the main providers of social housing.

The government has also provided central funds in order to assist local authorities to set up 'social' companies to run housing estates. These new-style companies will be allowed to raise money in the open market to finance house repairs and upgrade the surrounding environment. Financing will be provided partly by banks and building societies and, though tenants will have a voice in the management of the new housing companies, they have been criticized by traditional Labour supporters as 'backdoor privatization' (Hetherington 1998).

However, Labour policy has accepted that there is a need to improve housing for people who cannot afford to purchase it and who remain in rented accommodation. Blair's first administration allowed £800 million to be released from the capital receipts local authorities had gained from earlier sales of council housing (the former Conservative administration had prevented local authorities from using this money). These funds were used partly in order to pay for the repair and renovation of the existing stock of local authority housing and also to fund a modest increase in new social housing.

There is little doubt that without substantially greater capital investment, social housing – especially the large, run-down council estates that still exist in parts of the English Midlands and northern England, Wales and Scotland – will become even more unattractive and 'residualized'. It is not only the condition of the housing but also the image or reputation of social housing and housing estates that is deteriorating. As the twentieth century drew to a close, Glasgow alone was demolishing 2500 unwanted council homes annually (18,000 were lost between 1990 and 2000); a further 80,000 council houses stood empty in England (Hetherington 1998). There is a growing problem of 'unlettable' houses and blocks of flats, affecting not only the older 1960s properties but also council housing stock that was built relatively recently, in the 1970s and 1980s. Therefore, both central government and social landlords face a sharp dilemma. Is it worth spending millions of pounds on improving houses in certain areas when there is a strong possibility that they will still have to be pulled down?

This brings us to the second prong of New Labour housing policy, which is to target government effort on tackling the problems of social exclusion and disadvantage faced by people living in a selected number of communities. As noted above, a dominant theme of New Labour policy thinking has been the idea of social exclusion and a concern with mitigating it.

A stark manifestation of social exclusion in relation to housing is homelessness. On this basis, New Labour policy might appear to have failed. The overall number of households defined as homeless in 2003/4 was 137,000 (Office for National Statistics 2005b: 140). (However, this represents a fall in numbers from a decade earlier; in 1990 over 170,000 had been officially accepted as homeless – see Ford 2003: 144, Table 8.1.) The number of families defined as homeless and granted temporary accommodation increased from 41,000 in March 1997 to 97,000 in March 2004. This increase was due to a decline in the number of available social sector lettings (Office for National Statistics 2005b: 141).

The SEU, a significant New Labour institutional creation, published a consultation document on neighbourhood renewal in 1998, emphasizing area-based strategies and the need for 'joined-up' approaches to urban renewal. ('Joined-up'-ness was of course, like 'social exclusion', another significant New Labour slogan or mantra.) This was followed by a report from the Urban Task Force in 1999 (Social Exclusion Unit 1998; Urban Task Force 1999). The policy product of these rethinks came in 1999, when the government launched its 'New Deal for Communities' (NDC) programme for 17 of the poorest estates, and this was followed by a second round that brought the total of communities involved to 24 in the year 2000 (Atkinson 2003: 165). The NDC programme made funding available for its various projects. That year also saw the publication of the government's urban White Paper, which proposed a vision of urban living and created a framework for joint policy-making and implementation (DETR 2000b; Atkinson 2003: 165–6). Money for community regeneration was available for the first three years from the Single Regeneration Budget, a fund, introduced by the Conservatives in 1994, that succeeded the former urban programme. The latter made government funds available from four different government departments, mainly for environmental improvements to the streets and surroundings of poor neighbourhoods. The Single Regeneration Budget, which came to an end in 2000, simplified matters in that all the funds came from a single government department, the Department of Environment, Transport, and the Regions (DETR) (now Communities and Local Government, CLG). This money could be used for a wider range of purposes than it could under the urban programme, and the Single Regeneration Budget was used to fund the large variety of community regeneration projects mentioned at the beginning of this section. This source of funding was replaced by the Neighbourhood Renewal Fund in 2000, as a result of the Comprehensive Spending Review of that year, as well as by NDC funds (Atkinson 2003: 165).

There is also a separate flow of central government funds to local authorities and RSLs to maintain and improve their social housing stock – and this might be seen as 'housing' money rather than 'community regeneration' money. Taken together, however, these two sources of funding were substantially increased (an extra £5 billion over the three years from 1999 to 2002) by New Labour (Kemp 1999: 142), as part of the government strategy to increase spending on selected public services such as education and health.

Therefore it would be wrong to conclude that the government has paid only lip service to the principle of improving social housing or of putting public money into local communities. In 1999, a local government act, in addition to giving local authorities the freedom to spend gains from the sale of council houses (as mentioned above), required local authorities to promote the well-being of their communities. The strategy for realizing this aim is shaped in part by the government's 'national strategy for area renewal'. Local authorities must now draw up plans to show how they are planning with residents in local communities to develop supportive networks of care, provide better community services and facilities (for example, child care and family centres) and improve health and educational opportunities.

Not only has the government devoted a lot of energy and considerable amounts of money to its efforts to remove the causes of social exclusion and disadvantage in selected areas but also it has arguably succeeded in being innovative in the way social problems and needs are being thought about. For instance, previous governments had not developed quite the same links between housing policy, community development and local networks to provide or improve social care, as New Labour aimed to do (for an examination of these policies, see Barr et al. 2001).

Although new ways of tackling social deprivation and social exclusion on housing estates were developed, however, critics of the government pointed to a number of limitations to their 'community regeneration' strategy. First, at the same time as the government developed community regeneration, restrictions on both the amount of housing benefit and the eligibility of claimants to this benefit were introduced. Consequently some socially disadvantaged groups – for instance, young tenants on low incomes – argued that they were no longer able to afford rising rents. Admittedly housing benefit has often been identified as an example in which fraud and wrongful claiming has been particularly common. However, as Kemp (1999) and others pointed out, an 'Old' rather than 'New' Labour strategy would have been to put less emphasis on means-tested housing benefit in the first place. Increasing across-the-board, 'bricks and mortar' benefits – that is, benefits that are payable to all residents in certain categories of housing irrespective of income – would have reduced poverty to a greater extent, even though it would have been at the cost of paying benefits to some people above the poverty line.

Second, any policy that targets particular kinds of community is bound, to a greater or lesser degree, to be a piecemeal, selective one. As a result, government policies in this area were vulnerable to the charge that used to be laid at the door of community development projects in the 1970s, that they were only palliative policies – a substitute for more effective, universal policies to reduce poverty and to improve people's environments.

Only time will tell how effective New Labour's policies have been in tackling the structural, deep-seated causes of both social exclusion and housing problems. However, according to Page's (2000) research, resources are still not getting through to social housing estates on a sufficiently large scale to reverse a two-decade period of decline towards poorer services and a poorer physical environment. Public services provided by local authorities have been kept on a tight budget since the late 1970s and this, together with a lot of internal restructuring and reorganization, has left them poorly equipped to make sudden improvements in areas of social housing. And while extra money is now being provided by central government, critics add that the rate of increase is little different from that added to the housing and environment budgets by the previous Conservative administration (Kemp 1999).

Finally, even if regeneration and housing improvement policies do begin to work in selected areas, their very success can lead to contradictory outcomes. This is because reducing the jobless rate, improving people's incomes and raising their aspirations leads to the out-migration of the more successful members of the community. At last they can escape the run-down estates and poor housing in which they have been living. Therefore, while community regeneration efforts might make a real difference to the lives of a considerable number of people, they are less likely than might be imagined to fundamentally change the neighbourhoods in which they are applied. Whether these are inevitably the results of community regeneration and development, however, will depend partly on the kind of community that is involved in the project, and how far local people identify with it and want to remain there. Also, the long-term effects of community regeneration will also depend on the type of resources that are developed. For instance, developing a credit union, child care services or cooperative food purchasing are examples of community resources and services that make life easier and encourage people to stay in their local areas.

Conclusions: housing and the environment in a postmodern society

No other aspect of social policy in the UK reflects dramatic change in quite the way that housing does. Alcock (1996: 36) describes housing as 'a kind of policy football – first kicked one way and then another'. But while this is historically true, the housing policies of the two main political parties have converged since the early 1970s. There has been convergence towards the idea of the private market being the dominant way of providing housing, and of owner-occupation being the desired type of tenure for all but a few. Any real differences in approach have been more a matter of emphasis or the speed with which governments have implemented policies such as the sale of council housing.

Currently, New Labour's broad policy on housing differs little from that of the preceding Conservative administration. There is a new emphasis on the regeneration of certain types of local community, and on the interface between housing, neighbourhood and other areas of welfare (for example, social care, health, education and training opportunities), but no reversal to a policy of planning on the grand scale.

As we have seen, there are signs that demand for additional housing will increase greatly in some parts of Britain, and especially in South-East England, in the first quarter of the twenty-first century. Yet the government appears to prefer to look the other way, as far as this looming problem is concerned, rather than open up a debate or deal with the intense conflicts that will inevitably arise when housing shortages become even more critical.

A number of social trends are combining to put additional strains on the housing market and to increase the need for extra dwellings. They include a high rate of divorce, separation and family break-up, increasing mobility and the need to move to realize job opportunities, and an ageing population in which more very old people will survive in their own homes than they did in the past. At a time when the population needs an ever more flexible supply of housing to meet the rapidly changing family and work demands of a postmodern society, the inflexibilities of the market system are becoming particularly evident.

For instance, house prices have become prohibitively expensive in some parts of the UK, and especially in London, with the result that young house purchasers are being excluded from the market. There is a knock-on effect in terms of rising demand for private rented accommodation, which then encourages steep rises in rents. In turn, demand for rented social housing has escalated, with the result that tens of thousands of people in London, for instance, are on long waiting lists for social housing and are living in very inadequate temporary accommodation. As a result, one London borough, Camden, recently signed an agreement with Kirklees, a northern local authority, to offer alternative accommodation to Camden families in Yorkshire, where there is a surplus of empty social housing. This illustrates the point made above, about the problems some local authorities have in trying to let unwanted social housing, while others are struggling to combat a growing housing shortage.

There are even signs that, in areas such as inner London, where the demand for affordable housing is very high, some council estates are losing what has been unfairly termed their 'piss-and-pitbull' image (Bennett 1996). In the year in which English

Heritage listed 67 council estates or tower blocks for architectural merit, Bennett adds, 'there are signs that certain council blocks are becoming coveted places to live. By way of purchasing or letting schemes, council flats are socially mobile as never before'.

While such trends might remain a mainly 'London phenomenon' for the foreseeable future, they do indicate a deeper swell of changes in attitudes to housing that will come to affect housing policy in the near future. On the one hand, as suggested by the above examples, there is a growing search for more flexible housing alternatives, especially among the young. On the other, there appears to be a growing concern with environmental aspects of housing.

Among architects, designers and environmental pressure groups there is growing concern with how to apply 'green' principles in housing – for instance, with the ways in which house design could be improved to limit energy loss and emissions of greenhouse gases. There is also concern about the environmental sustainability of local communities and the need to improve public transport, cycle paths and footpaths. Lewis (1992) and Atkinson (1995) discuss the possibilities of developing new kinds of partnership between businesses and voluntary or grassroots organizations to regenerate cooperative community ties.

In some ways, environmental and green objectives conflict with other policy objectives of reducing social exclusion and poverty. For instance, the decision to reduce VAT on domestic electricity and gas to 5 per cent has helped poorer households, and especially older people, who particularly need to maintain an adequate level of heat in their homes. However, this policy is hardly consistent with green objectives and contradicts the aims of levying much higher taxes on motor vehicle fuels.

With regard to the latter, high taxes on petrol and diesel fit in with a green objective of trying to discourage the use of cars and, by implication, will reduce harmful pollutants and emission of the greenhouse gases that contribute to global warming. However, the high cost of fuel affects poorer sections of the community very adversely and works against the government's aims of social inclusion.

A study by Lucas *et al.* (2001) found that, while half of the poorest fifth of the population do not own or have access to a car (and often find that high fares prohibit the use of public transport), the other half do. Most of the people on low incomes with cars own them because they cannot meet their basic commitments without them. This applies particularly to people in rural areas, and also to people working in outer suburban districts where public transport is very often inadequate. Such is their dependence on the car that people on low incomes are prepared to cut down on other necessities in order to maintain and fuel their vehicles.

Thus high fuel taxes reduce the living standards of poorer households in a very direct way, and help to compound social disadvantage. Being unable to use a car, and finding that public transport is either woefully inadequate or too expensive, can mean that people in poorer households cannot get to work – and problems of social exclusion are exacerbated. Improving transport is therefore emerging as one of the more important public issues, as successful progress in this area will not only help to further the cause of social inclusion, and the welfare of poorer groups in society, but also improve the quality of life for the majority. At the time of writing, however, transport was proving to be one of the government's weakest areas of performance. New Labour is particularly vulnerable to the charge that it has failed to deal with the disastrous results of the previous Conservative administration's approach to the privatization of bus and rail transport.

As Wolmar (2001: 17) observes, 'Despite the promise of extra money for all methods of transport promised in the Government's groundbreaking ten-year plan, the actual amounts are insufficient to make a significant difference'. Improved public transport links can increase take-up of employment, access to health care and education facilities, improve the integration of older people in society, and cut down the amount of disaffection and crime in run-down areas of social housing. In general, better transport reduces the isolation of poorer neighbourhoods. However, as Wolmar reminds us, investment and improvements in public transport need to take place *before* restrictions on car use or higher fuel taxes are introduced. Otherwise, people are unwilling to abandon their use of the car for essential purposes but, if they do, are hard hit by the failings of an expensive and unreliable system of transport.

In concluding this discussion of housing policy, therefore, it is important to note how the problems experienced by low-income groups in particular kinds of disadvantaged communities – inadequate transport, limited employment opportunities, a neglected physical environment and sub-standard housing – are all interrelated. If the trends of the 1980s and 1990s continue, the *marginalization* of the poor in these socially excluded communities will continue to be a marked feature of British society.

The Labour government's strategy for tackling the problems of social polarization and exclusion is largely focused on problems in areas of social housing and council estates. However, it is also worth noting briefly that housing problems can also be severe among people who are on low incomes but who are owner-occupiers rather than tenants in social housing. A study by Revell and Leather (2000), for instance, found that almost a third of homes in England need urgent repairs, and approximately the same proportions of homes in Scotland and Wales also need repairs of the same order. The authors also point out that the number of grants for housing renovation has dropped to a third of the level of the early 1980s, as a result of restrictions on local authority finances. Consequently, a significant number of houses in Britain are in poor condition, having problems of dampness, inadequate insulation, weather-proofing, heating and sanitation.

Therefore, while the majority of people in the UK are relatively well housed, neither the housing market nor government housing policy has served the minority very well. This minority includes poorer owner-occupiers as well as some of the groups renting private and social housing.

Key terms and concepts

autonomy
council housing
homelessness
industrial paternalism
marginalization
philanthropy
postmodern

residualization
social engineering
social housing
tenure

Suggestions for further reading

For authoritative guides to the history of housing in Britain and to recent housing de-velopments, consult Peter Malpass and Alan Murie's *Housing Policy and Practice* (4th edn, 1994) and Paul Balchin's introductory but comprehensive book, *Housing Policy* (1995). For a historical treatment of housing policy, see Malpass's *Housing and the Welfare State* (2005). A thorough but approachable overview of housing policy under New Labour has been written by Peter Kemp, in a chapter for Martin Powell's book, *New Labour, New Welfare State?* (1999). A more recent discussion of housing policy is provided by Brian Lund's chapter in *Evaluating New Labour's Welfare Reforms*, edited by Powell (2002). See also the most recent editions of *Social Policy Review*, an annual publication, which con-tains a chapter on housing policy. The 2004 edition, *Social Policy Review* 16, contains a chapter by Lund; the 2005 edition, *Social Policy Review* 17, has a chapter by Malpass.

A more specialized study of the fate of council housing and the prospects for the future can be found in Ian Cole's and Robert Furbey's book, *The Eclipse of Council Housing* (1994). A book of short readings edited by Carol Grant, *Built to Last?* (1992), gives a readable and stimulating overview of housing history, including chapters on Octavia Hill, the development of building societies and the history of 'prefabs', as well as chapters on current issues such as the housing experience of black people. Similarly, *Cities of Pride*, edited by Dick Atkinson (1995), provides a set of imaginative and interesting views on topics related to housing and urban regeneration: for instance, there are chapters on community development and the sustainable city.

11 COMMUNITY AND SOCIAL CARE

Introduction

Imagine whisking someone forward in time from the late 1940s to today. Though many things in the welfare system would be vaguely familiar – NHS funding crises, for one – a puzzling change would be heated debates about something called *community care* or social care. 'What or who is a *carer*?' the 1940s person might wonder (the rather specialized meaning of this term appeared well after the 1940s – see Bytheway and Johnson 1997). They would be similarly puzzled over terms such as 'continuing care', and even 'community' itself, for what exactly is a 'community' service – a service provided by local government, or perhaps by central government through a Ministry of Community Care?

Our visitor from the past could also be forgiven for being puzzled by holes in the net of 'caring' services. They would be able to catch up with newspaper and television reports on 'community care scandals', including sad stories of mentally ill people who have harmed themselves and others when released into 'the community' with inadequate support. Talking to a sample of older people, our visitor would be astonished to discover that a considerably lower percentage of people would be 'going into a home' in their old age, compared to the 1940s. They would be told that, even if they wanted to do this, so many residential and nursing homes have closed in recent years that, in some parts of the UK, it is almost impossible to find a place. Instead, older people in daily need of care and help with 'daily activities of living' are supposed to be able to receive it at home from a range of service providers organized by the local authority. To find that this network of domiciliary care services had grown up in the community since the 1940s would be surprising enough to our time-traveller. But even more surprising would be the news that, in some areas, older people in need of these services would be expected to pay relatively high charges for them and, because of the cost, would be able to afford only a limited amount of home care.

If our visitor had read George Orwell's *Nineteen Eighty-Four* (written in the late 1940s), they could be forgiven for thinking that something Orwellian had happened to the social services. Our visitor might think that a Ministry of Community Care was presiding over the opposite, Community Neglect, just as a Ministry of Love was overseeing perpetual war and political repression.

If our time-traveller from 1948 did form this impression, would you wish to reassure them that things today are not quite as bad as they might seem? Or would you argue that, in your view, community care policy and its successor, social care, represent one of the most glaring failures of the welfare system set up in the 1940s?

It is these opposing points of view, and what we would decide to tell our imaginary person from the past, that are the focus of this chapter. At the end you should be better able to decide how far social care policies have succeeded in reaching the goals set by government and other interested parties. As with other areas of social policy, we shall find that conclusions are 'messy' – inevitably so, as judgements partly rest upon political values and the evidence is conflicting. However, an informed view is possible and can be developed in two ways. First, we can examine the way in which community and social care have been *implemented* in Britain. This means looking at what type of care reforms were brought in and what the implications were, for both carers and the cared-for, of the market framework that was designed for service provision. Second, we are able to assess *outcomes* of the community care reforms in the 1990s, and finally the development and likely outcomes of more recent and current New Labour policies on social care. A little more historical background is necessary, though, to understand more fully these two main aspects of community care.

The development of community and social care

The Victorian legacy: care in institutions

Although the language and the social conditions have changed a great deal, today's debates about social care reveal an age-old tension. What are the benefits, to society at large and to the people who are the objects of care and control, of residential care or institutional solutions on the one hand, and 'community' solutions on the other?

The main difference between now and 'then' (the nineteenth century) is that policy since the early 1960s has been to *deinstitutionalize* care and to rely increasingly on the community. In the nineteenth century, the main aim was to build institutions and to separate paupers, the destitute and those judged to be either mad or morally wayward from the rest of 'respectable' society. As we saw in Chapter 3, however, a large majority of those who received help under the Poor Law system did so outside Poor Law institutions.

The sheer expense and organization involved in putting everyone who needed help into institutions thwarted the Victorians' aim. By the same token, one of the main causes, if not *the* cause, of deinstitutionalization and the modern policy of community care was the cost savings that resulted from closing residential care institutions (Scull 1984).

At the beginning of the twentieth century, a much higher proportion of those in need of care were in institutions, compared to the proportion today. For instance, about three times more older people (about 8 per cent of over-65s) were in workhouse accommodation, homes for the aged or hospitals or infirmaries, compared with under 3 per cent in residential or nursing home care today.

Gradually, geriatric medicine emerged as a specialty, there was a boom in hospital building and, with the coming of the NHS, older frail people were more likely to be hospitalized than in the past and less likely to be placed in workhouse-type accommodation.

The 1950s and 1960s: deinstitutionalization gains momentum

With the medicalization of problems of ageing came the pressure to reduce length of stay. Hospital and nursing care are expensive, and in the medical world older people began to be labelled as 'bed blockers'.

There were parallel trends in other areas of care, such as psychiatric medicine and hospital care for mentally ill people. In fact, as the welfare system developed in the 1950s and 1960s, a number of factors worked together to put increasing pressure on residential and hospital care. First, there was mounting concern about spiralling increases in public spending on welfare. Second, the costs of residential care were rising particularly rapidly. Third, there were worries about the demographic and economic outlook (rapid increases in numbers of very old people combined with a slowing down of economic growth). And fourth, there emerged a strong critique of the negative and controlling aspects of residential and long-stay hospital care, as exemplified by liberal sociologists such as Goffman and critics of psychiatry (see Chapter 6).

Such critics of institutions had a point. A series of well-publicized scandals about abuse of older people and children in residential homes and revelations of the brutal degradation of people with learning difficulties and mentally ill people in hospitals seemed to bear out the oversimplified view that residential care is always a bad thing. Supporting those in need of long-term care to live freely in the community began to be seen as the best policy in almost all cases.

As Scull (1984) concludes, this consensus emerged during the 1960s. Both liberal or progressive opinion on the one hand and conservative opinion on the other could agree that, on the grounds of either human liberty or saving money, residential institutions of all sorts should be closed down.

It is possible to trace the development of this thinking, and of community care as the alternative, in a number of official studies of policy and in significant pieces of legislation. The Mental Health Act 1959 sought to establish community care for the mentally ill and this led to a significant reduction in long-stay hospital facilities. In 1963, the Conservative government produced a White Paper on the development of community care (Ministry of Health 1963), though an incoming Labour government in 1964 did not follow this up with legislation. And in 1968, local authorities were required (under the Health Services and Public Health Act) to provide a home help service to older people.

Some of these policies led to improvements in services. Governments did not cynically close institutions solely in order to save public money. There *are* strong reasons for concluding that the needs of those who are frail, ill or disabled can usually be better met with help in their own homes, or in some other community setting. However, nothing like a concerted policy on community care emerged in the 30 years after the welfare state was born. Although the benefits of well-organized community care were acknowledged, the priority was more to close institutions than to divert substantial resources into personal social services for community care. As one indication of this, for instance, many local authorities never managed to provide home help services on the scale required by official targets before 1980 (Tinker 1981: 101–6).

Finding ways of getting health and social service departments to work together at the local level to plan, pay for and provide community services proved to be difficult – despite the introduction of joint financing arrangements in 1976 (Challis *et al.* 1995: 10). This underlined the point that health authorities in particular were more concerned with shifting the 'burden' of long-stay patients or residents than in developing a flexible policy of community care.

Thus, as a result of these attitudes, a basic idea that all institutional care is bad became firmly entrenched policy. However, with the closing down of many of Britain's Victorian asylums and other long-stay facilities, quite a lot has been lost as well as gained. Take Bill Bryson's memory, from 1973, of the effects of a large mental hospital – now closed – on an affluent commuter area near London, for instance. It offers a different perspective on both patients and local residents:

> *What lent Virginia Water a particular charm back then, and I mean this quite seriously, is that it was full of wandering lunatics. Because most of the residents had been resident at the sanatorium for years, and often decades ... most of them could be trusted to wander down to the village and find their way back again. Each day you could count on finding a refreshing sprinkling of lunatics buying fags or sweets, having a cup of tea or just quietly remonstrating with thin air. The result was one of the most extraordinary communities in England, one in which wealthy people and lunatics mingled on equal terms. The shopkeepers and locals were quite wonderful about it, and didn't act as if anything was odd because a man with wild hair wearing a pyjama jacket was standing in a corner of the baker's declaiming to a spot on the wall or sitting at a corner table of the Tudor Rose with swivelling eyes and the makings of a smile, dropping sugar cubes into his minestrone. It was, and I'm still serious, a thoroughly heartwarming sight.*
> *(Bryson 1996: 80–1)*

The 1980s: 'community' and 'care' redefined

Bill Bryson's sketch of the relationship between a local community and a large mental hospital show us that the boundary between 'community' life and 'residential' or institutional life can be blurred. Unless inmates are incarcerated in prison-like conditions, there is bound to be a degree of interaction between the two. This point is important, because it is all too easy to assume what is meant by the respective terms 'community' and 'residential' care, when in fact their meanings are problematic.

In Knapp *et al.*'s (1992) study of 28 community care pilot projects, for instance, living in the 'community' is assumed to mean anything except long-term hospital care. Thus 'community' care in this study included residential homes, sheltered housing, hostels, staffed group homes and home care (foster) placements (Knapp *et al.* 1992: 342). Similarly, Parker (1990: 11) notes that in a Department of Health and Social Security (DHSS) consultative document of 1977, *The Way Forward*, 'The term "community" covered a range of provisions which included community hospitals, hostels, day hospitals, residential homes, day centres as well as domiciliary support'.

In the 1980s, however, official policy came to define community care in a different way. It was no longer to be regarded as the struggle to extend local authority services or district health services into people's homes, decentralized community facilities or *day centres*. The new policy was to aim for care *by* the community (primarily through family and neighbourhood support) in partnership with the state, rather than care *in* the community (the provision of state-run services to people in their homes or nearby).

These significant changes in policy occurred partly because the trends noted above were still at work: that is, concern about rising numbers of very old people coupled with a lack of resources, and so on. However, the 1980s in Britain ushered in additional pressures to find cheaper alternatives, not only to institutional care but also to expensive personal care delivered by the social services to people at home.

First, there was the impact of what was then called 'New Right' thinking about welfare. As discussed elsewhere in relation to the health service (see Chapter 9), Mrs Thatcher's government emphasized certain pro-market priorities and goals. These included privatization, seeking value for money in government expenditure, setting up market-style arrangements for purchasing and providing services at the local level, and treating users of social services as *consumers*.

Though expressed in impartial and diplomatic language, these goals were woven into the two most influential government reports on community and residential care in the 1980s, the Audit Commission (1986) report and the Griffiths (1988) report.

Second, however, the push for fundamental reforms in community and social care did not come solely from the rightward shift in thinking about welfare. The need for more care in people's own homes was made particularly important by the increasing costs of public spending on private residential care. In 1979 the cost to the public purse of subsidizing older people's use of private residential homes was only £10 million. By the mid-1980s this figure had increased alarmingly to £500 million per year, and by the end of the 1980s it was approaching £1000 million per year. As the Audit Commission (1986) and Griffiths (1988) soberly reminded everyone, this open-handed subsidy had created 'perverse incentives' not to develop community care alternatives which, as well as being cheaper, would as likely as not be a better form of care.

Both reports succeeded in convincing government and the social services community that there had been an unplanned drift into providing too much residential care. This perception took hold despite the findings of another government report (Firth 1987) showing that the overall provision of residential home places for older people (by private, local authority and voluntary sectors) had *not* risen very much in the 1980s in proportion to rising numbers of people aged over 75.

Therefore, the impression that large numbers of active older people, well able to support themselves in their own homes, were moving into private residential care at public expense was wrong. Actually, Britain has long had a comparatively low proportion of people in residential care, and there is now an argument for expanding residential accommodation. As Wistow *et al.* (1994) show, the ratio of beds in residential homes to older people (aged over 75) was static in the 1980s, mainly because local authority provision shrank dramatically relative to the growth of the independent sector (the private and voluntary sector homes combined).

Johnson (1999) reminds us that, in the UK in 1980, local authorities provided nearly two-thirds of all the places in residential care for older people, and the private and voluntary sectors provided about a fifth each. By 1995 the private sector was providing well over half of all the places, while local authorities were providing only just over a quarter, and the voluntary sector less than a fifth (Davies 1999: 84). This, as Davies points out, represents a rapid privatization of social services, not in the sense of a sell-off of government institutions but more in terms of a rapid replacement of state-provided services with private sector ones.

As far as organizing community care more effectively was concerned, the Audit Commission (1986) report and especially the Griffiths report (1988) were very influential in shaping government thinking about how to reform the funding and provision of care services. Their influences are clearly apparent in the government White Paper *Caring for People: Community Care in the Next Decade and Beyond* (DoH 1989), which prepared for the legislation of the NHS and Community Care Act 1990.

At the time, the Griffiths report was seen by some as ideologically biased and, despite its neutral and fair-sounding language, more concerned with finding cheaper solutions to the problem of social care than with human welfare. Such criticisms had some justification, but Wistow *et al.* (1994: 5) remind us that Griffiths was 'not entirely unsympathetic with the views of those critical about the adequacy of funding'.

But while the Griffiths report did show a concern that community care provision should be 'needs led' rather than entirely dictated by financial considerations, there was a failure or an unwillingness to spell out the full *social costs* of community care. It made rather bland assumptions about family support when, according to some research, an unequal burden of care often falls upon women in families. For instance, Qureshi and Walker's (1989) study of patterns of care in a sample of families in Sheffield showed that female relatives are more frequently expected than men to cut down or leave paid work to perform a wider range of care tasks.

Interestingly, however, in many households supporting people who need long-term care now, the only available carer is a man. This is becoming more common because a higher proportion of older people in their eighties and nineties continue to live as couples, rather than as dependants with younger members of their families, than might have done in the past. As a result, gender inequalities in giving care at home might not be as marked as is often supposed. Arber and Gilbert's (1988) study, for instance, based on a national sample of households and titled 'Men: the forgotten carers', showed that men take on almost as much care work at home as women do.

The same survey also showed that, with one or two exceptions such as 'meals on wheels', provision of domiciliary services is also more gender equal than is often supposed. The proportion of men in need of care who receive domiciliary services is not significantly greater than the proportion of women who receive help from outside the home. Inequalities between households, however, are much more significant. Irrespective of whether the person in need of care is a man or woman, those who live alone are much more likely to receive domiciliary services than people who live with others. This is the case even though there are substantial numbers of people living with a spouse or family who have greater needs than some of those living alone.

This underlines a significant point about the government's definition of community care and expectations of care by families. Officially, every individual in need has a right to be assessed in their own right, but in practice 'community' care assessments usually put *family* circumstances before individual needs. Thus the care plans for two disabled people with identical needs will often be quite different if one happens to live with family while the other lives alone.

According to this definition of community care it is only right that the family should be asked to step in to provide help wherever possible, while care funded by the state is targeted on people living alone. However, the problem with this view is that it can lead to situations in which unfair assumptions are made about the willingness or ability of carers to provide sufficient support. Carers have needs too – an important point that is mentioned again in the next section.

The community care reforms: implementation and outcomes

The NHS and Community Care Act 1990 can be portrayed as a new version of an old tune: how to save money by replacing expensive institutional care with cheaper alternatives. However, it has transformed the landscape of care and the personal social services, mainly because it made sure that a market system would operate throughout. The changes made from 1993 onwards (implementation of most of the 1990 Act was delayed until April 1993) still structure the social services and have been retained by New Labour – though Labour has also introduced further changes.

This Act was at least partly a genuine attempt to rationalize a system for coordinating services that previously had been far too poorly coordinated. The main changes brought about by the NHS and Community Care Act 1990 were as follows.

- It was the first attempt to treat community care as a distinct entity and to bring comprehensive change to this area of social policy. Above all, the Act was supposed to bring the social services and the NHS together under one umbrella – a coordinated set of services that would focus on care in the community.
- The core aim of the Act was to give people the choice, wherever possible, of being cared for in their own homes.
- Local authorities were required to draw up care plans for their areas. These plans were to include an overall assessment of clients' needs irrespective of the

facilities or resources actually available. Assessment was supposed to be client-led or needs-led.

* The Act brought a full change towards the introduction of an internal market in social services. The community care reforms required local authority social service departments to act mainly as the purchasers of care services (though local authorities were to continue to provide services where it was not possible to find other providers, or where people with the highest levels of dependency were involved).

Thus, as in the health services, a purchaser–provider split was introduced, with local authorities being responsible for ensuring that care needs were being addressed and purchasing services accordingly. A diversity of other agencies, either private (for profit) or voluntary (non-profit) increasingly fulfil the role of providing services and engaging in face-to-face work with service users and their families.

Sometimes the phrases *welfare pluralism* and *mixed economy of care* are used to describe these arrangements. However, it would probably be more accurate to view the changes brought about by the 1990 Act as the introduction of a *social care market* (Wistow *et al.* 1994: 2). This is because the whole picture has been changed, rather than parts of community care remaining as islands of publicly-run services. *All* services provided in the community, including local authority services, are now thought of in market terms.

Another central aim of the community care reforms was to establish care management. Care managers' responsibility is to draw up tailor-made 'care packages' for individual service users. The care manager is someone who will set targets and priorities, deciding who will get a service and what the aims of service provision are. They are supposed to plan and manage the delivery of services to avoid either duplication, or inefficient overlaps in services, or gaps in provision of care.

Another key change to be brought about by the 1990 Act was the return to local authorities of the power to decide who will receive state-supported long-term care in institutional or residential settings. No longer were people able to claim social security benefits directly from the DSS to pay for private residential home fees. Only those who are judged to be in need may enter a private or voluntary sector home at public expense.

More recently, there have been further changes by the Labour government in the policy on how much, and what kind, of financial support people may receive to pay for the costs of care if they are in a nursing home or residential home. New kinds of distinctions have emerged between health/nursing care, social care and personal care (see pp. 00–00). Public support for residential and nursing home care is also becoming more complex as different policies are being developed in England, Scotland and Wales (see Chapter 12).

Before these more recent changes, however, the 1990 Act had introduced a system that gave local authorities an incentive to place people in private or voluntary sector homes rather than in their own residential institutions. Where residents' incomes fell below the means-tested level and were to be given support by the local authority, local authorities could recoup some of the 'hotel' (board and lodging) costs – but only if the residents were in private and voluntary sector homes. If local authorities' own homes were used, from 1993 the local authority had to meet the *whole* cost ('hotel' and 'care' costs) if the resident was unable to do so.

Thus the residential care market was rigged in favour of the private sector. This meant that the government was able to claim that it had not 'pulled the plug' on support for private home owners, who had previously been able to count on a steady flow of publicly (DSS) funded residents into their homes. The abruptness of the government's change of policy was also lessened by the decision that people already receiving social security payments for fees in 1990 could continue to do so under the old arrangements (that is, direct payment from the DSS).

Outcomes of the community care reforms: the early years

Two main impressions of the early years of community care stand out. The first was the lack of any clear public endorsement or popular acclaim for the policy. If the new community care arrangements were successful, they were a very quiet success. Lack of public support for community care was also seriously weakened by isolated cases of attacks by dangerous mentally ill people on others. Though few and far between, these cases tragically resulted in deaths and injuries, both to the patients themselves and to unsuspecting members of the public. They caused headline news and public dismay about the ways in which dangerous patients had been discharged from hospital without any firm arrangements for managing their care or monitoring their behaviour.

The other main impression was of widespread dissatisfaction with the gap between the official rhetoric of community care as a needs-led policy and the reality of stringent controls on the resources available for home care and other community services. As deinstitutionalization gained pace in the 1990s, local authority social service departments were faced with rapidly rising bills for services to people who would have previously stayed in hospitals (and whose care would have been met by the NHS) or other long-stay institutions. As a result, they had little choice but to ration services to service users, mainly older people, who had previously been eligible for a range of domiciliary services such as meals on wheels, lunch clubs and home care at relatively low cost.

An illustration of these cutbacks was Gloucestershire County Council, which sent out a standard letter withdrawing services from a block of service users (Thompson and Dobson 1995). In a high court case in 1995, five pensioners won a test case on this action and, as a result, local authorities may no longer cut community care services indiscriminately. However, the court judgment also ruled that local authorities 'can and ought to take resources into account both in the assessment of need and the provision of services' (Thompson and Dobson 1995: 20). As a result of this and other test cases affecting local authority responsibilities, local authorities must honour existing decisions to provide community services once needs have been assessed. However, if an authority is faced with a shortfall in resources, it is quite within its rights to reassess individuals' needs and withdraw services, even though it is forbidden to send out a standard letter to whole groups, as in Gloucestershire.

Financial constraints on local authorities and the effects of a social care market meant that many individual service users faced increased charges for home care and other services as the community care reforms took effect. Charges present a particular hardship to older people whose incomes fall just above the level at which they are eligible for social security assistance. An older person looking after a severely disabled spouse, for instance, might have to struggle along with a minimum of home care because a few more hours of help each week would be too expensive.

Other aspects of community care reform caused concern in the early years. For instance, there was a major concern that the goal of providing consumer choice from a variety of providers was not being addressed. The new community care policy seemed to put more consumer power in the hands of care managers and their superiors than in clients' hands. This shortcoming paralleled the health reforms, and the way in which they led to GPs and other doctors making 'consumer' choices on behalf of the patient, rather than patients themselves. Consumer complaints procedures have been instituted by social service departments, as required under the 1990 Act. However, they vary in their effectiveness and still have a long way to go before they are even known about by the majority of service users (Dean and Hartley 1995).

Also, being able to make individual complaints about existing services is not the same as being able to participate in policy-making or in decisions about changing the direction, approach or content of services. Involvement of service users in planning community care in the early 1990s was minimal, according to Henwood's survey. She found that service users and carers wanted more genuine involvement and empowerment. There was a widespread desire for a chance to make actual changes to the services provided, so that 'people [could] get the help and support that they want, rather than the support which professionals believe they need' (Henwood 1995a: 19).

However, government rhetoric about consumer choice and empowerment set up certain expectations and demands in the public mind. As the pressures on community care resources increased significantly after 1993, these demands and contradictions in the policy had to be managed largely by local authorities. To many older people, for instance, the levying of relatively high charges for community care services represented a betrayal of welfare state values, and a withdrawal of care that many had supposed would be provided free at the point of use.

While conflicts over lack of resources and charges for services represent important issues, though, it is possible in some ways to overstate the amount of change directly brought about by community care policy in the first few years of implementation. As Henwood concluded, community care reforms brought greater flexibility in service provision and 'perhaps an improvement on past practice', though two years after implementation the changes were 'still only marginal' (1995a: 18).

The Carers' National Association (Warner 1995) reported disappointment in carers' experiences of the reformed system of community care. Many did not feel that they were fully understood or appreciated by care managers, and a considerable number did not know that full-time carers (approximately 1.5 million in total) had been given a right to have their own needs assessed. According to a Carers' National Association survey in 1994, only 13 per cent of carers had received a separate assessment of their needs (Brindle 1995). Similarly, many reported that they had never seen or had an opportunity to discuss a written assessment of the person they were caring for. In general, carers did not appear to be treated as equal partners in the process of making decisions about community care plans, despite the fact that so-called 'informal care' (support from family, neighbours and friends) is of enormous significance in ensuring the workability of government policy.

In recognition of the importance of carers, though, the Conservative government's support of a Labour MP's private member's bill (the Carers Recognition and Services Bill moved by Malcolm Wicks MP) made full-time carers' rights to assessment a legal requirement. Recording unmet needs among carers, as well as the cared for, was an important first step, as recognition of the strain borne by carers spurs local authorities into providing services such as respite care (Hancock 1995). As with the community care programme as a whole, however, the severe financial problems that local authorities faced from the outset hindered any substantial improvements for carers.

Finally, the community care reforms seemed to bring mixed results in the early years as far as the outcomes for care managers, practitioners and service providers were concerned. In one survey of 600 care managers, Marchant (1995) found mixed attitudes to the community care reforms rather than widespread disillusion or collapse of morale.

On the negative side, the same survey found evidence of considerable levels of stress among care managers as a result of budget cuts and financial restraints. As Marchant points out, 'it falls to the care managers to turn down a care package for a client if there is not enough money' (1995: 16). In their new roles as purchasers, they found that they were much more the rationers of care than before.

A second source of strain has emerged from the expansion of bureaucratic work involved in separating the functions of assessment, purchasing and providing. In the survey reported by Marchant (1995), an overwhelming majority – 96 per cent – of care managers reported an increase in administrative work as a result of the implementation of the community care reforms. Stress results not only from form-filling but also from the restriction in opportunities for helping people in the direct, personal way that many social service employees had joined their profession to do.

However, an evaluation of the changes in community care between 1994 and 1995, reported by Henwood (1995b), noted some improvement in joint working between social service departments and health authorities, though significant difficulties in managing care across the health and social care divide remained. This was especially so where hospitals had increased pressure on community services by altering discharge policies without telling social service and community health agencies. Problems also remained in the negotiations between community health service providers and home care providers on the matter of 'who does what' when caring for people in their homes.

Thus the reforms introduced some new complications and showed up the differences between the health and social services in their skills and cultures. These were patently too deeply entrenched to be transformed by a few years of community care reform, and the early stumbling blocks to 'joined-up working' were to prove to be of lasting significance.

Social care and social services after 1997

The New Labour Government of Tony Blair elected in 1997 inherited the institutional framework for social care just described and continued with it. However, Labour have also been concerned to put their own stamp on policy. Social care, or community care, and the social services have seen a large number of new initiatives. Changes since 1997 have included the following.

- New arrangements for the joint working of social and health care services and provision of social care in the community through care trusts.
- The development of a social services performance framework and a new emphasis on standards of care.
- A *divergence* of policies in England, Scotland and Wales on paying for residential care and care in nursing homes.
- A shake-up of the regulation and training of social workers.
- Measures to give service users a greater say in the delivery of services – for instance through the development of the 'direct payments' scheme introduced by the Conservatives. This allows users of services or their carers to apply to their local authority to be paid directly for the services they need; they then take responsibility for engaging and paying for home care or other services themselves.

There have been additional important changes to the examples mentioned above, and a stream of reports, guidance and training packs from the DoH on a host of topics in the area of social care.

While much of the detail of developments in the fast-changing area of social care is not covered here, it can be accessed by looking at the information provided by organizations in the field (see suggestions for further reading at the end of this chapter).

Modernizing social services

There has, arguably, been less fundamental change than might be supposed from the welter of government activity in relation to social care and social services. Labour's thinking on social care was contained in its White Paper of 1998, *Modernising Social Services* (DoH 1998a), one of a number of policy statements in the health and social care field that appeared early on in the government's first term. This identified and listed a number of problems with Labour's inheritance and expressed a commitment to dealing with these. Most of these problems – abuse and neglect of vulnerable adults, poor interagency coordination, service-led rather than individualized needs-led provision, territorial inconsistency in eligibility and care standards, inefficiency – were of long-standing and even predated the Thatcher and Major governments.

New Labour's policy has been to continue with the broad framework for community care built by the Conservatives in the NHS and Community Care Act 1990. The 'social market' has been retained, and there has been no attempt to return to the days when local authorities were the main providers of social care. The trend towards privatization of social care has continued.

Labour preferred to talk about 'social' care rather than community care and, after election to power in 1997, portrayed the Conservatives' approach to community care as a discredited one. But on balance the government's policies have tried to shore up an inadequate community care system rather than aiming to replace it with a different approach. Despite the rhetoric, therefore, the inherited framework of values and broad policy goals has been maintained. In fact social and community care is an area of social policy which, arguably, exhibits a higher degree of party-political consensus than any other.

Social services expenditure

The direction in which the New Labour government was to proceed with community care became evident in 1998 when Frank Dobson, then Health Secretary, announced that an extra £700 million would be spent on care services in the following three years. Though this was a substantial increase it represented only about a fifteenth of the total (between £10 billion and £11 billion) spent annually on community care and social services, and was seen as disappointing and inadequate by mental health charities such as the National Schizophrenia Fellowship (Brindle 1998).

Moreover, this extra money was to be directed toward an increase in the number of beds in secure units for mentally ill people rather than to care 'in the community'. The strategy included assertive 'outreach teams' with new legal powers to detain mentally unstable people thought to be a risk to others. Much of the impetus for this policy came from public concern about the killings of Lin and Megan Russell in 1996 by Michael Stone, a man with a personality disorder previously considered untreatable and highly dangerous, who had been discharged from hospital to live in 'the community'.

The prime concern of government was, some argued, less focused on finding the right mix of services for mentally ill people or others in need of care than on public safety and the government's credibility. Organizations defending civil liberties, for instance, were concerned about the new legal powers brought in by government to enforce treatment of people with mental disorders (Brindle 1998). Others were concerned about the purse strings that came with the extra money, because central government was to retain control of a substantial amount of the additional £700 million.

Expenditure on social care is substantial, if small by comparison with that on other public programmes such as the NHS and education. In 2004–5, £14.4 billion was spent on local authority provided social care in England, of which £10.6 billion was on adult social care (DoH 2005: 40). Of this, £8 billion was spent on older people, of which £1.6 billion was recouped through means-tested charges. Another £3.7 billion in help towards the cost of care was paid to elderly individuals on non-means-tested benefits.

It is estimated that, in addition, £3.5 billion was spent privately on residential and home care (Wanless 2006: xxi). The government has subsequently continued to promise additional resources for social care. The Treasury's 2004 Spending Review forecast an additional £1.8 billion of expenditure between 2004–5 and 2007–8 for England, bringing the projected total for the personal social services to £12.47 billion in the latter year, and representing a real-terms annual increase of 2.7 per cent (HM Treasury 2004: 100). The future for social care spending is likely to be somewhat bleaker after that, however, in common with that for other public programmes, as public spending is forecast to grow more slowly than national income, and more slowly than that for the period since 2000. It is likely that ministers will seek to protect spending on the NHS and acute services before that on adult social care.

Regulation, monitoring and inspection

The theme of increasing regulation and supervision of local services from the centre was continued in the Care Standards Act 2000. This legislation was a product of the 1998 *Modernising Social Services* White Paper's concern to establish national, common standards in all branches of social and residential care (DoH 1998a). At this time, the Waterhouse report (2000) on long-term physical and sexual abuse of young people in residential homes in North Wales in the 1970s was being prepared. This report recommended improvements in the inspection of children's homes and young people's residential units, some of which had been 'hidden' from effective supervision in the local authority care system.

The main change brought about by the Care Standards Act 2000 was a separation of *inspection* of social services (which had formerly been in the hands of local authorities, but with independent checks by the Social Services Inspectorate) from their *provision* by local authorities and other bodies. The Act introduced an independent watchdog, the National Care Standards Commission, which is responsible for inspection of social services in England. There are equivalent bodies in Northern Ireland, Scotland and Wales (see Chapter 12). The care standards commissions work through local and regional offices and conduct inspections of social services for children and child protection, private and voluntary health care (for example, in nursing homes), home care and residential care services for older people, and services for adults with disabilities and other needs.

The 2000 Act also set up a General Care Council in England – again with equivalents in the other countries of the UK. These regulatory councils oversee the education and training of professionals (social workers) and other care workers, deal with matters of professional misconduct, and apply a code of conduct. This measure reflects – among other things – government concern about the abuse of young people and other service users in care and has tried to establish a new framework for making sure that serious abuse and inefficient supervision are reduced to a minimum.

It will take time to assess the impact of all these attempts to toughen the regulation of social care and the work done by social and health services in 'the community'. It would be wrong to expect quick results, as social care covers a disparate range of services managed in different ways and by many different agencies. The total of workers employed in providing social care is huge, and is commonly estimated to be between three-quarters of a million and a million.

The need for improvement in the supervision of social and community health services was underlined in the same year as the Care Standards Act by the tragic case of Victoria Climbié – a young girl who was brought to live in London, via France, from the Ivory Coast. Victoria was murdered, after months of physical abuse and mental torture, by her great-aunt, Therese Kauao, and Carl Manning, Kauao's partner.

However, the lesson of this case not only seemed to be that tougher regulation of social and health services is required, but also underlined the point that inadequate levels of staffing, support services and the organizational capacity of the local authority (in this case Haringey, in London) are also keys to a full understanding of failures in care. There were many other reasons for the failure to detect and take action against the terrible abuse that Victoria suffered, such as a failure of the health practitioners who treated the girl to follow up her case. But the fact that the social services department in Haringey was very stretched in terms of staffing and a supply of experienced social workers seems to have been a crucial factor.

Thus the government's concern with 'quality control' and its attempts to impose a tougher, more centralized way of monitoring social care work are understandable. But if this policy is not matched by an even more substantial boost in social services staffing and other resources there is a strong argument that the confidence and morale of social services workers will continue to decline.

Relatively low wages and salaries in social services and social care work deter would-be employees. But in addition, and perhaps more important, is the perception that this type of work means having to carry the can for the local authority or other employer, yet in a work environment where there is insufficient support and where services are often inadequate.

Funding of long-term care

From the beginning of the 1980s to the end of the twentieth century, the availability of 'free' or publicly-supported long-term care services in a person's own home was increasingly restricted to those in most need or people on low incomes. And once the system of direct payment of residential care fees from the DSS was abandoned at the end of the 1980s, a rising number of older people faced more stringent rationing of 'free' residential care by local authorities.

This is partly because many more people now have substantial savings than used to be the case in the past. More own houses and other property above the value of £21,000 – which in 2006 in England was the cut-off point above which those going into residential care or using other care services had to pay their own costs in full (while those owning property or capital between £12,750 and £21,000 paid a proportion of these costs, according to a sliding scale, and those with assets below £12,750 did not have to contribute).

The problem of having to sell one's house to pay for care was a very politically sensitive issue for governments that have traditionally stressed the virtues of home ownership and the individual's right to keep their property. This issue also touched the political nerves of both main parties because of the anomaly of residents of nursing homes having to pay for their nursing care. If a person is treated as a 'patient' in NHS facilities, all health and nursing care is provided free. But while one person could receive free NHS care, another with very similar needs but in a different location could be asked to pay the steep monthly fees of a private nursing home, which would not come under the NHS umbrella.

As on other important election issues, New Labour's strategy in 1997 was to match the Conservatives' rather vague promises to do something about the problem of paying for long-term care. When elected to power, New Labour decided to set up a Royal Commission to investigate the whole question.

Arguably this was a stalling device, but the Royal Commission on Long Term Care, headed by Sir Stewart Sutherland (1999), did rethink the problematic distinction between health and social care, and re-label both as 'personal care'. The report also made a distinction between personal care on the one hand and, on the other, the living and housing costs to be met when disabled or older people are receiving long-term care (whether in their own homes or in residential or nursing homes).

The Royal Commission recommended to the government that all personal care costs should be met free of charge for everyone, irrespective of their incomes. However, the government rejected the Commission's main proposals. They claimed that the costs of providing free personal care to everyone who needed it, whether in their own homes or a residential setting, might be manageable in the short term, but in the future would represent too great a burden on the taxpayer and the welfare system. Significantly, however, the independence now enjoyed by the Scottish Parliament, as a result of devolution, allowed Scotland to decide to introduce a policy of paying for the long-term personal care costs of everyone in need (see Chapter 12).

Though not going as far as the Scottish proposals, the government has now undertaken to pay for the *nursing care* costs of people in need, though in England different levels of payment are still subject to a complicated assessment and means test. The thorny questions of trying to determine what exactly 'nursing' care is, how it differs from 'social' or 'personal' care, and how much nursing a particular individual needs, have not been solved but rather thrown into the limelight by this policy.

In sum, as far as institutional or residential care is concerned, the government has made modest efforts both to improve standards and to meet the costs of care for those in greater need or with fewer financial resources. However, a variety of pressures – not all of the government's making – are bringing about a serious crisis in residential and nursing care. Individual managers of homes, and the larger private companies that own and manage 'chains' of homes, are now pointing out that it is impossible for them to provide 'free' care to residents with the amounts of money paid on their behalf by government. At today's prices it would be difficult to find bed and breakfast accommodation or one night's stay at a hotel of a basic standard for the amount provided to support residents – and yet residential homes must include the provision of all meals and 'hotel' services, *and* personal care.

Also, as a result of the Care Standards Act 2000, many owners of residential and nursing homes have had to make further adaptations and improvements to their premises to meet the new standards. Faced with this additional burden, an increasing number of residential and nursing homes – especially the smaller private homes – have been forced to close. The knock-on effect of home closures and a shortage of places in residential care has been to worsen the 'bed blocking' problem in hospitals, where chronically ill people cannot be discharged to their own homes because they are too frail or disabled to look after themselves. The residential/nursing home crisis is also throwing additional strains on to the community care system. Social services struggle to meet the needs of a growing number of older and disabled people who are living in their own homes but who, in some cases, desperately need care in a residential setting but cannot find a place.

A crisis such as this suggests that the handling of social care since 1997 by New Labour has been marred by the same faults as the previous Conservative administration – and chiefly by a reluctance to devote substantially greater resources to social care. As mentioned above, however, this conclusion would not be entirely fair. The government has energetically set about trying to improve the quality and standards of social services. It has continued to increase the resources available to certain categories of people in need. For instance, in 2000 the Carers and Disabled Children Act widened the scope of direct payment schemes. The carer premium (additional allowance) payable to people receiving the invalid care allowance was increased, and direct payments became more widely available to disabled 16- and 17-year-olds, and to the parents of disabled children up to the age of 18.

On balance, though, the issue of personal care and its funding has continued to be a thorn in the government's side. The Health Service Ombudsman produced a critical report in 2003 on the maladministration involved in assessing some people for NHS continuing care (i.e. care in which the medical and nursing element was substantial enough to qualify for funding by the NHS).

The DoH was subsequently criticized and accused of slowness in reviewing the cases of people wrongly denied 'free' NHS funding of their care, notably in a Parliamentary Health Select Committee Report in 2005 (House of Commons Health Committee 2005). This called for the abolition of the distinction between health and personal care.

Meanwhile, six years after the Royal Commission report on the issue, the King's Fund set up an independent inquiry into the whole issue of the funding of long-term care for older people, under the chairmanship of Derek Wanless, the banker who had already conducted two notable inquiries into aspects of NHS funding and public health under Treasury auspices. This reported in March 2006 (Timmins 2006b; Wanless 2006). It is interesting that, in contrast to the earlier inquiries, the Treasury refused to be involved in this exercise, despite urging, and that it had to become an unofficial inquiry, organized under the auspices of a voluntary body (Carvel 2005; Timmins 2006b) – which is reminiscent of policy-making in the Thatcher years. The Treasury's apparent lack of enthusiasm for a social care funding review probably stems from its plans to rein in public spending after 2007, referred to earlier; it probably also reflects the lower degree of priority afforded to adult social care by comparison with the NHS and acute care.

The government subsequently appeared to execute a partial retreat from its initial position of neutrality, anticipating Wanless's recommendations by announcing, in the same week as the report's publication, its own wide-ranging, 'zero-based' review of long-term care funding, as part of the Treasury's Comprehensive Spending Review for 2007; this will look at funding needs for the care of all vulnerable groups. Wanless's recommendations will be among the options to be considered by the review, and Wanless himself has been co-opted on to the review working group (Timmins 2006a).

The Wanless report noted that 'there is little information about whether . . . spending achieves the government's desired aims for older people of promoting choice, independence and prevention'(Wanless 2006: pxxi). The report examined and compared a number of alternatives and proposed what it called a 'partnership' model of funding for care of the elderly, together with a large increase in funding, from £10 billion a year to £30 billion a year by 2026. This is necessary because of demographic change, the substantial burden of unmet need that exists and popular dissatisfaction with the present system.

The basic idea of 'partnership' funding is that higher spending by individuals should be matched by higher spending by the state. This is different from the Scottish model of 'free' personal care. A core level of free, non-means-tested personal care, amounting to 66 per cent of a benchmark package of care, would be universally available; individuals would then be able to top this up with their own money, the state matching individual additional contributions pound for pound. Low-income individuals would acquire the resources for additional care, if wanted, through the benefits system. This would obviously entail some means testing, but means testing would be transferred from the social care system to the benefits system, which is where it belongs, according to Wanless (2006: 285).

Wanless's conclusions and recommendations may be regarded as in some respects a partial re-run of the Royal Commission (Sutherland) inquiry seven years earlier, and has been viewed as such by Wanless's Royal Commission predecessor, as well as by its Minority Report critics (Benjamin and Carvel 2006).

The health and social care divide

Labour has sought to deal with the long-standing problem of divided health and social care responsibilities, which we have already referred to. Legislation in 1999 (Health Act) and 2001 (Health and Social Care Act) attempted to establish a framework for co-ordination.The latter marked a determined step by the government toward a unification of health (NHS) and social services (local authority) organizations. The aim is to provide a coherent framework of community care through the formation of care trusts. The Act also carried forward the government's intentions to provide 'free' nursing care.

The impact of the first of these important measures, however, will depend on how the administration and budgeting of care trusts will actually be agreed between the various partners – local government, NHS trusts and other health service representatives, and central government (the DoH).

These reforms have been criticized. First, worries have been expressed that health concerns will predominate over social aspects of care and support. Second, there is the issue of accountability – local social services are electorally accountable in a way which the NHS and PCTs are not. Third, it has been argued that PCTs lack the capacity to develop partnerships with social service agencies (Morris 2003: 216).

Labour and the future of social care

Whether the Labour government elected in 2005 is destined to be the one that finally solved the puzzle of how to bring together the distinctive sectors of health and social care, and forced them to work together effectively, is doubtful.

The Wanless report and the government's subsequent, somewhat belated, care funding review form part of a cluster of recent policies and initiatives, which include a report from the Prime Minister's Strategy Unit in 2005 on improving the life chances of disabled people (Prime Minister's Strategy Unit 2005) and a report from the House of Commons Health Select Committee on NHS continuing care (House of Commons Health Committee 2005).

The government's most recent views on the future of social care were set out in a Green, or consultation, Paper in 2005 (DoH 2005) and a White Paper in 2006. The Green

Paper rehearses and reiterates a number of policy themes: for instance, independence, choice, social inclusion, partnership between health and social care services, and expanding the role of direct payments. All these aims have implications for the role of social work, and the document is to some extent about a reconfigured role for social workers. The Green Paper was careful to stress that the changes sought will be 'cost-neutral' and that no substantial increase in expenditure is envisaged.

The White Paper, *Our Health, Our Care, Our Say* is concerned with health as well as with social care. One of the interesting things about this and the Green Paper reviewed above was their policy-making style, which involved substantial public consultation, including a 'Citizens' Summit' and a 'Citizens' Advisory Panel' – the 'our say' aspect of the initiative. The results of these consultations were fed into the policy-making process and influenced the policies, or so it is claimed. It is easy to be cynical about such exercises and to assume that the participants in them are likely to be highly self-selecting and unrepresentative of the population as a whole, but the DoH surely deserves some credit for attempting to involve the community in this way. The 2006 White Paper puts forward four main goals for the health and social care services: better prevention, greater choice, reducing inequalities and improving access, and providing more support for people with long-term needs (DoH 2006: 7–8). It highlights the importance of integrating health and social care services, via the development of Personal Health and Social Care Plans and integrated health and social care records, and the establishment of joint health and social care teams. More support will be given to carers (Department of Health 2006: 8).

The achievement of any degree of integration will depend on a reasonably stable level of resources. It has already been suggested above that the public spending climate will become less favourable after 2007, and there is evidence that current financial deficits among some NHS commissioners and providers are undermining social care provision. Scepticism has been expressed about the extent to which genuinely 'joined up' working between health and social care is capable of being realized, and the depth of the government's commitment, in the light of the apparent prioritization of the NHS and acute care. It remains to be seen how far the White Paper is able to overcome the fragmentation of policy-making in the area of health and social care, and a recent discussion concludes that 'the future prospects for adult social care are not promising' (Glendinning and Means 2006: 26).

Conclusions

You will recall that at the beginning of the chapter you were confronted with the idea of someone visiting us from the 1940s – someone who would be rather confused about the terms 'community care' and 'social care'. This person would want to know whether policies on 'care' and social services had brought genuine improvements or not. How far is 'care in the community' an ideological cloak masking a reduction in government commitment to public welfare services?

First, the balance of evidence discussed in this chapter suggests that, despite government rhetoric about community care being a needs-led policy, it is in fact resource-led. This does not mean that we should point the finger only at recent policy as a way of explaining why community care has become a way of saving public money. The history of community care from the 1950s onwards shows that there are long-standing pressures to deinstitutionalize care and to limit government commitments to providing services to people in their homes.

However, it would also be wrong to tell our 1940s visitor that no improvements have come about as a result of community care policy. Just because policy has been driven more by underlying economic pressures than need does not mean that the *idea* of care in one's own home is a bad one. Pilot schemes of community care in many different settings and with different client groups have demonstrated clear advantages of care at home over care in institutional surroundings. However, it will also be recalled that the advantages are not always clear cut, and that they depend on levels of funding many local authorities are unable to provide. Community care can be 'cheaper and better' than residential care, but only when the transition to 'the community' is well managed, or when staying in one's own home is sufficiently well resourced.

The advantages of the market system of social care introduced in the 1990s and continued by New Labour into the twenty-first century over the previous system of domiciliary care are much less clear. This seems to be the case whether one is looking at the market from the point of view of those who operate the system, or of service users and carers.

Just as much depends on finance and resources as it did in the days before the introduction of a social care market. As pointed out in this chapter, New Labour has substantially increased the total amount of government expenditure on social services and social care, though this area remains – in relation to social security, health, education and many other areas of government spending – the 'Cinderella' service.

It will be interesting to see how far the ideas of user empowerment referred to in this chapter will make a difference to the outcome of the struggles between central and local government over providing enough resources for social care. As discussed above, significant steps have been taken towards a fuller recognition of the contribution of carers. New Labour has brought tax credits, additional carer allowances and other benefits to carers on low incomes. The government has also continued to subscribe to the rhetoric of consumer rights and choice in a social care market, though in rather different language and using somewhat different terms than the former Conservative administration. Neither the extra carer allowances nor the ideology of empowerment will transform the landscape of social care, but they do reflect government concern to respond to the increasingly combative and consumerist attitude among service users and carers. While empowerment can be portrayed as empty rhetoric, it can nevertheless be exploited to criticize the limitations of official policy.

Changes have also occurred in one of the most contentious 'trouble spots' in social care, the question of who should fund continuing care of people who are initially looked after in NHS facilities or by NHS staff. One way out of the confusion about who is responsible for paying for and providing the different elements of long-term care was signalled by the Royal Commission on Long Term Care, as discussed earlier. However, as the government rejected the Commission's proposals for a simplified system of making all personal care free, some confusion and much variation in practice looks likely to continue.

The introduction of care trusts and free nursing care might go some way to resolving these problems, together with increasing central regulation and control of local authorities by government. However, at the time of writing, the degree to which these more recent policy changes will improve matters remains to be seen. What is more evident, as far as the present situation of social services is concerned, are widespread strains in the system. For instance there are widespread problems in the recruitment and retention of social workers and social care staff. An adequate supply of residential and nursing care places for the future is seriously threatened. And the ability of some cash-strapped local authorities to deliver services to people in their own homes, except for those in extreme need of care, means that the goal of a fair and equal standard of good quality social care across the UK is still a distant one.

Our visitor from the 1940s would probably be left with the impression that something had been lost from the ideals of the welfare state that had been newly-built in their decade. From a time in which the emphasis was on collective responsibility, mutual support and access to 'free' health care, they would find our contemporary emphasis on the idea of social care as a 'package' of services in a market very strange.

On the other hand, the 1940s were a time in which no one had anticipated just how much chronic illness would replace acute illness as the main burden of the NHS, or how the needs for long-term care in the population would have grown. There would also be one element of continuity, despite changing needs and changing social policies. Our visitor would find, in the continued willingness of millions of relatives and others to provide care, a strand of altruism and responsibility that linked their decade with ours.

Key terms and concepts

care management
carer
community care
consumers (of care services)
day centre
deinstitutionalization
domiciliary care (home care)
empowerment
mixed economy of care
needs-led assessment
purchaser–provider split
residential care
sheltered housing
social care market
welfare pluralism

Suggestions for further reading

There is now a rich variety of books on community care policy and the impact of community care on different social groups, such as disabled people or minority ethnic groups. One of the best all-round books to consult, especially in relation to different groups' experience of care policies, *Understanding Care, Welfare and Community* (2002) edited by Bill Bytheway and colleagues, is a reader containing short pieces on a wide range of topics. Similarly, *Community Care: A Reader* (1997) edited by Joanna Bornat and collegues is a useful source for of ideas and information about this subject.

For more detailed coverage of policy development in community care following the 1990 Act, see *Social Care in a Mixed Economy* (Wistow *et al.* 1994). Also, for a thought-provoking discussion of the nature of care and its relationship to social policy, it is well worth reading Julia Johnson's chapter, 'Care as policy' in *Care Matters*, a book edited by Brechin and colleagues (see Johnson 1997).

The historical background to the development of community care is well observed in Scull's *Decarceration* (1984), a book that is still interesting to read. Finally, the weekly publication *Community Care* provides a lively journalistic overview of topical issues in the field of social care and social services.

12 DEVOLUTION AND SOCIAL POLICY

Introduction: devolution and its significance

In 1999 the UK saw the creation of devolved governments of various types, affecting Scotland, Wales and Northern Ireland (the last only briefly). Devolution represents a historic change to the government and character of the UK. Its impact has been felt in many ways, and especially in the area of social policy and welfare. Nor has the impact of devolution been restricted to the countries with devolved administrations. Policy *divergence* from a standard 'UK model' in Northern Ireland, Scotland and Wales has increasingly had implications for social policy in England. As devolution takes effect, people in England may begin to realize that, in some cases, what they have been told is not desirable or cannot be implemented in their own country *is* being adopted or implemented in one or more of the other countries in the UK. The same, of course, is true for inhabitants of the devolved nations in relation to what is happening in England. Thus one way that social policy in England has gradually become distinctive is by default, as the other countries have tried out new arrangements, but England has also innovated in ways in which the other countries have not.

In education policy, for instance, a policy such as the introduction of specialist schools or the setting of SATs for 9-year-olds applies only to England. The other countries might choose to continue with existing policies towards education or other services and, by remaining the same as they were, accentuate their differences from England.

In this chapter, further examples of the growing differences in health, education and social services between England, Northern Ireland, Scotland and Wales will be examined. However, in the limited space available here, a comprehensive guide to all the distinctive policies and services in each country will not be provided. The chief aim of the chapter is to discuss the broad implications of devolution and its impact on social policy in the UK.

Key examples illustrate the different effects devolution seems to be having in different areas of welfare (such as education, health and social services) in the different countries of the UK. As devolution is a fast-changing area of government and politics, any detailed description of policies and services in the different countries dates very quickly – new policies are coming on stream at a rapid rate. To obtain updates on new policy developments, or to find details about particular policies or services, it is a good idea to consult official, annual publications by the devolved administrations or to consult their websites and other internet sources.

What is devolution?

The term 'devolution' refers to a transfer of government powers to make laws and policy. In the case of the UK, this means a transfer and loss of certain powers and functions from the Westminster Parliament and the government in London, which are at the centre of the UK's administration.

Devolution can be thought of as a process of transferring power and responsibility *upwards* as well as *downwards*. Upward devolution involves giving up some of the independence of the nation-state. The right to take certain important decisions is passed to a supranational or international organization such as the EU. By becoming a member of the EU in 1973, the UK Parliament agreed to regulation by EU laws and policies in key areas of economic and social life. Latterly, this has included wider areas of social policy, and the broad impact of EU social policy on the UK will be discussed toward the end of this chapter.

Devolution downwards – which is the main subject of this chapter – has been achieved in recent years by other Acts of Parliament that have transferred a limited range of powers and responsibilities from Westminster to elected assemblies or parliaments in each of the constituent countries of the UK. These legislatures are the Northern Ireland Assembly, the Scottish Parliament in Edinburgh and the Welsh Assembly Government in Cardiff.

Note that devolution in the case of Northern Ireland, which was supposed to result from the 1998 Good Friday Agreement, was suspended in 2002 because of continuing difficulties in securing agreement among the political parties, mainly relating to the issue of weapons decommissioning by the IRA. The Assembly did not meet and Northern Ireland was therefore subject to 'direct rule' and governed from Westminster, as it was between 1972 and 1999. A measure of administrative and policy devolution, however, continued. At the time of writing, the Northern Ireland Assembly was on the brink of a power-sharing agreement between the main political parties that promised a resumption of the Assembly's government.

A case for elected regional assemblies in England has been made, and was accepted by the government, but the government's proposals for an elected North Eastern Assembly were rejected in a referendum in 2004, effectively killing the issue for the time being.

Though devolution has advanced significantly in the UK in recent years, a degree of self-rule in certain parts is not a new phenomenon. For instance, the Isle of Man and the Channel Islands (Jersey, Guernsey and other smaller islands) are not part of the UK. They are Crown Dependencies and, though the UK Parliament retains the right to legislate for them, they have their own legislatures and historic rights to follow independent policies in many important areas. These include not only separate taxation and economic policies but also distinctive social policies. For instance, in Guernsey and Jersey there are quite different arrangements for running health services than those which pertain to the NHS in England and other parts of the UK.

Scotland, in terms of its size and political distinctiveness, is perhaps an even more significant example of historic 'devolution'. Strictly speaking, however, the Act of Union 1707 that joined together the two royal families, parliaments and administrations of England and Scotland was supposed to be an equal partnership rather than devolution of power from Westminster to Edinburgh. In practice, as England became the leading industrial economy and London the centre of political power in the UK, the principle of equal partnership of two nations was smothered by English dominance. However, the terms of the Act of Union meant that Scotland was able to retain its own distinctive laws and legal system, and a distinctive (and some would say superior) education system.

Northern Ireland also represents an example of a historic devolution of power from Westminster to a locally-elected government in the province. However, as mentioned above, Northern Ireland is a special case because of its troubled history. However, despite periods of direct rule from Westminster, it has long been recognized by the British government – since the splitting away of southern Ireland as the Irish Free State in 1922 – that because of its distinctive history, geography and social make-up, Northern Ireland needs its own administration and electoral system.

What type of devolution does the UK have?

As Northern Ireland, Scotland and Wales developed substantially different historic relationships with England, and with the UK as a whole, the more recent devolution reforms have been grafted onto these different historical relationships and political differences. Consequently, the type of devolution that the UK has chosen is called *asymmetric devolution*.

Symmetric devolution, on the other hand, is a type of government in which the constitution grants the same powers to each of the devolved states or administrations. In such cases more or less the same rules govern each devolved administration in its relationship with central government – as in the USA, for instance, where a written constitution prescribes the distinctive responsibilities and powers of all the US states and the federal government.

Why did the UK decide to take the road of asymmetric devolution, rather than scrap the existing constitution and start again with a more symmetric approach? This is perhaps a question of more interest to historians and political scientists than it is to social policy analysts. However, it can be said with certainty that a change to 'symmetric' devolution would have been very far-reaching. It would almost certainly have led to the federal government of the United Kingdom. A federal state is one in which there is a separate federal government, and in which there is a state or provincial government for *every* region or major province. Thus, federal UK government would have automatically led to the setting up of a (state) government of England – or, more likely, the splitting up of England into state governments of different English regions. In addition, federal government would mean state governments in Wales, Scotland and Northern Ireland and a separate federal administration to govern the UK as a whole.

As far as the future development of social policy is concerned, the main implications of the asymmetric pattern of devolution chosen by the UK are as follows.

First, the powers of the devolved administrations to make their own social policies vary, with the Scottish Parliament having the most independence and the Welsh Assembly Government the least. The Edinburgh Parliament can pass primary legislation on important areas such as education, health and the social services. It can also raise or lower the rate of income tax by up to 3 pence in the pound, giving it the opportunity to raise additional money from Scottish taxpayers to fund any new, distinctively Scottish, social policies. This is an option that would carry considerable political risks for any Scottish administration. The Assembly Government in Cardiff, on the other hand, has no tax-varying powers and can pass only secondary legislation – though a recent Government of Wales Act will extend some primary legislative powers to the Cardiff Assembly in 2007. Until then, however, all legislation in the Assembly must follow legislation at Westminster. For instance, an Act of Parliament in Westminster that changes policy on health services must be followed up with a Welsh equivalent that is broadly in line with the Westminster legislation. From 2007, though, the Welsh Assembly will have considerable powers to set its own priorities as well as adapt Westminster legislation. The ways in which the Welsh Assembly has already made a difference to the implementation of social policies are illustrated later in this chapter, for instance in relation to health and education policy.

Second, even though some government responsibilities have been devolved, the British government and the Westminster Parliament have retained control of some of the most important functions of central government – notably taxation, National Insurance and defence. In these matters – the so-called 'reserved powers' – the government in London continues to exercise its control in the whole of the UK.

Third, the election of members or representatives to each of the devolved assemblies or parliaments is based on systems of proportional representation. This has resulted in a more even distribution of seats in each of the devolved assemblies, according to the various political parties, than is the case at Westminster – where the traditional 'first past the post' method of election can lead to a large majority of seats for the winning party. In the National Assembly of Wales and the Scottish Parliament, on the other hand, the Labour Party – despite forming the largest single group in both places – does not have enough members to form outright majorities. Therefore, power sharing between parties and coalition politics are the hallmarks of government in Northern Ireland, Scotland and Wales. Coalition government makes both the political atmosphere and the kinds of policy that are considered in the three devolved legislatures distinctively different from that at Westminster. In Scotland and Wales, coalition government by Labour and Liberal Democrat members has forced each administration to consider policies that were not the agreed policy of the Labour government in London (for example, a reversal of policies on higher education students' tuition fees in Scotland).

A fourth point concerns the content of devolved politics. In large measure, devolved politics is social politics or policy. Most of the policy-making activity of the devolved governments is concerned with health, education and other social policy areas.

Important policy areas – foreign and defence policy and economic policy, for example – are wholly or mainly reserved to Westminster. (Note that social security policy has also not been devolved and remains a Westminster responsibility.) So in discussing the social policies of the devolved governments, we are in fact describing their main activities (Chaney and Drakeford 2004: 121).

A fifth point is that social policy was to some extent devolved already, before the creation of the devolved assemblies. This is most obvious in the case of Northern Ireland, which existed as a devolved 'state within a state' with its own representative assembly – Stormont – from 1921 to 1972 and pursued a partially distinctive social policy path (incidentally illustrating the dangers of devolution, because to some extent social policy, for example, in relation to housing, was used as a tool to reinforce sectarian divisions and to disadvantage the Catholic and nationalist minority).

The historical distinctiveness of Scottish education has already been noted. The Scottish Office was created in 1885 and the Welsh Office in 1964 as departments of Whitehall/Westminster government headed by secretaries of state; these agencies re-presented administrative rather than political devolution, but to some extent policies, for example in relation to health, were allowed to differ from the English model. It is sometimes hard, in reading some of the accounts of post-devolution social policy, to determine whether what is being described is some genuinely new departure or the continuation of trends and tendencies from the pre-devolution situation.

One further important point about the nature of devolution in the UK is that per capita public spending in Northern Ireland, Scotland and Wales has been significantly higher than in England. These imbalances in spending have a long history, beginning with the introduction of formula funding of Scottish expenditure in the 1890s, and have been permitted to grow incrementally thereafter from an initial baseline of equal spending. Formula funding for Northern Ireland and Wales was established in the 1930s and 1960s respectively, and became subject to similar processes of incremental upward drift. The reasons for higher spending levels in the devolved nations are complex, having more to do with political expediency than with any principled approach to the sharing of resources. Past secretaries of state for Scotland have, for example, used the spectre of resurgent nationalism, secession and defence of the Union to wring more resources out of Whitehall and Westminster (McLean 2001: 431). In recent decades spending has been regulated by a central (UK) government funding formula introduced in 1978 by the Labour politician Joel Barnett, Chief Secretary to the Treasury 1974–9 – the 'Barnett formula' – which grants Scotland, Wales and Northern Ireland additional amounts of the UK's public money every year (Glennerster 2003: 190). In fact the purpose of the Barnett formula was not to redistribute resources from England to Scotland and the other nations but to equalize spending between England and the other nations, a purpose in which it has failed. The main social services affected by the Barnett formula are health and education. Social security, as a national service, is outside this framework. These spending inequalities have survived devolution and the creation of national assemblies and have come to look increasingly anomalous, particularly so in the case of Scotland, which was given a measure of tax-raising powers. The Barnett formula has been subjected to powerful criticism on various grounds, including inefficiency, inequity and perverse incentives, and critics have argued that it is unsustainable in the long run (McLean 2005:

356–7). The Blair government reiterated its commitment to the Barnett formula in 1997 and has tried in various ways to narrow the public spending gap between England and the other countries, but these attempts have failed: 'Public spending in Scotland remains 23% above the English average, while Northern Ireland and Wales are 39% and 18% above, respectively' (Hetherington 2001a: 1).

A sense of unfairness in England about the privileged status of Scotland, Wales and Northern Ireland as the 'big spenders' of the UK is not restricted to border regions. English discontent has spread more widely, taking two different forms. First, there have been calls for renewed efforts to narrow the spending gap between England and the remainder of the UK, and perhaps to abolish the Barnett formula. Second, a strong case has been made by those representing English regions to give them devolution and additional spending too. As it stands, current arrangements seem to discriminate against the more disadvantaged parts of England with declining industry and agriculture. Also, special financial incentives can be used in Wales, Scotland and Northern Ireland to attract new businesses, whereas such incentives are not available in regions such as the South-West or North-East of England.

Whether devolution in England and matched funding to new English regional governments will occur in the future is, however, very doubtful. As Bogdanor (2001) suggests, the kind of regional identity that would guarantee the development of regional assemblies and governments in England is not present in sufficient strength. Also, regional devolution in England would necessitate further local government reforms that have already been achieved in Scotland and Wales. However, as he concludes, these factors do not rule out the piecemeal development of devolution in England in the future – whereby one or several regions gain a measure of self-government, rather than the whole of England being subdivided into devolved regional governments.

There is also another point to bear in mind, when comparing public spending and social services in England with those in the other UK countries. Although the Barnett formula grants a higher amount of public money to Scotland, Wales and Northern Ireland overall, this does not mean that spending on a particular *service* or category of 'service user' is always higher in all the 'Celtic' countries. This can be seen in education, for instance. In 2000–1, the system of funding universities resulted in £145 less per student for Welsh institutions than their English counterparts. The gap between Welsh and Scottish higher education funding was even less favourable to Wales (Association of University Teachers 2001). Similarly, the stronger grip of Welsh local authorities on social services and education spending than obtains in England has resulted in *lower* per capita spending on certain services in certain parts of Wales, compared to the English average.

Devolution and education policy

The education systems of Scotland and Northern Ireland have long followed their own paths. Devolution of education policy in these two examples has therefore built upon foundations that were already very different from those in English education. In Scotland particularly, much of the driving force behind support for the whole project of devolution was a determination to preserve Scottish distinctiveness in education.

In Wales, on the other hand, schools have traditionally been run on English lines, in terms of the structure of the school system, the curriculum and the system of administration. However, Welsh distinctiveness has long been apparent in the ethos and culture of the education system in Wales. This is particularly apparent in the teaching of the Welsh language and literature, which used to occur in some, and now in all, primary and secondary schools (with some schools teaching entirely in the medium of Welsh). But Welsh distinctiveness is also demonstrated by the development of a nationwide, 'federal' university – the University of Wales – and in other significant ways such as a widespread commitment to the value of education, as manifested in traditions of adult education and a desire for learning.

However, of the three countries, Scotland had the most distinctive education system before devolution was agreed in 1998. Scottish education already had:

- no statutory or centrally imposed national curriculum, along the lines introduced by the Education Act 1988 in England and Wales (see Chapter 7);
- its own examinations and qualifications system, leading to a broad curriculum of subjects or Scottish Highers (presently under review) – rather than to 'A/S' and A-level examinations, as in England and Wales;
- an earlier school leaving age (17) for those completing the high school or secondary stage of education, and a tradition of four-year rather than three-year degree courses;
- a significantly lower proportion of children being educated in private (fee-paying) schools, compared to England (though this is not distinctive in comparison with Northern Ireland and Wales, where the percentages of the privately educated is 4 per cent or below);
- a low level of Church involvement in state schools compared with the rest of the UK.

Starting from a base that was distinctively different from the rest of the UK, the Scottish Parliament has already introduced several reforms in education that have had significant repercussions beyond Scotland as well as within the country.

The first was to reverse the policy to introduce up-front tuition fees for higher education that had been brought in by New Labour in London. The main argument for this change was that up-front fees are particularly discouraging to potential students from disadvantaged backgrounds, or families with no tradition of attending university. At the time of writing, students from Northern Ireland, England and Wales were paying up-front means-tested fees of £1050 a year towards their tuition costs. But Scottish students do not have to pay tuition fees before university courses are taken. Instead, graduates will have to contribute to a 'graduate endowment' scheme after they have graduated, but only if they earn over a certain amount. Some Scottish students will get all their tuition fees paid from public funds, following a means test.

Scotland also took a distinctive path in funding higher education students by introducing bursaries (grants). The bursaries payable to Scottish students replace part of the student loan and do not have to be repaid after graduation. In 2002, the maximum bursary was £2000. It falls to £1174 when family income rises above £15,000, and no bursary is available if the family income is above £25,800. By reintroducing student grants for higher education students from less well-off backgrounds, Scotland was the first of the 'Celtic' countries to challenge UK government policy in this area, and thus provided a concrete example of what could be achieved through devolution. Higher education policy is arguably the area of greatest divergence (McLean 2005: 353).

English higher education policy has subsequently diverged further from Welsh and Scottish policy with the introduction of so-called 'top-up' fees in England in 2006, after legislation narrowly passed in 2004, by which English universities are permitted to charge annual fees of up to £3000. Most have chosen to do so. Although this is an England-only policy, there are implications for higher education in the devolved nations. No account was taken by English policy-makers of the possible consequences for Scotland and Wales – for example, an increase in the number of English students choosing to attend Scottish and Welsh universities in order to avoid top-up fees. There are also other significant, unforeseen, resource consequences. All this amounted to, in the words of one observer, 'quite a failure of government – of all four governments involved' (McLean 2005: 354).

A second major innovation in education policy in Scotland has been in relation to teachers' pay and work contracts. In 2001, the Scottish Executive (government) approved a pay increase for Scottish teachers of 23 per cent over three years, combined with a reduction in their working week to 35 hours. There is also a guarantee that primary school teachers will not have to spend more than 22.5 hours a week in front of their classes.

Thus the changes in higher education fees policy and teachers' pay and working conditions illustrate the way that Scotland has recently struck out in its own direction. But Scottish distinctiveness in education is also being maintained by important decisions *not* to change in line with the direction English education is taking. Not only has the National Curriculum remained non-statutory, as mentioned above, but also the Scots have decided not to follow the English system of SATs at ages 7, 11 and 14. As Slater (2001: 20) puts it, 'Despite the mania for testing south of the border, Scottish pupils still do not sit national tests until 14 or 15'. Similarly, the policy of the literacy hour centrally enforced on English schools has been ruled out in Scotland as being too much of an intrusion on professional freedom and the ability of Scottish teachers to decide for themselves how best to teach. And though there is a small number of specialist high schools and colleges in Scotland, the Scottish Executive has no plans to increase the number of this type of school.

Therefore, in significant ways Scottish education has been protected from the impact of the type of reform introduced by Mrs Thatcher's government in the 1980s and continued vigorously by New Labour more recently. As discussed in Chapter 7, recent education policy in England is characterized by the continued break-up of the comprehensive school system through expansion of the numbers of specialist and 'faith' schools, the readiness to privatize 'failing' schools and LEAs, and constant scrutiny of schools' and teachers' performance. As Scotland has been able to turn its back on these changes, Scottish education policies offer a comparative test of the value of the English reforms. If the performance of the Scottish education system is at least as good as that in England, what does this tell us about the wisdom of the government's approach to education in England?

Before the impact of devolution can be assessed, however, education policy in Wales and Northern Ireland also needs to be put into the picture. The Welsh example is interesting because, despite the more limited powers of the National Assembly compared with the Scottish Parliament, considerable divergence from English education policy has already occurred since devolution became a reality in 1999. As in Scotland, much of this divergence is coming about because of Welsh decisions not to follow the English educational road. Though the Education Act 1988 led to the introduction of opted-out, grant-maintained schools (see Chapter 7) in Wales, there is no Welsh plan to continue to diversify the secondary school system, as in England. Wales will continue with the established system of comprehensive schools and there will be no encouragement to develop specialist schools and colleges. Similarly, and as in Scotland and Northern Ireland, the National Assembly for Wales has ruled out the idea of involving the private sector in running state education.

These are two major planks of English education policy. But education in Wales now differs from English practice in other ways too – for instance, in the decisions to suspend SATs, to abolish published league tables of school performance, and to abandon the system of literacy and numeracy training used in England (see summary in Table 12.1).

Table 12.1   Education in the UK – how countries compare

	England	Scotland	Wales	Northern Ireland
Private companies allowed to set up state schools	Y	N	N	N
Specialist schools	Y	N	N	N
Limit on teachers' working week	N	Y	N	Y
Performance-related pay for classroom teachers	Y	N	Y	N
Secondary league tables	Y	Y	N	N
Statutory curriculum	Y	N	Y	Y
Primary school literacy and numeracy strategies	Y	N	N	Y
National tests for 11-year-olds	Y	N	Y	Y
Selective education	Y*	N	N	Y
Class size limits for 7- to 11-year-olds	N	N	Y	Y

Note: *In some areas
Source: Slater (2001: 21). The information in Table 12.1 has been reproduced with kind permission of the *Times Educational Supplement.*

In February 2002, the Welsh Assembly Government took another significant step in higher education policy and decided, like Scotland, to reintroduce means-tested maintenance grants for students. Up to £1500 will be available for each student's living costs per year of full-time study (including some further education, as well as university courses), but on a mean-tested basis so that only those on low incomes will receive the full amount. As in Scotland, this measure will not fully restore the student maintenance grant – students will still need to take out subsidized loans to meet the larger part of their maintenance or living costs. However, it is likely to have considerable impact, and should help to remove some of the financial barriers that discourage students from poorer and working-class backgrounds from continuing with post-school education.

The Welsh proposal to restore limited grants is also significant because it shows what can be achieved with a devolved administration that has only secondary powers. As will be recalled, the Welsh Assembly, unlike the Scottish Parliament, cannot make entirely new laws of its own, and it cannot levy its own taxes. However, the new policy on student maintenance demonstrates that the Assembly has considerable freedom to change spending *priorities* even though it cannot determine the overall amount of public money at its disposal. The student maintenance proposals are estimated to cost £41 million in the first year, and this amount will have to be drawn from other social spending and other departments.

Finally, in Northern Ireland there is also a mood of significant educational change and a widespread desire to set education policy in new, distinctive directions. However, unlike the changes envisaged in Wales and Scotland, the plans for education in Northern Ireland are deeply affected by the legacy of selective education in the province. In Northern Ireland, not only are most schools identified with having either a largely or wholly Catholic or Protestant intake of children, but also they are divided by a selective system of grammar and secondary schools. While the rest of the UK gradually introduced comprehensive education in the 1960s and 1970s, Northern Ireland did not. It has retained its long-standing system of selection, which includes a 'transfer test' at the age of 11 (the eleven-plus).

The Northern Irish system produces better GCSE and A-level results than the education systems of England and Wales (Woodward 2001c). Despite this, however, leading opinion in Northern Ireland is now promoting the need to change to a non-selective – or at least a less selective – system. As Woodward points out, research commissioned for the Northern Ireland Assembly underlined the drawbacks of the old selective system. These include narrowing of the primary school curriculum (in order to focus on the selective examination at age 11), the biases in the test itself and underachievement among the 'failed' students in secondary schools.

The Northern Irish system differs from that of England in many other ways. As in the other 'Celtic' countries, there is currently no teacher shortage in Northern Ireland, for instance (Woodward 2001c: 7). Nor are the province's teachers affected by the interventions of Ofsted, the standards watchdog (see Chapter 7), which does not exist in any of the three 'Celtic' countries. Also, as in Wales and Scotland, Northern Ireland has very few independent or private schools – it has an almost entirely state-run education system. All these characteristics will have an impact on the progress of Northern Ireland's education reform programme.

However, setting aside these factors, the educational debates in the rest of the UK can seem irrelevant in Northern Ireland. The success or otherwise of the proposed educational reforms there still depends a great deal on the development of the peace process, and the ability of the Northern Ireland Assembly to work out a widely accepted set of policies.

Devolution – health and social care

There is a long-running public debate in the UK about the problems of the NHS and the funding of social care. In the second Blair administration this debate grew particularly intense. Problems such as waiting lists for treatment, adequate care for older patients and the doctor shortage (see Chapter 9) were increasingly seen not only as a comment on the NHS and social care system, but also as a test of the government's general credibility.

The health systems of the four devolved nations have always been slightly different in terms of policy emphasis, although sharing the same basic features. The NHS was fundamentally the same in all countries, although, as noted above, the English system is less generously financed than the rest (Ham 2004: 102). Particular areas of policy, such as public health and community care, have been allowed to vary, and administrative structures relating to, for example, social care, have differed from the English model. It is noteworthy, however, that the Thatcher–Major reforms of the NHS implemented in 1991 were imposed on the whole of the UK.

In February 2002 the BBC conducted an opinion survey to find out the public's views on priorities in health and social care. Interestingly, the goal of providing 'free' care to older people – whether in a hospital, nursing home or residential home – topped the poll by a wide margin. This was significant for two reasons. First, it showed that, though the government has put a higher priority on health service spending than on social services (see Chapter 11), public attitudes in England as well as the rest of the UK reflect continued concern about both halves of the health and social care equation. There is a surprisingly large amount of public support for attending to the 'social' as well as the 'health' care needs of an ageing population. Second, public endorsement of 'free' care showed widespread support for a policy that is already being developed in Scotland, and is being considered in Wales and Northern Ireland as well.

As in education policy, Scotland's recent policies on social care show how devolution is leading, in some ways, to a return to a traditional, universalistic welfare state philosophy. In Scotland it has been agreed that all older people will be entitled to free personal care if they are in need of it in their own homes, or in residential or nursing home facilities. Personal care costs will include such items as cooking and laundry costs, or 'hotel' costs in residential homes. At the time of writing, this benefit will remain means tested in the rest of the UK.

This is because the government in London had rejected a Royal Commission's key recommendation (see Chapter 11; see also Sutherland 1999) that personal care should be provided 'free' to all older people in the UK. It was agreed by the government in London that *nursing* care will be provided free of charge – though, as noted in Chapter 11, this has led to continuing wrangles over what counts as 'nursing' and as 'social' care in different areas.

In terms of public image and approval, then, the Scottish policy to provide free personal (that is, social and nursing) care to everyone who needs it seems to win hands down when compared with the niggardly and variable means-tested approach in England. From July 2002 there were no charges for personal care in Scottish older people's own homes, and free nursing care is provided whether the patient is at home or in a care home. Also, Scottish older people who are in residential and nursing homes, and who contribute to the cost of their care, receive free personal/nursing care payments of £145 per week (residential homes) and £210 per week (nursing homes).

Though this policy met with a very positive response from the public, however, it is worth noting that it is an example of 'middle-class welfare state' provision. The main beneficiaries are relatively well-off older people who own substantial property or have above-average savings and retirement incomes. 'Free' personal care helps this group of older people to avoid using their own money or assets to pay for their care. Older people living on low incomes and with fewer assets would not have had to pay means-tested care costs under the former system in Scotland. Therefore a policy that has given considerable political and electoral rewards to the politicians who have introduced it, and a policy that *appears* to promote equality and fairness, in fact subsidizes the care costs of affluent older people.

The Scottish policy on long-term care has been favourably reviewed (Scottish Assembly Health Committee 2006). Policy in England on long-term care of the elderly is once more in the melting pot, with the publication of the Wanless report on social care in England in 2006 (Wanless 2006), which recommended greater state financial support for long-term care, and the government's recent commitment to review its policy in this area (see Chapter 11) (Timmins 2006a). The report provides a careful and critical analysis of the Scottish policy (Wanless 2006: 225). Its recommendations, which of course may not be adopted by the government, differ from the Scottish policy, although they are interpretable as a movement in a Scottish direction. It is not clear that the government's decision to launch a policy review owes anything to the Scottish experience.

In Wales there appears to be considerable support in the National Assembly for policies on health and social care that will be distinctively different from those in England, and which will seek to address the hardship faced by some older people when faced with care costs. The National Assembly does not have, however, either the degree of financial independence or the level of resources that are at the disposal of the Scottish Parliament. The way that nursing care costs are met is already different in Wales. A standard amount is payable to older people in care to help meet these costs. In England, a more complicated – and, some suggest, a less fair – system operates. Those qualifying for means-tested help to pay for nursing care are paid according to their level of need. As a result, residents of a single residential or nursing home in England can find that relatively small and sometimes arbitrary differences in their nursing care needs have led to marked differences in the amounts of money they receive (or rather that the home receives on their behalf). Managers of residential and nursing homes find the system difficult to cope with. In some cases they have begun to allocate an equal amount of money to each resident, per week, to pay for nursing care, and have decided to ignore the variations in amounts paid to individual residents. The example of the Welsh solution to this problem – a flat-rate sum to help people with nursing-care costs – shows how devolution is beginning to develop opportunities to experiment with different ways of *implementing* or *administering* policies, as well as opportunities to make different policies in the first place.

An interesting Welsh attempt to diverge from English policy by eliminating all home care charges for disabled people – a commitment contained in the 2003 Welsh Labour manifesto – was abandoned in 2006 amid considerable recrimination. A less generous package of support, which nevertheless diverges from English policy, was provided (Constitution Unit 2006: 17–18).

However, the more significant changes resulting from devolution will come from divergence in *policy* rather than as a result of different ways of interpreting or implementing common UK policies. In this respect the devolution of health and social care policy, like education, is building on rather different foundations in each of the 'Celtic' countries.

One recent observer of health politics in the UK has suggested that the style of politics has started to vary among the four countries, and, among the three devolved nations, to revert to pre-Thatcher styles of policy-making, which can be characterized as *professionalism* in Scotland, *markets* in England, *localism* in Wales and *permissive managerialism* in Northern Ireland (Greer 2004: 78, 156, 193; McLean 2005: 354–5). So a *status quo* established under the Thatcher and Major governments regarding the organization of the NHS has dissolved; all four systems have been in movement, the English one taking a more radical direction, the others in various ways trying to put the clock back.

In Scotland, however, it is perhaps more significant that the NHS is beginning to seem to be distinctively different from the NHS in England and Wales because the Scottish system is not being reorganized at the same pace or on the same scale as it is in England and Wales. The Scottish Executive has decided to use the independence that it has to avoid many of the upheavals and changes being planned south of the border.

Recent NHS reforms in England have included the development of PCTs to commission most health services in local areas. PCTs will also take over an increasing amount of devolved responsibility for commissioning and providing community health services in England. Added to this are plans for more decentralization of management and funding arrangements for hospitals and health trusts in England, with the objective of allowing the better-performing hospitals to build on their financial independence and, where appropriate, to form partnerships with private sector companies and health service providers (see Chapter 9).

In Scotland, on the other hand, the NHS has not been pushed so vigorously towards these kind of changes. As in the rest of the UK, the internal market that used to operate in the NHS (following the earlier Conservative health reforms of the 1990s) was suspended. The Scottish NHS is now centrally managed by the Scottish Executive, and comprises 15 area health boards and 28 self-governing NHS trusts. The NHS and local authority social services work together to develop policies on health and social care, and to provide community care 'packages'. In this area, much has been done since 2000 to integrate the organization of health and social services in Scotland.

Although the NHS in Scotland does not appear to be absorbed in the amount of internal restructuring now being attempted in England and Wales, this does not mean that there is no change in the Scottish health care system. One of the main effects of devolution appears to be the development of a wider range of local initiatives and health service developments than might have otherwise occurred. In both Scotland and Northern Ireland (where health and social services were grouped together long ago), there have been innovations in the care of people with mental health problems, for instance. There have also been targeted preventive strategies to improve the poor health record in both countries in terms of heart disease and cancer, with additional money for these programmes from the devolved administrations. In Scotland, mental health laws are being reviewed with the aim of strengthening the rights of patients and carers. An Advocacy Safeguard Agency and a Scottish Independent Advocacy Alliance will provide advocacy services for vulnerable patients, such as those with learning disabilities or mental health problems, and will help to protect their interests.

In Wales, however, progress in developing such initiatives has been somewhat hampered by the task of reorganizing the structure of the NHS. Because of its more limited independence than that of the Scottish Parliament, the National Assembly in Wales must provide a Welsh equivalent to the main NHS reforms being carried out in England. Unlike England, however, the NHS in Wales has been structured around local health groups rather than PCGs. These groups are to have the same boundaries as the 22 unitary local authorities that have been established in Wales (Leathard 2000: 239). At the same time, it has now been decided that health authorities will be scrapped. But rather than reducing the number of managing organizations in the NHS or the various levels of bureaucracy, these proposed changes have been criticized for being likely to result in over-complicated, wasteful extra tiers of management.

However, there are also signs that devolution has encouraged innovations and distinctive changes in Wales despite the time-consuming task of NHS reorganization. For instance, Wales is distinctive in instituting a Children's Commissioner – a role similar to that of an 'ombudsman' who can monitor the quality and effectiveness of educational, health and social services for children, respond to individual cases of abuse, mistreatment or injustice, and protect children's interests generally. Also, Wales has taken innovative steps in several other ways – for instance, in developing unified budgets for the provision of social, educational and health services for children, and more generally in terms of building statutory (that is, legally required) partnerships between the National Assembly, the voluntary sector and business organizations. These partnerships are intended to build a foundation for further developments in urban renewal and employment in poorer communities, as well as health improvement and social or community development.

An interesting recent health policy divergence between Wales and England is the Welsh Assembly Government's decision in 2005 to detach itself from NICE requirements. NICE is the body established in 1999 to assess new medical technology and make recommendations about its use. The reasons for this withdrawal are not clear, but the Assembly Government has stated that it will take account of NICE recommendations, but does not wish to be bound by them. Some concern has been expressed by Assembly members that the decision may result in the return of so-called 'postcode rationing', to the detriment of Welsh patients (Constitution Unit 2005: 24).

Some recent commentaries on devolved health policy suggest that a degree of scepticism about the benefits of devolution hitherto may be in order. The performance of the NHS, measured by such criteria as waiting lists, appears to be improving in England while worsening in the three devolved countries (McLean 2005: 355). In Northern Ireland, for example, waiting list lengths increased during the period of devolved government and improved after the reintroduction of direct rule in 2002 (Constitution Unit 2005a: 43). In relation to Scottish health policy there is some suggestion that delivery failures may be encouraging a degree of Scottish interest in the English approach (Constitution Unit 2005b: 42).

The end of British social policy? The impact of devolution and of the EU

As this brief survey of examples of recent social policy in Northern Ireland, Scotland and Wales has shown, there are now clearly detectable trends in the development of devolution in the UK. Some of the changes are relatively small scale and subtle. They have involved behind-the-scenes changes in management or funding arrangements rather than obvious or far-reaching changes in the way welfare or health services are provided or experienced by service users. But all these relatively minor changes are mounting up, and are leading to a gradual divergence of the social policies of England and the three 'Celtic' countries. In time, important social institutions – the NHS, social services, the education system – that used to share at least parts of a common 'national' (British) identity may lose much of that common identity. The NHS and the social services, for instance, may begin to look different in the different parts of the UK, and they will have increasingly different patterns of provision, goals and ways of working.

In summing up the impact of devolution, however, some caution is needed before reaching the conclusion that a very diverse patchwork of social policies and social services will develop across the English regions, and between Wales, Northern Ireland and Scotland. This is for the following reasons.

First, devolution is still in its early days. Some distinctively different policies have been launched, especially in Scotland, in such areas as higher education and funding of care for older people. Also, devolution seems to be having a significant effect in terms of putting a brake on changes that would have come about if the 'Celtic' countries had had to follow the English lead. Examples of this are rejecting the involvement of the private sector in education that is taking place in England, or rejecting school league tables. But as some of these policies have been introduced by the devolved administrations only since the late 1990s it is too early to form judgements about their likely success or outcomes, or their impact on public opinion – either in the relevant 'Celtic' country or in England.

Second, devolution in the UK is asymmetrical. Only Scotland has enough independence to become a semi-autonomous country within the UK. The National Assembly for Wales can pass only secondary legislation and has none of the tax-varying powers of the Scottish Parliament. The Northern Ireland Assembly has the potential to develop a considerable degree of autonomy for the province but the troubled political history of Northern Ireland casts doubt on how quickly any radically new policies could be agreed by the different sides of the community. It would be wrong to be too optimistic about the Northern Ireland Assembly given the difficulties in forming a government with a working majority.

Third, one of the main ways in which devolution has an impact is by *example*. As discussed in this chapter, for instance, the examples of the reintroduction of student maintenance grants in Scotland and Wales, or of free personal care for older people in

Scotland, seem to show in both a concrete and obvious way that 'devolution works'. One argument is that people in one country will draw unfavourable conclusions about their own social policies from the social progress and improvements in welfare being made in neighbouring countries. However, there are some flaws in this argument. They boil down to a question of whether people in one country will notice what is happening in the other countries. In population terms, England is the giant of the group. Not surprisingly, English politicians and policy-makers tend to be preoccupied with the much larger population on their own doorstep, or in their own regions, than they are with developments in what can be seen, ethnocentrically, as the 'Celtic margins'. Historically, the English have dominated the Union, and to this day there is still some cultural distance – increased by national differences in newspapers, radio and television output – between English people on the one hand, and Scottish, Welsh and Irish people on the other. Therefore even if the growing distinctiveness of the 'Celtic' countries in politics and social affairs is going to be noticed, it is not yet clear what the impact of this will be. One possibility is that, rather than demand that similar welfare policies to those in Scotland, Wales or Northern Ireland are developed in England, the English will demand the scrapping of the Barnett formula.

Fourth, it is commonly assumed that devolution will bring increasing, never-ending divergence in social policy, not only between England and the rest of the UK but also between the three main 'Celtic' countries. Taken to its logical limits, this argument would suggest that future differences between England, Scotland, Wales and Northern Ireland will be as marked as between, say, the social welfare systems of Sweden, Norway, Denmark and Finland today. Increasing divergence is not inevitable, however, for a number of reasons. First, the 'Celtic' countries might converge on approximately similar solutions and policies for common issues and problems – there is already a considerable amount of 'policy learning' and sharing of experience among the three devolved administrations. Second, the impact of devolution might be one of allowing one of the countries in the UK to experiment with certain limited areas of social policy but with the end result that the others also adopt the same kind of innovation. For instance, England and Wales could 'converge' on some of the developments pioneered in Scotland, rather than forging ahead with increasingly different social policies.

Finally, there is the unifying effect of EU social policy.

None of the above reasons means that it is certain that devolution will have a limited impact on social policy in the UK. They are simply reasons for exercising caution about any claims that devolution will inevitably and completely transform the map of British social policy.

The significance of the EU

As mentioned at the start of this chapter, devolution can be seen as the passing of state power and responsibility 'upwards' as well as 'downwards' to devolved administrations, as in Scotland, Wales and Northern Ireland. Some have argued that the ceding of authority by the UK government and Parliament to the EU is at least as significant as the recent devolution of power to the 'Celtic' countries of the UK. Are the Westminster

Parliament, and British governments led by prime ministers in London, going to be increasingly powerless and irrelevant in the future, when it comes to deciding important social issues?

As with 'downward' devolution, however, it is quite difficult to judge whether the impact of EU policy will lead to the end of the British welfare system as we know it. In one way Europe is becoming pervasive. The number of social policy areas and the depth of involvement in policy areas have all increased in recent years. This is especially the case since 1997, when the Labour government signed the 'Social Chapter' (section) of the Single European Act 1986. The Single European Act was a key piece of legislation and has been 'acclaimed as the most important and successful step in the process of European integration since the Treaty of Rome' (McCormick 1999: 77). Blair's signing up means that legislation agreed under the Social Chapter since the 1991 Intergovernmental Conference (Maastricht Treaty) will now apply to the UK.

The EU has become less of a foreign policy issue and is now more a part of domestic politics and social administration than formerly. However, despite the increasing impact of the EU on social policy and politics in the UK, it would be wrong to portray the EU as an all-powerful juggernaut that flattens all domestic or national policies in its path. There are strong limitations to the impact of the EU. These limitations are both practical (limits to the effective capacity of EU institutions and organizations to enforce legislation) and constitutional (all member states – not just the UK – retain significant controls).

The balance between the EU's and nation-states' powers is not settled and there is still a major question as to whether the UK will fully participate in the process of further European integration and will be prepared to secede more national policy-making powers to the EU. An alternative to a single, unified and increasingly powerful 'superstate' is a two-speed Europe, or a two-*tier* Europe, or some variation of the two things. This is possible, given the recent enlargement of the EU from 15 to 25 member states, including, among others, the Czech Republic, Cyprus, Hungary, Malta and Poland. Two more countries, Romania and Bulgaria, are set to join the EU in 2007. These possibilities allow for an inner core of countries to press ahead with integration, whether in terms of defence, economics, or social policy and domestic issues such as immigration control and policies on refugees and asylum.

Thus, any estimation of the impact of the EU on the UK, and on British social policy, needs to include discussion of what role the UK itself wants to play in the Europe of the future. Will the UK be committed to being a member of any inner core of member states, alongside France and Germany for instance, or will it wish to continue to deal with the EU at arm's length?

The EU and social policy

There has been a lot of interest across Europe in the effect that the growing powers of the EU will have on social policy and on existing welfare states. As far as the UK is concerned, the impact of EU social policy on British social policy can be described as limited, but significant in particular areas such as employment conditions and equality at work. As Timonen (1999: 253) points out, the direct effects of EU policy are limited because 'EU social policy does not for the most part fall within the traditional definition of social policy (a structure of transfers and services aimed at redistribution among the entire population)'.

The EU's impact is more in terms of establishing a common framework of standards and goals in social welfare rather than imposing a blueprint of how each country should run its system of social security, education, health care, housing and so on. EU legislation is governed by a principle of subsidiarity, which means that member states build European law into their own legislation and policies. Key areas of EU legislative action include the following.

- *Free movement of workers*: all nationals of EU member states have the right to live and work in any member state. If they do, they have the same rights to social security, working conditions and access to jobs as nationals in the country they have moved to (with certain exceptions, such as access to employment in defence, law and police forces).
- *Equal pay*: an Equal Pay Directive (1975) requires member states to abolish all overt discrimination between men and women in pay. After 1975 they also had to introduce legislation to recognize equal pay for work of equal *value* – a point that had a particular impact in the UK, which had to replace previous equal pay legislation with a new law that fell in line with the Directive.
- *Equal treatment*: an Equal Treatment Directive established the principle of equal treatment between men and women in access to employment and training. It also governs working conditions.
- *Social security*: Article 119, a Social Security Directive, covers not only wages but also overtime, sick pay, bonuses and occupational pensions. The main aim of this Directive is to eliminate sex discrimination in the calculation of benefits for men and women. In 1986 this legislation was extended to cover private pension and insurance schemes. As a result of one successful challenge to the UK under this legislation, the UK government was ordered to treat single and married carers equally in payment of benefits.
- *Parental leave*: EU Directives in this area are part of a wider programme of EU initiatives to help both men and women balance the demands of work and home. For instance there has been a Directive (1992) on the protection of pregnant women at work and on employment protection for such women. This establishes a minimum 14-week period of leave, and prohibition of dismissal on grounds of maternity. There has been a noticeable impact in the UK in relation to this. Several leading court cases involving wrongful dismissal of pregnant women from the armed forces have been referred to the European Court of Justice and have resulted in the payment of large compensation sums to the women involved.
- *Part-time work*: now that the UK has accepted the Social Chapter, Directives on part-time work since 1991 will become binding on British employers. They mean that part-time workers must be given the same rights to pensions, employment benefits and health and safety protection as full-time workers.
- *Working hours and welfare at work*: there have been a number of Directives from

the EU on the subject of working time (the maximum number of hours per week permitted in most occupations, with some agreed exceptions) and on employee participation in decision-making at work.

When we look at other areas of social policy – that is, outside the areas of social security, welfare in employment, or equality laws and sex discrimination – the impact of the EU is much less noticeable.

The European Social Fund was set up in 1960 to assist member states with the provision of retraining schemes, job creation and migration assistance – all designed to meet the social and human costs of industrial restructuring and the consequences of unemployment. Two main groups have been helped over the years: the long-term unemployed and unemployed young people. The Social Fund takes less than 10 per cent of the total EU budget (far less than the 50 per cent or so going to support agriculture) and it has been criticized for being cumbersome and inefficient. On the other hand, it has had considerable impact on the development of innovative schemes to address youth unemployment.

The EU has also funded a wide range of other initiatives – for example, to support disabled people in employment and to remove the obstacles that prevent disabled people from obtaining work. Similarly, the EU funds schemes to tackle economic disadvantage and to revitalize inner-city and other economically depressed areas. These initiatives often have a 'social' element and include such things as community development schemes, community transport projects and funds to develop child care services or facilities.

Conclusions

Devolution, both 'upwards' to the EU and 'downwards' to the elected legislatures in Scotland, Wales and Northern Ireland, poses some important questions about the future of the British welfare state. As stated at the outset, devolution to the 'Celtic' countries is beginning to lead to some exciting changes in the way social policies are formulated and how services are going to be delivered in the different parts of the UK. There are already signs of considerable divergence in education, health and social care policies, though for a variety of reasons we must be cautious about how much difference devolution is going to make, until the devolved administrations have had more time to make their mark.

A key question raised by devolution within the UK is how far the independence of the devolved administrations in Wales, Scotland and Northern Ireland will be used not only to develop their own distinctive approaches in social policy, but also to *protect* the 'traditional' welfare state. There are certainly signs in the 'Celtic' countries of a greater commitment than in the New Labour Westminster government to supporting older, or existing forms of social provision – rather than following a New Labour drive towards ever more 'modernization' and involvement of the private sector in welfare management and provision.

For instance, as will be recalled, the Scottish Executive's approach to the NHS and the Welsh approach to favouring the retention of standard comprehensive schools are illustrations of this more traditional welfare strategy. Also, the use of public money to fund improvements in personal care and student maintenance show a similar commitment to more traditional pro-welfare values and a commitment to investment in the social infrastructure. How strongly devolution will protect or revive the 'old' social democratic approach to building a welfare state, and how far the devolved administrations will be able to resist the centralizing pressures of the UK government, remains to be seen.

As far as the effect of devolution upwards to the EU is concerned, there has been little or no discussion of the EU weakening or watering down Britain's welfare services or social security provisions. This is because Britain's welfare system underwent a considerable squeeze and restructuring by Mrs Thatcher's government in the 1980s, and UK social expenditure is only average for comparable developed countries.

Not surprisingly, in countries that joined the EU more recently and that have more developed welfare systems than in the UK – notably Finland and Sweden – the debate has been quite different. Here, concerns have focused on the worry that the EU's impact would lead directly to considerable erosion of their advanced welfare systems (Gould 1999; Timonen 1999).

Thus we may sum up the impact of upward and downward devolution as follows. First, for the minority of the UK's population living in the 'Celtic' countries there will be perceptible changes in the health and social care system, and in education, compared to England. Most of these changes will have a practical impact and a mostly beneficial effect on certain groups in the Scottish, Welsh and Northern Irish populations.

For the majority of UK citizens – the English – neither devolution nor the growing influence of the EU look like making as much difference. Of the two sorts of influence, however, the EU is likely to have a greater impact, if only in specific areas such as parental leave or new regulations governing working time. Otherwise, it is hard to see how devolution within the UK will much affect English social policy, except by example and unless there is some regional devolution in England. However, the ability to draw comparative examples, and to see how things can be done differently, will perhaps turn out to be one of the most underrated effects of devolution. For everyone in the UK, the examples of EU social policy and the policies being worked out in the devolved administrations offer alternatives to the social policies emanating from central government in London.

Key terms and concepts

asymmetric devolution and symmetric devolution
divergence

primary legislation and secondary legislation
subsidiarity

Suggestions for further reading

An edited book by Jonathon Bradbury and John Mawson, *British Regionalism and Devolution: The Challenges of State Reform and European Integration* (1996) is, like other books on this subject, a rather specialist discussion of the political and constitutional implications of devolution. However, it is worth looking at because it includes chapters both on the question of devolution in England and on the European context of devolution. Vernon Bogdanor's *Devolution in the United Kingdom* (1999) also concentrates on political aspects, but has substantial sections on social policy as well. It is perhaps the most accessible, all-round book on devolution available. However, there are other readable and interesting discussions. For example, from a Welsh perspective, Ron Davies has written a 'think piece' on devolution, *Devolution: A Process, not an Event* (1999), and Paul Chaney and colleagues have collected together chapters on recent aspects of devolution in a book titled *New Governance: New Democracy?* (2001). Greer (2004) provides a valuable discussion of devolved health policy. Stewart (2004) provides useful material on Scottish social policy. Valuable updates on policy devolution are contained in the quarterly devolution monitoring reports published by the Constitution Unit at University College, London. These, which also contain much other devolution-related material, are available on the web at www.ucl.ac.uk/constitution-unit/research/devolution.

Compared to devolution in the UK, there is a much wider literature on all aspects of the EU. As a start, and in order to build a basic understanding of the history, institutions and current policies of the EU, John McCormick has produced a very readable and clear guide, *Understanding the European Union* (1999). Although it is now rather dated, Colin Brewster's and Paul Teague's *European Community Social Policy and its Impact on the UK* (1989) is a useful reference book and source of information on the earlier impact of EU social policy on the UK. Finally, *Social Policy in the European Union* (2nd edn, 2000), by Linda Hantrais, provides an excellent, in-depth discussion of current social policy in the EU and member states.

13 CONCLUSION: THE FUTURE OF SOCIAL POLICY

Social policy and rapid social change
  'Not so New' Labour and social policy: a loss of direction?
The changing context of social policy: a 'postmodern' era?
  Endnote: a postmodern government and postmodern social policies?
Key terms and concepts
Suggestions for further reading

Social policy and rapid social change

This book has aimed to introduce you both to the academic subject of social policy and to 'real' social policies evident in the world around us. It has included discussion of recent developments in social security, criminal juistice, education, employment policy, health services, housing and social care. It has also included discussion of key themes in the subject of social policy and some of the academic debates that have developed in the discipline.

Years ago, in the era of welfare consensus (a term still of use in understanding mid-twentieth-century social policy: see Deakin 1994), studying social policy meant learning about the workings of the welfare state: a growing giant of welfare service provision in the postwar years. In more recent years, fundamental changes have begun to undermine old assumptions about both the subject of social policy and the welfare state itself. As suggested at the beginning (see Chapter 1), it is probably better to think of welfare today as a *system* of more or less connected agencies in different sectors (the public, private, voluntary and informal) than as a 'welfare state' that is almost entirely a government-run operation.

As the old welfare state fragments and changes, it will be increasingly important to rethink the subject of social policy. If social policy continues to define itself as a subject that concerns itself only with traditional areas of study, focusing on need, inequality and social services in well-demarcated areas such as education and health, important aspects of social change and reform will be missed. The old association between the subject of social policy and the welfare state needs to be questioned seriously. 'Social policy' will become much more concerned than it is now with such themes as the role of NGOs in providing welfare, with the changing nature of work, or with other aspects of human welfare, including leisure, transport and patterns of consumption (see Cahill 1994).

The changing and broadening nature of the subject matter of welfare is indicated by the inclusion of a chapter on criminal justice in this edition. Having said that, you will have noticed that this book has concentrated for the most part on the traditional fields of social policy, from education and health to housing and community care. This is because there are continuities in social policy and, though the pace of change has been very rapid in the context of welfare (the economic and political scene), it makes sense to look forward from a well-understood base to developments on the horizon. It is also dangerous to make too many guesses, even about the near future, when a week is as long in the politics of social policy as it is in anything else.

This concluding chapter therefore aims to encourage you to look over your shoulder at recent policy in such areas as education, the health service and social care, as discussed earlier in this book. However, it is important to try to reflect on these recent changes in a way that helps us to think about the general direction of social policy – and to see the 'bigger picture' as it unfolds.

As a start, it may help to review the context in which British social policy finds itself following a third victory for Labour in the general election of 2005. What are the implications of this political context for social policy?

Second, and tied to the thesis that the old welfare state is crumbling away, is a set of debates about the emergence of a *postmodern social order*. Depending on one's viewpoint, the notion of postmodernism is either a very useful way of summarizing trends that have great significance for social policy, or a set of ideas that cloud the picture and obscure such realities as growing inequality and exclusion from welfare.

'Not so New' Labour and social policy: a loss of direction?

The election of a Labour government in May 1997 seemed to herald the dawn of a new political era. This was especially the case because Labour's victory over the Conservatives was so decisive and because it followed nearly 20 years of uninterrupted Conservative government.

As mentioned in Chapter 7, the British electoral system allows governments with large majorities to do what they want to a degree that other constitutions with more checks and balances do not. Thus the Labour government seemed to set out in 1997 with a free hand to change policy. Tony Blair's newly-elected government promised bold changes in a number of areas.

First, it gave the impression that one change of policy would be to break with the 'Old Labour' approach of 'tax and spend' in dealing with the economy and public services. Labour's 1997 election manifesto stated that a Labour government would not raise basic and higher income tax rates to fund an expanded welfare budget (Labour Party 1997: 11–13), a commitment reiterated in the 2005 manifesto (Labour Party 2005: 16–17). At the time, an anti-taxation stance seemed vital to Labour's campaign to win the general election. The political mood in 1997 was anti-Conservative but not, apparently, supportive of any kind of radical programme for social reform. The tax commitment was in fact quite ambiguous and perfectly compatible with a policy of increasing the tax burden – precisely what has happened. The manifesto also stated a commitment to increased spending on health and education.

Second, the Labour Party under Blair had built its ideas for change around a rejection of the Conservative approach to economic management and welfare reform. Blair insisted that New Labour did not want to follow the neo-liberal, free market principles that had become a marked feature of Conservative thinking and strategy in the governments led by Margaret Thatcher and John Major. Instead, New Labour would follow a 'Third Way' (see Powell 1999) – a new, distinctive approach to both economic and social policy that would be neither a version of 'Old Labour' socialism nor another kind of free enterprise, laissez-faire version of Conservatism.

Not much is heard of the Third Way now. Instead, the government prefers to talk about 'pragmatic' policies, and to justify its actions on the principle that 'whatever works' is the best policy choice. For instance, New Labour has justified the policy of involving private sector companies in takeovers of 'failing' schools or LEAs in this way.

Some observers argue that this suggests that New Labour did not so much lose direction after 1997 but never had a clear direction to follow in the first place. Powell (1999: 298) and others have suggested that New Labour's supposedly big idea was never built around 'a coherent concept that can be applied more or less uniformly to different policy sectors. Instead, it appears to be … a poorly specified, pick and mix strategy, largely defined by what it is not'.

The reluctance of the government led by Blair to commit itself to a particular direction seems to have had two main effects in the political context. First, the strategy seemed to work, in some ways, in helping to secure the second and third terms in government for New Labour. The government's 2001 and 2005 election strategies, as in 1997, were to make some modest commitments but not to promise the earth. This at least succeeded in not scaring away voters by raising concerns about higher taxes or (in 2001) about the UK adopting the common European currency.

Second, however, this strategy seemed to foster voter apathy. Labour voters grudgingly gave the government another chance to continue in office in 2005, but more out of a sense that there was no credible alternative to Labour than as a result of strong support for the Labour programme. Blair's promise to quit some time after the general election also helped to shore up support for Labour among many voters, as by 2005 Tony Blair had become less popular than the party he led.

The lack of a clear programme of policies all aiming in one direction suggests that the government's achievements have been few and far between, but this was not the case. The government did succeed in passing a great deal of legislation and introducing many policy reforms, including reforms in the area of social welfare. The point is rather that the social policy achievements of New Labour turned out to be both modest and to be working in different directions.

For example, the Labour government's strategy after 1997 included some remarkably right-wing policies. Abolishing the lone parent premium in income support for new claimants, the introduction of student loans and tuition fees, and adoption and expansion of the Conservatives' PFI to fund hospital building and other public infrastructure are all examples of policy in which New Labour 'out-Conservatived' the Conservatives.

On the other hand, some left of centre policies aiming to redress decades of increases in social inequality and poverty were introduced. The minimum wage, an extension of disabled people's rights, commitments to reduce child poverty and to improve access to child care facilities, and tax credits to working families on low incomes are all examples of this kind of policy.

Therefore New Labour's period in government so far has been like a river marked by swirling currents and eddies rather than a river flowing strongly and consistently in one direction. Another example can be found in contrasts between aspects of education policy on the one hand, and employment, New Deal and anti-poverty policies on the other. The latter policies are all aimed at improving the social inclusion of disadvantaged and socially excluded groups – for instance by improving their chances of a good education, and of access to worthwhile employment and training opportunities. But recent policies to increase 'diversity' in the secondary school system, and to foster selection (by 'aptitude' if not 'ability') seem to be aimed at pleasing New Labour's middle-class constituency. It is hardly a recipe for social inclusion to continue to break up the comprehensive school system (in England) and to widen the social divisions that already exist between the intakes of schools in better-off and poorer neighbourhoods.

No government's policies are ever entirely consistent, and every government has policy failures as well as successes. For example, as mentioned in Chapter 3 (see concluding section), even Mrs Thatcher's single-minded approach did not mean that all her government's policies were working in the same direction.

As discussed in Chapter 5, New Labour did succeed in introducing a lot of specially targeted measures to improve the earnings and employment prospects of people on low incomes. Some of these measures have made a substantial difference, but the likely outcome of present government policies is that any improvements in health and social services will take place against a backdrop of sharp and persistent social and economic inequalities. The gap between rich and poor in the UK, you may recall, is one of the highest in the world. The needs and social problems that are increased by poverty – for instance, poor health, illiteracy, crime and social exclusion – will continue to put pressure on stretched public services.

It remains to be seen how rapidly, after two or three decades of relative underfunding, the public services – notably, education, health and social services – can be helped to recover in the government's period in office post-2005. As mentioned in the various chapters of this book dealing with these services, all of them face critical shortages of professional practitioners – doctors, nurses, teachers, social workers and other staff.

Given Labour's record in involving the private sector in funding and managing health, education and social services, and its determination to continue and extend the Conservatives' strategy of building a market in welfare provision, any substantial investments in the welfare system will be made with strings attached. In this respect there is at least one consistent thread in government policy – a steady increase in central government control of the various services. This, combined with the use of the private sector to fund and run services, is likely to result in the continued break-up of the old structures of local authorities, professions and managers that used to run the welfare system.

The changing context of social policy: a 'postmodern' era?

The 'modern' world has proved to be bewildering and confusing, if we take the twentieth century to be representative. In that century there were two world wars, numerous acts of barbarism and mass murder, and stupendous rises not only in agricultural and industrial production but also in human population. There were mighty clashes of political ideology accompanying the rise of mass democracy in many states and – in the industrialized world – the rise of 'welfare states'.

At the beginning of the twenty-first century, though, a possibly even more bewildering, anxious and insecure world awaits us. It is therefore not surprising that, at the end of the twentieth century, commentators referred to the 'end' of almost everything: the end of socialism, for instance, or the end of the industrial age (*postindustrialism*).

However, before we leap to the conclusion that social policy, along with everything else, really is being swept into a new world order, it is worth contemplating what theories of postmodernism have suggested and whether they ring true in helping to explain both recent policy and emerging trends. Postmodernism as an intellectual and cultural phenomenon and its relation to other 'post' entities is hard to summarize and embraces a number of different ideas. In the 1990s there was a brief surge of interest in academic journals in postmodernism and its possible applicability to the understanding of social policy, an interest which seems now to have subsided. Social policy experts differed about the value of the idea of postmodernism. For example, Mishra (1993) found the concept useful, while Taylor-Gooby (1994) was strongly critical.

First, it may be helpful to make a distinction between postmodernism, a general term implying the end of the 'modern' era as we have known it in the twentieth century, and *postindustrialism*. The latter term refers more specifically to certain trends in the economy and the world of work (Penna and O'Brien 1996). The theory of postindustrialism can be summarized as follows.

- The collapse of manufacturing as a major source of jobs and the rise of service sector jobs.
- Associated with this, a fundamental set of changes in the ways both organizations and work itself are structured. The earlier industrial world provided work based on principles of mass manufacturing (Fordism). That is, people tended to work in organizations or factories run as hierarchies. Each worker had an allotted role and a predictable work pattern. But in the postFordist world, the old hierarchies based on traditional skills or on bureaucratic organizations are disappearing. Organizations are said to have become 'flatter' (less like pyramidal power structures) and decentralized, while part-time work has expanded at the expense of full-time; people will increasingly move from one workplace to another and develop more flexible portfolios of skills.
- As a result of the two trends identified above, old class and gender divisions based on industrial society are breaking down. However, new divisions are arising: there is likely to be a well-rewarded section of the workforce who are the more skilled in postindustrial, knowledge-based employment, while a poorer section will be relegated to casual, temporary and part-time work.
- The postindustrial world, it is suggested, will also be increasingly affected by *globalization*. This means that revolutions in production and information transfer permit production of goods and services on a worldwide basis. In the new world order, the nation-state will become increasingly unable to manage or control the economy within its own borders. The pressures to compete in a

global market will force the more 'expensive' countries to reduce their welfare and labour costs. As a result, according to this view, not only will nation-states find it increasingly difficult to independently run their own economies, they will also find that their social policies (which are largely determined by economic success and failure) slip out of their grasp too.

All the above points represent a *theory* about what is happening in the world today, not a set of firm conclusions. How much can be explained convincingly by this theory, and what use is the idea of postindustrialism in understanding social policy trends?

For those such as Penna and O'Brien (1996) and Fitzpatrick (1996), who believe that the concept does have some value, postindustrialism helped to explain a number of recent trends in the way the welfare system is developing. For instance, the *casualization* of employment in welfare services, as a result of the imposition of short-term and part-time work contracts, reflects wider changes in the workforce. The development of internal markets in most areas of welfare provision is resulting in the break-up of the old welfare bureaucracies. These changes also reflect the broader postindustrial trend towards working in fragmented, decentralized organizations. More generally, the emergence of a postindustrial type of economy is eroding the old norms of secure, permanent employment for men and leading to a situation in which the former 'Beveridgian' welfare state (see Chapter 3) is increasingly outmoded and unsuited to people's needs.

For such authors as Hillyard and Watson (1996) it is vitally important to include what are termed *poststructural* accounts and ideas in the study of social policy. Poststructural accounts of contemporary social life and society have appeared to call into question such universalistic creeds and norms as socialism, social justice and equality. These were the master narratives or so-called 'grand narratives' of 'modernist' societies, associated with the 'Fordist' economic production and the classic welfare states that arguably dominated much of the twentieth century. (The historical dimension to the popularity of poststructuralist/postmodernist theorizing may be significant; it emerged in the 1970s and 1980s, when 'the system' appeared to be in crisis, and also under challenge from various quarters.) Poststructuralism allegedly challenges the universalistic ways of thinking that underpinned the old 'Beveridgian' welfare state, for instance, the assumption that all people who fit a certain category (for example, older people, or women) have similar needs, and that a universalistic welfare state should provide for everyone's needs in a similar way.

For some commentators on social policy these ideas, although bold and interesting, obscure more than they reveal. For instance, Carter and Rayner (1996) take as an example a particular area of social policy (education) to see whether concepts of postFordism and postindustrialism help to interpret recent changes in the education system. They conclude that these theories downplay important elements of continuity in British policy-making. According to them, there is little evidence of the scale of change anticipated in theories of a postmodern society, either in the way the education system is being run or in the content of the system. Postmodernism may therefore exaggerate the idea of a complete change from one era to another, with associated social policy changes.

Taylor-Gooby (1994) also argues this point, suggesting that postmodernism is a set of ideas that is likely to deflect attention from such continuities as poverty and inequality.

Far from ushering in a new postmodern era, Taylor-Gooby argues, the market economy and its accompanying values that now so dominate the world have led to a re-emergence of social conditions and relationships that are reminiscent of the period before the welfare state. The 're-emerging past' includes such things as a deregulated and exploitative labour market and a retreat from the idea of using universal, society-wide policies to reduce poverty.

Postmodernist styles of thinking have influenced social policy analysis in a number of indirect ways for example, the highlighting of 'social construction' and 'social constructionist' methodological and theoretical approaches found in some recent texts (Saraga 1998). In so far as social constructionism as an approach to social analysis amounts to anything significant, it is probably in its emphasis on pluralism and diversity of viewpoints and its highlighting of social differentiation and division. In social policy this is associated with the discovery of 'identity' politics, the highlighting of new rather than old social divisions and inequalities, and the questioning of the traditional redistributionist agenda in terms of socioeconomic or class inequalities. The embrace of 'diversity' and multiculturalism, the recognition of disability, age and sexuality as well as gender as social divisions might be taken as evidence of 'postmodernist' influence. In this sense postmodernist or poststructualist social policy thinking represents the impact of the 'new social movements'. Of course, it might seem inconsistent and incoherent for poststructuralist-influenced writers to appear to offer a critique of 'modernist' values like equality on the one hand, while highlighting and apparently deploring a variety of 'new' social divisions on the other.

Endnote: a postmodern government and postmodern social policies?

In the persistence of poverty there is certainly a lot of evidence to support Taylor-Gooby's scepticism about postmodernity and its value as a concept in understanding the present-day world. As discussed in Chapter 5 there is still a lot of 'old-fashioned' poverty about in the UK today – the poverty of older people trying to live on inadequate pensions, for instance, or the poverty of people who are working on low incomes.

However, it would be wrong to write off postmodernism and associated ideas about the social changes resulting from the drawing to a close of the industrial era. As pointed out in Chapter 5, 'new' poverty and increasingly different experiences of poverty mean that it is no longer the 'mass experience' of, say, the 1930s. 'The poor', never a homogeneous social group, are becoming an increasingly fragmented and differentiated mixture of categories or groups in society. For instance, with regard to one major social category – older people – divisions in this group are becoming more significant than they were. Some older people – an increasing number in today's society – are relatively well-off. Among those who are not so well-off, there are rising numbers of older people who are 'asset rich but income poor' – those who own their own homes but are on low pension incomes. And there are yet other subgroups, such as older people on varying levels of pension income but with few savings and no substantial property.

Not surprisingly, therefore, there is a sound argument to suggest that the old universalistic policies of the welfare state will look increasingly anachronistic in a postmodern world in which new social distinctions and a greater diversity of values and social groups are emerging. But it might be helpful to picture this as a change in which the old, or traditional, elements of the welfare state continue to shape the postmodern welfare system. The development of the NHS (see Chapter 9) in the twenty-first century – a much-adapted 1940s-style health system that still retains its basic design – is a case in point.

Similarly, it would be misleading to conclude with the view that Blair's New Labour government is a pure and simple example of a postmodern approach to politics and social policy. There are certainly some strong signs of postmodernity in the way that New Labour has developed its appeal to the public and angled its policies to suit a range of opinion. As discussed in the first section of this chapter, New Labour seems to have adopted a 'pick and mix' approach (Powell 1999) to selecting its priorities.

The 'postmodernity' of Labour's approach to making policy can also be seen in the rapidity with which the government can change direction. Sometimes this has been done without much public consultation and with no piloting or careful consideration of policy options. An example of this can be seen in health policy, where abrupt changes of direction took place after 2000 regarding levels of funding, the role of the private sector, the value of choice and the role of market mechanisms.

Further signs of the government's postmodern approach to politics can be seen in its preoccupation with style, appearance and mass media reactions to its policies. As with the government's ability to change direction to suit the needs of the moment, pre-occupation with style and presentation is nothing new in politics. However, there is certainly an argument that the *degree* to which New Labour is preoccupied with style rather than substance, and with firmly controlling MPs so that their views are 'on message', marks a significant change from old-style party politics.

But as suggested above, none of these postmodern characteristics neatly sums up the nature of the Blair government and its policies. In social policy, the New Labour approach has not only been marked by a flexible, pick and mix approach, but also affected by surprisingly old-fashioned assumptions. For instance, welfare *paternalism* is evident in many of New Labour's policies. A strong thread of paternalism can be seen in government legislation and guidance on its various New Deal, community regeneration and neigh-bourhood renewal schemes. It can also be seen in such initiatives as the obligatory lit-eracy hour in English and Welsh primary schools, or in some Sure Start schemes that seem to work on the principle of advising (mainly working-class) parents about how best to bring up their children.

This kind of paternalism is far from postmodern. It has echoes of 1940s Britain, and of times when government used to tell people what was best for them, in their own interests. New Labour paternalism has been accompanied by the increasing centralization of government power mentioned above. Devolution and the growing significance of EU social policy are weakening or diluting this trend, but only to a limited degree, or in relatively minor ways to date (see Chapter 12).

Another view about New Labour after ten years in office is that it is really much more consistent, and traditional, than it appears. It is, from this perspective, essentially an old-fashioned social democratic 'tax and spend' government, little different from its pre-decessors in the 1960s and 1970s. The level of public spending, as a share of national income, has risen steadily since 1997 and is forecast to reach 43 per cent of GDP (it was 36 per cent of GDP in 1996, the last full year of Conservative government). Although New Labour pledged in 1997, and has continued to pledge, that top rates of income tax will not rise, the tax burden has in fact steadily increased to match the increase in public spending. So-called 'stealth taxes' – taxes that (it is hoped) nobody will notice – have done the work of raising money for additional spending on public services, and have in fact been much more effective for this purpose than any increase in top rates of income tax could be. The period of New Labour rule has, for example, seen the rediscovery of 'fiscal drag', last heard of in the 1970s. Fiscal drag, a term which conjures up pleasing images of cross-dressing Revenue officials, is actually an easy and painless way for governments to raise taxes without appearing to. As incomes from earnings rise, as they have done in a period of uninterrupted economic growth like that experienced since 1993, people pay more tax. They also move from lower to higher income tax bands. The tax thresholds between bands are indexed – increased – annually, but in line with prices, rather than average earnings (which have increased faster than prices over the period), ensuring that earners will therefore, over time, be dragged into higher tax bands. This has ensured that income tax yields have been buoyant. The increase in National Insurance contribution rates for both employers and employees in 2002 is another stealth tax. Yet another has been steep rises in Council Tax to pay for local authority-provided services (rather less successful as a stealth tax, since there has been some recent public backlash, particularly from pensioners).

Labour has clearly prioritized public spending, and been prepared to accept the fiscal consequences of doing so. In this respect there is 'clear blue water' between Labour and the Conservatives, at least until the advent of David Cameron as Conservative leader at the end of 2005, since when there appears to have been a shift in Conservative policy. The Conservatives consistently favoured tax cuts under Cameron's predecessors. Labour's tax policies appear to be in accord with the public's expressed desires for improved public services, and Labour in this respect has been closer to mainstream public opinion than the Conservatives. Just as the Blair-led Labour Party contesting the general election in 1997 felt it necessary to adapt, chameleon-like, to prevailing policies on taxation and social welfare that had been created by the Conservatives, so a Conservative Party led by Cameron a decade later is apparently being forced to adapt to the political 'realities' of higher public spending that have been shaped by Labour. What looks like recent Conservative repositioning under Cameron on the tax issue suggests that New Labour's lack of openness about its stance on taxes may not be electorally necessary.

There is a good case for saying that New Labour is quite traditional in another sense as well, and that is in its concern for equality. Conventional wisdom suggests that New Labour is unconcerned about equality, taking its cue from such remarks as that by Blair to the effect he had no interest in limiting the earnings of star footballers such as David Beckham, but this is misleading. New Labour has arguably been concerned about equality, not necessarily in the 1970s sense articulated by Denis Healey when he was reported to have said that a Labour government would 'squeeze the rich until the pips squeaked', but in the sense of equality of opportunity and equality of status or citizenship. New Labour has pursued equality agendas in relation to gender, race, disability, sexuality and age, not perhaps to the extent desired by lobbies and movements, and perhaps with limited success, but nevertheless with some vigour. The Human Rights Act

1998, the concern with 'work–life balance' and nursery education, anti-discrimination legislation and initiatives affecting race, disability and age point to an underlying commitment. In this sense New Labour could be said to be both traditional and postmodern. The 'grand narrative' of equality as a component of social justice could be said to be alive and well, indeed livelier than ever, despite poststructuralist doubts. Intolerance of inequality is the prevailing mood, and New Labour's policies reflect this. In the texture of social life and in what can loosely be described as 'culture', this is manifested in many ways – the content of TV soaps, the disappearance of received pronunciation, replaced or modified by 'Estuary English' or even varieties of African-Caribbean dialect, the dumbing-down of the print and broadcast media, Gordon Brown's attack on Oxford University in 2000 for its alleged bias against pupils from state schools, the decline of deference and the apparent disappearance of a tightly-knit traditional 'establishment', or social and political elite, surrounding a respected and trusted royal family. There is no doubt that Britain has become, in these respects, a more equal society than it was even 30 years ago (another way of putting it is to say that social life and culture have been democratized). These developments have been presided over and encouraged by New Labour, even if they did not begin with them.

Of course this does not imply that serious social divisions do not still remain. As students of social policy, even of a postmodern generation, we may feel that these dimensions of inequality are relatively unimportant, perhaps just cosmetic or surface changes, and that the underlying material reality of poverty and socioeconomic inequality are more important. As we saw in Chapter 5, New Labour's record here is ambiguous, but not contemptible: little improvement in overall income inequality (but the growth of inequality has been halted), some improvement in indices of child poverty, no improvement in non-family rates of poverty (Stewart 2005). Much remains to do.

In the final analysis, therefore, welfare paternalism no more sums up recent government policy than the tag of Third Way government or postmodern government. New Labour and the social policies it has developed and implemented are a combination of all these things, and more. Waiting to find out what the actual combination is, how the character of the government will change, and how this will affect the policies and the people of the future, is what makes the study of social policy so exciting.

Key terms and concepts

casualization
globalization
paternalism
postfeminism
postFordism
postindustrialism
postmodernism
poststructuralism

Suggestions for further reading

There are now a number of academic studies of the performance of the Blair government and its impact on social policy. Although it was written midway through Blair's first term in government and therefore does not include more recent developments, an edited book by Martin Powell, *New Labour, New Welfare State?* (1999) remains one of the best. It includes an overview of New Labour, written by Martin Powell, and a series of chapters on the various branches of the welfare system, such as education and health, by other authors. Powell's *Evaluating New Labour's Welfare Reforms* (2002) is an update of this, with some useful articles. A comprehensive discussion of New Labour's successes and failures in relation to poverty and inequality is provided by the contributors to John Hills's and Kitty Stewart's *A More Equal Society? New Labour, Poverty, Inequality and Exclusion* (2005). A useful summary of much of this material is provided by Stewart's chapter 'Equality and social justice' in *The Blair Effect 2001–5* edited by Seldon and Kavanagh (2005). Although journalistic and not in-depth in its approach, Polly Toynbee's and David Walker's *Better or Worse? Has Labour Delivered?* (2005) updates their earlier *Did Things Get Better?* (2001) and provides a very readable and informative summary of Labour's successes and failures. It is written from a standpoint that is largely sympathetic to New Labour, so this has to be taken into account, but does not pull its punches where necessary.

To follow the debate about postmodernism in social policy, try to obtain the issues of the *Journal of Social Policy* which include the articles by Taylor-Gooby, Penna and O'Brien, Fitzpatrick, and Hillyard and Watson, which were mentioned in this chapter.

On a final and more general note, you will find that the *Journal of Social Policy* is well worth consulting for any research or coursework that you may have to do, or just to keep up to date with current policy issues and debates. Each issue contains a section titled 'Digest', which helpfully summarizes key changes in various policy areas such as the health services, education, housing, gender issues and so on.

Glossary

The key terms and concepts in this glossary are also listed at the end of the particular chapter(s) in which they have been most used. Therefore, by reading the text of the relevant chapter(s) you will be able to find examples of the ways in which they can be applied. Relevant chapter(s) are indicated after each definition with an abbreviation (for example, 'Ch. 1' for Chapter 1).

The definitions that follow are summaries of the way concepts are used in *social policy*. You may find different interpretations of terms in a dictionary or a reference book.

Where terms are closely related (for instance, 'maximalist' and 'minimalist' types of equal opportunity policy), they have been placed together for convenience. Otherwise, the terms are arranged alphabetically.

Active labour market policy: a term that sums up a variety of government policies to maximize the number of people in employment. These policies include initiatives to improve people's employability through additional training and to give personal advice to individuals on the types of work they could do. They may also include (for example, in Sweden) incentives to take paid employment such as providing grants for travelling to work or moving house, or child care facilities. This type of policy includes groups who have previously experienced difficulties in finding work – for instance, disabled people, lone parents, older workers and the long-term unemployed. Active labour market policies represent a state interventionist philosophy that assumes that the job market alone cannot be relied on to maximize the number of people in work. They connect economic and social policy, and operate on the principle that welfare and social security are enhanced through being employed rather than being unemployed and dependent on 'passive' welfare benefits. (Ch. 8)

Acute illnesses: serious life-threatening illnesses which are resolved in a relatively short period of time (usually a matter of days or weeks), either by death or by the patient regaining health. Medical intervention may help either to restore health or to manage acute illness, which may then become a chronic condition (see **chronic illnesses**). Acute infectious illnesses were common in Britain up to the early part of the twentieth century. (Chs 3, 9)

Asymmetric devolution and symmetric devolution: devolution is a process in which certain central government powers and functions are granted to regions or countries within the larger nation-state. If devolution is *asymmetric*, central government grants more powers of self-rule to some regions or countries than to others. If it is *symmetric*, each part of the country and each devolved administration has the same powers and functions. (Ch. 12)

Autonomy: when applied to individuals, this term refers to the ability of a person to decide their own fate; the autonomous individual has the freedom and the ability to make decisions independently or to exercise choices for themselves. 'Autonomy' can also be used to refer to government institutions and organizations (see **quangos**) or to devolved administrations (see **asymmetric devolution**). See **oppression** and **social control**. (Chs 2, 6)

Basic needs: these are universal human needs that are considered to be fundamental, not simply to enable human beings to survive, but as basic requirements for the development of independent individuals. Autonomy has been seen as a basic need, as well as adequate nutrition and housing, for instance. (Ch. 2)

Business cycle: this refers to the tendency for economic activity (including production, rates of employment and unemployment, profit rates) to rise and fall over time. Both economic and social policies are concerned to smooth out the 'bumps' and crises in the business cycle. For instance, policies may aim to stimulate employment in times of high unemployment and sluggish economic growth (see **active labour market policy**). Or government policies might try to reduce the problems of 'overheating' of the economy in times of rapid growth by raising taxation (thus reducing consumer demand) or by trying to solve shortages of skilled labour. (Ch. 8)

Care management: a term associated mainly with the provision and organization of services in the community, or with managing services for people who are moving in or out of hospital or institutional settings. Care management is an approach which stresses the importance of coordinating health and social services in ways which not only best serve the interests of service users but also maximize the efficiency of service delivery. Care managers are often social workers, but can be appointed from other fields, such as occupational therapy, and their job is to take the lead responsibility for coordinating the various services needed. (Ch. 11)

Carer: this is a formal way of defining the role of someone who either willingly and voluntarily cares for someone, usually on a continual and permanent basis, or feels obliged to provide care or is paid to do so. The invention of the term 'carer' has had some unfortunate consequences, in that it tends to suggest that all the 'care' goes in one direction (from carer to 'cared for'), and it can overemphasize the helplessness and passivity of people who need help with managing their daily activities. (Ch. 11)

Casualization (of employment): a process of change in working conditions and work contracts. It refers to the way in which permanent work contracts and full-time jobs are replaced by short-term and part-time work. When work is casualized, employees tend to lose important rights and the protection of laws that should safeguard their welfare: for instance, laws against instant or unfair dismissal, laws to ensure safety at work and contributions by employers to social security, insurance and pension schemes. See **deregulation**. (Ch. 8)

Chronic illnesses: these are illnesses which are, in most cases, incurable. However, they may or may not be disabling and often they can be successfully managed by medical intervention. Chronic illnesses are thus long-term problems, in that they are not immediately life-threatening (for instance, Parkinson's disease), and they have replaced **acute illnesses** as the main causes of illness in modern society. (Chs 3, 9)

Civil rights: the rights of individuals to liberty and security under the law: for instance, the right to move freely from one place to another, freedom from arbitrary arrest or detention without legal cause, and the right to own property. T.H. Marshall (1950) saw civil rights as a first step to the development of other rights (**political rights** and **social rights**). (Ch. 2)

Coercion: this term can be used to define a wide variety of methods with which those in power constrain or force people without power to do something or to act in a particular way. Coercion may be subtle and may be exercised as a result of the way a particular organization or institution is run (for instance, a residential home for disabled people), or it may be direct and consciously applied by those with power. (Ch. 6)

Community care: this refers to caring activities or services that exist outside large-scale institutions such as hospitals. The 'community' may be defined as a wide range of non-institutional settings (for instance, **day centres**, 'halfway houses' or **sheltered housing** schemes, foster homes), but in most cases 'community care' is another way of describing the care of people living alone or in families. See **domiciliary care** and **residential care**. (Ch. 11)

Comparative analysis: the study of the institutions or policies of more than one country, usually identifying and exploring similarities and differences, for the purpose of policy learning or to throw light on the causes of institutional or policy change. (Chs 3, 4)

Comparative need: a way of defining need in a group in relation to what other comparable groups have, or do not have. An observer may find that one group of disabled people, for instance, receive very little help in the form of social services even though it is clear that they need such services. Finding a second comparable group that does receive services may help to establish a case for providing services to the first group as well. (Ch. 2)

Consumers (of services): the idea of portraying users of public services as 'consumers' gained importance as a result of the introduction of market-style reforms of the **welfare system** in the 1980s. Its significance lay in the goal of giving individual service users greater choice of services or a greater say over how services should be delivered to them. Thus people who used public services such as NHS hospitals, schools or social services were to be seen *as if* they were purchasing goods or services in the private market, even though (in the case of 'free' services) they were not paying for them at the point of use. (Ch. 11)

Contract state: A role for government which seeks to ensure that certain services are provided (such as education), but not by the government itself. Instead of public provision, the contract state draws up contracts with private and voluntary organizations to provide services. These organizations are then paid for services by government, which restricts its role to regulating providers and to making sure that value for money is obtained. (Ch. 3)

Contributory benefits and non-contributory benefits: payment of social security benefits to people is based on two different principles. *Contributory* benefits work on the principle that people qualify for them because they have paid (contributed) National Insurance payments to the government's social security scheme. The state retirement pension is an example of a contributory benefit. To qualify for benefit, the recipient must also belong to a certain social category or group (for example, be over retirement age). *Non-contributory* benefits work on a different principle. They are payable to anyone who qualifies on grounds of **need** and do not depend on having paid contributions to the National Insurance scheme. Income support is an example of a non-contributory benefit. (Ch. 5)

Convergence and divergence: As countries develop, they become more alike, or perhaps *converge* on a uniform model of social organization, institutions and policies. This might be because of either certain imperatives in the process of development (for example, arising from technology or market forces, or perhaps because of 'social' or 'policy learning' – exchange of policy ideas between societies). The question might be asked of international institutions like the EU, whether it is promoting convergence of member countries because of such policies as the single market, imposed on all member countries. In comparative studies *divergence* refers to a process of change in which the social policies of the countries or other units being compared become increasingly different from one another. However, it is a process and does not mean that the policies of the different countries become completely different from one another – they are just less alike than they were. Equally, convergence does not mean that policies in different countries or regions become the same or similar. Convergence is also a process in which policies become more alike than they were, but still might retain a lot of difference and distinctiveness. (Chs 3, 4)

Corporatist welfare states: a model or type of welfare state that is based on the principle of legal or informal agreements between the major 'corporate groups' of society: for instance, organized labour (trade unions), employer organizations, voluntary organizations (such as leading churches or religious organizations) and government. Germany is an example of a corporatist welfare state. Some welfare and service provision is in the hands of Church organizations, while employers' and workers' organizations come to agreements with government over **social security** benefits and other aspects of welfare. (Ch. 3)

Council housing: rented accommodation provided and owned by elected local government councils. See **social housing**. (Ch. 10)

Critique: a critical discussion of someone's idea, position, theory or set of findings. A critique appraises others' ideas and suggests new insights. (Ch. 1)

Curative medicine: an approach in medicine that emphasizes the treatment of disease to effect cures and restore health. The 'curative model' or approach implies a policy that puts more resources into treating sick people (with doctors, other medical practitioners, hospitals and drug therapy) than into preventing the onset of disease. (Ch. 9)

Day centre: a social services term to describe a facility which provides services during the day (for instance, meals, recreation, therapy) for people who continue to reside in their own homes. See **community care**. (Ch. 11)

Deinstitutionalization: a policy or process of change through which institutions such as mental hospitals and residential homes are closed down. It can also refer to a process of personal change in which former residents or patients lose their 'institutionalized' identities and behaviour patterns. (Ch. 6)

Democratic pluralist model of power: this is one of several perspectives on the way power is distributed and exercised in society (see also **elite control** and **political economy** models of power). The democratic pluralist view suggests that power is distributed widely among a large number (plurality) of different groups in society (for example, business interests, political parties, campaign groups). No one group monopolizes power or decision-making. Democratic elections make governments accountable to ordinary citizens. (Ch. 7)

Deregulation (of employment): this refers to the abolition or suspension of rules and regulations governing work contracts. Those in favour of deregulation suggest that it is a necessary process to eliminate restrictive 'red tape' that often prevents employers from hiring more workers or expanding their businesses. Those who are critical of deregulation see it as an attack on the legislation that protects workers' welfare – for instance, health and safety legislation, or rules about working time or unfair dismissal. See **casualization**. (Chs 5, 8, 11)

Deserving poor and undeserving poor: a terms from the nineteenth century that imply a distinction between those who are destitute and have a moral right to state welfare or charitable support (for instance, orphaned children or disabled people unable to work), and those who could support themselves but do not do so, preferring to make undeserved claims on the state or on charities. See **dole**. (Ch. 3)

Deterrence: approach to crime control and criminal justice which states that the aim of punishment is to deter the offender (from offending again), or to deter other would-be offenders. (Ch. 4)

Devolution: see **asymmetric devolution and symmetric devolution**.

Disciplines: used in this book to discuss the status and identity of different academic subjects or fields of study, such as social policy. A discipline is a recognized university subject that has generated its own body of research and has developed a distinctive set of theories. (Ch. 1)

Disposable income: the money that people have and are able to spend or invest (including the cash benefits they receive), minus any direct taxes they have to pay (see Figure 5.1). (Ch. 5)

Divergence: see **convergence**.

Dole: one of the earliest terms related to welfare. 'The dole' was the daily or weekly payment (in bread or money) to the poor of the parish. The dole was given to those who were regarded as the **deserving poor** and who could receive 'outdoor relief' (assistance from the parish or Poor Law authorities while continuing to live at home, rather than in an institution such as the workhouse). (Ch. 3)

Domiciliary care: home care, that is, social services delivered by a local authority, voluntary or private sector agency to the home (domicile). See **community care** and **residential care**. (Ch. 11)

Dual labour market: in some countries or economies – particularly in developing countries – the labour market is segmented. In the formal sector of employment, workers normally receive wages on a regular basis and work according to formal contracts; they are also protected by legislation governing their terms of employment and retirement. In the informal sector, there are no permanent jobs with regularly-paid wages. Workers in the informal sector either are self-employed, or work for employers who are not bound by formal contracts governing wages, job security, health and safety, working hours, leave and so on. (Ch. 8)

Due process: term more often used in the United States than the UK, meaning approximately the same as Rule of Law. (Ch. 4)

Economic activity and the economically active: these terms refer to employment. The total of 'economically active' in the population is a combination of everyone in paid employment *and* the unemployed. When counting unemployment, the International Labour Organization recommends that everyone aged over 16 and below retirement age is included, as long as they are seeking a job and are available to start work within two weeks' time. This is a more comprehensive measure of unemployment than counting only those who have registered as unemployed to claim state benefits. The economically active, then, normally means everyone in work plus everyone who is employable and is seeking paid work. (Ch. 8)

Economic growth: the size of an economy can be measured by statistical estimates of the total value of all the goods and services produced every year. Economic growth occurs when one year's total production exceeds a previous year's. However, economic growth measures can be criticized because they are usually based on what is known as the 'formal economy' and production or work that has been statistically measured by economists. Official economic estimates often neglect the millions of hours and the resources devoted to family care and domestic work – an 'informal economy' of welfare. (Ch. 5)

Egalitarianism: a broad term which encompasses a variety of socialist points of view. However, all egalitarians believe in the importance of absolute equality and of creating a society which minimizes distinctions of rank or status, and of income and wealth. (Ch. 2)

Eligibility: see **less eligibility**.

Elite control model of power: an analysis or view of power in society which suggests that power is concentrated in the hands of an elite, or several connected elites. Elites may be defined as extremely small groups of people who occupy the leading positions in business, government and political parties, cultural institutions and the military. (Ch. 7)

Empirical research: research (on the natural or social world) which is based on observation, experience and testing of hypotheses against factual evidence. Empirical research is used to test theories, but is not itself highly theoretical. (Ch. 1)

Empowerment: a process of change in which oppressed groups discover their ability to challenge those who oppress them. Empowerment can be brought about by change in the power structures which govern communities and social service organizations. For instance, women living in a housing estate who were previously isolated and powerless might bring themselves together to form their own campaigning group to challenge street crime, domestic violence, a lack of community services and inadequate housing maintenance. See **oppression**. (Chs 10, 11)

Equality: when applied to human societies, equality describes a state in which people are closely similar in social status, income, wealth, opportunities and living conditions. See **egalitarianism**. (Ch. 2)

Equality of opportunity: exists if everyone has the same or near-similar chances to achieve their ends or goals (for instance, through educational success or seeking employment). Therefore, equality of opportunity says nothing about final outcomes, which may be highly unequal in terms of success, educational qualifications or income. Equality of opportunity is often a measure of how fair or equal conditions are at the 'starting gate' before the race, though it can also be applied to promotion, career development and further opportunities after people have entered the job market. (Ch. 2)

Equity: this term refers to justice and fairness in the distribution of something (for instance, social benefits, jobs, income and wealth). It may be just and fair for one individual or group to receive more than another because needs differ. (Ch. 2)

Expressed needs: needs which are publicly known and which have been identified as important by an individual or a group. Not all expressed needs are met, but the expression of need is an important first step in placing a demand on government or some other body. (Ch. 2)

External benefits: a term often used by economists to refer to additional benefits that could be gained from a particular policy or course of action. Rather than being a narrowly defined or individual benefit, an external benefit is likely to be something that brings a gain or payoff to the community as a whole. For instance, education brings individual benefits or payoffs (because it allows people with qualifications to obtain higher pay) but it also brings external benefits such as a general increase in productivity and efficiency. (Chs 5, 7)

Felt need: this is need which not only objectively exists (i.e. there would be agreement among observers that a particular individual or group needs something) but also the people or groups in question realize that they have, and consciously express their feelings about. See **wants**. (Ch. 2)

Flat-rate (contributions and benefits): a rather old-fashioned term which refers to everyone paying in the same amount to a social security scheme and, if benefits are also flat-rate, all beneficiaries receiving the same amount. (Chs 3, 5)

Freedom: this may be defined 'negatively' as the absence of restraint or **oppression** (for instance, freedom from crime, freedom from arbitrary arrest), or 'positively' as freedom to do certain things, such as the freedom to follow educational courses to one's full potential. Positive freedoms have greater resource implications than negative freedoms because they often involve increases in welfare and educational spending. See **social rights**. (Chs 2, 6)

Full employment: this term describes a state of the economy and the job market in which there is plentiful employment and in which almost everyone who is economically active (except for a very small percentage who are changing jobs) is in paid work. Not only is there negligible unemployment, but also there may even be labour shortages in some areas and a slight surplus of jobs compared to the numbers of people available for work. (Ch. 8)

Globalization: a world trend in which national barriers to international trade and production are being eroded away. At the same time as an international or global market in goods, services and capital is being developed, it is also argued that globalization will lead to an erosion of national differences in ideology, culture and politics. According to this argument, distinct differences in social policy between countries will gradually disappear. There could be an overall reduction in welfare provision, among industrialized countries, towards the lowest common denominator. (Chs 2, 8, 13)

Gross domestic product (GDP): a measure of the total value, in money terms, of all the goods and services produced in a country, excluding exports and 'invisible' earnings (for example, from insurance services provided to other countries). (Ch. 5)

Home care: see **domiciliary care**.

Homelessness: lack of a home, which may exist even if people have a place to stay or 'a roof over their head'. People who inhabit overcrowded or hazardous dwellings, or who are unable to enjoy freedom of movement, may be described as homeless. (Ch. 10)

Human rights: fundamental moral claims – for example, the rights to life, right to a fair trial, freedom of speech, freedom of worship, right to vote, and in some cases rights to welfare, for example, health care or education, often or usually presented in constitutional documents or international declarations such as the UN Declaration of 1948 or the European Charter of 1961 and in the UK in the 1998 Human Rights Act. (Ch. 4)

Hypothecated taxation: a way of linking or pledging the revenue gained from taxation to public spending on clearly specified services or developments. For instance, the Liberal Democrat Party proposed an increase in income tax that could be hypothecated to increased spending on education. In this example all the extra revenue gained from the tax increase would be spent on education services and none of it could be spent on anything else. There has been a public debate about whether most taxes should be hypothecated or linked to particular services or items of public spending, or whether this would introduce too much inflexibility into the government's management of the economy. The main attraction of hypothecated taxation is an apparent greater certainty for the taxpayer about 'where all the money goes' after it has been collected in taxes. (Ch. 5)

Hypothesis: an assumption or guess which is used to explain something. Hypotheses are 'working assumptions' that need to be tested against evidence. They are developed as ways of finding out whether broader theories are correct. (Ch. 1)

Iatrogenic disease: disease which is caused or aggravated by medical treatment. (Ch. 9)

Implementation (of policy): the process of carrying out a policy and turning it from a written policy statement, law or guideline into action 'on the ground'. Note, however, that even when implemented, some policies do not bring about much change. (Chs 1, 7)

Income (original, gross and final income): the distinctions between original, final and gross income help to illustrate the effect of welfare provision upon people's incomes. *Original* income represents the sum that a household receives (including cash benefits). *Gross* income is the sum before taxes and other deductions are taken away. *Final* income is what is left after **taxation**, plus an estimate of the value of social/welfare services and **social security benefits** that the household receives. A year's primary schooling, for instance, might be valued at £5000 and added to the household's final income (see Figure 5.1). (Ch. 5)

Industrial paternalism: this term refers to the examples of employers in the nineteenth and twentieth centuries who sought to improve the living and working conditions of their employees and their families. Such concerns have been termed 'paternalist' because employers tended to assume that they knew what was best for their workers. Further, in accepting improved conditions, workers were expected to show deference and loyalty to employers. Modern industrial paternalism can be seen in the management styles of Japanese companies. See **paternalism**. (Ch. 10)

Industrial relations: a useful but now rather outdated term to describe employer–employee relations. It does not have to be restricted to 'industrial' companies or organizations, and can be used to describe the state of relations between management and trade unions in service industries – for instance, the health service. Industrial relations cover such things as wage bargaining and negotiations over work contracts. (Ch. 8)

Institutional care: see **residential care**.

Internal market: this term is used to define the way in which competition and market-*like* ways of operating have been introduced into state-run organizations and services. Thus an internal market can be developed without any privatization. Public services (for example, local authority social services) are divided into 'purchasing' and 'providing' divisions. The 'purchasing' side of the organization is then free to 'shop around' to find the service provider that will provide the best value in terms of costs and quality of services provided. See **purchaser–provider split**. (Chs 7, 9, 11)

Justice: in social policy, justice is discussed with reference to the fairness or rightness of policies. A socially just policy, for instance, will result in the fairest possible distribution of welfare, services or resources. See **equity**. (Ch. 2)

Keynesian strategy/policy: named after the famous economist John Maynard Keynes on whose theories it is based, this is a policy to use government borrowing and public money to manage the economy. In times of economic slow-down or recession, for instance, Keynes advocated the careful use of public spending to generate employment and stimulate production. When unemployment is reduced, more people are able to pay tax, thus replenishing government income and enabling the government to repay its debts. This strategy was used to good effect in various countries both before and after the Second World War. More recently, there have been attempts to apply Keynesian principles in new ways (neo-Keynesianism), but the advent of a global economy (see **globalization**) has made it difficult for national governments to follow Keynesian strategies as they did in the past. (Ch. 8)

Less eligibility: a term used in the framing of the 'New' Poor Law of 1834. Eligibility in this old-fashioned usage can be taken to mean 'satisfactory'. The argument put forward by those who wanted to reform the old (pre-1834) Poor Laws was that the income and living conditions of those in receipt of public assistance (poor relief) should always be 'less eligible' (satisfactory) than the lowest paid labourer's. (Ch. 3)

Liberal welfare states: one of several major categories or types of welfare system. A country with a 'liberal' welfare system typically has minimal welfare provision. Where public services and welfare benefits are provided, they tend to be strictly means tested (see **means tests**) and restricted to the poorest sections of society. The dominant philosophy is one of laissez-faire, and the majority make their own arrangements (through private insurance and private facilities, or reliance on family support) to safeguard their welfare. Esping-Andersen's *The Three Worlds of Welfare Capitalism* (1990) refers to this type of welfare system. (Ch. 3)

Marginalization: a social and political process in which weaker or poorer groups and individuals are excluded from, or pushed to the margins of, mainstream society. Marginalization means that the views and the needs of excluded groups tend not to be taken into account in policy-making. See **social exclusion**. (Chs 5, 6)

Maximalist policies: see **minimalist policies and maximalist policies**.

Means tests: rules which are used to target benefits or services upon people whose incomes (means) fall below a certain level, so that only poorer groups are eligible. Means-tested benefits may be contrasted with universal benefits, which are available to all. See **selective benefits** and **social security benefits**. (Chs 3, 5)

Medicalization: a process of social change in which perceptions of human and social problems shift towards the view that problems can best be explained as 'illnesses' which must be dealt with by medical treatment. For instance, much deviant behaviour that might once have been described as 'evil' or 'mad' is now portrayed as illness that must be treated. Natural phenomena such as childbirth have also been extensively medicalized. (Ch. 9)

Minimalist policies and maximalist policies (of equal opportunity): the terms 'minimalist' and 'maximalist' could be applied to any kind of policy, in that the former suggests the idea of doing the minimum and the latter suggests maximum government intervention and effort. In relation to equal opportunities, a minimalist policy is one that seeks to ensure that competition for jobs or education is fair and not openly discriminatory in any way. Maximalist policies are those that seek more ambitiously to change outcomes by equalizing numbers of men and women, ethnic and 'racial' groups and other under- and over-represented groups in the workforce. See positive action. (Chs 2, 8)

Mixed economy of care: a phrase that summarizes the complex modern system of social and health services, which are provided and funded by a variety of different types of organization in the local authority or central government, voluntary and private sectors. The idea of a 'mixed economy' was developed originally to describe countries that combined capitalism with nationalized (state) industries. See **social care market**. (Ch. 11)

Models (of welfare or social policy): in academic discussion the term 'model' is used to describe a set of ideas that summarizes the essence or essential characteristics of something. A model is not expected to be an accurate or detailed description: it is a way of picturing or generalizing basic types. In welfare, we may therefore develop ideas or models of different types of welfare system, such as the 'Scandinavian model' of social policy. (Chs. 1, 3)

Need: in social policy, the term 'need' is usually reserved for objective definitions of resources, skills or other things that are required and which an individual or a group lacks: for example, psychological needs for security or personal development, or physical needs for adequate nutrition. See **comparative need**, **expressed needs**, **felt need** and **normative needs**. (Ch. 2)

Needs-led assessment: a principle of basing assessment of people's eligibility for services or welfare upon an objective definition of their needs – as opposed to 'resource-led assessment', which works on the principle of assessing need on the basis of what limited services or resources are available. (Ch. 11)

Non-contributory benefits: see **contributory benefits**.

Normative needs: needs defined by professionals' standards and their judgement of what is lacking and what ought to be provided. (Ch. 2)

Normative policies: policies that express social norms and strong public views of what ought to happen in society. (Ch. 2)

Objectivity: this is a key term in any discussion of social science. It is particularly important in social policy because the assessment of policies is often influenced by values and political opinion rather than by objective assessment. Although complete objectivity may be impossible, this does not mean that all statements have equal validity or that one person's observations are always as valid or reliable as another's. An objective appraisal or piece of research is one that is as free of prejudice as possible. Objectivity is attained when evidence and reasoned argument show that a particular phenomenon – a government policy, for instance – has certain characteristics that exist independently of the perceiver's mind or personal opinions. (Ch. 1)

Oppression: this term is now widely used in sociology and politics, and in social work training, where 'anti-oppressive practice' is a key training goal. Oppression refers to a wide variety of behaviours and practices that unfairly deprive others (the oppressed) of their rights to **autonomy** and self-expression. In traditional and wider usage, oppression suggests tyranny and extremes of cruelty. However, in social science and social work, oppression is used to imply a broad range of discriminatory behaviour and prejudiced beliefs that exclude and demean powerless groups and individuals. See **empowerment** and **social control**. (Ch. 1)

Outcomes: the results or achievements of policies: for instance, health policy outcomes can be measured in terms of rates of various illnesses, or education policy outcomes can be measured by rates of literacy or by percentages of the population attaining various skills. (Ch. 9)

Parliamentary democracy: a form of democratic government in which almost all elected representatives are members of political parties which compete for power (although independent representatives or MPs who do not represent any political party are sometimes elected). The party that has the largest group of elected members after an election then forms the government, though it may have to rely on the support of another party if it does not have an overall majority in Parliament. In a parliamentary democracy, elected members are bound by the policies and discipline of their parties rather than by the wishes of their constituents. If there were a democracy in which those elected to power *directly* represented the wishes of the voters (for instance, to restore capital punishment), representatives would become 'delegates'. (Ch. 7)

Paternalism: a general term meaning any kind of policy or politics that is based on the view that a leader, government or influential group knows best what is in the public interest, or in the interests of less well-informed classes or social groups. Paternalistic policies tend to impose the views and policy solutions of an elite or dominant group on the rest of society, and such policies are usually shaped without much public consultation or participation. See **industrial paternalism** and **welfarism**. (Chs 6, 13)

Pauperism: a state or condition of absolute poverty and of dependence on public welfare. The Victorians drew a distinction between general poverty, which many experience, and pauperism. (Ch. 3)

Payment by results (in education): a phrase associated with education policy in the last quarter of the nineteenth century. Public funding of schools was based on a system of assessing school attainment (the numbers of pupils passing tests in the 'three Rs' – mainly tests of numeracy, literacy and rote learning of basic facts) and school attendance. The more pupils a school could 'process' successfully through the tests of rote learning, the more money was received from government. (Chs 3, 7)

Penal welfare state: term employed by sociologists influenced by Foucault to describe modern societies, which combine high levels of welfare with surveillance and regulation or social control of the population through criminal justice policy. Welfare and crime control go together; crime control is the dark side of the welfare state. (Ch. 4)

Philanthropy: charity and the practice of 'good works' in the community, either by donations or benevolent action. (Ch. 10)

Policy agenda: the main public issues or topics that are seen as a priority by government and/or the general public and the mass media. There is no completely objective way of defining which issues are on the policy agenda at any particular time, because there is a constantly changing list of concerns that drift in and out of the limelight. The absence of public issues from the policy agenda may have nothing to do with their importance. Many important issues or examples of need are ignored and never reach the policy agenda. (Ch. 7)

Policy learning: a concept of policy development, often used in comparative analysis, implying transfer or exchange of policy ideas between one country and another. Implies that the policies of other countries provide lessons or examples on how to do things which a policy-maker can use. (Ch. 4)

Political economy model of power (see also the **democratic pluralist** and **elite control** models of power): this view suggests that vested political and economic interests tend to be the dominant influences on decision-making and policy. For instance, the deep-seated interests of capitalist business exert a strong influence on government decisions about public spending and social welfare. However, these influences may be subtle and hard to detect. For various reasons, including a political ideology that supports the prevailing economic system, those who are relatively powerless might nevertheless support dominant interests (for instance, by voting for political parties that are pro-business and which reduce state-provided welfare). The political economy model is primarily a Marxist view of power. (Ch. 7)

Political rights: these are rights to political expression and freedom: for instance the right to organize and to hold political meetings, to demonstrate publicly in groups, to organize political parties, to publish political views, to hold elections and to vote without being intimidated. See **civil rights** and **social rights**. (Ch. 2)

Positive action: a term used to define a particular approach to equal opportunities policy. Positive action includes measures which go further than minimalist policies. Positive action encourages people from under-represented groups to apply for jobs or for educational places (whereas a minimalist policy would simply try to ensure fairness or similarity of treatment of applicants). However, positive action does not go as far as positive discrimination or 'reverse discrimination', which is a policy to ensure that formerly under-represented groups are equally represented in the workforce or in educational institutions. (Chs 2, 8)

Postfeminism: feminist perspectives show how inequalities between men and women are constructed and maintained. Postfeminist perspectives do not deny that major inequalities remain as a result of traditional patterns of male dominance. However, postfeminist perspectives point to the growing instability of men's and women's identities in the 'postmodern' world (the identity and economic status of many men has been profoundly affected by changes in the nature of manual work, for instance). Rather than taking for granted the idea that existing gender divisions will continue, postfeminism suggests that a greater variety of male and female roles and identities will develop. (Ch. 13)

PostFordism: 'Fordism' refers to the dominant pattern of work organization in modern society. Whether one works in a factory or not, Fordist organizations tend to be large-scale, hierarchical and bureaucratic, and to divide work into specialized units. However, as a result of profound changes in the economy and in technology, the nature of work is changing. To manage these changes, organizations – whether private firms or public organizations such as NHS hospitals or social services departments – are also changing. A postFordist economy or society is one in which the majority of organizations are becoming less centralized than before, and in which employees are expected to work flexibly with a range of skills rather than as specialized workers with narrowly defined skills. (Chs 8, 13)

Postindustrialism: a term that sums up key changes in the world of work and work organization. It is held that, as the industrial society of the twentieth century gives way to a postindustrial society, work and production will no longer take place in centralized plants and offices. Increasingly, work will be performed in decentralized units and in less hierarchical or bureaucratic working environments. Knowledge-based work and ability to use and control information will become increasingly important, while 'traditional' patterns of work in manufacturing industry will decline in significance. (Chs 8, 13)

Postmodernism: a term that refers to a wide variety of ideas about the ways in which society is changing from a 'modern' period to an emergent, postmodern period. Postmodern society is characterized by the break-up or fragmentation of all the major social institutions and social groups. For instance, working patterns, social class groups and even categories such as 'older people' are undergoing major transformations. Lifestyles, expectations and social groups are becoming increasingly diverse. This will have major implications for social policy. The 'modern' notion of centralized government and universal or 'one size fits all' policies may have to give way to more diverse patterns of government intervention (for instance, partnerships between business and government) and flexible policies. (Ch. 13)

Poststructuralism: a way of thinking that challenges the idea of universal truths. Poststructural ideas question the assumption that there is an underlying rationality in the social structures that we live with (such as government and state policies). A post-structural approach suggests that different ideas and views of a subject (such as poverty) all have a certain validity (even if they are not all equally valid). There may be no single or most authoritative view of a problem such as poverty and what to do about it. Therefore poststructural thinking, like **postmodernism** in general, poses questions about the basic idea of having a commonly defined policy that is based on a single, 'rational' set of goals. (Ch. 13)

Poverty (absolute and relative definitions): *absolute* definitions of poverty are ways of measuring poverty that are based on the idea that it is possible and valid to identify an objective, fixed 'poverty line'. People or groups above the line are judged not to be in poverty, those below it are. The poverty line is therefore a supposedly objective standard of living, and it may be expressed in terms of income or money, percentage of household income that has to be spent on 'basics' such as food, heating or rent, or measurements of food consumption and diet. Absolute definitions can be regularly updated to keep up with changing standards. *Relative* poverty, on the other hand, is a concept that tries to move beyond the idea of a fixed standard at a particular point in time, or poverty line. Relative definitions stress that poverty can be understood only in relation to the standard of living of the majority in society, and what society as a whole sees as necessary items or patterns of consumption to fully participate in social life. For instance, not having a television set could be seen as a valid indicator of poverty even if a family has enough food to eat and adequate housing. See **pauperism**. (Ch. 5)

Preventive health policies/services: an approach to designing, planning and delivering policies which aims above all to prevent people from becoming ill. 'Secondary' prevention refers to the concept of preventing further illness among people who have already contracted a disease. (Ch. 9)

Primary legislation and secondary legislation: these terms have become important in debates about devolution in the UK. When laws can be made independently by a parliament or legislature in matters over which it has authority, this is *primary* legislation. For instance, the Scottish Parliament has the authority to pass primary legislation in certain policy areas (for example, education) but not others (for example, defence, foreign relations). When laws have to be made with reference to primary legislation in another legislature or parliament, as occurs in the National Assembly for Wales with reference to the UK Parliament at Westminster, then this is *secondary* legislation. (Ch. 12)

Principles: as used in this book, the term 'principles' refers to the rules or guiding ideas that govern or inform social policies. (Ch. 2)

Public administration: the subject or field of study that is concerned with the ways in which government policies are administered: that is, how government is organized and run, how decisions are made and how services are delivered. See **social administration**. (Ch. 1)

Public health: this term refers to governmental and medical concern with maintaining a healthy environment and with preventing outbreaks of disease in the community. (Chs 3, 9)

Purchaser–provider split: the formal separation of the two separate functions of purchasing (paying for) services and providing and delivering them. This term gained currency as the internal market was developed in health and social services during the 1980s. Formerly integrated departments (for instance, social services departments in local authorities) were divided into separate units, some of which played the 'purchaser' role, while others provided services (such as home care teams). (Ch. 11)

Quangos (quasi-autonomous non-governmental organizations): these are public bodies or organizations that have been created by government but which are not actually part of central government. Therefore, the appointees who run quangos are not civil servants. Some are experts and professionals, but many are drawn from the business world. Quango managers usually work part-time for a quango while continuing to work for other employers or as managing directors of business firms. The phrase 'quasi-   au-tonomous' means that these organizations are partially free of government control. Quangos function at arm's length from government to oversee and manage a wide range of services. (Chs 1, 7)

Real increases/decreases (for example, in spending, wages or benefits): a technical term to indicate that, when amounts of money are compared from year to year, inflation and other distortions have been removed from the calculations. For instance, when government expenditure in 1950 and the year 2000 is compared 'in real terms', it means that like is being compared with like, in terms of the currency values that are being referred to. (Ch. 5)

Recession: a term used to identify when a country's economy has produced less in one year than the previous year. A recession is when an economy slows down so much that it actually 'shrinks', in GDP terms (see **gross domestic product**). Unemployment and other social problems associated with economic slow-down tend to get worse in times of recession. (Chs 5, 8)

Redistribution: simply, a distribution or sharing out which is different from before. It is important to remember that redistribution of resources does not necessarily mean a shift from the rich to the poor; wealth and resources can be redistributed in favour of better-off groups. (Ch. 5)

Rehabilitation: a model or theory of criminal punishment, implying reform of the offender, through, for example, education, training for employment, counselling, psychiatric or social work-type interventions, to restore them to being a 'useful' member of society. Distinguished as a justifying aim of punishment from the deterrence and the 'retributivist', 'just desserts' models of punishment. (Ch. 4)

Residential care: a broad term to describe a variety of living arrangements and social care for people who cannot, or do not wish to, live in their own family homes. The term 'residential care' tends to be reserved for descriptions of social service establishments (including the private and voluntary sectors), whereas 'institutional care' is an even broader term that can include not only social services but also health care establishments such as hospitals and nursing homes. See **community care** and **domiciliary care**. (Ch. 11)

Residual (approach to state services): a residual approach or policy is one that assumes that most people will purchase welfare services, care or social security from the private sector (the market), or will look after themselves, or obtain help and care from their families. However, those who cannot fend for themselves or who cannot afford to do so form a residual (remaining) group, and a residual safety net of public services is provided for them. (Ch. 3)

Residualization: a process of change in which public services or facilities are increasingly restricted to the poor, who cannot afford better quality private services or other forms of welfare. (Chs 10, 11, 12)

Resource-led assessment: see **needs-led assessment**.

Reverse discrimination: see **positive action**.

Risk society: term coined by the German sociologist Ulrich Beck to describe modern or perhaps postmodern societies in which concern about risks grows and intensifies. Old risks may be less salient, but are replaced by newer risks, for example, the environment, terrorism, crime and health risks. May have a link with the concept of 'moral panic'. (Ch. 4)

Rule of law: basic principle of a liberal society and politics. Decisions are made according to law, a system of public rules, rather than being the product of unlimited discretion by powerful individuals, groups or a political elite. For example, individuals can only be prosecuted for known offences. (Ch. 4)

Secondary legislation: see **primary legislation** and **secondary legislation**.

Selective benefits: these are means-tested social security benefits. They are 'selective' in that they target or select for assistance only those people who cannot afford to pay fees or charges, or who cannot provide for themselves. See **means tests**, **targeting** and **universal benefits**. (Ch. 5)

Sheltered housing: a form of accommodation for people who are relatively independent and can manage most of the tasks of daily living by themselves, but who may be frail or vulnerable in some way. Sheltered housing is usually adapted in various ways to meet the needs of those who have physical or mental impairments, or who may benefit from having access to a supervising warden. See **community care**. (Chs 10, 11)

Social administration: the subject or field of study which focuses on the structure and organization of social welfare services (in particular, health, education, the personal social services, housing and community care services). While social administration has a theoretical element (administrative theory), it has traditionally been seen as less theoretical than the discipline of social policy, and more concerned with the study of the 'nuts and bolts' of service provision – the content of social services and how they are administered. See **public administration**. (Ch. 1)

Social care market: the concept of a 'social care market' suggests competition among a number of care providers. Consumers of care, or service users, may therefore choose between providers (assuming that they have the means and resources to do so). See **mixed economy of care**. (Ch. 11)

Social consensus: general agreement. When applied to welfare policy, the idea of social consensus suggests that there is no support for any reversal or significant change to the direction of policy. (Ch. 6)

Social contract: an agreement between major social groups which may be binding (and expressed in legal terms) or may exist more loosely as a set of 'understandings' and political compromises. For instance, a social contract may develop in which trade unions expect government to follow certain economic and welfare policies in order to protect their members' livelihoods; in return, government may expect trade unions to moderate their wage demands. However, this is only one example; a 'social contract' can develop between government and any major sectional interests, or between government and the community as a whole. (Ch. 6)

Social control: Any kind of relationship or social setting in which an individual's or a group's behaviour is brought into line with social norms and general expectations. Social control may be highly visible, direct and coercive (for instance, if police tactics get out of hand and become brutal and confrontational), or it may be more subtle and generally acceptable (as in preventive or community policing). See **autonomy** and **oppression**. (Ch. 6)

Social democratic welfare states: 'social democracy' is difficult to define in precise terms, but all social democratic states and political parties stress the importance of equality, openness and participation, and of the role of a centrally managed welfare state. Social welfare in social democratic states therefore tends to be inclusive and available to all on an equal basis. The best known examples of the social democratic model (such as Sweden) are renowned for the comprehensiveness and generosity of their social services and social security benefits. (Ch. 3)

Social engineering: a philosophy or approach to government which suggests that it is possible to plan solutions to social problems and to create a new social order. (Ch. 10)

Social exclusion: a process that results in certain social groups and individuals being marginalized (see **marginalization**) and separated from 'mainstream' society. When disadvantaged and powerless groups are socially excluded, this can be observed in high rates of unemployment and the geographical concentration of excluded groups in certain types of housing or urban areas. See **underclass**. (Chs 5, 6, 10)

Social housing: housing provided for people in need who, for one reason or another, cannot purchase accommodation on the open market. Social housing may be built by and/or rented from the private sector, but usually the term 'social housing' refers to accommodation provided by, or rented from, housing associations and the voluntary sector of housing. Social housing can mean voluntary and public sector housing – in which case it is a wider category than **council housing**. (Ch. 10)

Social rights: these rights are associated with the development of the welfare state. In welfare states, full citizenship is expressed in rights to certain services (such as 'free' education) and social security. See **civil rights** and **political rights**. (Ch. 2)

Social security benefits (contributory, non-contributory, income-related and non-income-related): entitlement to and size of *contributory* benefits is worked out on the basis of need and also on how much an individual has previously contributed to the scheme through taxes and National Insurance contributions. *Non-contributory* benefits are provided on the basis of need only; neither the amount of benefit nor a person's right to it are affected by the contribution record. *Income-related* benefits are adjusted in amount according to the recipient's means (a means test is applied so that poorer benefit claimants receive more and the better-off receive less). *Non-income-related* benefits are standard and are calculated irrespective of income. (Ch. 5)

Speenhamland system: an informal system, widespread in Britain before the introduction of the 'New' Poor Law in 1834, to supplement the income of poorer agricultural and rural workers. Public money, gathered in the form of local rates or taxation, was used to subsidize poorer workers' pay on a 'sliding scale' (the lower the wage, the higher the subsidy). (Ch. 3)

Stigmatization: Social stigmata are public and obvious signs of 'spoiled identity' and shame. Stigmatization refers to a process of applying such signs of deviant status and shame either to groups and individuals or to particular kinds of public services. In residual welfare systems, for instance, both those who rely on public welfare and the services themselves are likely to be stigmatized. (Chs 6, 10)

Subsidiarity: the concept of allowing policies to be applied or implemented in ways which are decided at a lower (subsidiary) level of decision-making. The EU, for instance, has developed a range of social policies and (depending on their status) some of these must be adopted by member states. However, the principle of subsidiarity allows each country to develop the policy in its own way, as long as the main aims and objectives of the policy are achieved. 'Subsidiarity' also refers to the idea (underlying many social policies in European countries) of expecting the family and local community to meet welfare needs wherever possible. (Ch. 12)

Symmetric devolution: see **asymmetric devolution**.

Targeting: developing policies and services (in particular social security benefits) that are aimed to meet the needs of particular groups only. See **selective benefits**. (Ch. 5)

Taxation (direct, indirect, progressive and regressive): income taxes are examples of *direct* taxation, while *indirect* taxes are levied on goods and services. *Progressive* taxes are those that become progressively higher as income and wealth rise, so that better-off groups pay high taxes and the low paid relatively little. *Regressive* taxes, on the other hand, take similar amounts from everyone, so that the less well-off end up losing a higher proportion of their income in tax than the better-off. (Ch. 5)

Tenure: a legal expression of the claim or right that someone has to live in a property, for instance by ownership, or by renting or leasing. (Ch. 10)

Theory: an idea to explain phenomena or facts that have been observed. (Ch. 1)

Third age: Intended to promote a positive view of later life, this concept suggests that the life course can be divided into different phases – a first age of learning, growing up and socialization, a second age of work, production and acquiring responsibility, and a third age of creative development and further learning, leisure and fulfilling activity. One drawback of the 'third age' concept is that it prompts thoughts of a 'fourth age' of decline and dependency – and has been criticized because it promotes a view of ageing that relies too much on sharply divided stages of life. (Ch. 8)

Underclass: a sociological term to describe a category or group that is excluded from the labour force. This term is highly contentious because there is disagreement about whether an underclass exists as a single group. The socially excluded comprise many different groups, such as older people, the long-term unemployed, some minority ethnic communities and lone parents. Also, there has been much disagreement about what the causes of **social exclusion** and a possible underclass might be. For instance, some suggest that members of the underclass exclude themselves from the rest of society by adopting a deviant and/or criminal lifestyle. But others suggest that if an underclass exists, it is composed mainly of people who wish to work and to join the mainstream but are prevented from doing so for various reasons – for instance, by discrimination. (Ch. 6)

Undeserving poor: see **deserving poor**.

Universal benefits: universality implies that a service or benefit is available to everyone irrespective of their income or social position, so universal benefits are available to all without **means tests**. See **selective benefits**. (Ch. 5)

Utilitarianism: a school of thought which developed in the early nineteenth century, largely through the efforts of Jeremy Bentham. Utilitarianism aims to assess the value of all human action (including government policy) in terms of its 'utility' or use. Briefly, utility or usefulness is itself assessed by the ability of an action or a policy to bring 'the greatest happiness to the greatest number'. (Ch. 2)

Values: ideas and standards which are highly important in a social group or culture. Certain values may be evident in social policies: for instance, US policies on poverty express core American values concerning self-reliance and individualism. (Ch. 1)

Wants: wants are (in social policy terms) expressions of a subjective desire for something (resources, care, a service) irrespective of need. For instance, a person might want to have a particular surgical operation but not need it. **Felt need** occurs when the person subjectively feels an actual need for something. (Ch. 2)

Welfare: An extremely difficult term to define briefly. Almost every commentator has a different definition of the main ingredients or components of human welfare. However, a comprehensive definition would include not only measures of well-being in the present, such as health and material well-being, but also opportunity and autonomy. (Ch. 1)

Welfare capitalism: a 'late' stage in the development of capitalist society in which the provision of welfare becomes an integral and essential part of that society and its market economy. (Ch. 6)

Welfare dependency: A term which suggests not only financial dependence on welfare benefits and services but also a state of mind – a psychological state on which those dependent on welfare lose motivation, skills, independence and self-reliance. (Chs 3, 6)

Welfare pluralism: this is a useful term that sums up the way in which many observers see the future of welfare. 'Welfare pluralism' suggests that welfare provision will increasingly become the responsibility of a number – a plurality – of providers (state, voluntary, private and informal) rather than being mainly the responsibility of the state. (Ch. 11)

Welfare system: a phrase which can be used to suggest that a structure of welfare services and social security exists, but that this is not provided by, or organized solely, by, government. Where welfare *is* still mainly a government-run concern, we may continue to use the term 'welfare state'; otherwise, 'welfare system' may be more appropriate. (Ch. 1)

Welfarism: a set of political and social values that strongly support the existence and continuation of a comprehensive welfare state. Sometimes welfarism may underpin paternalistic, condescending attitudes towards certain social groups – for instance, disabled people. Welfarism might lead to the assumption that everyone in a particular group such as disabled people needs support and is bound to be dependent on welfare services. See **paternalism**. (Chs 1, 2, 6)

'Whole system' comparisons: as an alternative to comparing individual social   policies in one country with those of another (for instance, policies in the Netherlands and Britain towards the idea of decriminalizing certain drugs), it is possible to compare the 'whole systems' of each country (or groups of countries). This means comparing their economic systems, political systems, belief or value systems and so on. This will help to put their respective social policies in context (see Jones 1985). (Ch. 3)

Workfare: policies which seek to make eligibility for benefits and welfare conditional upon willingness to work – in other words, claimants receive benefits only if they have completed a specified total of hours of work per week. (Chs 3, 5, 6)

Workhouse: a centuries-old social institution which provided shelter and subsistence to the poor. If able-bodied they were usually expected to work in the institution at menial and/or backbreaking tasks, but workhouses were also a form of residential care for the non-able-bodied. (Ch. 3)

References

Abel-Smith, B. and Titmuss, K. (eds) (1987) *The Philosophy of Welfare: Selected Writings of Richard M. Titmuss*. London: Allen & Unwin.

Addison, P. (1994) *The Road to 1945: British Politics and the Second World War*. London: Pimlico.

Alcock, P. (1996) *Social Policy in Britain: Themes and Issues*. Basingstoke: Macmillan.

Alcock, P. (1997) *Understanding Poverty*, 2nd edn. Basingstoke: Macmillan.

Annesley, C. (2003) Americanised and Europeanised: UK Social Policy since 1997, *British Journal of Politics and International Relation* 5(2): 143–65.

Arber, S. and Gilbert, N. (1988) Men: the forgotten carers, *Sociology*, 23(1): 111–18.

Arch, J. (1986) *From Ploughtail to Parliament: An Autobiography*. London: The Cresset Library (first published 1898).

Atkinson, D. (ed.) (1995) *Cities of Pride – Rebuilding Community, Refocusing Government*. London: Cassell.

Atkinson, R. (2003) Urban policy, in N. Ellison and C. Pierson (eds) *Developments in British Social Policy 2*. Basingstoke: Palgrave.

Audit Commission (1986) *Making a Reality of Community Care*. London: HMSO.

Association of University Teachers (AUT) (2001) Swansea AUT News, unpublished Newsletter, 7 June.

Baggott, R. (1994) *Health and Health Care in Britain*. London: Macmillan.

Balchin, P. (1995) *Housing Policy – an Introduction*, 3rd edn. London: Routledge.

Barnett, C. (1986) *The Audit of War*. London: Macmillan.

Barr, A., Stenhouse, C. and Henderson, P. (2001) *Caring Communities: a Challenge for Social Inclusion*. York: York Publishing Services.

Barr, N. (1998) *The Economics of the Welfare State*. Oxford: Oxford University Press.

Benjamin, A. and Carvel, J. (2006) The cost of cutting edge, *Guardian*, 5 April.

Bennett, F. (1998) Social policy digest, *Journal of Social Policy*, 27(3): 397–420.

Bennett, F. (2000) Social policy digest, *Journal of Social Policy*, 29(4): 669–96.

Bennett, O. (1996) It's really nice once you get inside, *Independent on Sunday* (Real Lives section), 8 September: 3.

Bentham, J. (1982) *An Introduction to the Principles of Morals and Legislation*, edited by J.H. Burns and H.L.A. Hart. London: Methuen.

Best, G. (1979) *Mid-Victorian Britain 1851–75*. London: Fontana.

Bevan, S. (2000) *Family-Friendly Employment – the Business Case*. Research Report No. 136. London: DfEE.

Beveridge, Sir W. (1942) *Social Insurance and Allied Services* (Beveridge report), Cmnd 6404. London: HMSO.

Blair, T. (1993) Why crime is a socialist issue, *New Statesman* 29 January: 27–8.

Blakemore, K. and Boneham, M. (1994) *Age, Race and Ethnicity*. Buckingham: Open University Press.

Blakemore, K. and Drake, R.F. (1995) *Understanding Equal Opportunity Policies*. Hemel Hempstead: Prentice Hall.

Blank, R. H. and Burau, V. (2004) *Comparative Health Policy*. Basingstoke: Palgrave.

Bogdanor, V. (1999) *Devolution in the United Kingdom*. Oxford: Oxford University Press.

Bogdanor, V. (2001) England may get its turn, *Guardian*, 23 April: 17.

Bornat, J. *et al.* (eds) (1997) *Community Care: A Reader*, 2nd edn. Basingstoke: Macmillan.

Boseley, S. (2000a) Cancer diagnosis errors no worse than average, *Guardian*, 15 June: 6.

Boseley, S. (2000b) Doctor's errors led to agony and death, *Guardian*, 21 October: 6.

Boseley, S. (2001) Alzeimer's patient in NHS lottery, *Guardian*, 29 May: 5.

Bradbury, J. and Mawson, J. (1996) *British Regionalism and Devolution: The Challenges of State Reform and European Integration*. London: Jessica Kingsley.

Bradshaw, J. (1972) The concept of social need, *New Society*, 30: 640–3.

Brewster, C. and Teague, P. (1989) *European Community Social Policy and its Impact on the UK*. London: Institute of Personnel Management.

Brindle, D. (1995) Government backs bill to recognise carers, *The Guardian*, 3 March: 7.

Brindle, D. (1998) Civil liberty row on mental health law, *Guardian*, 9 December: 14.

Brown, G. (2003) State and market: towards a public interest test. *Political Quarterly*, 74(3): 266–84.

Browne, A. (2000) Ageist NHS lets elderly suffer, *Observer*, 13 August: 3.

Bryson, B. (1996) *Notes from a Small Island*. London: Black Swan.

Budge, I., Crewe, I., McKay, D. and Newton, K. (1998) *The New British Politics*. Harlow: Addison Wesley Longman.

Bulmer, M. and Rees, A.M. (eds) (1996) *Citizenship Today: The Contemporary Relevance of T.H. Marshall*. London: UCL Press.

Burchardt, T. (2000) *Enduring Economic Exclusion: Disabled People, Income and Work*. Joseph Rowntree Foundation Report. York: York Publishing Services.

Burden, T. (2000) Poverty, in J. Percy-Smith (ed.) *Policy Responses to Social Exclusion – Towards Inclusion?* Buckingham: Open University Press.

Bytheway, B. and Johnson, J. (1997) The social construction of carers, in A. Symonds and A. Kelly (eds) *The Social Construction of Community Care*. London: Macmillan.

Bytheway, B. *et al.* (eds) (2002) *Understanding Care, Welfare and Community – A Reader*. London: Routledge.

Cahill, M. (1994) *The New Social Policy*. Oxford: Blackwell.

Callender, C. (1992) Redundancy, unemployment and poverty, in C. Glindinning and J. Millar (eds) *Women and Poverty in Britain in the 1990s*. Hemel Hempstead: Harvester Wheatsheaf.

Carter, J. and Rayner, M. (1996) The curious case of post-Fordism and welfare, *Journal of Social Policy*, 25(3): 347–67.

Carvel, J. (2001) 'Tories dispute waiting list fall', *Guardian*, 12 May, 4.

Carvel, J. (2005) "Age shall not weary him..." *Guardian*, 2 February.

Carvel, J. and MacLeod, D. (1995) Learning swerve, *Guardian*, 14 June: 15.

Casserley, C. (2000) The Disability Discrimination Act – an overview, in J. Cooper (ed.) *Law, Rights and Disability*. London: Jessica Kingsley.

Cavadino, M. and Dignan, J. (2000) Penal systems: a comparative approach, in W. E. C. A. Valkenburg, M. Cavadino and J. Dignan (eds) *Comparative Criminal Law*. Tilburg: Katholieke Universiteit Brabant.

Challis, D., Darton, R., Johnson, L., Stone, M. and Traske, K. (1995) *Care Management and Health Care of Older People – the Darlington Community Care Project.* Aldershot: Arena.

Chaney, P. and Drakeford, M. (2004) The primacy of ideology: social policy and the first term of the National Assembly for Wales, *Social Policy Review,* 16.

Chaney, P., Hall, T. and Pithouse, A. (eds) (2001) *New Governance: New Democracy?* Cardiff: University of Wales Press.

Citizens' Advice Bureau (1998) *Flexibility Abused.* London: National Association of Citizens' Advice Bureaux.

Cole, C. and Furbey, R. (1994) *The Eclipse of Council Housing.* London: Routledge.

Colwill, J. (1994) Beveridge, women and the welfare state, *Critical Social Policy,* 14(2): 53–78.

Constitution Unit (2005a) Devolution monitoring programme, *Northern Ireland Report,* 23 July.

Constitution Unit (2005b) Nations and regions: the dynamics of devolution, *Quarterly Monitoring Programme, Scotland: Quarterly Report,* April.

Constitution Unit (2005c) Nations and regions: the dynamics of devolution, *Quarterly Monitoring Programme, Wales: Quarterly Report,* April.

Constitution Unit (2006) *Wales Devolution Monitoring Report,* May.

Cooper, J. (ed.) (2000) *Law, Rights and Disability.* London: Jessica Kingsley.

Crosland, J. (2005) Leader of the opposition, *The Sunday Telegraph,* 18 December: 4.

Crowther, A. (1988) *Social Policy in Britain 1914–1939.* Basingstoke: Macmillan.

CSO (Central Statistical Office) (1996) *Social Trends 26.* London: HMSO.

CSO (Central Statistical Office) (1994) *Regional Trends 29.* London: HMSO.

Curtis, B. (2005) Government to revamp academy schools plan, *Guardian,* 23 July: 8.

Dahl, R.A. (1961) *Who Governs? Democracy and Power in an American City.* New Haven, CT: Yale University Press.

Dale, J. and Foster, P. (1986) *Feminists and State Welfare.* London: Routledge.

Davies, R. (1999) *Devolution: A Process, not an Event.* Cardiff: Institute of Welsh Affairs.

de Swaan, A. (1989) The reluctant imperialism of the medical profession, *Social Science and Medicine,* 28(11): 1165–70.

Deakin, N. (1994) *The Politics of Welfare,* 2nd edn. Hemel Hempstead: Harvester Wheatsheaf.

Dean, H. (1991) *Social Security and Social Control.* London: Routledge.

Dean, H. and Hartley, G. (1995) Listen to learn, *Community Care,* 30 March: 22–3.

Dearing, Sir R. (1994) *National Curriculum and Assessment: Final Report.* London: School Curriculum and Assessment Authority.

Denny, C. (2000) Tories' legacy of poverty, *Guardian,* 12 January: 2.

DETR (Department of Environment, Transport and the Regions) (2000a) *Housing Policy Statement: The Way Forward for Housing.* London: The Stationery Office.

DETR (Department of Environment, Transport and the Regions) (2000b) *Our Towns and Cities: The Future. Delivering an Urban Renaissance,* Cm 4911. London: The Stationery Office.

DETR/DSS (Department of Environment, Transport and the Regions/Department of Social Security) (2000) *Quality and Choice: A Decent Home for All.* London: DETR/DSS.

DfES (Department for Education and Skills) (2005) *Schools – Achieving Success.* London: The Stationery Office.

DHSS (Department of Health and Social Security) (1977) *The Way Forward.* London: HMSO.

DHSS (Department of Health and Social Security) (1983) *NHS Management Inquiry* (the Griffiths Report). London: DHSS.

Dilnot, A. (2001) Our unequal society, *Guardian*, 2 June: 20.

DoH (Department of Health) (1989) *Caring for People: Community Care in the Next Decade and Beyond*. London: HMSO.

DoH (Department of Health) (1996) *The National Health Service. A Service with Ambitions*, Cm 3425. London: The Stationery Office.

DoH (Department of Health) (1997) *The New NHS: Modern, Dependable*. London: DoH.

DoH (Department of Health) (1998a) *Modernising Social Services*. London: The Stationery Office.

DoH (Department of Health) (1998b) *Our Healthier Nation: A Contract for Health*. London: The Stationery Office.

DoH (Department of Health) (2001) *Shifting the Balance of Power within the NHS: Securing Delivery*. London: DoH.

DoH (Department of Health) (2005) *Independence, Well-being and Choice*, Cm 6499. London: The Stationery Office.

DoH (Department of Health) (2006) *Our Health, Our Care, Our Say: A New Direction for Community Services*, Cm 6737. London: The Stationery Office.

Donnison, J. (1988) *Midwives and Medical Men*, 2nd edn. London: Heinemann.

Dornan, P. (2006) Social security policies in 2005, *Social Policy Review*, 18.

Douthwaite, R. (1992) *The Growth Illusion*. Bideford: Green Books.

Downes, D. (1988) *Contrasts in Tolerance: Post-War Penal Policy in the Netherlands and England and Wales*. Oxford: Oxford University Press.

Downes, D. and Morgan, R. (2002) The skeletons in the cupboard: the politics of law and order at the turn of the millennium, in M. Maguire, R. Morgan and R. Reiner (eds) *Oxford Handbook of Criminology*. Oxford: Oxford University Press.

Doyal, L. and Gough, I. (1991) *A Theory of Human Needs*. Basingstoke: Macmillan Education.

Drabble, M. (1988) *Case for Equality*. Fabian Tract 527. London: The Fabian Society.

Drake, R.F. (1999) *Understanding Disability Policies*. Basingstoke: Macmillan.

Drake, R.F. (2001) *The Principles of Social Policy*. New York: Palgrave.

DSS (Department of Social Security (1994) *Households Below Average Income: a Statistical Analysis 1979–1991–92*. London: HMSO.

DSS (Department of Social Security) (2000) *Opportunity for All*. Cm 4865. London: DSS.

DWP (Department for Work and Pensions) (2004) *Work and Pension Statistics*. London: DWP.

Elliott, L. (2000) It's working, *Guardian*, 17 October: 19.

Esping Andersen, G. (1990) *The Three Worlds of Welfare Capitalism*. Cambridge: Polity Press.

Faulkner, D. (2001). *Crime, State and Citizen*. Winchester: Waterside Press.

Field, F. (1995) The poison in the welfare state, *Independent on Sunday*, 14 May: 27.

Finn, D. (2003) Employment policy, in N. Ellison and C. Pierson (eds) *Developments in British Social Policy 2*. Basingstoke: Palgrave Macmillan.

Firth, J. (1987) *Public Support for Residential Care: Report of a Joint Central and Local Government Working Party*. London: DHSS.

Fitzpatrick, T. (1996) Postmodernism, welfare and radical politics, *Journal of Social Policy*, 25(3): 303–20.

Ford, J. (2003) Housing policy, in N. Ellison and C. Pierson (eds) *Developments in British Social Policy 2*. Basingstoke: Palgrave Macmillan.

Forrest, R. and Murie, A. (1988) *Selling the Welfare State*. London: Routledge.

Foucault, M. (1977) *Discipline and Punish: The Birth of the Prison*. Harmondsworth: Penguin.

Fraser, D. (1984) *The Evolution of the British Welfare State*. Basingstoke: Macmillan.

Fraser, D. (2003) *The Evolution of the British Welfare State*, 3rd edn. Basinstoke: Macmillan.

Friedman, M. (1962) *Capitalism and Freedom*. Chicago: University of Chicago Press.

Garland, D. (2001) *The Culture of Control: Crime and Social Order in Contemporary Society*. Oxford: Clarendon Press.

Gatrell, V.A.C. (1990) Crime, authority and the policeman state, in F.M.L. Thompson (ed.) *The Cambridge Social History of Britain 1750–1950*. Cambridge: Cambridge University Press.

GHS (General Household Survey) (1983) *General Household Survey 1983*. London: OPCS.

Gibbs, G. (2000) Doctor blundered in more than 200 cases, *Guardian*, 14 May: 4.

Gillborn, D. and Youdell, D. (2000) *Rationing Education*. Buckingham: Open University Press.

Gilmour, Sir Ian (1992) *Dancing with Dogma*. London: Simon & Schuster.

Glendinning, C. and Means, R. (2006) Personal social services: developments in adult social care, *Social Policy Review*, 18.

Glendinning, C. and Millar, J. (eds) (1992) *Women and Poverty in Britain*. Hemel Hempstead: Harvester Wheatsheaf.

Glennerster, H. (1995) *British Social Policy Since 1995*. Oxford: Blackwell.

Glennerster, H. (2003) *Understanding the Finance of Welfare: What Welfare Costs and How to Pay for It*. Bristol: Policy Press.

Glennerster, H. (2005) The health and welfare legacy, in A. Seldon and D. Kavanagh (eds) *The Blair Effect 2001–5*. Cambridge: Cambridge University Press.

Glennerster, H. *et al.* (eds) (2004) *One Hundred Years of Poverty and Policy*. York: Joseph Rowntree Foundation.

Goffman, E. (1991) *Asylums: Essays on the Social Situation of Mental Patients and Other Inmates*. Harmondsworth: Penguin.

Gordon, D. and Pantazis, C. (1997) *Breadline Britain in the 1990s*. Aldershot: Ashgate.

Gordon, D. *et al.* (eds) (2000). *Poverty and Social Exclusion in Britain*. York: Joseph Rowntree Foundation.

Gough, I. (1979) *The Political Economy of the Welfare State*. London: Macmillan.

Gould, A. (1999) The erosion of the welfare state: Swedish social policy and European Union, *Journal of European Social Policy*, 9(2): 165–74.

Grant, C. (ed.) (1992) *Built to Last? Reflections on British Housing Policy*. London: ROOF Magazine/Shelter.

Gray, J. (1986) *Liberalism*. Milton Keynes: Open University Press.

Gray, J. (1995) Beggaring our own neighbours, *Guardian*, 17 February: 12.

Greer, S. (2004) *Territorial Politics and Health Policy*. Manchester: Manchester University Press.

Griffiths, R. (1988) *Community Care: Agenda for Action*. London: HMSO.

Hallett, C. (1995) *Women and Social Policy: an Introduction*. Hemel Hempstead: Prentice Hall.

Ham, C. (2004) *Health Policy in Britain*. Basingstoke: Palgrave.

Ham, C. and Hill, M. (1993) *The Policy Process in the Modern Capitalist State*. London: Harvester Wheatsheaf.

Hancock, C. (1995) Who'll take care of the caring? *Guardian*, 8 March: 2–3.

Hantrais, L. (2000) *Social Policy in the European Union*, 2nd edn. Basingstoke: Macmillan.

Harris, J. (1977) *William Beveridge: a Biography*. Oxford: Oxford University Press.

Hasluck, C. (2000) Early lessons from the evaluation of New Deal programmes, *Labour Market Trends*, 108(8): 353–80.

Hayek, F.A. (1944) *The Road to Serfdom*. London: George Routledge & Sons.

Heidensohn, F. (2002) Gender and crime, in M. Maguire, R. Morgan and R. Reiner (eds) *Oxford Handbook of Criminology*. Oxford: Oxford University Press.

Hennessy, P. (1992) *Never Again. Britain 1945–51*. London: Jonathan Cape.

Henwood, M. (1995a) Measure for measure, *Community Care*, 6–12 July: 18–19.

Henwood, M. (1995b) *Making a Difference? Implementation of the Community Care Reforms Two Years On*. London: Nuffield Institute for Health/King's Fund.

Hetherington, P. (1998) Council houses unloved, unlettable, *Guardian*, 10 November: 9.

Hetherington, P. (2001a) Scots and Welsh face subsidy axe, *Guardian*, 24 April: 1.

Hetherington, P. (2001b) English learn the Scottish way, *Guardian*, 24 April: 3.

Hill, M. (1990) *Social Security Policy in Britain*. Aldershot: Edward Elgar.

Hills, J. (1997) *The Future of Welfare: A Guide to the Debate*, 2nd edn. York: Joseph Rowntree Foundation.

Hills, J. (2004) *Inequality and the State*. Oxford: Oxford University Press.

Hills, J. and Stewart, K. (eds) (2005) *A More Equal Society? New Labour, Poverty, Inequality and Exclusion*. Bristol: Policy Press.

Hillyard, P. and Percy-Smith, J. (1988) *The Coercive State: the Decline of Democracy in Britain*. London: Fontana.

Hillyard, P. and Watson, S. (1996) Postmodern social policy: a contradiction in terms?, *Journal of Social Policy*, 25(3): 321–46.

HM Treasury (2004) *2004 Spending Review*, Cm 6237. London: The Stationery Office.

HM Treasury (2005) *Public Expenditure Statistical Analyses*, Cm 6521. London: The Stationery Office.

Hodgson, A. and Spours, K. (2005) Divided we fail, *Guardian*, 1 March: 4.

Home Office (2000) *The Criminal Justice System of England and Wales*. London: Home Office.

Horowitz, R. (1995) *Teen Mothers: Citizens or Dependents?* Chicago: University of Chicago Press.

House of Commons Health Committee (2005) *NHS Continuing Care Sixth Report 2004–05 Vol. 1 HC 399-1*. London: The Stationery Office.

Hudson, B. (2002) Punishment and control, in M. Maguire, R. Morgan and R. Reiner (eds) *Oxford Handbook of Criminology*. Oxford: Oxford University Press.

Hunter, D. (1992) Lost tribes of the NHS, *Health Service Journal*, 20 August: 19.

Hutton, W. (1995) *The State We're In: Why Britain is in Crisis and How to Overcome It*. London: Jonathan Cape.

Ignatieff, M. (ed.) (2005) *American Exceptionalism and Human Rights*. Princeton, NJ: Princeton University Press.

Illich, I. (1990) *Limits to Medicine – Medical Nemesis: the Expropriation of Health*. London: Marion Boyars.

Islam, F. and Mathiason, N. (2001) Labour spending less than Thatcher, *The Observer*, 27 May: 1.

Jack, A. (2006) Decision on Herceptin to come 'within six months', *Financial Times*, 16 February.

Jack, A. and N. Timmins (2006) Alzheimer's decision a test for ministers, *Financial Times*, 24 January.

Jack, R. (1992) Case management and social services: welfare or trade fare? *Generations Review*, 2(1): 4–6.

James, O. (1998) *Britain on the Couch*. London: Arrow Books.

Johnson, J. (1997) Care as policy, in A. Brechin, J. Katz, S. Peace and J. Walmsley (eds) *Care Matters*. London: Sage.

Johnson, J. and Slater, R. (eds) (1993) *Ageing and Later Life*. London: Sage.

Johnson, N. (1999) The personal social services and community care, in M. Powell (ed.) *New Labour, New Welfare State?* Bristol: Policy Press.

Johnson, P., Tanner, S. and Thomas, R. (2000) Money matters: measuring poverty, wealth and unemployment, in S. Kerrison and A. Macfarlane (eds) *Official Health statistics: an Unofficial Guide*. London: Arnold.

Jones, C. (1985) *Patterns of Social Policy: an Introduction to Comparative Analysis*. London: Tavistock.

Jones, K. (1994) *The Making of Social Policy in Britain 1830–1990*, 2nd edn. London: The Athlone Press.

Joseph, K. and Sumption, J. (1979) *Equality*. London: John Murray.

Kangaspunta, K. *et al.* (eds) (1998) *Crime and Criminal Justice in Europe and North America 1990–1994*. Helsinki: European Institute for Crime Prevention and Control (HEUNI).

Kemp, P. (1999) Housing policy under New Labour, in M. Powell (ed.) *New Labour, New Welfare State?* Bristol: Policy Press.

Kennedy, I. (1980) The Reith lectures – unmasking medicine, *The Listener*, 13 November: 641–4.

Kennedy, I. (1983) *The Unmasking of Medicine*, 2nd edn. St Albans: Granada Publishing.

Kennedy, I. (2001) *The Report of the Public Inquiry into Children's Heart Surgery at the Bristol Royal Infirmary 1984–1995*, Cm 5207. London: The Stationery Office.

Kennett, P. (2001) *Comparative Social Policy*. Buckingham: Open University Press.

Kesey, K. (1962) *One Flew Over the Cuckoo's Nest*. London: Methuen.

Kincaid, J. (1984) Richard Titmuss 1907–73, in P. Barker (ed.) *Founders of the Welfare State*. London: Heinemann Educational.

Kitwood, T. (1997) *Dementia Reconsidered*. Buckingham: Open University Press.

Klein, R. (1984) Edwin Chadwick, in P. Barker (ed.) *Founders of the Welfare State*. London: Heinemann Educational.

Klein, R. (1993) The goals of health policy: church or garage? in A. Harrison (ed.) *Health Care UK 1992/93*. London: King's Fund Institute.

Klein, R. (1995) *The New Politics of the NHS*, 3rd edn. London: Longman.

Klein, R. (2006) *The New Politics of the NHS*, 5th edn. Oxford: Radcliffe Publishing.

Klein, R. (ed.) (1998) *Implementing the White Paper: Pitfalls and Opportunities*. London: King's Fund.

Knapp, M. *et al.* (1992) *Care in the Community: Challenge and Demonstration*. Aldershot: Arena.

Labour Party (1997) *New Labour: Because Britain Deserves Better*. London: Labour Party.

Labour Party (2005) *Britain Forward not Back*. London: Labour Party.

Laurance, J. (2001) Routine abuse of elderly in NHS, *The Independent*, 28 March: 1.

Lawson, R. (1995) The challenge of 'new poverty': lessons from Europe and North America, in K. Funken and P. Cooper (eds) *Old and New Poverty*. London: Rivers Oram Press.

Le Grand, J. (1982) *The Strategy of Equality*. London: Allen & Unwin.

Le Grand, J. *et al.* (eds) (1998) *Learning from the NHS Internal Market: A Review of the Evidence*. London: King's Fund.

Lea, J. (2003) Institutional racism in policing: the Macpherson report and its consequences, in R. Matthews and J. Young, *The New Politics of Crime and Punishment*. Cullompton: Willan.

Leathard, A. (2000) *Health Care Provision*, 2nd edn. Cheltenham: Stanley Thornes.

Lewis, J. (1980) *The Politics of Motherhood: Child and Maternal Welfare in England, 1900–1939*. London: Croom Helm.

Lewis, J. (1983) *Women's Welfare, Women's Rights*. London: Croom Helm.

Lewis, J. (1992) *Inner-city Regeneration: The Demise of Regional and Local Government*. Buckingham: Open University Press.

Lister, R. (1998) *Citizenship: Feminist Perspectives*. Basingstoke: Macmillan.

Lloyd, T.O. (1993) *Empire, Welfare State, Europe: English History 1902–1992*, 4th edn. Oxford: Oxford University Press.

Loader, I. and Sparks, R. (2002) Contemporary landscapes of crime, order and control: governance, risk, and globalisation, in M. Maguire, R. Morgan and R. Reiner (eds) *Oxford Handbook of Criminology*. Oxford: Oxford University Press.

Lowe, R. (1993) *The Welfare State in Britain since 1945*. Basingstoke: Macmillan.

Lowi, T.J. (1966) Distribution, regulation, redistribution: the functions of government, in R.B. Ripley (ed.) *Public Policies and their Politics: Techniques of Government Control*. New York: W.W. Norton.

Lucas, K., Grosvenor, T. and Simpson, R. (2001) *Transport, the Environment and Social Exclusion*. York: Joseph Rowntree Foundation/York Publishing Services.

Lukes, S. (2005) *Power: a Radical View*, 2nd edn. Basingstoke: Palgrave.

Mabbett, D. and Bolderson, H. (1999) Theories and methods in comparative social policy, in J. Clasen (ed.) *Comparative Social Policy: Concepts, Theories and Methods*. Oxford: Blackwell.

Mack, J. and Lansley, S. (1985) *Poor Britain*. London: Allen & Unwin.

Maguire, M. *et al.* (eds) (2002) *Oxford Handbook of Criminology*. Oxford: Oxford University Press.

Malpass, P. (1984) Octavia Hill, 1838–1912, in P. Barker (ed.) *Founders of the Welfare State*. London: Heinemann Educational.

Malpass, P. (2005) *Housing and the Welfare State*. Basingstoke: Palgrave.

Malpass, P. and Murie, A. (1994) *Housing Policy and Practice*, 4th edn. London: Macmillan.

Marchant, C. (1995) Care managers speak out, *Community Care*, 30 March: 16–17.

Marshall, T.H. (1950)*Citizenship and Social Class, and Other Essays*. Cambridge: Cambridge University Press.

Marshall, T.H. (1963) *Sociology at the Crossroads*. London: Heinemann.

Marshall, T.H. (1964) *Class, Citizenship and Social Development*. Chicago: University of Chicago Press.

Marshall, T.H. (1970) *Social Policy*. London: Hutchinson.

McCormick, J. (1999)*Understanding the European Union*. Basingstoke: Macmillan.

McKeown, T. (1979) *The Role of Medicine: Dream, Mirage or Nemesis?* 2nd edn. Oxford: Blackwell.

McLean, I. (2001) The national question, in A. Seldon (ed.) *The Blair Effect*. London: Little, Brown.

McLean, I. (2005). The national question, in A. Seldon and D. Kavanagh (eds) *The Blair Effect 2001–5*. Cambridge: Cambridge University Press.

Meikle, J. (1994) Puppets on a string? *The Guardian*, 8 November: 2.

Midwinter, E. (1994) *The Development of Social Welfare in Britain*. Buckingham: Open University Press.

Ministry of Health (1963) *Health and Welfare: The Development of Community Care*, Cmnd 1973. London: HMSO.

Mishra, R. (1990) *The Welfare State in Capitalist Society*. Hemel Hempstead: Harvester Wheatsheaf.

Mishra, R. (1993) Social policy in a postmodern world, in C. Jones (ed.) *New Perspectives on the Welfare State in Europe*. London: Routledge.

Morris, J. (2003) Community care or independent living? in N. Ellison and C. Pierson (eds) *Developments in British Social Policy 2*. Basingstoke: Palgrave.

Morris, T. (1983) Crime and the welfare state, in P. Bean and S. MacPherson (eds) *Approaches to Welfare*. London: Routledge.

Morris, T. (1989) *Crime and Criminal Justice Since 1945*. Oxford: Basil Blackwell.

Morris, T. (1994) Crime and penal policy, in D. Kavanagh and A. Seldon (eds) *The Major Effect*. London: Macmillan.

Morris, T. (2001) Crime and penal policy, in A. Seldon (ed.) *The Blair Effect*. London: Little, Brown.

Murray, C. (1994) *Underclass: The Crisis Deepens*. London: Institute of Economic Affairs.

Nelken, D. (2002) Comparing criminal justice, in M. Maguire, R. Morgan and R. Reiner (eds) *Oxford Handbook of Criminology*. Oxford: Oxford University Press.

Novak, T. (1988) *Poverty and the State: an Historical Sociology*. Milton Keynes: Open University Press.

Nozick, R. (1974) *Anarchy, State and Utopia*. Oxford: Blackwell.

O'Donnell, O. and Propper, C. (1991) Equity and the distribution of NHS resources, *Journal of Health Economics*, 10: 1–19.

Office for National Statistics (2000) *Economic Trends No. 557*. London: The Stationery Office.

Office for National Statistics (2001) *Social Trends No. 31*. London: The Stationery Office.

Office for National Statistics (2005a) *The Effects of Taxes and Benefits on Household Income, 2003–04*. Basingstoke: Palgrave.

Office for National Statistics (2005b) *Social Trends No. 35*. Basingstoke: Palgrave.

Oliver, M. (1990) *Politics of Disablement*. London: Macmillan.

Page, D. (2000) *Communities in the Balance: The Reality of Social Exclusion on Housing Estates*. York: York Publishing Services.

Pantazis, C. *et al.* (eds) (2006) *Poverty and Social Exclusion in Britain: The Millennium Survey*. Bristol: Policy Press.

Parker, R. (1990) Elderly people and community care: the policy background, in I. Sinclair, R. Parker, D. Leat and J. Williams (eds) *The Kaleidoscope of Care: a Review of Research on Welfare Provision for Elderly People*. London: HMSO.

Pascall, G. (1986) *Social Policy: a Feminist Analysis*. London: Tavistock.

Paton Walsh, N. (2001) UK matches Africa in crime surge, *The Observer*, 3 June: 11.

Peach, C. and Byron, M. (1994) Council house sales, residualisation and Afro-Caribbean tenants, *Journal of Social Policy*, 23(3): 363–83.

Pease, K. (2002) Crime reduction, in M. Maguire, R. Morgan and R. Reiner (eds) *Oxford Handbook of Criminology*. Oxford: Oxford University Press.

Peel, Q. (2005) America's exceptionally poor choice of friends, *Financial Times*, 11 August.

Penna, S. and O'Brien, M. (1996) Postmodernism and social policy: a small step forwards? *Journal of Social Policy*, 25(1): 39–61.

Phillimore, P., Beattie, A. and Townsend, P. (1994) Widening inequality of health in northern England, 1981–91, *British Medical Journal*, 308: 1125–8.

Phillipson, C. (1982) *Capitalism and the Construction of Old Age*. London: Macmillan.

Philpott, J. (ed.) (1997) *Working for Full Employment*. London: Routledge.

Piachaud, D. (1981) Peter Townsend and the Holy Grail, *New Society*, 10 September: 419–21.

Pickvance, C.G. (1986) Comparative urban analaysis and assumptions about causality, *International Journal of Urban and Regional Research*, 10(2): 162–84.

Pierson, C. (1991) *Beyond the Welfare State?* Oxford: Blackwell.

Piven, F. and Cloward, R. (1971) *Regulating the Poor: the Functions of Public Welfare*. New York: Pantheon Books.

Powell, M. (1995) The strategy of equality revisited, *Journal of Social Policy*, 24(2), 163–85.

Powell, M. (ed.) (1999) *New Labour, New Welfare State?* Bristol: Policy Press.

Powell, M. (ed.) (2002) *Evaluating New Labour's Welfare Reforms*. Bristol: Policy Press.

Prime Minister's Strategy Unit (2005) *Improving the Life Chances of Disabled People*. London: PMSU.

Qureshi, H. and Walker, A. (1989) *The Caring Relationship – Elderly People and Their Families*. Basingstoke: Macmillan.

Ranson, S. and Travers, T. (1994) Education, in P. Jackson and M. Lavender (eds) *Public Services Yearbook*. London: Chapman & Hall.

Rawls, J. (1972) *A Theory of Justice*. Oxford: Oxford University Press.

Rawnsley, A. (2000) *Servants of the People – The Inside Story of New Labour*. London: Hamish Hamilton.

Rawnsley, A. (2001) A conspiracy that threatens democracy, *The Observer*, 13 May: 29.

Revell, K. and Leather, P. (2000) *The State of UK Housing*, 2nd edn. York: Joseph Rowntree Foundation/Policy Press.

Revell, P. (2005) Beyond the school gates, *Guardian*, 25 October: 32.

Riddell, M. (2001) *The New Statesman* interview – Peter Morris, *New Statesman*, 10 December: 20–1.

Riley, R. and Young, G. (2001) *The Macroeconomic Impact of the New Deal for Young People*. Discussion paper 184. London: National Institute for Economic and Social Research.

Robinson, R. and Le Grand, J. (1994) *Evaluating the NHS Reforms*. London: King's Fund Institute.

Robertson Elliott, F. (1996) *Gender, Family and Society*. Basingstoke: Macmillan.

Routledge, P. (1997) The cruellest test, *Independent on Sunday*, 28 December: 17.

Rowntree, B.S. (1937) *The Human Needs of Labour*. London: Longman.

Royle, E. (1987) *Modern Britain: a Social History*. London: Edward Arnold.

Rust, V. and Blakemore, K. (1990) Education reform in Norway and in England and Wales: a corporatist interpretation, *Comparative Education Review*, 34(4): 500–22.

Saraga, E. (ed.) (1998) *Embodying the Social: Constructions of Difference*. London: Routledge.

Scottish Assembly Health Committee (2006) *Tenth Report. Care Inquiry*. Edinburgh: Scottish Assembly.

Scruton, R. (1984) *The Meaning of Conservatism*, 2nd edn. London: Macmillan.

Scull, A.T. (1984) *Decarceration: Community Treatment of the Deviant – A Radical View*, 2nd edn. Cambridge: Polity Press.

Seldon, A. and Kavanagh, D. (2005) *The Blair Effect 2001–5*. Cambridge: Cambridge University Press.

Sen, A. (1980) Equality of What? in S. M. McMurrin (ed.) *Liberty, Equality and Law*. Salt Lake City, UT: University of Utah Press.

Sen, A. (1987). *The Standard of Living*. Cambridge: Cambridge University Press.

Sherman, J. (2001) Internet and TV blamed for NHS claims bill, *The Times*, 3 May: 4.

Simon, B. (1990) *Education and the Social Order, 1940–1990*. London: Lawrence & Wishart.

Simon, J. (1997) Governing through crime, in L. Friedman and G. Fisher (eds) *The Crime Conundrum: Issues in Criminal Justice*. Boulder, CO: Westview Press.

Slater, J. (2001) Thriving out of the slipstream, *Times Educational Supplement*, 5 October: 20–1.

Sly, F. and Stillwell, D. (1997) Temporary workers in Great Britain, *Labour Market Trends*, September. London: The Stationery Office.

Smithers, R. (2005) Researchers raise more doubts on city academies, *Guardian*, 30 June: 7.

Smithers, R., White, M. and Ward, L. (2004) Blair insists A-Levels will stay in shakeup, *Guardian*, 19 October: 1.

Social Exclusion Unit (1998) *Bringing Britain Together: A National Strategy for Neighbourhood Renewal*, Cm 4045. London: HMSO.

Spicker, P. (1993) *Poverty and Social Security*. London: Routledge.

Stainton, T. (1994) *Autonomy and Social Policy*. Aldershot: Avebury.

Steintrager, J. (1977) *Bentham*. London: George Allen & Unwin.

Stevenson, J. (1984) *British Society 1914–45*. Harmondsworth: Penguin.

Stewart, J. (2004) *Taking Stock: Scottish Social Welfare after Devolution*. Bristol: Policy Press.

Stewart, K. (2005) Equality and social justice, in A. Seldon and D. Kavanagh (eds) *The Blair Effect 2001–5*. Cambridge: Cambridge University Press.

Summerskill, B. and Hinsliff, G. (2001) An impossible dream? *The Observer*, 24 June: 13.

Sutherland, S. (1999) *With Respect to Old Age: Long-Term Care – Rights and Responsibilities*, Cmnd. 4192. London: The Stationery Office.

Tait, N. (2006) Cancer sufferer loses drug fight, *Financial Times*, 16 February.

Tawney, R.H. (1964) *Equality*, 4th edn, with an introduction by R.M. Titmuss. London: George Allen & Unwin.

Taylor, M. (2005) New blow to city academies, *Guardian*, 3 December: 3.

Taylor, M. (2006a) Parents rebel at 'Dickensian' school run by millionaire evangelist, *Guardian*, 30 May: 12.

Taylor, M. (2006b) Academies fail to improve results, *Guardian*, 22 May: 4.

Taylor, S. and Field, D. (1997) *Sociology of Health and Health Care: an Introduction for Nurses*, 2nd edn. Oxford: Blackwell Scientific Publications.

Taylor-Gooby, P. (1994) Postmodernism and social policy: a great leap backwards? *Journal of Social Policy*, 23(3): 385–404.

Thane, P. (1996) *The Foundations of the Welfare State*, 2nd edn. London: Longman.

The Guardian (2001) Better late than never, 3 January: 19.

Thompson, A. and Dobson, R. (1995) 'Death of an ideal', *Community Care*, 6–12 July: 20–1.

Thompson, N. (1998) *Promoting Equality*. London: Macmillan.

Timmins, N. (1995) *The Five Giants – a Biography of the Welfare State*. London: HarperCollins.

Timmins, N. (2006a) Review of social care funding launched, *Financial Times*, 27 March.

Timmins, N. (2006b) Scrap means-testing on care of old, says study, *Financial Times*, 25 March.

Timonen, V. (1999) A threat to social security? The impact of EU membership on the Finnish welfare state, *Journal of European Social Policy*, 9(3): 253–61.

Tinker, A. (1981) *The Elderly in Modern Society*. London: Longman.

Tinker, A. (1997) *Older People in Modern Society*, 4th edn. New York: Addison Wesley.

Titmuss, R.M. (1950) *Problems of Social Policy*. London: HMSO.

Titmuss, R.M. (1958) *Essays on the Welfare State*. London: Allen & Unwin.

Titmuss, R.M. (1968) *Commitment to Welfare*. London: Allen & Unwin.

Titmuss, R.M. (1970) *The Gift Relationship*. London: Allen & Unwin.

Tomlinson, S. (2001) *Education in a Post-welfare Society*. Buckingham: Open University Press.

Tomlinson, M. (2004) *14–19 Curriculum and Qualifications Reform (Final Report)*. Annesley: DfES Publications.

Townsend, P. (1979) *Poverty in the United Kingdom*. London: Allen Lane/ Penguin Books.

Toynbee, P. (2000) Targets for pensions, *Guardian*, 22 September: 19.

Toynbee, P. (2005) 'I don't want schools to do to children what they did to me', *Guardian*, 20 December: 27.

Toynbee, P. and Walker, D. (2001) *Did Things Get Better? An Audit of Labour's Successes and Failures*. London: Penguin.

Toynbee, P. and Walker, D. (2005) *Better or Worse? Has Labour Delivered?* London: Bloomsbury.

Ungerson, C. (1987) *Policy is Personal: Sex, Gender and Informal Care*. London: Tavistock Publications.

Urban Task Force (1999) *Towards an Urban Renaissance. Final Report of the Urban Task Force chaired by Lord Rogers of Riverside*. London, E. & F.N. Spon.

Vickerstaff, S. (2003) Work and welfare, in J. Baldock, N. Manning, S. Millar and S. Vickerstaff (eds) *Social Policy*, 2nd edn. Oxford: Oxford University Press.

Vidal, J. (1994) Health over wealth, *Guardian*: 4–5.

Wadham, J. and Mountfield, H. (1999) *Blackstone's Guide to the Human Rights Act 1998*. London: Blackstone Press.

Wainwright, M. (2001) Bradford warned on segregation trend, *Guardian*, 20 June: 6.

Walker, A. (1990) The benefits of old age? Age discrimination and social security, in E. McEwen (ed.) *Age – the Unrecognised Discrimination*. London: Age Concern England.

Walker, P. (1994) What happens when you scrap the welfare state? *Independent on Sunday*, 13 March: 17.

Wanless, D. (2006) *Securing Good Care for Older People: Taking a Long-Term View*. London: King's Fund.

Warner, N. (1995) *Community Care: Just a Fairy Tale?* London: Carers' National Association (unpublished report).

Warnock, M. (ed.) (1966) *Utilitarianism*. London: Collins/Fontana.

Waterhouse, R. (2000) *Lost in Care: Report of the Tribunal of Inquiry into the Abuse of Children in Care in the Former Country Council Area of Gwynedd and Clwyd since 1974*. London: DoH.

White, M. and Taylor, M. (2005) Blair sweeps aside critics of school reform, *Guardian*, 25 October: 1.

Wilkin, D., Hallam, L., Leavey, R. and Metcalfe, D. (1987) *Anatomy of Urban General Practice*. London: Tavistock.

Williams, Z. (2005) She's being a total Kelly, *Guardian*, 14 June: 21.

Wintour, P. (2005) Blair's public service crusade, *Guardian*, 25 October: 12.

Wintour, P., Smithers, R. and White, M. (2005) Blair prepares retreat on education, *Guardian*, 19 November: 1.

Wistow, G., Knapp, M., Hardy, B. and Allen, C. (1994) *Social Care in a Mixed Economy*. Buckingham: Open University Press.

Wolmar, C. (2001) Collision course? *Search*, 35. York: Joseph Rowntree Foundation.

Woodward, W. (2001a) UK spending on education lags behind rivals, *Guardian*, 14 June: 8.

Woodward, W. (2001b) Schools 'resemble third world', *Guardian*, 1 June: 8.

Woodward, W. (2001c) Test paper, *Guardian*, 23 October: 6–7.

Woodward, W. (2006) View from on high, *The Guardian*, 14 February, 1–2.

Worrall, L. and Cooper, C. (1998) *The Quality of Life: 1997 Survey of Managers' Changing Experiences*. London: Institute of Management.

Worsthorne, P. (1971) *The Socialist Myth*. London: Cassell.

Wragg, T. (ed.) (2005a) *Letters to the Prime Minister – the Future of Education*. Place of publication not specified: The New Vision Group.

Wragg, T. (2005b) Opinion, *Guardian*, 1 March: 7.

Wyn, H. (1991) Women, the state, and the concept of financial dependence, in J. Hutton, S. Hutton, T. Pinch and A. Shiell (eds) *Dependency to Enterprise*. London: Routledge.

Young, J. (2002) Crime and social exclusion, in M. Maguire, R. Morgan and R. Reiner (eds) *Oxford Handbook of Criminology*. Oxford: Oxford University Press.

Young, J. and Matthews, R. (2003) New Labour, crime control and social exclusion, in R. Matthews and J. Young (eds) *The New Politics of Crime and Punishment*. Cullompton: Willan.

Index

This index is in word by word order. Page numbers in italics indicate tables and diagrams. The letter 'b' after a page number indicates a text box; the letter 'g' indicates a glossary entry.